China and Intervention at the UN Security Council

China and Intervention at the UN Security Council

Reconciling Status

COURTNEY J. FUNG

OXFORD
UNIVERSITY PRESS

Great Clarendon Street, Oxford, OX2 6DP,
United Kingdom

Oxford University Press is a department of the University of Oxford.
It furthers the University's objective of excellence in research, scholarship,
and education by publishing worldwide. Oxford is a registered trade mark of
Oxford University Press in the UK and in certain other countries

© Courtney J. Fung 2019

The moral rights of the author have been asserted

First Edition published in 2019

All rights reserved. No part of this publication may be reproduced, stored in
a retrieval system, or transmitted, in any form or by any means, without the
prior permission in writing of Oxford University Press, or as expressly permitted
by law, by licence or under terms agreed with the appropriate reprographics
rights organization. Enquiries concerning reproduction outside the scope of the
above should be sent to the Rights Department, Oxford University Press, at the
address above

You must not circulate this work in any other form
and you must impose this same condition on any acquirer

Published in the United States of America by Oxford University Press
198 Madison Avenue, New York, NY 10016, United States of America

British Library Cataloguing in Publication Data

Data available

Library of Congress Control Number: 2019937227

ISBN 978-0-19-884274-3

Links to third party websites are provided by Oxford in good faith and
for information only. Oxford disclaims any responsibility for the materials
contained in any third party website referenced in this work.

For my parents

Acknowledgements

Despite presenting a set of neat explanations and insights in the book that follows, I must recognize that the path to publication was nowhere as logical or clear. Indeed, I was lucky with much good fortune. At just the right time, I received a General Research Fund grant (#17612518) from the Research Grants Council of Hong Kong to focus on finishing this book project. My grateful thanks to the RGC for the award.

This book grew out of my doctoral thesis, though much of that text does not remain here. It was my time working on my dissertation at The Fletcher School of Law and Diplomacy, Tufts University, that taught me to put less weight on academic fads and work on intellectual projects in service to a greater, practical good. My dissertation advisors—Alan M. Wachman, Daniel W. Drezner, Ian Johnstone, and Alastair Iain Johnston—all deserve my deepest thanks for their patience with me and my work. It was all the unanswered questions of my dissertation—and in particular during my oral defense, where my committee wanted to discuss the Chinese role in addressing the unfolding Syrian civil war—which prompted me to change my research question entirely.

I am eternally grateful that Alan took me on as a doctoral advisee, and for always encouraging me to move on to my next phase of research ("Why wait until everyone says it's your turn, Courtney? If you're ready, you should try"). Alan was not only generous enough to offer his own peers as initial points of contact during my first round of fieldwork in Beijing, but then followed up with individual email messages thanking them all for their time. A decade on from my first trip, and I still meet those who remember me as Alan's student, given his proper attention to detail with those thank you messages. In Alan's own unassuming sure-handedness, he left a very high standard for me to aspire to as a productive and thoughtful scholar. Dan offered succinct feedback during my numerous visits with him ("You've mixed up variables and observable implications. What's the next question?"). I hope to impart insights the way he does in a ten-minute meeting; one day! Dan's argumentative curiosity, clear thinking and total impatience for half-baked work are solid reminders for why we engage in social science to begin with. Ian's reputation as one of the most generous, kind, and thoughtful scholars is entirely deserved. Ian's introduction to the Center on International Cooperation gave me the launch pad for fieldwork, and he *always* made time to read my (many) drafts and meet in person. Those of you who know Ian will be unsurprised; and those of you who know what a scholar-practitioner's schedule looks like will be rightfully impressed. I'm grateful for Ian's mentorship to say the least.

Iain's work is a continual source of inspiration for me. Alan was right that while others see the world in black and white, Iain is watching in color. Iain spent hours discussing my Darfur case with me, and in asking probing questions about my interview minutiae, he showed me first-hand how to actually *do* process-tracing. The months (or let's be honest here, years) spent reworking and rethinking this single case, meant that the growing pains for the next case studies were nowhere near as bad. I thank each of my teachers for letting me observe and learn as I became my own independent researcher. I will always be a student in their company, and their unanimous assumption that I would write a book was a touchstone for me upon my departure from Boston for new responsibilities and time pressures in Hong Kong.

A number of fellowships and visiting positions gave me respite to work on the ideas contained here. Some of my initial fieldwork was supported by a Konosuke Matsushita Memorial Foundation grant (#11-003), which enabled me to start data collection. I was a research fellow in the International Security Program at the Belfer Center for Science and International Affairs, Harvard University, under the guidance of Steven E. Miller and Stephen M. Walt. The program provided an intellectual environment to contemplate larger implications of my research, and an excellent opportunity to present initial ideas to an audience skeptical that China could be interested in such vague things as 'status' and 'responsibility.' I was a pre-doctoral research fellow at the Center on International Cooperation, New York University, and thank Richard Gowan, Jake Sherman, and Ben Tortolani in particular. They all nudged along my thinking and emphasized the policy relevance of my research. I had an eye-opening summer serving in the UN Department of Peacekeeping Operations–Policy and Best Practices Section under the guidance of David Haeri, Roxaneh Bazergan, and Rebecca Jovin. It was there that I truly realized that outcomes in the real world are idiosyncratic and fortuitous, and that even apparently insignificant, private moments have ripple effects for policy. Both Iain and Thomas J. Christensen supported me for a year-long fellowship at the Fairbank Center for Chinese Studies, Harvard University through the now Columbia-Harvard China and the World Program funded by the Carnegie Corporation of New York. I am so grateful for that uninterrupted opportunity to think, collect data, and write. I thank both Iain and Tom for the mentorship over the years, and for reminding me of the importance of having work-life balance, something not really valued in the academe. It was Tom who wisely reminded me to work six days a week while I could still justify it, and then not to feel guilty when other priorities prevailed. I am also glad for the CWP friendships and scholarly network; the jolt of energy from the workshop sessions are always worth the dreaded jetlag. Colin Wight had me as a visitor in the Department of Politics and International Relations at the University of Sydney when I was rethinking the research framework, and Jingdong Yuan was a generous host there too. I also thank Young Hwan Shin of the East Asia Institute in Seoul for my fellowship in the Program on Peace, Governance, and Development in East Asia funded by the Japan Foundation, the Chiang Ching-kuo Foundation for International Scholarly Exchange of Taiwan, and YBM/KIS, which gave me the valuable opportunity to think through background ideas for the project.

Many people have supported me, in big ways and small, and without them I wouldn't have figured out where I was going. Thanks go to my seniors—Steve Chan, Rosemary Foot, and Ja Ian Chong—who offered encouragement for the project and read various drafts along the way. Thank you to Jenifer Burckett-Picker, Lydia M. Chen, Jessica Daniels, Ann Decembrele, Noah Gall, Laurie Hurley, Susan Lynch, Ellen McDonald, Carol Murphy, Miriam Seltzer, Sharon To, Daniel Tsang, and May Yim for all keeping the literal and figurative trains running on time.

At Oxford University Press, Dominic Byatt was a joy of an editor to work with, and I am so grateful that he saw promise in this project and kept up the hunt for reviewers. Matthew Williams and Céline Louasli ably pulled together all the different files and kept production humming. Rob Wilkinson admirably cleaned my text. I am indebted to all four reviewers for their comments and queries that undoubtedly improved this book. Some initial drafts of my research were published as journal articles. My 2018 article, "Separating Intervention From Regime Change? China's Diplomatic Innovations at the UN Security Council Regarding the Syria Crisis," *The China Quarterly*, 235, 693–712 is reprinted with permission from Cambridge University Press. My 2016 article, "Global South solidarity? China, regional organisations and intervention in the Libyan and Syrian civil wars," *Third World Quarterly* 37: 1, 33–50, is reprinted by permission of the publisher Taylor & Francis Ltd. Copyright © Southseries Inc., www.thirdworldquarterly.com, reprinted by permission of Taylor & Francis Ltd, www.tandfonline.com on behalf of Southseries Inc., www.thirdworldquarterly.com. v1.9. My 2016 article, "Explaining China's Deployment to UN Peacekeeping Operations," *International Relations of the Asia-Pacific* 16: 3, 409–41 is reprinted by permission of Oxford University Press and the Japan Association of International Relations. This project also benefited from a number of scholars who gave their time to challenge my work. Thank you to the participants at seminars at the Fletcher School of Law and Diplomacy, the National University of Singapore, the Saltzman Institute for War and Peace Studies at the School of International and Public Affairs at Columbia University, the China and the World Center at the Australia National University, the Asia-Pacific Centre for the Responsibility to Protect at the University of Queensland, and the Security Studies Group at the University of Sydney, Keio University, Peking University, Seoul National University, The University of Nottingham-Ningbo, and at NYU-Shanghai.

I am lucky to have a supportive research environment at the Department of Politics and Public Administration at the University of Hong Kong. Thank you to colleagues past and present, in particular John Burns, Joseph C. W. Chan, Peter

Cheung, Yvonne Chiu, James Gledhill, Enze Han, Will Hayward, Ian Holliday, Inwook Kim, Danny Lam, Helen Liu, Kai Quek, Uwe Steinhoff, and Injoo Sohn for discussing different phases of the project with me. Thank you to Thomas S. Wilkins, who was visiting faculty in the Department, for so graciously facilitating my time at the University of Sydney. Thank you to Eliza W. Y. Lee for supporting my mini-sabbatical and to Richard W. Hu for making my application to the RGC possible. Thanks in particular to both Joseph and Ian for their sense of perspective on academic life and mentorship over the years. Both believed in the value of this monograph and gave steady guidance on managing my competing professional demands as I embarked on this multi-year project. I am indebted to Debby S. W. Chan, Christelle Chartrand, Yudi Feng, and Shing-Hon Lam for the yeoman's work of research assistance. This category of tasks included ferreting down dead-ends, chasing winding paper trails, and forever explaining software to this tech dinosaur. In particular, Debby and Shing-Hon dealt with the brunt of my off-the-cuff and short-notice requests, of which there were many. I am honored to have learned from such bright, young scholars and foreign-policy practitioners.

Many colleagues, friends, and family cheered me on along the way. Thank you to Nichole Argo Ben Itzhak, Yan Bennett, Susanna P. Campbell, Jonathan T. Chow, Enda Curran, Leif-Eric Easley, Joe Gagliano, Nancy W. Gleason, Elke Jahns-Harms, Tiffany Kam, Jung Eun Kim, Jeehye Kim, Alanna Krolikowski, Jada Lam, Marc Lanteigne, Tabitha Mallory, Ben Mazzotta, Elizabeth McClintock, Bex Metcalf, Dipali Mukhopadhyay, Jenny Powlesland, Xiaoyu Pu, Ivan W. Rasmussen, Mihaela Papa, Tracy Richardson, Daniel Suchenski, Sarah Teitt, Marina Travayiakis Melidonis, and Sean Wong for all of their support. I thank Wilfred Wan in particular for reading drafts, putting up with *all* of my WhatsApp messages, and for always making the time to call and commiserate. Thank you also to Jennifer L. Erickson for offering frank insights on the book publishing odyssey and for all of her encouragement via email, ISA catch-ups, and skype calls. Thanks to Kei Koga for all of his sage advice over the years ("just write it, Courtney!") and for always setting a pace for me to follow.

The research that follows is impossible to do without the time and observations from the decision-makers addressing these foreign-policy crises. I am indebted to all of my interviewees for their insights, contacts, and reflections as to how foreign policy actually happens. Numerous cigarette breaks, coffee and tea appointments helped me understand just how complex, tenuous, and at times fortuitous, the work of day-to-day international relations actually is. I left many Beijing and New York research trips thinking it was frankly a marvel that any international response is offered at all for crises in these perennially 'far away places.' Thank you to each of my interviewees for their generosity and patience with my questions, and repeated contact throughout the years. Many interviewees not only recommended others to call on next, but actually vouched for me to facilitate my appointments.

Thank you to my two little loves for being the embodiment of joy and the best form of distraction—two things that all writers need in great quantities. My real commitment to work on this book began when my first was still teething, and I was pregnant with our second. Never did I think I would write singing nursery rhymes, bouncing a baby desperate to 'help' by jabbing at the keyboard—and never did I think that I would find it hilarious to do so. My children, and their curiosity, exuberance, and persistence ("I do it myself, Mama!") have given me a true sense of purpose about my day. My husband deserves much gratitude. Writing is an inherently selfish task: staring into space, attempting to clear your head, and dismissing wandering thoughts in order to type a few sentences. All of this looks much like time-wasting to the untrained eye. My husband never once asked if I could write faster. And he gave me the one thing I couldn't find anywhere else when the real crunch came: time. Time for me to think, write, and sleep—a true luxury when you face a killer combination of writer's block, half-finished drafts, and a growing brood. My husband's own curiosity and zest for life keeps me buoyant when buffeted. I am so grateful that our stars aligned.

My deepest thanks go to my first teachers, my parents. My parents have always encouraged me to believe in myself and to be unafraid of 'stretch.' They had faith that I knew what I was doing—even as a 16-year-old choosing to move to London to read the fuzzy stuff of International Relations. In particular, I will always be grateful for my parents taking care of everything during my junior sabbatical, my one precious opportunity to focus on the book's foundation. Mom in particular selflessly took care of me and my growing family—and kept me in good company walking to the station and going for tea. Daddy was the first to read the whole manuscript. Both my parents remain my most steady guides, listening to me debate about how to proceed in work and life. I dedicate this book to my parents with love.

Table of Contents

List of Graphs — xv
List of Tables — xvii
List of Abbreviations — xix

Introduction — 1

I. BACKGROUND

1. Historical Overview of China and Intervention at the UN Security Council — 15
2. Chinese-Language Discourse on Regime Change — 29

II. THEORY

3. Theory and Empirical Strategy — 39

III. CASES

4. Status and Intervention in Darfur, Sudan 2004–2008 — 63
5. Status and Intervention in Libya, 2011–2012 — 88
6. Status and Intervention in Syria, 2011–2015 — 108

IV. CONCLUSION

7. Conclusion — 135

Appendix: PRC Ambassadors to the United Nations, 1971–2019 — 149

Endnotes — 151
Bibliography — 225
Index — 275

List of Graphs

2.1. Chinese National Knowledge Index keyword search for "regime change" in the core newspaper database for 2000–2015, without duplicates — 30

2.2. Chinese National Knowledge Index keyword search for "regime change" in abstracts of the academic journals database for 2000–2015, without duplicates — 30

4.1. Factiva database search of English-language sources regarding "Darfur" and "regime change" within five words, 2004–2008, without duplicates — 67

4.2. Factiva database search of English-language sources regarding "China" and "Darfur" as headline/lead terms, 2004–2008, without duplicates — 83

5.1. Factiva database search of English-language sources regarding "Libya" and "regime change" within five words, 2000–2014, without duplicates — 93

5.2. Factiva database search of English-language sources regarding "Libya" and "regime change" within five words by month, 2011, without duplicates — 93

6.1. Factiva database search of English-language sources regarding "Syria" and "regime change" within five words, 2000–2014, without duplicates — 112

6.2. Factiva database search of English-language sources regarding "Syria" and "regime change" within five words by month, 2011–2014, without duplicates — 112

List of Tables

1.1.	China's abstentions on sanctions-related UN Security Council resolutions in the 1990s	23
3.1.	Separating status, reputation, honor, and prestige	40
3.2.	Summary of the case universe of China's responses to intervention	57
4.1.	Key UN Security Council Resolutions regarding the Darfur crisis	70
5.1.	Key UN Security Council Resolutions regarding the Libya crisis	94
6.1.	Key UN Security Council Resolutions regarding the Syria crisis	116

List of Abbreviations

AMIS	African Union Mission in Sudan
ASEAN	Association of Southeast Asian Nations
AU	African Union
CCP	Chinese Communist Party
DPRK	Democratic People's Republic of Korea
EU	European Union
FRY	Federal Republic of Yugoslavia
GCC	Gulf Cooperation Council
HIPPO	High-level Independent Panel on Peace Operations
ICC	International Criminal Court
KFOR	Kosovo Force
LAS	League of Arab States
MINUGUA	UN Verification Mission in Guatemala
MINUSTAH	United Nations Stabilization Mission in Haiti
MONUC	UN Organization Mission in the Democratic Republic of Congo
NATO	North Atlantic Treaty Organization
NLD	National League for Democracy
OIC	Organization of Islamic Cooperation
OSCE	Organization for Security and Cooperation in Europe
P3	P3 (the United States, the United Kingdom, and France)
PLA	People's Liberation Army
RPF	Rwandan Patriotic Front
SADC	Southern African Development Community
UN	United Nations
UNAMET	UN Mission for East Timor
UNAMID	UN–AU Hybrid Mission in Darfur
UNAMIR	UN Assistance Mission in Rwanda
UNFICYP	UN Peacekeeping Force in Cyprus
UNIFIL	UN Interim Force in Lebanon
UNITAF	United Task Force
UNMIL	United Nations Mission in Liberia
UNMIS	UN Mission in Sudan
UNOSOM II	United Nations Operation in Somalia II
UNPREDEP	UN Preventative Deployment Force
UNPROFOR	UN Protection Force
UNSC	United Nations Security Council
UNSCR	United Nations Security Council Resolution
UNSMIS	UN Supervision Mission in Syria
UNTAET	United Nations Transitional Administration in East Timor

Introduction

China is increasingly forthright about the specter of regime change at the UN Security Council. China was outraged with the toppling of Colonel Muammar Gaddafi in October 2011, consistently condemning the escalation of the bombing campaign as overstepping the UN Security Council mandate.[1] The no-fly zone and protection of civilians mandate implementation were proof for some Chinese officials that "Western countries have long harbored the intention of dethroning Libya's Muammar Gadhafi regime."[2] When debating possible modes of intervention into the Syria crisis, Chinese officials have often stressed that "China opposes any externally imposed solution aimed at forcing a foreign-imposed regime change."[3] In escalating UN Security Council sanctions against the Democratic People's Republic of Korea, China pointedly reminded fellow Council members "don't seek foreign-imposed regime change; don't incite a collapse of the regime."[4] Repeated statements like these belie a serious concern for China about the tensions between regime change and UN Security Council intervention. While China has gradually eased into accepting intervention, China remains reluctant to condone regime change.[5] Amongst other reasons, a leading concern for China is that being permissive in cases of regime change could set precedent for such actions against China, where Chinese Communist Party control and stability is arguably the most important core interest for Beijing. As one Chinese Ministry of Foreign Affairs advisor plainly stated: "when we vote on Syria, we are thinking of China."[6]

China's concerns are driven by an awareness that the UN Security Council could directly or indirectly address regime change: the forcible or coerced removal of the political leadership of a state by outside actors.[7] Broad changes in the international system, mean that norms like protection of civilians, accountability, and the responsibility to protect are consistently invoked to protect populations under threat of mass abuse by their governments. No longer are UN efforts limited to inter-state threats to international peace and security, but include addressing internal threats like genocide, ethnic cleansing, and state failure, for example. Scholars wryly observe that in the post-Cold War era, a much more targeted use of force against senior government officials, as opposed to whole states, would have saved much blood and treasure.[8] In an era where states themselves deliberately abuse their populations, often with the direction and support of senior government officials, the UN Security Council has authorized resolutions that fundamentally challenge government leadership structures *in order* to address the mass human rights abuse at hand, rather than assuming the host state government as a partner in resolution.[9] For example, International Criminal Court referrals for Sudan and Libya led to the indictments of both states' leaders;[10] peace enforcement missions in the case of Côte d'Ivoire gave way to UN helicopters firing on government military installations and the presidential palace where the incumbent was sequestered to enforce a transfer of power to the newly-elected head of state.[11] Such interventions mean to apply pressure on the regime, leading to a blurring of regime change and UN-led intervention.[12]

Given this evolving normative context, this book is primarily interested in cases of non-consensual intervention in cases of mass atrocities perpetrated by or with tacit support of the state. Cases without host state consent mean that the UN Security Council must coerce the state that is perpetrating the mass abuse through a violation of state sovereignty, which is a core principle for China.[13] This definition draws from the humanitarian intervention literature, though I do not concentrate on military means as the only tool for coercive intervention against the state.[14] In these cases of non-consensual intervention, I focus on activities and the threat of activities under Chapter VII of the UN Charter to include sanctions (diplomatic and economic), legal measures (International Criminal Court country case referrals) and the use of military force (peacekeeping operations and no-fly zone enforcement, for example)—all of which do not require host state consent.[15] As scholars note, the use of this variety of military and non-military tools represent a "compromise of sovereignty…that are exceptional in some way,"[16] disrupting the "conventional pattern of international relations."[17]

In contemporary international affairs, "responsible" members of the international community display a commitment to protecting collective goods like human rights, non-proliferation, development, and climate management.[18] These activity areas and their attenuating regulations and norms are recognized as legitimate by members in international society, and therefore, states that engage in these practices also have standing of good international citizenship.[19] The norms of accountability,[20] the responsibility to protect,[21] and protection of civilians challenge sovereignty boundaries in privileging peoples' rights—even in the face of their state—and by implication holding states and their leaders responsible for mass abuse. Although China may be reluctant to support norms challenging sovereignty, China is conscious that it cannot dismiss them altogether. Even if these norms are not fully internalized, states may still comply with these normative standards in order to reduce social opprobrium and maximize social benefits from their peers (praise, recognition and prestige, for example).[22] Although China may be more engaged with the intervention regime and displaying a deepening commitment to its international responsibilities, China is still reluctant to promote activities, like regime change, that are antithetical to state sovereignty.

Chinese officials are keenly aware that regime change can occur via a "Trojan horse" of intervention: when apparently legitimate requests for intervention push through regime change on the sly.²³ As one Chinese official noted: "regime change in Libya left [us] with this feeling that...we had been fooled."²⁴ UN Security Council-authorized resolutions were used as stepping stones to remove Gaddafi. Interviews reveal that potential cases of intervention with a surrounding public discourse presenting regime change as a viable policy choice are some of the most difficult crises for China to address at the UN Security Council, as China does not want to condone or support regime change via UN efforts.²⁵ Discourse, and the narratives that follow, make some facts appear as more relevant than others.²⁶ Discourse "work to define and to enable, and also to silence and exclude, for example by limiting and restricting authorities to some groups, but not to others, endorsing a certain common sense, but making other modes of categorizing and judging meaningless, impractical, inadequate or otherwise disqualified."²⁷ Public discourse calling for regime change—whether implying that regime change is "inevitable" given the arc of the crisis, or framing it as "necessary" in order to resolve the crisis—present regime change as a viable and logical goal in the context of debates about how to intervene in a particular crisis.²⁸ Public discourse helps create a policy window, when decisionmakers can switch policy tracks at much lower costs—away from tolerating or accepting heads of state to pursuing debates about forcibly removing them.²⁹ To be clear, my emphasis on public discourse as an element of contextual constructivism is not to say that material conditions do not matter, or that ideas and narratives always matter. I want to emphasize that social constructions by way of public discourse of regime change matter when embedded in wider material conditions. This occurs when a host state appears "ripe" for regime change (i.e. when the head of state directs or supports mass human rights abuse). And although regime change may not actively be discussed on the UN agenda in regards to the host state—a logical choice given China's veto—these dominant narratives cast long shadows on actual live negotiations for intervention in the host state.³⁰ As one advisor to the PRC Ministry of Foreign Affairs noted, "talking heads in Washington and London are important for what we achieve in [UN Security Council deliberations in] New York...it's not just noise."³¹ It is not the case that public discourse supersedes discussions in chambers,³² but that public discourse represents a signal that regime change could end up a distinct possibility for the host state—even if this is not part of the negotiating agenda amongst the UN Security Council.³³

The Puzzle

Despite a repeated commitment to the Five Principles of Peaceful Coexistence, and repetitions for intervention under UN Security Council authorization, host state consent, and regional support, China's record on intervention is fundamentally inconsistent, driven by a pragmatic weighing of principles versus national interests.

China now has a much more diversified position on intervention, voting for robust peace enforcement missions,[34] committing combat troops on mission,[35] and is actively engaging in the discourse regarding the responsibility to protect.[36] Yet even with China's repeated discontent regarding regime change, China has varied its response to UN Security Council intervention in the trinity of post-September 11 cases where heads of state have been marked for dispatch. Advocates asserted that "regime change alone can end genocide as the domestic security policy of choice in Sudan";[37] that the United Nations must "ensure the ouster of Libyan leader Muammar Gaddafi,"[38] and that Bashar al-Assad of Syria was a "'dead man walking'."[39] However, despite the robust public discourse in these cases identifying these strongmen for dispatch, China acquiesced to an International Criminal Court referral for Sudan in 2005 and largely supported intervention into Darfur by way of a Chapter VII peace operation; supported an International Criminal Court referral and acquiesced to a no-fly zone in the Libya case in 2011, but halted any interventions into the Syria crisis, issuing repeated vetoes since 2011.

China's record of responses regarding intervention cannot be robustly explained by existing theory. If realist theories guide decision-making, then one would expect vetoes in the cases of Sudan and Libya, where China had the most significant financial investments and close political ties with both leaders. Yet, these were the cases where China either permitted or actually supported intervention. If liberal theories guide China's decision-making, then one would expect that the United Nations institutional setting would clarify information, reduce transaction costs, and identify focal points so as to modify China's preferences to comply with emerging norms regarding accountability for massive human rights abuses, motivating China to cast at least abstention votes consistently across all these cases.[40] Yet China has cast votes in all the different voting categories, including multiple vetoes in relation to the Syria crisis. The Chinese foreign policy literature offers few insights. China did not support intervention into all three crises in the face of US pressure to do so,[41] nor is this a straight-forward story of learning or adaptation—despite the realization that China had enabled regime change in the case of Libya, China contended with difficulties in casting its Syria vetoes.[42] Fundamentally, China's range of responses is inconsistent with rational security-maximizing calculations. As these explanations fall short, we are left with a puzzle: for a state so reluctant to condone intervention—especially in the extreme of cases identified in the public discourse as targets for regime change—what explains China's response to intervention at the UN Security Council?

Argument in Brief

This book argues that status is an overlooked determinant in understanding the variation in China's position on intervention at the UN Security Council. I start with the unoriginal assumption that states are rational actors in a social context.[43] The desire to take actions that comply with status, and related social factors like self-image and identity, can mean that states select policy options even if it means bearing material costs.[44] Status—a state's "standing or rank in a status community"[45]—can have independent and significant effects for China's position on intervention. Status can shape China's response to intervention by way of China's peer groups. Under certain conditions, China's peer groups are able to modify China's preferences, even getting China to permit action. China's pursuit of status is in part driven by a consequentialist calculation to maximize China's standing as a group member, but it is also inherently social, with China driven by a logic of appropriateness and a desire to conform to an intersubjective standard of good behavior as a member of the peer group. To this extent, status is causal (i.e. external to actors) *and* constitutive (i.e. part of who actors are). I draw upon the status and Chinese foreign policy literatures, using a constructivist lens in so far that this approach unpacks aspects of international life that are taken as natural, given or embedded, allowing me to probe agency and social constructs.[46] Status highlights the connection between social and strategic drivers in foreign policy decision-making, as states' actions are framed by a normative context. By better understanding the impact and scope conditions of status we can answer fundamental questions of *why* China took certain positions regarding intervention and *how* these positions were justified. Therefore, the book is guided by a secondary research question, how does *status* affect China's response to intervention at the UN Security Council?

Though China's focus on status is not a new proposition,[47] this book offers greater analytical purchase on two grounds. First, I show that China is not motivated by a singular status concern by unpacking the effects of China's twin statuses as *both* a great power *and* as a developing state—therefore, China is focused on recognition from *both* its intervention peer groups: the United States, the United Kingdom, and France—the western, permanent members of the UN Security Council, the so-called "P3"—and *also* representatives of the Global South, which include geographic-specific regional organizations and often the host state.[48] Second, this book takes status seriously as a variable, and does not treat status as a constant value to China. The UN Security Council is an excellent social environment to examine China's status considerations, and I isolate the causal mechanism and conditions under which status can matter enough to China to impact its response to intervention. China is most concerned about securing status in the wake of a status trigger, and when its peer groups congregate around the same policy position; when its peer groups remain cohesive, with no individual state defections, and when peer groups can make an unresponsive China pay social costs for bucking group standards of good behavior. With this insight, I address a broader question about the limits of status as a variable in Chinese foreign policy.

Working inductively, I develop my theory based on an extensive collection of data, accepting the bounded transparency regarding ongoing, sensitive foreign policy matters. For the history of China and intervention, the book relies on primary sources to include UN Security Council resolutions, verbatim records and official statements, and secondary documents from news reports to academic texts. In order to uncover the "dogs that didn't bark"—those voting options *declined* by Beijing, for example—I conducted over 200 interviews with UN officials and Chinese foreign policy elites during multiple fieldtrips—primarily in Beijing and New York. Respecting interviewee anonymity, and also that readers may prefer sources that they can cross-check, I cite these interview materials sparingly. Participant observation at UN Headquarters was crucial to understand the near deference given to China because of its position as an anti-intervention, veto player. I created a dataset of Chinese-language analysis on regime change and intervention using the Chinese National Knowledge Index database, coding each article in order to understand how regime change was considered across time by Chinese analysts, scholars, and foreign policy elites. With these data sources, I am able to distill a rich study, going beyond works available in breadth and in depth, primarily focusing on the 2000–2015 period.

Contributions

This book makes three broad contributions to the International Relations literature.

First, it shows how status—often conceived of as a cause for conflict—is a determinant for cooperation. By treating status as a variable and not an unproblematic given in international politics, I take seriously the need to analyze and specify its effect on achieving cooperation at the international level. In key cases, China's behavior is inconsistent with rationalist arguments that emphasize a consequentialist calculation of material interests. By detecting and explicating this variable, I am able to offer better explanations than those outcomes predicted by the traditional lens of state security. The book highlights the effects of holding more than one status at a time—as China is simultaneously a great power and a Global South state in regards to intervention—and unpacks how status works in practice. Much of the status literature focuses on how a state can gain entry to a new peer group through status signaling, status-seeking behavior, and status attribution—but "requesting membership" to a peer group is not the same thing as *being* a member of the group. China's membership in its intervention peer groups is explicitly negotiated by its self-identification and behavior. But what does it mean to be a member of the peer group that itself is debating its intersubjective standard of good behavior? Or when that standard of good behavior suddenly shifts in favor of robust action, which China is reluctant to support?

The book shows how the process of negotiation and normative contestation within peer groups affects China's assessments of its desire to maintain status.

Second, the book offers a new lens to analyze how rising powers wrestle with attaining great power *and* maintaining "lower" status. After all, rising powers are states in status transition per se, and the assumption that these states automatically seek to "drop" lower status should be considered. Understanding how rising powers reconcile their status dilemmas—by this I mean the dilemma of how they secure status recognition from *all* their groups, as opposed to *which* of their status groups—is one of the broader issues under scrutiny here. In so doing, the book considers at what costs rising powers are willing to pursue status goals, even when the definitions of being in-status are changing or ill-defined. Addressing status dilemmas is a means to categorize these rising power states, differing from traditional definitions that typically emphasize material factors as identifiers—specifically preponderance of global military capabilities;[49] changes in relative material capabilities and influence;[50] global rather than regional interests,[51] or seeking recognition as a great power.[52]

Third, I extend analysis into the relationship between UN Security Council-sanctioned intervention and regime change, which is surprisingly under-studied. Both subjects often require the use of force in explicit violation of state sovereignty—the cornerstone of modern international relations—and are costly in blood, treasure, and have the potential to exacerbate existing conflict.[53] However, the literature largely approaches regime change from the lens of US foreign policy, reflecting the experience of the dominant state in the system.[54] Shifting the focus to the UN Security Council—the one institution explicitly and directly charged with governing international peace and security—allows us to reflect on the reality that the UN Security Council, and its composite members, must navigate such matters in consideration of intervention.

In terms of the Chinese foreign policy literature, I make three key contributions also. First, I contribute to our understanding of under what conditions status is pursued by China. China's focus on status is an obsession: since the 1990s, Chinese elites have "evoked 'international status' (*guoji diwei*) as if it were the most desirable value, the one that leads to power, security, and respect."[55] Suzuki notes that there is "a curious fixation" with status within China,[56] while Deng notes that "[j]udging by the frequency of the term's use in official Chinese discourse and scholarly analyses, [China] may very well be the most status-conscious country in the world."[57] Indeed Chinese analysts have attempted all sorts of measures to establish China's status.[58] Scholars have long noted that China is a state particularly concerned about its status,[59] but have been unable to explain the occasional willingness of China to sacrifice status and stand alone in foreign policy decisions at the UN Security Council.[60] When it comes to outlining scope conditions for when a state should care most about its status, the literature offers scant guidance: either when states are novices to a community, therefore, they are most eager to comply with norms to prove their membership,[61] or peer groups can only exert pressure on matters that are not behind China's "firewall" of core interests.[62] Once China perceives UN Security Council issues to touch upon Taiwan, for example, China is assumed to be immune to pressures from peer groups. As one senior UN official noted, "China needs to be a good citizen—but only up to a certain point; 'One China' is an existential issue... diplomatic relations with Taiwan are the red line not to be crossed."[63]

However, China is no longer a novice at the United Nations. Having assumed its seat at the UN Security Council over forty years ago, China has a steady record of gradual, scaled engagement with intervention problems. Furthermore, the concept of the core interests "firewall" is also unclear. In the Libya case alone, the UN Security Council unanimously referred a sitting head of state to the International Criminal Court, and with even more of a surprise, China abstained on imposing a no-fly zone on the regime.[64] Both these votes occurred against a vivid public discourse on regime change calling for the explicit overthrow of Gaddafi. If the core interest scope condition should hold, then one would expect vetoes against both proposed resolutions—after all protecting the longevity of the Chinese Communist Party, by ensuring *against* precedent for such coercive regime change abroad, is the paramount interest for China.

Second, I contribute to our understanding of China as a rising power and its involvement in multilateral security institutions. Despite China's growing importance for the intervention regime, China position on intervention remains poorly understood, with only a small body of sporadically produced, primarily historical scholarly works.[65] The copious research into intervention and the literature on the workings of the UN Security Council has scant mention of China.[66] Examining China and intervention contributes to the debate on the rise of China and what type of global security provider China will be.[67] For the most part, the literatures on rising powers and global governance have been left separate.[68] While there is a growing literature on China and peacekeeping, intervention, and specialist security regimes—there is yet to be a systematic investigation of China's response regarding regime change and intervention. The book explores China's reluctance to condone regime change. As Philpott argues, sovereignty is conceptualized in phases, with periods of "revolution," where its normative content is redesigned.[69] Sovereignty is a social construct open to reinterpretation by states that populate the system.[70] Periodically, the UN Security Council inserts itself in overriding state sovereignty, and since the 1990s, the UN Security Council has sometimes viewed mass violations of human rights as threats to international peace and security to be addressed through even non-consensual intervention. The limits of intervention are rigorously contested and a complex normative landscape links intervention to a broader discussion concerning regime change. Regime change is explicitly focused on fundamental transformations of domestic institutions—so not only is it about relinquishing control over territorial sovereignty (as in the case of intervention), but regime change goes to the heart of the matter of unseating governments. A core interest for China remains securing "state sovereignty, national security, territorial integrity, and national reunification, China's political system established by the Constitution and overall social stability."[71] Arguably, the first priority for the Chinese Communist Party is regime survival:[72] Chinese Communist Party sensitivity to regime survival is translates into concerns about regime change elsewhere.

Third, I examine China's sensitivity to regime change in the context of non-consensual intervention, an understudied theme in Chinese foreign policy.[73] Considerations of regime change appear to be an important element in Chinese foreign and security policy,[74] with Chinese strategists discussing concerns about "constant 'regime change' pressure" from the West.[75] Christensen suggests that one of the keys to stable US-China relations is for the United States to convince China that it is not pro-actively targeting China for regime change.[76] The regime change debate captures the edge of what China considers feasible in its normative framework. Counterintuitively, this debate reflects China's efforts as a norm entrepreneur of sorts,[77] where China contests the emerging pro-intervention, pro-human-rights-first status quo. In this crucial phase of China's rise—where China is not only expected to "do more," but has shown a willingness to do so, the book shows China's response and adaptation to the shrinking rhetorical space for its previous justificatory discourse limiting intervention. I illuminate the quandaries faced by China as it engages forcefully with attempts at new diplomatic measures and efforts to regain rhetorical advantage by establishing additional criteria for intervention. The book captures how China navigates this "status quo in transition" as its peer groups attempt to redefine the boundaries for intervention against a public discourse for regime change.

Plan of the Book

Chapter 1 sets the scene regarding China's record on intervention at the UN Security Council since China assumed its seat in 1971. The chapter illustrates how the UN Security Council has taken an increasingly expansive view as to what is under its purview—including massive domestic human rights abuses as threats to international peace and security—and the different tools to address these threats. The chapter reveals that for all its changes in regards to intervention, China prefers UN Security Council authorized, consent-based interventions, supported by regional players.

In Chapter 2, I turn to my original dataset of Chinese-language sources to understand Chinese views on the connection between regime change and intervention, and unpack why China finds regime change so problematic. I find that China's controversies over regime change fall into five categories: defining which actor has the authority to impose regime change; critiques about the aftermath of regime change; misgivings about how regime change affects China's overseas interests; the role of the United Nations in executing regime change; and how regime change presents challenges to China's core interests. Most importantly, Chinese writings reflect concerns regarding cases of regime change setting a precedent for actions against China.

In Chapter 3, I first define status and situate it in the literature against oft-interchanged concepts like honor, prestige, and reputation. Next, I identify gaps in the status literature, and explain my theory about status as a variable, defining peer groups and status triggers. The chapter discusses how social influence is the causal mechanism for status. Then the chapter specifies why the great powers and the Global South are China's peer groups for intervention, and debunks the popular assumption that Russia stands as China's peer in regard to intervention. The chapter closes on the research design and empirical strategy.

The remainder of the book examines the total number of contemporary, post-9/11 cases where intervention occurred against a public discourse of regime change in Sudan, Libya, and Syria. These cases represent an extreme of the recent crises at the UN Security Council—in which the state itself perpetrated mass atrocity crimes against civilians, spurring debate about the feasibility and legitimacy of intervention against a public conversation calling for enforced political transition.[78] These are also cases that have troubled Chinese foreign policy analysts with the surprising turns in China's behavior and the lack of systematic explanation for China's shifting stance. The three cases show variation on the dependent variable, China's response to intervention. Each of these chapters illuminate specific critical junctures in the cases. I discuss the weaknesses of alternative arguments and show how China's status considerations is the key variable to explain China's policy response.

Chapter 4 analyzes China's decision to shift its position on intervention in Sudan over the Darfur crisis. China went from viewing Sudan's problems as domestic affairs not for the UN Security Council's purview, to actively supporting intervention. China wrangled and effectively "enforced" consent from Khartoum for a UN Charter Chapter VII peacekeeping mission, and acquiesced to a referral of the Sudan case to the International Criminal Court, which led to an indictment of sitting President Omar al-Bashir. Though this case is popularly understood as being determined by material drivers—like shielding the Sino-Sudanese economic relationship, or addressing the reputational threat to the 2008 Beijing Olympic Games as the "Genocide Olympics," I demonstrate that status is the key variable to explain China's shifting position. Under mounting pressure from both the P3 and the African Union, in particular, China gravitated to supporting and permitting intervention with a yes vote for the UN-AU Hybrid Peace Operation and an abstention vote for an International Criminal Court referral in 2005, and again in 2008.

Chapter 5 analyzes China's support for an International Criminal Court referral of Gaddafi and its acquiescence to a no-fly zone during the 2011 Libya crisis. Though China initially had a muted position on the anti-Gaddafi protests within Libya,[79] in the space of three weeks Chinese officials would vote on two landmark resolutions: a yes vote for a unanimous referral of a sitting head of state to the International Criminal Court, and shortly after, an abstention vote permitting sanctions and a "no-fly zone plus" imposed on the regime. China's votes were largely a surprise—many analyses had predicted that China and Russia would cast tandem vetoes.[80] Status is key to China's response. China was particularly sensitized to status due to a well-publicized speech by Gaddafi citing his domestic repression as a parallel to the Tiananmen Square Incident of 1989. Against this status trigger, the P3 came out forcefully for intervention, and representatives of China's Global South reference group—the League of Arab States, the Organization of Islamic Cooperation, and the Gulf Cooperation Council—were among the first to call for intervention. China was able to move past its concerns regarding an International Criminal Court referral of the Libya case as it was isolated from its great powers peers at the UN Security Council *and* from its Global South peers in regional organizations. When the Global South reference group disagreed about the call for a no-fly zone, the basis of the "no-fly zone plus" resolution—with Middle East groups calling for action, and the African Union rejecting any physical intervention—China viewed the next most feasible option as an abstention vote, so as to offend no peer.

Chapter 6 analyzes China's decision to halt intervention into the Syria crisis, issuing repeated vetoes against calls for verbal censure, sanctions, compliance with peace plans, and referral of the Syria case to the International Criminal Court. I challenge the popular view that these vetoes were simply due to the Libya case, which ultimately had led to regime change. The vetoes were not automatic per se; China reconsidered its position, weighing factors against one another before each landmark vote. However, China's status concerns were largely discounted in this case: there was no status trigger, and concerns about acting within peer group status did not come into play. China rejected the P3 position that Assad was no longer a legitimate ruler, and Middle East regional groups were in internal disarray with individual member states selecting different policy positions. None of China's peer groups could exact social costs on an unresponsive China. China reconciled status concerns against other interests, and sought to protect the norm of intervention as separate from the norm of regime change.

Chapter 7 offers the conclusion, summarizing the findings of the book regarding China's status dilemma: pinpointing when status matters to China and how status affects China's position on intervention, dealing with other case sketches to show external validity. The chapter then contextualizes China's engagement with intervention against a broader theme of China as an actor in global governance, reflecting on to what extent China is seeking to "rewrite the rules of the game."

Next, the chapter considers the regime change problem at the UN Security Council, and the feasibility of the UN Security Council's response to such incidences—especially in light of China's hardening turn to separate intervention norms from regime change. Moving beyond the China case, I next highlight how the status dilemma is generalizable to other states' foreign policy decisions, and how states reconcile their competing status groups, with a particular focus on rising powers. The chapter closes on further research avenues regarding the status dilemma, intervention, and China's behavior at the UN Security Council.

PART I
BACKGROUND

1
Historical Overview of China and Intervention at the UN Security Council

Introduction

This chapter outlines China's approach to intervention since assuming its seat at the UN Security Council in October 1971. China remains committed to the principles of host state consent, UN Security Council authorization and regional support when governing decisions to intervene. However, these principles are applied pragmatically, against an assessment of China's interests, the circumstances of each country case, and a changing normative framework regarding intervention. It was only after the 1990s that intervention was viewed with increasing legitimacy in response to mass rights violations. The UN Security Council has, at times, taken it upon itself to override state sovereignty. In response to these violations of sovereignty over the last decades, there are three traits in China's approach to intervention: enduring skepticism about the benefits of Chapter VII non-consensual activities; a preference to not make Chapter VII intervention a trend; and the persistence of status as a concern in China's decision-making: whether it be an acute awareness of China's international isolation, or a commitment to account for peer group positions.

1971–1979: Non-Participation at the UN Security Council and Support for the "Third World"

Cold War dynamics prevented UN Security Council action into the three cases often coded as significant examples of intervention: India's 1971 intervention into East Pakistan, birthing Bangladesh; Tanzania's 1978 intervention into Uganda; and Vietnam's 1978 intervention into Cambodia.[1] China's initial years at the UN Security Council showed its "strict moral opprobrium"[2] regarding intervention. China cast abstention votes or pursued the so-called "fifth-voting style," simply not casting a vote while present in chambers. This position of non-participation and emphasis on rhetoric led to China's moniker as "Ambassador Look Out The Window."[3] These "moral vetoes" did not require China to take a stand and isolate itself amongst UN members for blocking potential action, but gave China the opportunity to give lengthy polemics against superpower abuse of the Third

World. China emphasized its solidarity and leadership over Third World politics by supporting efforts by the Non-Aligned Movement against colonial oppression in South Africa and Southern Rhodesia/Zimbabwe, and issuing an August 1972 veto at the behest of Pakistan against Bangladesh's admission to the UN, and a September 1972 veto against modifications to a Non-Aligned Movement backed resolution that sought to condemn Israel.

Explanations for China's behavior point to China's novice position as a self-labeled "student" of the United Nations bureaucracy,[4] coupled with China's lack of strategic interests in the country cases discussed at the UN Security Council. China's main objective was to use the United Nations to build stronger relationships with Third World states, establishing China as a leader of its peer group.[5]

1980–1989: Passive Support for Intervention

China gradually eased into supporting intervention, casting its first vote to support a mandate extension for the UN Peacekeeping Force in Cyprus (UN-FICYP) in 1981, almost a decade after its arrival at the UN Security Council.[6] China was the only permanent member to not use its veto during this period, and it voted in favor of all subsequent UN Security Council Resolutions concerning traditional, consent-based peacekeeping.[7] China began contributing to the UN peacekeeping budget and participating in other specialist UN agencies.[8] China shifted its rhetoric to discuss issues of sovereignty, reducing its polemics against the West as a source of abuse. China's position can likely be explained by its plans to chase greater strategic priorities of its independent foreign policy of peace, which promoted smooth relations with big powers and international institutions instead of ideological struggle.[9] The UN system provided China the means to develop its economy, promoting China's profile as a destination for foreign trade and investment.[10]

1990–1999: Pragmatic Flexibility

The post-Cold War euphoria led to a drive to implement intervention on the grounds of gross domestic human rights abuses, with a view to "right wrongs."[11] The number of UN peacekeepers—approximately 10,000 at the end of 1990, multiplied almost eight-fold by mid-1993. The Department of Peacekeeping Operations was established in 1992. The UN Security Council agenda quickly crowded with overlapping cases of intervention. Each of the cases set precedents for the motivations, means, and context of intervention. Peacekeeping, for example, moved from "keeping" peace to now "building" and "making" peace, and even nascent attempts at "enforcing" peace.[12] These changes in peacekeeping reflected the rise of a western liberal order and its focus on liberal democracy, institution building, good governance, and open markets.[13]

China defended its principles for intervention—UN Security Council authorization, host state consent, and regional support—but had to find ways to pragmatically apply these principles to the circumstances at hand.[14] Immediately after the Tiananmen Square incident, China's much diminished foreign policy stature limited its ability to offer its own views on just and correct intervention. During this time period, a trend can be seen of the great powers advocating for intervention and China using different logics to support, or more often than not, acquiesce to intervention. China sought to address its post-Tiananmen diplomatic isolation, which weighed considerably on foreign policy calculations at the UN Security Council by being seen as a more compliant player. It is key to note, however, that China remains steadfast to its principles, viewing these seminal moments of intervention as "exceptions." The United Nations primarily utilized three types of tools to address intervention: an extension of the use of force to include no-fly zones; non-traditional peacekeeping; and sanctions. This section deals with each of these in turn.

Addressing the Use of Force

China's concerns centered around the UN authorization for the use of force, and whether military interventions without an external threat would erode the norm of sovereignty. Morphet notes China's suspicions that such precedent could lead to an assault on China's sovereignty.[15] Wu Xinbo emphasizes that concerns about the use of force lie in China's negative experience with the UN-sanctioned Korean War and China's past as a colonized state by foreign imperialists.[16] However, though China raised its opposition to intervention, it would consistently capitulate: rhetoric signaled China's dissatisfaction, as did its emphasis on "exceptional circumstances" that could justify its lack of a veto.

For example, after the UN-authorized, US-led expulsion of Iraqi forces in 1991, the P3 initiated no-fly zones over northern and southern Iraq for humanitarian purposes,[17] citing UN Security Council Resolutions 678 and 688 to justify their actions,[18] as the latter was the first time that the UN Security Council referenced a humanitarian crisis as "threatening to international peace and security in the region."[19] China abstained on both these resolutions, acknowledging the humanitarian concerns in Iraq and the growing refugee flows into Turkey and Iran, but asserted that the UN Security Council should not act "on questions concerning the internal affairs of any state."[20] Oddly though, China gave no formal objection to the no-fly zone establishment,[21] nor its initial enforcement.[22] The Chinese Foreign Ministry spoke of China's "serious concern" and that actions should not "jeopardize Iraq's unification and territorial integrity,"[23] but otherwise did not escalate its criticism. China's initially muted position on the establishment of no-fly zones is most likely attributed to its post-Tiananmen isolation, and the support from regional representatives including the League of Arab States,[24] the Organization of the Islamic Conference,[25] and the Gulf Cooperation Council.[26] However, China's opposition to the no-fly zone measures grew as the purpose gradually shifted away from humanitarianism towards regime containment. For example, China saw that the no-fly zone imposition humanitarian driver as a "pretense" and "excuse" for what really "violated the UN Charter and norms of international relations and are in defiance of and trampling on Iraq's sovereignty."[27]

China raised similar criticisms of the no-fly zone imposition over Bosnia following ethnic cleansing and mass human rights abuses there. The UN Security Council incrementally expanded the UN Protection Force (UNPROFOR) mandate to address protection of humanitarian efforts and the protection of "safe areas" around Sarajevo and Srebrenica and other Bosnian towns in the Federal Republic of Yugoslavia.[28] China supported a number of resolutions broadening UNPROFOR's mandate through 1992,[29] though China registered its concerns about host state consent and enforcement actions.[30] While China showed a degree of flexibility for humanitarian purposes, voting for enlarging the UNPROFOR mandate and its scope for the use of force, it did so with unease, repeatedly discussing the "exceptional" nature of the Bosnian issue.[31] China emphasized its commitment to securing host state consent as the mandate included no-fly zones, as China perceived that sovereignty would be under threat.[32] China again emphasized the relevance of host state consent, issuing abstention votes over Resolution 781 when no-fly zones were to be established over Bosnia to limit Serbian air assaults[33]—the first time that the UN Security Council imposed these measures over another sovereign member state—and China abstained again when Resolution 816 called for "all necessary means" to enforce the no-fly zone.[34] Both votes were explained in reference to the lack of consent.[35] Though China was willing to criticize unilateral actions, it remained unwilling to prevent measures.

Following the Federal Republic of Yugoslavia's refusal to comply with the Rambouillet Agreement for a proposed peace between Yugoslavia and the Albanian majority of Kosovo, NATO intervened in the Kosovo crisis without UN authorization. NATO executed a bombing campaign from the end of March through early June 1999 to push Serbian forces out of Kosovo, paving the way for the protection of Kosovar Albanian and Serbian communities via the NATO-led Kosovo Force (KFOR). While key NATO members made the case for a right of humanitarian intervention[36] due to Belgrade's persecution of ethnic Albanians in Kosovo, China opposed designation of the Kosovo situation as a threat to international peace and security.[37] China routinely referenced the need to have "respect for the sovereignty and territorial integrity and noninterference in [the Federal Republic of Yugoslavia's] internal affairs under any pretext are in conformity with the principles of the United Nations Charter.[38] China saw that NATO unilateral actions were making "an extremely dangerous precedent in international relations," violating the sovereignty and territorial integrity of the Federal Republic of Yugoslavia.[39] The willingness of NATO to violate Yugoslavia's sovereignty was proof of "double standards,"[40] and China charged NATO bombings as "power politics whereby the strong bully the weak."[41] China warned that the "human rights over sovereignty theory serves... to promote hegemonism under the pretext of human rights. This totally runs counter to the purposes and principles of the United Nations Charter."[42]

China's approach of abstention, acquiescence, and rhetoric in these three cases regarding the expanded use of force relates to a number of factors. China had made a prudent calculation that achieving economic modernization was a priority beyond that of opposing the West,[43] and given China's interests in each case were fairly limited, acquiescence and a "detached attitude" was the best policy.[44] China also systematically cited the importance of regional players in advocating for such intervention, using regional opinion as a barometer for permissible action.

Peacekeeping

The 1992 report, *An Agenda for Peace*, expressly put the United Nations in the position of using "preventive deployment," "post-conflict peacebuilding" and armed peacekeepers to "respond to outright aggressions, imminent or actual"; prototypes of sort for multi-dimensional peacekeeping, robust peacekeeping, and peace enforcement operations that followed.[45] The report harkened a new era for peacekeeping, with a more circumscribed view of consent. *An Agenda for Peace* saw that peacekeeping no longer had to be limited by consent—"deployment of a United Nations presence in the field, *hitherto* with the consent of all the parties concerned"[46]—and that peace enforcement units should also be deployed in the field. Doctrinal changes pushed China to engage in activities beyond traditional peacekeeping. Scholars note that China most likely did "acquiesce to a series of interventions about which many in Beijing [had] real reservations" in this time period, with the priority on promoting China's profile as a good international citizen.[47] China's concerns for its international reputation and status therefore led to a pragmatic approach, reducing post-Tiananmen tensions as a pathway to breaking through sanctions. In three seminal cases—Somalia, Rwanda, and East Timor—China reinterpreted the meaning of consent in order to justify peacekeeping efforts, while consistently returning to the importance of regional opinion.

The UN pushed for a Chapter VII intervention on solely humanitarian grounds into Somalia,[48] leading to the US-led United Task Force (UNITAF).[49] China supported the establishment of UNITAF, pointing to human suffering, the position of African states, and the recommendations of the UN Secretary-General for "strong and exceptional measures"[50] in view of "the unique situation in

Somalia,"[51] which had no functioning government to offer host state consent. As the conditions in Mogadishu worsened, the UN Security Council established UNOSOM II, the first UN peacekeeping operation authorized for Chapter VII enforcement actions,[52] again with strong regional support.[53] China supported intervention, consistently emphasizing "the unique situation of the absence of any effective, functioning government in Somalia,"[54] the importance of regional input and that these measures were not to establish precedent for the use of Chapter VII in a peacekeeping context.[55]

In October 1993, the UN Security Council unanimously established the UN Assistance Mission in Rwanda (UNAMIR), to monitor a consent-based ceasefire between the Rwandan government and the Tutsi-led Rwandan Patriotic Front (RPF).[56] The UN-led effort was supported by the Organization for African Unity, as it recognized its own inability to deal effectively with the crisis due to limited resources, a lack of concerted political will, and the internal debate about the non-interference clause in its own Charter.[57] China abstained on the resolution that led to the deployment of a French-led multinational force, *Opération Turquoise*, with an all-necessary-means mandate to protect displaced persons, refugees, and civilians at risk,[58] following the genocide of at least 500,000 Tutsis and moderate Hutus in April 1994.[59] China asserted that "armed force or mandatory measures would only worsen the situation,"[60] calling for a traditional peacekeeping force over a Chapter VII enforcement mission.[61] China called for "securing the cooperation of all parties" as the French-led force "cannot guarantee the cooperation of the parties to the conflict."[62] The Chinese perspective was that the events were not genocide, but a civil war.[63] The Rwanda case highlights that without consent, China was unwilling to support intervention but was not unwilling enough to necessarily cast a veto. These peacekeeping failures led to the United Nations' temporary retreat from fielding ambitious peacekeeping missions. By 1996, less than 20,000 peacekeepers were deployed. A new UN Secretary-General Report, *Supplement to the Agenda for Peace*, reemphasized consent, impartiality, and non-use of force as "essential" components to peacekeeping success.[64]

Following agreements between Indonesia and Portugal on the status of East Timor in May 1999, the UN Security Council unanimously established the UN Mission for East Timor (UNAMET) with Indonesia's consent, to assist with the East Timorese independence referendum.[65] With the overwhelming vote for independence, the Indonesian military-sponsored militias began attacks on civilians to reverse the decision. As the UN Security Council debated next steps, China held to its position that Indonesian consent was imperative for any intervention via a UN peacekeeping force,[66] emphasizing the opinion of regional states.[67] Indonesia begrudgingly gave consent and requested the deployment of an international force,[68] and despite this being "induced consent,"[69] China praised the decision as "rational, respectable and responsible."[70] Shortly thereafter, China voted for the establishment of the Australian-led multinational peacekeeping force the International Force in East Timor (INTERFET)).[71] The East Timor case alone has been consistently cited as a turning point in Chinese foreign policy, which no longer denied the legitimacy of human rights and humanitarian intervention.[72] And that despite China's critiques of the Kosovo crisis, East Timor proved that China's "orthodox view of sovereignty might be less intractable than Beijing's rhetoric would otherwise indicate."[73] Even though this was only induced consent, China still permitted action, viewing that this was sufficient host state support.

China did cast two vetoes, both times to prevent peacekeeping efforts in states that had recognized Taiwan over China, violating the One China Policy and infringing on China's sovereignty. China vetoed the draft resolution regarding the dispatch of military observers to Guatemala to observe the peace accords that ended the thirty-year civil war in January 1997 via the UN Verification Mission in Guatemala (MINUGUA).[74] The motivation for this veto—the sole dissenting vote in the face of fourteen votes favoring establishing the UN peacekeeping mission, was Taiwan's relations with Guatemala. The Chinese representative noted at the UN Security Council discussions:

> The Government of Guatemala has, for four consecutive years, unscrupulously supported activities aimed at splitting China at the United Nations, in flagrant violation of the purposes and principles of the Charter of the United Nations and in disregard of the solemn warnings of the Chinese government.[75]

China was faced with overwhelming support throughout the UN system for MINUGUA,[76] and ten days of Sino-Guatemalan negotiations led to China reversing its veto.[77]

China cast the sole veto to deny the extension of the UN Preventative Deployment Force (UNPREDEP) to Macedonia at the end of February 1999.[78] China explained its veto with the view that the situation in Macedonia had

> apparently stabilized in the past few years, and its relations with neighboring countries had improved... the original goals of the Security Council in establishing UNPREDEP had already been met. In that context, there was no need to further extend the mandate of the mission... the United Nations already insufficient resources should be used where they were most needed.[79]

Though these comments allude to the Chinese commitment to "standardized standards" (i.e. "no playing favorites" amongst peacekeeping missions), Taiwan concerns cannot be discounted in China's decision.[80] Macedonia gave Taiwan diplomatic recognition just before the UN Security Council vote.[81] Although there was resounding support for the proposed resolution, China still vetoed the extension of the operation—only to receive regret and opprobrium from Macedonia, several UN Member States, and UN Secretary-General Kofi Annan.[82] As Zhao Lei notes, "the purpose behind China's two vetoes was to protect national sovereignty and dignity."[83] Wuthnow supports this view, pointing to the deteriorating cross-Strait relations in the mid-1990s as motivating China to cast vetoes on routine peacekeeping affairs that called into question the sanctity of the One China policy.[84]

Sanctions

China consistently expressed reservations regarding sanctions regimes, an activity that the UN Security Council pursued multiple times during this time period. China held to a consistent view that coercion was counterproductive, and so sanctions would not help international peace and security. However, China did not use its veto, instead favoring an abstention position (see Table 1.1).[85]

China refused to support "further Security Council action,"[86] possibly including sanctions, against the DPRK in 1993-4, following Pyongyang's withdrawal from the Non-Proliferation Treaty and refusal to submit to visits by the International Atomic Energy Agency. China pushed for weaker draft resolutions and presidential statements in order to guarantee a stable Korean Peninsula.[87]

In contrast, China supported sanctions against the Haitian government following the September 1991 *coup d'etat* ousting the democratically-elected president Jean-Bertrand Aristide. The Organization of American States lobbied the UN Security Council to address the ensuing Haitian crisis, which China initially opposed to adding to the Council's agenda.[88] The UN Security Council unanimously passed an embargo freezing the assets of the new government in June 1993.[89] Despite its yes vote, China saw the matter as "essentially...the internal affairs of that country, and therefore should be dealt with by the Haitian people themselves."[90] China again noted "the unique and exceptional situation in Haiti"[91] and the request of the exiled Haitian government for sanctions, which were an extension of existing regional measures.[92] National interests dictated a tough stance in regards to potential escalatory action into the DPRK crisis, and a lack of direct interests into Haiti permitted flexibility when pushed by regional opinion. These two cases constitute the notable exceptions during this period.

2000—Present: China Makes Diversified Commitments Regarding Intervention

The initial enthusiasm for intervention waned after the patchy record of the immediate post-Cold War period. The United Nations reduced its missions—with the UN Security Council only authorizing ten new missions in this interval. The 2000 *Brahimi Report*, the 2003 *Peacekeeping Handbook*, and the 2008 *Capstone Doctrine*[93] reconceptualized peacekeeping, reflecting changes that were

Table 1.1. China's abstentions on sanctions-related UN Security Council resolutions in the 1990s

Date	Topic	Purpose	Resolution	Vote (yes, veto, abstention)
31 Mar 1992	Libya	Impose aviation, arms embargo on Libya	748	10:0:5
30 May 1992	Bosnia	Impose economic, aviation, arms, cultural embargoes on Serbia and Montenegro (the FRY)	757	13:0:2
9 Oct 1992	Bosnia	Impose military flight ban over FRY airspace	781	14:0:1
16 Nov 1992	Bosnia	Impose sanctions to end external interference (from FRY) in Bosnia-Herzegovina	787	13:0:2
30 Nov 1992	Cambodia	Sanction Democratic Kampuchea for failure to comply with Paris Treaty	792	14:0:1
31 Mar 1993	Bosnia	Extend military flight ban	816	14:0:1
17 Apr 1993	Bosnia	Threaten sanctions against Bosnian Serbs for continued violence	820	13:0:2
11 May 1993	DPRK	Call on DPRK to rejoin Non-Proliferation Treaty	825	13:0:2
11 Nov 1993	Libya	Impose economic and financial sanctions on Libya for non-compliance with previous resolutions	883	11:0:4
2 Dec 1994	Bosnia	Affirm enforcement of economic sanctions adopted under Resolution 820	None	Russian veto
21 Apr 1995	Bosnia	Extend partial suspension of measures against the FRY	988	13:0:2
26 Apr 1996	Ethiopia-Sudan	Sanction Sudan for failure to extradite suspects	1054	14:0:1
16 Aug 1996	Ethiopia-Sudan	Impose aviation sanctions on Sudan for non-compliance with Resolution 1054	1070	13:0:2
20 Oct 1997	Iraq	Threaten travel ban on Iraq for non-cooperation with UNSCOM	1134	10:0:5
31 Mar 1998	Kosovo	Impose arms embargo on FRY due to Kosovo situation	1160	14:0:1
14 Oct 1998	Kosovo	Demand FRY comply with OSCE and NATO missions in Kosovo	1203	13:0:2

already underfoot in peacekeeping practice.[94] These official documents were ambitious in that they no longer required peacekeepers to assume continual consent of all parties as a precondition to action, nor remain impartial when acting. For example, the *Peacekeeping Handbook* noted that peacekeepers must "actively pursue the implementation of their mandate even if doing so goes against the interests of one or more of the parties."[95] The *Capstone Doctrine* went further, stating that peacekeepers should not "condone actions by the parties that violate undertakings of the peace process or the international norms and principles that a UN peacekeeping operation upholds."[96] These official documents were ambitious in their reinterpretation of impartiality and consent. Though the UN implemented high-profile and large-scale peace-support missions,[97] these were missions typically spearheaded by regional hegemons, reducing some of China's concerns about expansive reinterpretation of peacekeeping principles. In recognition of the ongoing issues in peacekeeping, in 2015 the High-level Independent Panel on Peace Operations (HIPPO) published its report, *Uniting Our Strengths for Peace: Politics, Partnership and People*, offering over 100 recommendations for improving peacekeeping.[98] The Panel was established so as to address the increasingly demanding environments and mandates that peace operations encounter, including stabilizing states, ongoing insurgency, and facing asymmetric threats.

China's voting record gradually converged with the P3 during this period, and China moved to reduce rhetoric in favor of more technocratic commentary, with reference to its guiding principles for intervention. China re-engaged with other facets of the intervention regime. China started increasing its troop contributions at a time of severe overstretch in UN peacekeeping operational capacity. In April 2004, China voted in favor of establishing the United Nations Stabilization Mission in Haiti (MINUSTAH),[99] and deployed on mission, marking the first time that China sent peacekeeping contributions to a state with which it had no diplomatic relations.[100] China supported the establishment of the International Force in East Timor (INTERFET) and the United Nations Transitional Administration in East Timor (UNTAET).[101] China deployed to these missions also, showing acceptance for enforcement mandates. Chinese participation in the United Nations Mission in Liberia (UNMIL),[102] the UN–AU Hybrid Mission in Darfur (UNAMID), the UN Mission in Sudan (UNMIS),[103] the UN Interim Force in Lebanon (UNIFIL),[104] and the UN Organization Mission in the Democratic Republic of Congo (MONUC),[105] for example, supported high-profile, large-scale missions short of desperately needed enabler units giving even greater support to Chinese statements of responsible power.

China's contributions to the UN budget grew in the 2000s, jumping from less than 1 percent in the 1990s, to just over 3 percent in 2008—a sizable commitment for China as the budget itself had reached $8billion by 2008.[106] Based on the UN-assessed funding system, which takes into account China's economic wealth and UN Security Council permanent position, by 2016 China was poised to become the second largest contributor to the UN peacekeeping budget, just behind the United States; and the third largest contributor to the overall UN budget, just behind the United States and Japan.[107] China is often within the top ten of all troop contributors to UN peacekeeping and leads the permanent members of the UN Security Council. While China's 2,419 troops are still a fraction of the total Chinese military,[108] China stands apart because it has typically provided hard-to-source enabler troops: the medical teams, engineers, and logisticians that provide the backbone to a peacekeeping mission, supporting all other troops to carry out the mandate. These high-value assets are typically sparse in developing country military profiles, and also cost more than the standard UN reimbursement rate to maintain and train.[109] China reached a "major breakthrough" from its previous decades of deployment,[110] dispatching comprehensive security forces to Mali in 2013 and a battalion of combat troops to South Sudan in 2014. China most recently committed 8,000 troops to the UN peacekeeping standby force—one fifth of the 40,000 total troops committed by fifty nations—and China allotted $100m towards the African Union standby force, along with $1bn to the China-UN peace and development fund, geared towards peace operations.[111]

Decisions to engage with peacekeeping contributions are taken at the senior most levels, with comment from the Joint Staff Department of the Ministry of National Defense, the State Council, and the Ministry of Foreign Affairs—though policy elites including former officers, researchers, and think-tank officials with expertise in the region or subject-matter offer guidance also. In complicated incidences of non-consensual intervention—where Chinese assets and nationals are in politically volatile countries facing high-security risks—the Standing Committee of the Politburo is likely to have the final word.[112] China's deployment to UN peacekeeping is motivated by a series of factors,[113] including bolstering local security, so as to "protect the rightful interests of Chinese people and companies."[114] Peacekeeping is an internationally acceptable platform for invaluable field experience and military-to-military cooperation. Troop contributions bolster China's status as a great power and leader of the Global South, blunting criticism of China's defense spending and confirming China's profile as a responsible player in international affairs.[115]

China signaled some flexibility with the emerging norms of the protection of civilians and the responsibility to protect, which became standard features in UN Security Council resolutions.[116] The protection of civilians sees the protection of the most vulnerable as a collective responsibility, and is now prioritized during missions, with multiple operations directed to develop their specific protection strategies.[117] The responsibility to protect recast state sovereignty as responsibility; if states failed to protect populations in their territories, then the international community can take on this responsibility to protect through prevention, rebuilding, and reaction measures.[118] China pushed for a diluted version of the norm. The World Summit Outcome Document charged the international community to act in a "timely and decisive manner," lifting the threshold on target states from being "unable and unwilling" to protect their citizens, to proving that these states are "manifestly failing" at doing so. The precondition of UN authorization remained, though the UN Security Council only had to *consider* action, with no requirement to act in the face of such cases. The norm could only be applied in four categories of specified crimes: genocide, war crimes, crimes against humanity, and ethnic cleansing, all of which were already covered in international law.[119] China saw the term as so watered down it was now meaningless, and only a topic for future discussion.[120] At this point, China had succeeded in limiting the responsibility to protect to be consistent with China's views on international politics, and as one Chinese official reasoned, the norm was "not such a challenge to sovereignty as we had thought."[121] China endorsed the responsibility to protect in various UN Security Council Resolutions when the language replicated the 2005 World Summit Outcome Document wording, and did so even while it could have used Russia for "veto cover".[122]

A new feature in this period was the International Criminal Court, a supranational, permanent court to prosecute states and their leaders for future mass crimes.[123] International legal efforts were previously limited to support of context- and geographic-specific ad hoc tribunals in Rwanda, Sierra Leone, and the former Yugoslavia.[124] Crucially, the International Criminal Court goes beyond these prior legal instruments,[125] which all rely upon state leaders essentially volunteering themselves for punishment. The International Criminal Court has judicial authority to determine whether or not particular uses of force by state officials are excessive and criminal violations of international law. Therefore, the International Criminal Court is designed to operate *regardless* of whether leaders elect to put themselves on trial.[126] Indeed, the Court has intervened in ongoing crises.[127] The UN Security Council can make a referral of any country case to the International Criminal Court, invoking authority to address international peace and security under Chapter VII of the UN Charter.[128] Once the UN Security Council refers a situation, the ICC prosecutor completes an investigation that can lead to individual indictments on one or more of the mass atrocity crimes. In effect then, a referral of a case can and has led to indictments that actually target heads of state.[129] As the detailed case studies show, China's consistent concerns regarding intervention reflected misgivings about the potential for this tool to segue into regime change; indeed commentators noted that "regime change appears to be a pre-condition for the ICC to achieve its goal of ever seeing leaders like Gaddafi and Bashir in the dock."[130] China worked to reduce ICC involvement in the case against President Laurent Gbagbo of Côte d'Ivoire, while it also delayed ICC investigations into the Sri Lankan civil conflict.[131]

During this time period, China cast two vetoes preventing censure of Myanmar in 2007 and sanctions on Zimbabwe in 2008. In the case of the potential UN Security Council rebuke of Myanmar for massive human rights violations in 2007, China justified its veto by arguing that human rights violations were not the concern of the UN Security Council unless there was a direct challenge to international peace and security.[132] The calls for Myanmar's military junta to stop persecuting minority and opposition groups was unjustified in China's eyes. In 2008, China again vetoed a draft resolution that sought to appoint a UN special envoy, impose an arms embargo, and apply travel and financial sanctions on President Robert Mugabe and other senior Harare officials.[133] China saw that "[the] development of the situation in Zimbabwe until now has not exceeded the context of domestic affairs" and that measures would lead to interference. China cited the need for "great attention and full respect" for African Union/Southern African Development Community-led mediation and good offices efforts, and the need to respect regional opinion that Zimbabwe was not a threat to international security.[134] China watered down resolutions sanctioning the DPRK for its nuclear weapons activities, and pushed back on similar measures against Iran for its nuclear developments.[135] China abstained on sanctions against Eritrea in 2009, and when China did support sanctions against the Democratic Republic of the Congo (DRC), it fell short of meeting compliance standards in not divulging its arms sale information.[136]

Popular explanations for China's harder turn emphasize China's material interests. As Wuthnow notes, many of these "pariahs" were key energy suppliers for China: Iran as a key source of liquid natural gas; Sudan and Libya as top providers of crude oil; and the DRC and Côte d'Ivoire were key sources of raw materials fuelling China's growth.[137] Therefore, the priority on China's "Go Abroad" policy called for Chinese government offices and businesses to search for new markets for Chinese exports and for new energy markets, leading to a harsher line against intervention.[138] Concerns about regional proximity are also cited: regime collapse could bring refugees and Republic of Korea-based US troops closer to China's border. Sri Lanka and Burma are both access points to the Indian Ocean, and the latter stands as a resource partner for China. Both of these factors ensure the Chinese incentive to reduce western-led pressure against these states.

Conclusion

China's gradual shift in attitude regarding intervention—from outright dismissal to guarded engagement and more robust participation with the facets of the intervention regime—shows China's flexibility in practice regarding intervention, while emphasizing its commitment to limiting intervention through the UN Security Council, under the ideal conditions of host state consent and regional support. However, China has made "exceptions" to its first preference of a non-interventionist stance, accommodating the international community's waxing and waning interest in intervention. Despite this flexibility, China remains consistent in framing its support for enforcement or violations of consent as exceptions due to the case at hand. China's persistent skepticism regarding the value of Chapter VII activities reflects China's views that the use of force is only acceptable as a last resort; and serves as a blunt instrument to resolve conflict *because* it disregards consent and state sovereignty. The brief record shows China's concerns about status—whether by standing with peer groups or reducing China's international isolationism—are also consistent with China's considerations for intervention.

2
Chinese-Language Discourse on Regime Change

Introduction

Regime change remains a central activity in international relations, with over 100 incidences of successful regime change in the last 200 years.[1] The United States attempted seventy-two covert regime change operations during the Cold War alone.[2] In the post-9/11 landscape, regime change has re-emerged as a foreign policy tool and goal applied to target dictators in Egypt, Iraq, Libya, and Sudan. Yet the relationship between regime change and non-consensual intervention is discussed in only a limited sense, despite the policy relevance for understanding the boundaries of intervention today. Both regime change and intervention often require the use of force in explicit violation of state sovereignty—the cornerstone of modern international relations—and are costly in blood, treasure, and potential to exacerbate existing conflict.[3]

An emerging literature discusses the problem of regime change and its ripple effects for China's foreign policy behavior. Wang and Lieberthal classify concerns about regime change as a major source of Sino-American friction and strategic distrust.[4] Christensen suggests that stable Sino-US relations hinges on the United States establishing China is not a target for regime change.[5] However, these writings have conceived of regime change as a problem in only Sino-US relations, overlooking a lively Chinese-language discussion that details *why* China harbors such concerns about regime change in other arenas also. While there is admittedly no sustained research agenda on regime change, there are a number of Chinese government-funded projects, producing individual cutting-edge analyses.

Chinese Sources on Regime Change

In order to unpack China's response to regime change, I use the Chinese National Knowledge Index database, and searched for the keyword "regime change" (translated as both *zhengquan gengdie* or *zhengquan gengti*),[6] across China's core newspapers and academic journals focusing on politics, military affairs, and law for the time period of study. This gave me a broad cross-section of data to analyze how Chinese thinkers, academics, and officials are conceptualizing and responding to incidences and discourses about regime change. A small number of articles discussing non-violent, domestic political transitions in the DPRK, Japan, and the United States were set aside. This left writings citing examples of regime change to include targeting Serbia, Georgia, Ukraine, Iran, Iraq, Libya, Syria, amongst others. While in admittedly small sums in both databases, "regime change" picks up traction as a keyword, reflecting reporting and editorials about various regime change crises in the core newspaper database (see Graph 2.1), with an academic discussion mirroring press analysis (see Graph 2.2). A spike in analysis

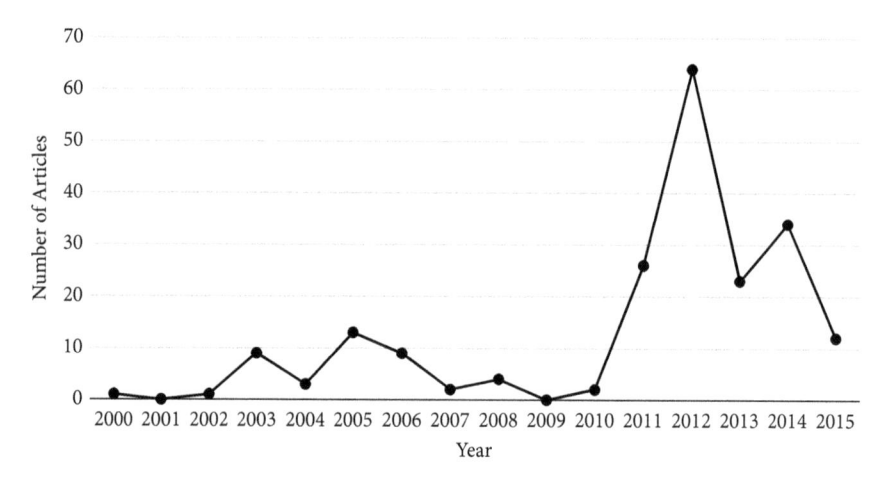

Graph 2.1. Chinese National Knowledge Index keyword search for "regime change" in the core newspaper database for 2000–2015, without duplicates

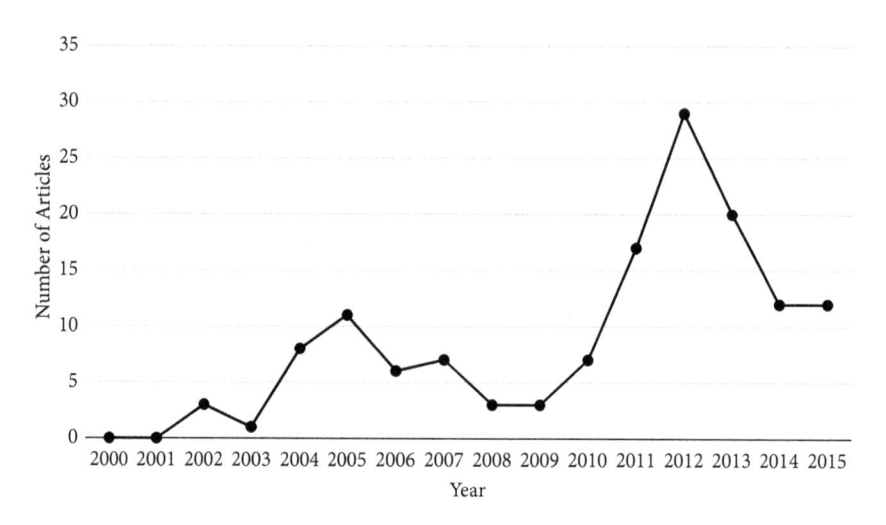

Graph 2.2. Chinese National Knowledge Index keyword search for "regime change" in abstracts of the academic journals database for 2000–2015, without duplicates

on regime change follows the colored revolutions in the early 2000s, with interest surging following the opening of the Arab Spring and the Ukraine crisis.

I find similar themes regarding regime change as there are in China's discourse regarding intervention—with one key difference, however. The systematic investigation reveals that unlike intervention, which may be permissible under certain conditions,[7] Chinese-language sources systematically dismiss any positive value in regime change. This outright rejection of regime change reflects China's "significant concern to delegitimize the regime-change mode of external intervention promoted by the Western powers."[8] Despite China's rise, suspicions about foreign or domestic hostile forces creating disorder at home remain "a paramount feature of Chinese leaders' foreign policymaking."[9] Therefore, refuting attempts to subvert sovereignty remains an integral commitment due to the need to protect China's sovereignty and political stability.[10] With such deeply-held beliefs that the "ultimate goal of 'Western powers' is to overthrow [Chinese leadership's] rule,"[11] China remains committed to preventing initiatives via the UN Security Council that could challenge China's security and stability.[12]

Analysis of these sources reveals thematic objections regarding regime change, often overlapping in each individual publication. The first set of concerns regarding regime change is focused upon the use of illegitimate authority to execute regime change on a target state. Writings systematically note that "Western" countries—typically identified as the United States, but also France and the United Kingdom—are the primary proponents of regime change. These states are routinely criticized for not only domestic interference in the target state, but for forcefully executing regime change for their own selfish interests. For example, one author argues that "the West is very elated with their success on Syria, however, they are gradually ceding rationality because of their flailing hegemonic ambition to make regime change"[13] and that

> the real goal of the West in doing this is not to (improve) the so-called human rights and democracy in Syria, but for reasons that are deeper and more complicated. First, Syria is of great geopolitical and military significance... Second, the al-Assad Government adopts an anti-America foreign policy... all of these have made America unhappy with Syria's current government. (The United States) has long been eager to subvert it and build a pro-West regime in order to permeate and control this significant spot more effectively.[14]

Commentators abide by the view that the only legitimate authority to regulate international peace and security is the United Nations Security Council. Therefore, efforts to "usurp" authority by western states for their own motives is entirely unacceptable.

A second theme in Chinese-language discourse is the misgivings about the aftermath of regime change. Once the original government has been targeted, modified or even deposed, Chinese scholars emphasize that the immediate result is social turmoil, chaos, and disaster. For example:

> However, after two years, countries (that have achieved regime change during the Arab Spring) have not realized their expected political stability and power, economic development and prosperity, and a peaceful and enlightened society. In contrast...conflicts resulting from all kinds of disputes have trapped this region into turmoil and chaos that no one has expected beforehand.[15]

Analysts see that these cases of regime change "sank [countries into] corruption and scandal of internal conflicts"[16] and are now examples of "continuous political instability."[17] Scholars argue that "[at] the same time, the United States has instigated 'regime change' in countries such as Libya and Syria, which has enabled Islamic extremist forces to gain more room for survival."[18] Chinese analysts challenge the "benefit" of regime change as a source of positive development for countries, and they point out that

> [many] Arab countries are increasingly aware that China's position and proposition is correct, recognizing that China is the great country that truly considers the interests of the Arab countries. Western countries that have been vigorously interfering in Syrian affairs and always seeking political change have finally had to admit that "political settlement is the only way out" and began related efforts.[19]

The virtual collapse of states post-regime change leads to a third theme in Chinese discourse: that foreign-imposed regime change brings unpredictability to the management of China's overseas interests in the targeted states. For example, in the context of the Libya and Syria interventions, commentators assert that:

> From the aspect of our own interests, China needs energy, light industry and labor markets. Also, it is possible that the Middle East is a market for China's sophisticated products such as large mechanical equipment, airplanes, and ships. Wars and chaos in this region is contradictory to China's national interests.[20]

Managing Chinese investments abroad and protecting Chinese nationals requires political stability within host states and politically stable relationships with foreign leadership. However, with the regularity of regime change, evidence suggests a gradual reassessment of how China maintains its interests abroad. Chinese government entities and firms now maintain contact with both the ruling parties and the opposition parties in certain states.[21]

A fourth theme in the Chinese discourse identifies that regime change does not occur just between individual enforcing states and those that are targeted for regime change, but stretch into the role of the United Nations in authorizing and executing regime change. Chinese-language sources reveal two strands of thought upon this theme. First, that the use of the United Nations as a venue to execute regime change is an abuse of the United Nations system built upon foundational principles like respect for state sovereignty. Plainly stated: "We cannot agree to regime change under the banner of the United Nations."[22] Authors remain skeptical of attempts to use "humanitarianism" as the excuse for regime change.[23] Using the excuse of UN authority for regime change is unacceptable to China.[24] A second theme reflects deeper anxieties with suspicions that the UN Security Council itself is focused on *purposefully inducing regime change* (i.e. that regime change occurs not because of an abuse or reinterpretation of a resolution—but was the actual goal of the UN Security Council all along).[25] Chinese-language sources argue that China must hold a firm line to prevent a trend of UN Security Council-authorized regime change.[26]

One last important theme is whether such regime change policies will set precedent that challenges the core interest of the Chinese Communist Party's control over China. Challenges to Chinese Communist Party control are conceived of in two ways: that examples of regime change can embolden internal challenges to state authority or that China itself will be targeted by powerful states as a regime change candidate. For example, "For China, Ukraine political upheavals and political games between Russia and the United States (Europe) in Ukraine have in fact touched China's core interests...that is...their spillover effect on China's national security...risks of separatism have long existed for China."[27] Authors variously list Taiwan, Xinjiang, the Diaoyu Islands, the South China Sea, and Sino-Indian territorial dispute as sites where secessionists could be emboldened to achieve their own interests at the expense of China's state stability. On the latter theme, Chinese analysts argue that

> if a ruler leaves office not because of the power of people of its own country but because of external power, the order of this world is lost. Once the principle of non-intervention in domestic affairs is broken through, you can randomly exert intervention to any country that you do not like.[28]

States like China, which challenge more liberal approaches to governance, can become a target itself. These writings reflect a central theme that even incidences of regime change that appear to be physically remote to China are a threat to China and its core interests.

Why the Rejection of Regime Change?

Having established the Chinese-language discourse wholeheartedly rejects regime change, the question remains why? Jia Qingguo asserts that a combination of China's negative modern experience with the outside world; its developing country position; the US-dominated international system; and China's domestic politics explain China's skepticism regarding regime change and intervention.[29] The experience of the "century of humiliation," when the Chinese state was shaped by war and unequal treaties, and fractured between different warlords, foreign concessions and invading colonizers is central to the myth of the founding of the Chinese Communist Party, as the protector of the Chinese people and territory.[30] As Wang Jisi points out, the Chinese leadership has a "persistent sensitivity to domestic disorder caused by foreign threats."[31] The Chinese wariness of "power politics," "hegemony," "gunboat diplomacy" and "might is right" are references to the Chinese experience of the "century of humiliation" at the turn of the twentieth century.[32] The weight of the Chinese state's traumatic entry into modern history is so great that "the loss or gain of sovereign rights by other actors was always seen through this prism of China's own sovereignty in a way that often overemphasized the possible implications of intervention elsewhere for China's own sovereignty claims."[33] Therefore, the firm line against regime change in Chinese discourse is fundamentally driven to protect China's sovereignty from future intervention.

Of fundamental concern here is the relationship of regime change to challenges of China's key core interest, Chinese Communist Party stability and authority.[34] As You Ji notes, at the center of a conceptualization of core interests is China's focus on "CCP security as the ruling party."[35] Concerns about internal security threats have led to a governing mentality that even "unexpected accidents may lead to a 'color revolution' and threaten state security."[36] The conflation of internal and external security concerns has meant a hyper-awareness that incidences of regime change elsewhere could only instigate such agitation against the Chinese state at home.[37] These concerns are reflected in the formulation of China's core interests, which consistently feature preservation of China's "basic state system and national security," "sovereignty and territorial integrity," and the "continued stable social and economic development" of China.[38] It is no coincidence that the first formal mention of the preservation of China's political structures occurred during the Sino-US Economic Dialogue: a reminder to the hegemon that China's existing state system was not for modification—despite the "constant 'regime change' pressure from the West."[39] Prior to the development of the term "core interests," the commitment to protecting China's mode of governance and the CCP as the agent of political governance were cited as part of China's "fundamental interests," which emphasized domestic order and stability, along with economic and social reform policies.[40] The formulation of core interests matter as these are "an important element of PRC diplomacy."[41] Chinese officials have repeated that China will "never waver, compromise, or yield" on core interests.[42]

Conclusion

Unlike intervention, which may be permissible at times, Chinese discourse systematically dismisses any positive value in regime change. Regime change is explicitly focused on fundamental transformations of domestic institutions in the target state. Not only does regime change concern relinquishing control over territorial sovereignty (as in the case of intervention), regime change goes to the heart of the matter of unseating and transforming governments. Therefore, regime change is routinely written off as an illegal activity taken at the behest of hegemons, leaving target states destitute and politically unstable, challenging China's ability to protect its overseas interests. Even worse is the sneaking suspicion that United Nations authorization is abused to achieve regime change—or worst yet—that the United Nations *willingly* takes part in regime change. This outright rejection of regime change goes beyond wider Chinese foreign policy tenets like the touchstone of Chinese foreign policy, the Five Principles of Peaceful Co-existence—and reflects China's "paramount concern to delegitimize the regime-change mode of external intervention promoted by the Western powers."[43] Yet these concerns have to be applied and navigated in practice when China must engage in country crises at the UN Security Council that occur against a public discourse on regime change. Developing a method and a theory to explain China's pragmatic adaptations of its absolutist anti-regime change stance occupies the next chapter.

PART II
THEORY

3

Theory and Empirical Strategy

Introduction

Disentangling Status

Status is central to many sub-debates in International Relations. Understanding how states are stratified in an international hierarchy is a core research agenda,[1] as is understanding status attribution and inconsistency and status conflicts effects on war.[2] Nuclear proliferation,[3] nuclear weapons testing,[4] the prestige effects of the non-proliferation treaty[5] and the purchase of conventional weapons platforms are also linked to status projections.[6] And though status has been mostly tied to a research agenda for great powers and rising powers, there is an emerging research agenda concerning status for small powers also.[7] Despite the relevance of status for the discipline, this term is often ill-defined and interchanged with prestige, reputation, and legitimacy.[8] Unsurprisingly, status is also defined differently by scholars: a reputation for power;[9] a rank or reputation attributed to an individual by others in the same social system;[10] esteem or credit associated by others;[11] recognition by others of one's strength;[12] or as a position in a social hierarchy, for example.[13]

Working with status means that "semantic confusion" must be first cleared away.[14] I adopt the hierarchy of beliefs system to delineate status from other overlapping, related terms like honor, prestige or reputation (see Table 3.1).[15] Take this hypothetical example:

> Zeroth level of belief: The number of vetoes that China has cast at the UN Security Council.
>
> First level of belief: The United States believes China will veto any draft resolution that pertains to Taiwan.
>
> Second level of belief: Many states believe that China will use its veto more frequently because it is a rising power.

In the example, the zeroth level of belief is a verifiable fact, regardless of an audience to observe the fact. For example, to date, China has cast a total of twelve vetoes at the UN Security Council since assuming its seat—and these vetoes exist whether states pay attention or not. The first level of belief is essentially one actor's belief about another actor's (China's) future actions, based upon its past or current actions or statements—i.e. China will likely veto any draft

Table 3.1. Separating status, reputation, honor, and prestige

	Perceptual	2nd Order Belief	Social Construct	Positional
Reputation	Yes	Sometimes	No	No
Honor	Yes	Yes	Yes	No
Prestige	Yes	Yes	Yes	No
Status	Yes	Yes	Yes	Yes

resolution pertaining to Taiwan, is derived from China's perceived reputation regarding Taiwan's sovereignty in international affairs. First-order beliefs now separate out the target (China) and an audience of *at least* one other actor, that perceives China's reputation to veto. The second level of belief relates to status—since many actors hold a shared belief about the beliefs of another actor or group. All of these actors have to share that same belief on how China is pursuing its rise in global politics—the community holds a shared belief about China's rising status.

With this heuristic, we can see that both prestige and honor differ from status in that they are not positional, but absolute values. Reputation also differs from status in that it is not necessarily a second-order belief: it only takes two actors for a reputation to exist, for example. Reputation is predominantly used as a tool to help states promote credibility. In security studies, the focus is on the use of reputation as a means to help states enforce their security through military credibility. Reputation is viewed as a key component to states producing credible, effective threats: a reputation is developed by past behavior in prior situations that are akin to current or future situations.[16] In contrast, the international political economy literature specifies reputation as a tool to promote cooperation as reputation is a proxy for state's reliability.[17] A reputation for consistency promotes belief in reliability, so it is "easier for a government to enter into advantageous international agreements; tarnishing that reputation imposes costs by making agreements more difficult to reach."[18] As Erickson notes, these literatures develop reputation as "primarily a proxy for past action"[19] that will help predict action of other states in future, similar scenarios. States select policy options that enable them to exploit their "good" reputations for future negotiations: maximizing reputational gains in order to accrue material ends in future scenarios. Erickson extends the rationalist account of reputation and develops a constructivist concept of "social reputation," where reputation is a "policy support as a means to enhance, maintain or repair reputation as a rational strategy for social ends."[20] She argues that states value their social reputation as "an end in and of itself, having an 'internal' feel-good effect on state identity, and as a means to additional social benefits in the international community."[21] These social benefits include "national self-esteem or international standing and legitimacy."[22] Erickson therefore makes an important innovation linking together constructivist and rationalist accounts of reputation, latent in the literature.[23]

While Erickson's definition of social reputation overlaps somewhat with the concept of status in its emphasis of social goods, it still differs from status on two accounts. First, in regards to status, states focus on maximizing social benefits from *specific peer groups*, rather than the unspecified singular entity of the "international community."[24] In so doing, status gives me the specificity to understand status pressures from different peer groups and how China reconciles status as it navigates its social position vis-à-vis a specific peer group. Second, Dafoe et al. note that while a reputation can be consciously nurtured or manipulated by an actor so as to acquire a new reputation, status is not as pliable by the actor themselves—status is inherently social, and is "accorded by others."[25] Last, Erickson's theory relies upon a causal mechanism developed from case studies of western democracies, where domestic groups shame their governments for falling short of their international reputations for compliance with human rights standards. It remains unclear if China's domestic audience replies to China's social pressures from abroad in similar ways.[26]

Definition of Status

I adopt the definition that status is the "standing or rank in a status community."[27] This definition is in line with the classic sociological definition put forward by Durkheim and Weber, and widely reproduced in International Relations literatures.[28] It captures the rank/standing aspects of status (emphasizing positionality vis-à-vis peers) *and* identity aspects of status (*as a peer*), as emphasized in social identity scholarship: China's status *as* a great power and *as* a developing state.[29] To clarify, a status community is "a hierarchy composed of the group of actors that a state perceives itself as being in competition with."[30] I use the term "peer group" or "reference group" as this encapsulates the social aspect of status: the peers that China views it belongs with matter in as far as they represent a collective guide for the good behavior and standards that group members should uphold. While corresponding with rationalist and constructivist accounts of International Relations, this definition emphasizes that status holds five qualities:

- it is relational to a particular peer group or a position in time,[31] and therefore, it is always relative as a "positional good";[32]
- it is perceptual and intangible, and therefore subjective (i.e. what actors think of another actor's beliefs); status cannot simply be calculated from material

attributes.[33] A state's understanding of its own individual status requires an understanding of what status is accorded to them by others;

- it is a social, shared belief amongst a group of actors,[34] and while the exact position of states within a hierarchy may be a matter of debate, there is a general agreement as to group membership.[35] Therefore, it is not the case that an individual state can confer status on another, status rests on "consensus of opinion within a group";[36]
- it is a means to an end (i.e. instrumental use of status to maximize another goal);
- and it is an end in and of itself (i.e. staying within status to maximize status markers is the pursuit).

This short definition of status highlights that multiple status standings within the international system at any given time are possible. Moreover, it is not so much that being of x status counts, but what matters is that x status is in relation to the x peer group of states, with specific recognition from that peer group. Recognizing this quality helps us investigate the sub-questions about status in China's case, i.e. *which* peer group and *under what conditions* is that peer group important to China?

States are motivated to stay current with evolving norms in the international community as these guides for appropriate behavior are key to states being seen as legitimate players. States that operate within the international community address norms through their activities, defining the "boundaries and distinctive practices" that shape international society.[37] By meeting these expectations of good behavior, states develop status that is aligned with their identities, enabling their peers to view them as equivalents. This position of peer status has additional benefits, giving the state the opportunity to distinguish themselves within the peer group rank as a leader within their peer group hierarchy garnering "respect, deference and social influence."[38] As Erickson asserts, when states seek to improve their status, they may "seek to outperform their peers, particularly with respect to policies on issues close to their self-image."[39] This desire to be a social leader amongst a peer group may mean that states adopt policies that seek to redefine what is viewed as "responsible": either by adopting "more responsible" policies, above and beyond the community standards, or by redefining what "responsible" means entirely. Both of these avenues permit states to enhance their ordinal position within their peer group as a leader. States seek status as both a means to an end, and as an end in and of itself. Accruing status markers—such as praise, esteem, prestige, and recognition from group members—delivers a state's interests in addressing the "need to feel good about itself, for respect or status."[40] This search for social approval from group members validates a state's identity as a group member,[41] which is in part grounded in the external perception of that identity by other actors.[42]

Theorizing Status Effects on China's Response to Intervention

A growing number of empirical works show how status can modify state's considerations of intervention.[43] Implicit to these arguments is that state interests are not fixed, but are socially constructed, guided by a sense of identity-based, peer group-enforced appropriate action. I argue that material factors shaping China's strategic choices regarding intervention are necessary, but ultimately insufficient to explain China's acceptance or resistance to intervention. Status, particularly in its most concentrated form, has independent and significant effects as China considers intervention in light of its role-based appropriate behavior. Yet status is not a constant driver for China; other considerations can outweigh status in importance on a case-by-case basis. Nor is status uni-directional as often implied—China seeks status as a great power *and* a developing state in regard to intervention.

I find a direct correlation that China is most status sensitive—i.e. that status drivers can trump other concerns regarding intervention—when there are two components. First, when China's *peer groups* are able to exact social costs or social benefits on China by way of social influence. China's peer groups are most able to affect China via social influence when they are *cohesive* with no significant defectors from the peer group, *unified around a single policy position*, and *willing to exact social costs* on China for not executing their policy prescription. With these conditions met, peer groups have narrowed and defined policy options for China, so China can clearly understand what the peer group expectations are. This also means communicating and establishing the group standard of acceptable behavior for a group member, clearly signaling what the peer groups see as the intersubjective normative consensus. The difficulty here is that the peer groups may be composed of multiple constituent players (engaging with not only one regional group, but multiple Middle East regional groups during a regional crisis, for example), which gives the opportunity for these constituent players to disagree about policy, while multiplying the chance for defections as there are more constituent players at hand.

A second component for when China is most status sensitive is the presence of a *status trigger*. Status triggers heighten or accentuate China's pre-existing status concerns *by emphasizing China's isolation from its peer groups*, making China more susceptible to status challenges. My concept of status triggers build upon the concept of "status deficits," when "a status ranking...falls below a level set by expectations."[44] While Renshon and others emphasize a state's perception of its ranking, my focus is on the *perceived isolation from the state's peer group community*. Status triggers heighten the social space between China and its peer group, as status triggers indicate that China could be shunned by its peer group. Status triggers are conceived of in primarily two forms: these are speech acts that draw a contemporary parallel to a low status time in China's foreign policy (i.e. references to the Tiananmen Square Incident of 1989) or attacks on China's high-profile status-rewarding events (i.e. attempts to tar the 2008 Olympic Games).[45] I will explain each of these in turn. Speech acts that draw a contemporary parallel to a low status time in China's foreign policy accentuate China's pre-existing status concerns because of China's negative expectations around this social rejection occurring a second time. The status trigger leads to anticipation of again being isolated internationally. For example, after the Tiananmen Square Incident of 1989, China was almost immediately bound by diplomatic and economic sanctions by the United States, its allies, and international bodies like the World Bank and the Asian Development Bank. These sanctions included halting official development assistance, sales of police and military equipment, and senior-level official visits. The ramifications of official sanctions was to further encourage private firms and individuals to reconsider their business efforts in China, leading to an immediate and sharp decline in direct foreign investment, foreign lending, and in-bound tourism.[46] China paid a steep price in figurative and literal terms for its use of force domestically, ultimately leading to a period of stigmatization in international politics.[47] Therefore, speech acts that attempt to draw contemporary parallels to the Tiananmen Square Incident can spark concerns about the potential for re-ostracizing China.

Another variation on status triggers are attacks on China's high-profile status-rewarding events. Rising powers in particular are recognized to make concerted efforts to secure high-profile, international events as a kind of status marker.[48] Each of these events present a precious opportunity and prestige of being the *only* host for that particular time period.[49] Because these events are scheduled so far in advance, states can largely control planning, using these events as platforms for "political imagineering" to showcase the political, societal, and economic development of these states within global politics.[50] China has made a concerted effort to secure such status markers, taking rounds of efforts to secure the 2008 Olympic Games in Beijing.[51] The 2008 Olympic Games were not an exogenous shock for Chinese foreign policy, however. China is hosting more and more international headline events—like the 2010 World Expo in Shanghai, the 2016 G20 Summit in Hangzhou, and the 2022 Winter Olympics in Beijing. Because of the importance of these events for China, especially in signaling its own arrival in global politics, such high-profile events provide the opportunity for status triggers if they are attacked, defamed or boycotted.[52] This status trigger builds upon the literature, which identifies that status perceptions are most likely "updated sporadically"[53] in response to a "status-altering event" that "must be highly visible...dramatic or salient, and convey unambiguous information."[54] Major, high-profile international events, like the Olympic Games, give the largest swath of bandwidth-deprived observers clear signals about a state's status as a recognized member of the international community. This again is a counter-intuitive take on the status literature, which emphasizes nuclear weapons, the initiation of conflict, and military technological developments as status-altering events.[55]

I also find the inverse to be true; China can discount status against other factors—even to the point of moving towards status insensitivity—when there is no status trigger and when peer groups have defectors, cannot agree on a single policy position, and when peer groups cannot exact social costs. Therefore, though status can be addressed along a spectrum—from when China is status sensitive to when China is status insensitive—it would be a mistake to generalize status sensitivity with acceptance of intervention by casting a yes vote, and the opposite, namely status insensitivity to rejecting intervention by casting a veto. Calibrating status sensitivity to voting outcomes can only be excavated by a case-by-case analysis, as the effects of status for intervention are tied to peer group interaction. However, it is key for this study to isolate status in action. Yet, this can be difficult to do: status is intangible; states may not publicly acknowledge decisions taken because of status; and status can easily appear to be reputation or another nested concept. I use the concept of *social influence*—the distribution of social rewards or punishments against China by its peer groups—as the causal mechanism to highlight status in action.

Social Influence as a Causal Mechanism for Status

I use social influence as the causal mechanism to isolate status effects. Social influence is the distribution of social rewards and punishments from the peer group to the target state, which can elicit the target state to modify its behavior.[56] The target state modifies its behavior due to "real or imagined group pressure."[57] These changes in policy position reflect a desire to not challenge the peer group position, rather than a deep persuasion that the peer group position is correct and should be followed. In short, social influence is defined by public conformity without private acceptance.[58] Therefore, social influence spurs calculations to boost status through maximizing a sense of well-being by conforming with the peer group and maximizing esteem through social praise for having done so. This micro-process captures China's own disquiet about supporting its status groups responses to intervention and using social influence separates out China's status drivers from other nested intangible motivators, like reputation. An assumption in the literature is that a prior condition for social influence is that it must be used by a peer group that the target state has an existing identification with, otherwise there is nothing social about critiques or shaming. However, this existing identification works both ways: an actor cannot continually shop to maximize status from any praise-giving player as status is sticky, constrained by role-based appropriateness and what "good behavior" peer groups dictate.

Social punishments are defined as "shaming, shunning, exclusion, demeaning or dissonance derived from actions inconsistent with role and identity."[59]

Punishments are social in nature—only the peer group that the target state identifies with and approves of can execute punishments on the target state. Conversely, social rewards include "psychological well-being, status, a sense of belonging, and a sense of well-being derived from conformity with role expectations."[60] Maximizing a social good of a positive self-image and accruing positive status markers from the various peer groups is the end in and of itself. There are two prior conditions grounding social punishments and social rewards. First, there must be an intersubjective normative consensus between the peer group and the target state about what good behavior looks like. Second, these social punishments must be made in public spaces, so that the target can be put under pressure for actions inconsistent with the group standard.

If social influence is at play and status maximization is pursued by China, we can look for three criteria. First, China's commitment to pro-social behavior is made when non-commitment means being in the minority—or in the extreme, China will end up alone if it stays on its original policy path. This criteria highlights the social aspect of being isolated from the peer group as the driver to modify China's position. Second, China should stress back-patting and opprobrium from members of its peer groups in its statements explaining its changes in behavior. These statements should emphasize China's actions in line with the peer group and China's success in achieving recognition from the peer group or acknowledge the social criticism of China. Third, commitments should take place in the absence of material gains and side payments. This is the key criteria that separates status from reputation—i.e. acting strategically to maximize material payoffs at a future bargaining scenario. To be clear, social influence accepts that China's pursuit of status can be taken even at cost to China's other material pursuits (i.e. reputation, maximizing other material markers of power—like territory, economic strength etc.). However, this move is not irrational per se.[61] Maximizing status can mean maximizing the social benefits of wellbeing and the sense of belonging of acting within the standards of good behavior of the peer group.

China favors the UN Security Council as the crucible for moderating global peace and security.[62] This preference for the UN Security Council is consistent throughout all the decades of China's involvement at the United Nations.[63] The United Nations is built upon a state-based international order, with states having equal opportunity through their membership in the UN General Assembly. The UN Security Council underscores that great powers bear greater responsibilities for the regulation of global peace and security.[64] China's permanent seat is proof that China is a great state,[65] where through the veto or threat thereof, permanent members can moderate solutions to issues. Because of the normative value placed in the UN Security Council's legitimacy as *the* venue for moderating global peace and security, it means that alternate platforms comparatively lack legitimacy.[66] China consistently refers to the importance of the UN Security Council, aware that its legitimacy is a "valuable means of taming American power."[67]

As an international institution, the UN Security Council systematizes status concerns as it acts as a social environment for states. Institutions help guide standards of appropriate behavior of good international citizenship by legitimating rules and norms.[68] First, the UN Security Council formally brings together all the potential status groups that could matter to China in regard to intervention. This is done with permanent or rotating seats at the UN Security Council, or through case-specific activities including special briefings or *Arria* formula meetings, which permit relevant stakeholders beyond the fifteen states at the UN Security Council, like the African Union or League of Arab States, to address the UN Security Council. Feedback assessments and briefings from UN Department heads and senior officials to the UN Security Council reaffirm policy expectations amongst peer group members also. In so doing, the UN Security Council's procedures shorten the distance between China and its peer group representatives through the regularized interactions between diplomatic representatives.[69] The UN Security Council follows the UN Charter regulations and evolving multilateral practice, that promote transparency and accountability for traditionally opaque diplomatic negotiations. For example, the UN Security Council voting procedures require votes to be recorded and made public, along with meeting minutes, press briefings, and working group efforts—in so doing, the structure of the UN Security Council makes public what could remain private, enabling policy choices for status appraisal by other actors.[70] In regulating diplomatic practice and procedure, the UN Security Council is a social environment that amplifies how social pressures and rewards can be exerted on China.[71] The relevance of having consistent policy and normative behavior is magnified when states take a leadership role, as they do at the UN Security Council.[72] After all, states that "value their social standing in international society seek to avoid negative social judgments,"[73] and will exhibit behavior according to the standards of good behavior by their peer groups. By holding this context constant, we have the opportunity to highlight the transmission of these pressures and China's response to them.

China's Peer Groups for Intervention

China's two peer groups for intervention include the great powers and the Global South. I will turn to each of these peer groups first before debunking the common misperception that China views Russia as a peer.

China's Status as a Great Power Peer and Its Great Power Peer Group

In regards to intervention, China self-identifies as a great power, a view of the Chinese state since modern times.[74] China stresses the permanence of its great power heritage, regardless of comparative short-term economic or military shortfalls—relying on China's demographic weight, geographic expanse, civilizational longevity, cultural attributes, and participation in international institutions as indicators of its superiority. Such arguments are "consistent with a long-running theme in Chinese foreign policy that China's inherent greatness as a civilization should translate to international standing and respect... regardless of domestic political, military or economic circumstances."[75]

China's self-view is also replicated in the wider International Relations literature, with prodigious materials arguing China's rise as a great power,[76] while debating what type of great power China will be—strong or fragile;[77] revisionist or status quo;[78] whether its intentions can be gleaned from its capabilities[79] and whether its rise is a matter of threat or opportunity in global politics.[80] The view that China is rising is recognition that "a rising power will, in the near future, become a great power."[81] China's position as a great power is reinforced by its permanent position at the UN Security Council, arguably the most legitimate international security institution in recent memory,[82] and so China has a privileged institutionalized perch in the elite decision-makers of global governance. The different schools of International Relations take the view that the great powers hold special responsibilities for the regulation and maintenance of the international system, the core idea behind the establishment of the UN Security Council permanent membership. Realists have an instrumental notion of great power responsibility, citing Waltz's comment that "those of greatest capability take on special responsibilities"[83]—even if those system-wide decisions are driven by their own interests. While the English School also accepts material components,[84] they in turn emphasize the social component to responsibility, noting that great powers are also shaped by the intersubjective understandings of their own social role.[85] Therefore, great powers execute system-stabilizing responsibilities partly out of enlightened self-interests that recognize the importance of international society and a smooth-running international order. To put it succinctly, great powers are "recognized by others to have, and conceived by their own leaders and peoples to have, certain special rights and duties."[86] As scholars have noted, it is not just that great powers are executing duties on behalf of international society, it is "that these rights and duties are *recognized* by both self and others."[87]

More recently, China's great power status has become equated with China's role as a responsible power.[88] Though it is popularly assumed that China's responsible power discourse was imposed by the United States,[89] there is strong evidence that responsible power (*fuzeren de daguo*) is in and of itself a Chinese-derived concept with "deep roots in Chinese traditions of statecraft and corresponding visions of world order."[90] The responsible power discourse appeared in the 1990s, initially referring to the Five Principles of Peaceful Co-existence and the need for positive bilateral relations.[91] Jiang Zemin made use of the term in 1997 in a speech, linking together China's major power position and its responsibilities to protect world peace.[92] Since then, Chinese scholars have engaged in an active debate about what "global responsibility" entails and what these notions mean for China.[93] In Yeophantong's detailed study of the Chinese discourse on responsible great power, she notes that the concept of responsibility falls into four different camps ranging from those that exhort China to embrace its position and responsibilities; those that see the need to execute domestic development before committing to international responsibilities; those that see responsibilities limited to only the Global South; and those that dismiss the responsibility discussion as simply a new means to limit China.[94] Despite the broad spectrum of views, these thinkers do not challenge the concept of "responsibility" itself.

What does responsible power mean? The term has come to signify that a deeper involvement in multilateral organizations, including the daily governance and norms that govern these institutions, is in fact in China's interests.[95] As China takes on greater responsibilities in the international sphere—from peacekeeping contributions, to anti-piracy missions in the Gulf of Aden, to aid deliveries after the 2004 Indian Ocean Tsunami and the 2010 Pakistan floods—Chinese officials have framed these actions as examples of China executing its "international obligations" as a responsible power.[96] Responsible power enables China to emphasize that it is an atypical great power, disinterested in destabilizing international politics for its own narrow self-interests, yet it should still be regarded as a great power peer.[97] In so doing, this responsible power concept has meant that China can simultaneously claim its special perch in the international hierarchy, while also fending off critiques or concerns of its rise.

If it turns out that China is motivated by its great power status, then it will focus on its great power peer group, and be particularly responsive to signals from France, the United Kingdom, and the United States, informally known as the "P3," and also senior UN officials (e.g. the UN Secretary-General; Under-Secretary-Generals, special rapporteurs etc.). No doubt, the United States features prominently for China as a member of the great power group; its military prowess, economic strength, and diplomatic resources are unparalleled in contemporary politics. For much of the post-war period, the United States has set the agenda at the UN Security Council. While the UN Security Council is indeed another venue to test the limits of US power and authority, Chinese views of the great power elite are not solely fixated on the United States. Ostensibly, the United States alone could address the bulk of China's status concerns; however, such a view overlooks how Chinese elites approach the *collective* relevance of the "western" permanent UN Security Council members and senior UN elites.

This set of actors is known for being comparatively more liberal in its preferences, as proponents of the liberal institution-building project, with the means towards executing intervention against massive human rights abuses. The P3 is composed of the traditional great powers that define the contours, processes and norms of the international system.[98] More often than not, these are the states that galvanize UN Security Council action, and circulate the drafts for deliberation and voting. Therefore, recognition from these gatekeepers is important as they represent the status club, and in part, this has its roots in Occidentalism, which essentializes Western standards as the baseline for success in international relations and prioritizes securing Western recognition.[99] Moreover, comparisons of China as a great power peer to the P3 came up consistently amongst interviews with Chinese foreign policy elites, as detailed in the book's empirical chapters, and reflects scholarly analysis of the Chinese foreign policy community, which praises the United States, France, and the United Kingdom as the standard bearers for success in the post-war order.[100]

China's Status as a Global South Peer and its Global South Peer Group

On matters of intervention, China continues to view itself as a member of the Global South, symbolized by its membership in the G77+China and observer position in the Non-Aligned Movement, for example. The Global South is not a fixed, homogenous entity, but rather a term that captures states with differing economic and political systems, drawn together by their experiences of a power disparity with the global elite.[101] The cornerstone of China's relationship with the Global South is an emphasis on the respect for sovereignty,[102] therefore, China is a vocal supporter of UN Security Council actions that have host state consent and regional support, and a preference not to support more robust interventions. Though China's stance on sovereignty is carefully applied in practice, and its erosion of an absolutist commitment is well documented,[103] even with China's rising economic might, its self-identification with the Global South is yet to waiver.[104]

If it is the case that China is motivated by its Global South reference group, then China would be particularly responsive to signals from regional organizations in the crisis area and the host state. Regional organizations are key components within China's political, military, and economic outreach strategies,[105] and China's UN Security Council activity often focuses on regional organizations.[106] For example, in the event of humanitarian crises, China notes "the opinions of the country and the regional organization concerned should be respected."[107] In the case of the potential UN Security Council rebuke against Myanmar for massive human rights violations in 2007, China justified its veto by noting that ASEAN did not see Myanmar's internal affairs as a threat to international peace and security.[108] In the case of intervention into Zimbabwe following worsening violence after elections in 2008, China explained its veto by emphasizing the need for "great attention and full respect" to be offered to African Union/SADC-led efforts.[109]

The common thread in these cases is that the Chinese anti-intervention position is in relation to regional organizations' positions against UN Security Council-sanctioned intervention.[110] Such a view is a logical extension of Beijing's "state-centric approach to global governance,"[111] which emphasizes states, regional organizations, and the United Nations as the units for international affairs. For its first thematic debate during its UN Security Council presidency,[112] China advanced a discussion of Chapter VIII of the UN Charter, and addressed how regional organizations could promote multilateralism and boost international security through closer cooperation and coordination with the UN Security Council. However, it is not the case that China is always responsive to regional groups; as the Syria case shows, China is willing to oppose its Global South peers.

Why Russia Is Not a Peer to China

With their authoritarian and centralized governments, similar security and political challenges, and focus on their global prestige and influence,[113] China and Russia are deemed individually to be problematic players in the current global order. Rejection of the western-led order is viewed as a motivating factor for Sino-Russian cooperation[114]—and the two states are seen to work together to project alternate norms through their international cooperation.[115] However, there is markedly little consensus about the nature of the Sino-Russian relationship. Scholars have simultaneously marked this as one of an "ominous anti-American alliance"[116] between two "comrades in arms,"[117] while others view the relationship as teetering on falling apart—seeing it as an "axis of convenience,"[118] "axis of necessity,"[119] or "axis of insecurity."[120] Since there is little consensus from scholars of Sino-Russian relations, it is no wonder that there is the open debate about their "rapprochement or rivalry"[121] or "rivalry or partnership."[122]

The small literature on the Sino-Russian relationship at the UN Security Council reflects a view that the two are "soft-balancing" against the P3,[123] with the Sino-Russian axis opposing addressing humanitarian emergencies. To this end, the Sino-Russian bloc at the United Nations presents a neo-Westphalian challenge,[124] with an intent to destabilize the western-led order.[125] With their common Cold War positions challenging western democracy promotion, misgivings about secessionism and memories of invasion, both authoritarian states are frequently the most outspoken against intervention, and dubious about emerging humanitarian doctrines that challenge traditional sovereignty.[126] The drive to balance against US power increased in the light of the 1999 Kosovo War and the 2003 Iraq War, and in response to US support for the colored revolutions in Ukraine and Georgia and NATO expansion.[127] While both states do tend to vote in the same direction, mostly favoring abstention votes, their joint vetoes are a measured occurrence: issued regarding proposed action into Myanmar in 2007;

Zimbabwe in 2008; Venezuela in 2019, and some of the multiple vetoes in the face of Syrian intervention since 2011.

However, Russia is not a peer state to China in regards to intervention at the UN Security Council. First, it is not the case that China and Russia always vote together. China refused to follow Russia in 2008 when it attempted to use the UN Security Council to legitimate its intervention into Georgia, nor has China recognized Abkhazia and South Ossetia as independent.[128] When Russia attempted to get China to endorse its actions at the 2008 Shanghai Cooperation Organization Summit, arguably a lower-grade of support than required at the UN Security Council, China again refused to condone Russia's maneuvers. China rejected Russia's lead regarding the Ukraine crisis in 2014, repeatedly stating that Ukraine's independence, sovereignty, and territorial integrity must be protected.[129] This split in opinion about how Russia should lead in its geopolitical sphere highlights fundamental discord between the two states. Even when China has little strategic interest at stake, it remains reluctant to get dragged into Russian affairs. Once clear calculations of national interests are made, Russia cannot move China, in part because the two do not have a prior identification of being status peers.

Second, when tandem votes do concur, these have not been a "given" per se, with coordinated, parallel positions from the start. Rather, Chinese and Russian votes were almost misaligned in the case of the recent Syria crisis, for example. And had it not been for high-level, repeated interventions up until voting time to align their positions, China and Russia may not have issued joint vetoes. This implies that the bloc is based upon measured calculations of self-interest, and perhaps not as much in peerage and decisions constrained by appropriateness. While China and Russia view the United Nations as the core component in governing through a multipolar international environment,[130] the Sino-Russian "marriage of convenience" at the UN Security Council is based on a negative position of ideological antipathy to great power intervention—not necessarily a relationship based on a positive relationship of peerage. Evidence suggests that in regards to intervention, it is not the case that China regards Russia as a peer, but rather China's actions are the result of a clear calculation of interests.

So while Russia will regularly rail against the instrumental approach of great powers towards intervention at the UN Security Council, taking on the role of a "loud dissenter," China instead stands as a "cautious partner."[131] Indeed, closer analysis of the Chinese and Russian explanations for their vetoes regarding the Syrian crisis reveal that while both staunchly oppose the possibility of regime change, China's concerns were focused on much more intangible concepts like equal culpability between the state and protesters; the need for negotiations and a win-win solution. In contrast, Russia's position was driven by hard practical interests about keeping a key military ally and its open-water port available in the Middle East. Fundamentally, Russia is satisfied to be a loud and public block against western action, but China is in favor of quiet, bilateral diplomacy and conscious of being deemed a spoiler.

Therefore, though Russia and China may turn to one another to avoid acting alone at the UN Security Council, "they do not see issues through identical eyes."[132] Indeed, it is more an "axis of convenience" [133] that draws the two states to vote together. In this sense, their alignment is based on a negative precept: the two states oppose creeping human rights norms and democracy promotion, but do not have a sense of peerage that unites them together.[134] Both states may have had a warming relationship in recent years, but "share neither a long-term vision of the world nor a common understanding of their respective places in it."[135] From China's perspective, Russia's decline in global politics and gradual overall weakness stemming from its *perestroika* political decisions are not a model for China to aspire to.[136] Though Russia was most recently undergoing a resurgence after its 1990s troubles, Russia's weakening position in international affairs highlights China's advantages in the global system. Interestingly, in preparation for this book, not one interview with Chinese officials invoked the idea of Russia as a fulsome partner for China, if Russia was mentioned at all.

Measuring China's Response to Intervention

China's response to intervention is conceived of as a degree of resistance or acceptance for intervention, captured by three measures: China's voting regarding intervention; China's diplomatic maneuvering; and Chinese elites' official discourse regarding intervention. This section turns to operationalize each of those measures in turn.

Voting Outcomes This measure is conceived of in three ways, including the veto: when China is the most resistant to intervention as China is willing to halt UN Security Council action. Abstention votes signal China's ambivalence regarding intervention, showing a lack of willingness to support or deny intervention. Yes votes are most accepting of intervention, offering support through condoning the resolution.[137]

Diplomatic Maneuvering

China's diplomatic maneuvering—the process of negotiating resolutions—can also signal a degree of resistance or acceptance for intervention. For example, diplomatic efforts to side-track and delay resolutions indicate ambivalence or resistance to intervention. These moves, for example, include weakening language in draft resolutions (i.e. from "sanctions for non-compliance" to "considerations of sanctions for non-compliance"); tabling resolutions from going to vote, and non-participation in negotiation sessions. In contrast, participating in negotiations with little or no push-back on draft language; volunteering assets to ensure resolutions can be executed; or working to secure support for the draft language from other UN Security Council members, indicates an acceptance for the resolution material.

China's Official Discourse on Intervention

A final measure includes China's discourse at the UN Security Council. This measure is thought about in two ways. First, these focus on explanations for the vote. Explanations that accompany non-support via the veto indicate resistance to intervention. Statements like China "sees no alternative to action" or "despite seeing problems with the resolution, we had to support it," are indications of ambivalence, for example, when addressing intervention. Explanations that China "fully supports the text" are indications of support. Second, official discourse also focuses on framing of the vote and China's use of rhetorical adaptation to try to control discursive power.[138] Efforts to use more evocative terms, like "humanitarian disaster," to push for intervention into a crisis, indicates a degree of acceptance for intervention, or "illegitimate regime change" – is indicative of a degree of resistance to intervention.

Research Design and Empirical Strategy

The following briefly outlines my research design and the empirical strategy employed to test the argument. First, I outline why comparative case studies presents the optimal empirical strategy before I turn to the study's scope. I then deal with the possible universe of cases, and discuss my case selection logic.

I use a primarily qualitative approach as it gives me the leverage to uncover causal processes and causal mechanisms, while minimizing the problems of measurement errors and maintaining conceptual rigor.[139] A qualitative approach enables me to test my hypothesis using a wider range of empirical implications, which is key since I am confronted with a constrained data environment: while there is much reporting speculating or correlating China's actions with hypotheses, research on China's voting decisions at the UN Security Council is still an exercise in relative data paucity. Votes are publicly recorded along with verbatim record, but China's considerations, bartering, and diplomatic backchat are not matters of the public record. Working with in-depth cases lets me assess the strength of my argument against alternatives using the Bayesian logic of process tracing.[140] With participant observation at UN Headquarters, multiple fieldtrips to intervention decision-making centers in Beijing and New York, supplemented by a thorough secondary material search, I have sufficient material to form the case studies to interrogate causal processes.

Defining the Case Universe

I commenced building the dataset of all the country cases that were at the UN Security Council for the period January 2000 through December 2014. I then used the Factiva news database to run a search for each of the UN Security Council country cases within five words of the term "regime change" across all fifteen years. This provides a crude indicator of public discourse linking regime change with each country case. The initial results separated out the cases into two categories for sorting: the first category of cases where there was no substantial public discourse about regime change, so these cases could be discarded altogether; then the second category of cases showed a short list of cases with some public conversation about regime change.

I then used UN Security Council press releases to code whether the UN Security Council addressed mass abuse in the individual cases. This allowed me to dismiss cases with a public discourse of regime change on primarily three grounds:

- When the UN Security Council intervention was *not* motivated by concerns of mass abuse. For example, intervention into the Democratic People's Republic of Korea was primarily in regards to its nuclear proliferation activities.

- When the UN Security Council was not privy to establishing intervention to address mass abuse. For example, the United States presented its military action in Afghanistan following the September 11, 2001 attacks as exercising the right to self-defense under Article 51 of the UN Charter, and not as a case of humanitarian intervention, thereby negating the authorization of the UN Security Council.[141] The UN Security Council unanimously supported the US position that "those responsible for aiding, supporting or harboring the perpetrators, organizers and sponsors of these acts will be held accountable."[142] However, the United States did not pursue the "implicit offer"[143] for Chapter VII coverage for the US military response. It was only after the US military response commenced that the humanitarian component was grafted on, so as to curry local favor and international support for the US campaign.[144]

- When there was no credible evidence of input from the UN Security Council. For example, the public discourse on regime change and Israel concerned Tel Aviv's position on executing regime change in Iran and Iraq, a discussion largely devoid of any active UN Security Council input. Zimbabwe is another case, where Harare accused the United Kingdom of trying to institute regime change, but Zimbabe was not an active matter on the UN Security Council agenda. The public discourse on regime change and Georgia is negligible until Russia sent forces into Abkhazia and South Ossetia, annexing these territories from Georgia. Russia then recognized both as independent states. Russia was harshly condemned by the United Nations. The surrounding regime change discourse was used to criticize Russia's foreign policy moves *after* the annexation of Abkhazia and South Ossetia, not as a consideration surrounding debates about how the UN should intervene in the crisis.[145] Russia also tried to persuade the UN Security Council to legitimize its intervention into Ukraine after the fact.

This then left the universe of country cases where China addressed intervention at the UN Security Council against a backdrop of public discourse calling for regime change: the Darfur, Sudan case of 2004–8; the Libya case of 2011; and the Syria case of 2011–14 (see Table 3.2). These cases also yield sufficient amounts of information on the independent and dependent variables in question, so to test both the hypothesized correlations and the processes proposed by my argument. In so doing, these three case studies in and of themselves, provide an opportunity for key tests of other alternative explanations because they establish a tough test in presenting three least-likely cases for status explanations. The least-likely cases can serve to support explanations for cases where the explanations should have little utility. The strongest evidence to support an explanation is a case that is least likely for that particular explanation, and where all alternate explanations predict a different outcome from that particular explanation, but those alternative explanation outcomes are *different* than what actually happened in that particular case. Therefore, if one explanation turns out to be accurate (i.e. predicted the actual outcome of the case), others can be ruled out (because they predicted different outcomes for the case).[146] This approach works well because there is an abundance of explanations for China's response to intervention, specified in each empirical chapter. As George and Bennett note, "[theories] that survive such a difficult test may prove to be generally applicable to many types of cases, as they have already proven their robustness in the presence of countervailing mechanisms."[147]

This approach has several theoretical advantages. Each of the three cases have within-case variations in China's response, while holding constant factors like autocratic governance structures and a period of general interest in addressing mass human rights abuses. With a collection of these cases, I could complement subnational, longitudinal, and cross-national variation, while addressing questions of the external validity of a single case.[148] In addressing cross-national comparison, I sought to hold constant—insofar as was possible—the other variables that might be affecting China's position on intervention, which I outline in each empirical chapter. These alternative explanations predict very different outcomes than those in these three cases. The three cases all had Chinese overseas

THEORY AND EMPIRICAL STRATEGY 57

Table 3.2. Summary of the case universe of China's responses to intervention

	Darfur/Sudan 2004–2008	Libya 2011	Syria 2011–2014
Calls for intervention	- ICC referral - Sanctions - Peace Operation (UNAMID)	- ICC referral - Sanctions - No-Fly Zone	- Sanctions - Implement peace plan + stop violence - Withdraw heavy weapons + sanctions - ICC referral - Humanitarian Corridors
Was there a status trigger?	Yes - "Genocide Olympics"	Yes - Gaddafi "Tiananmen Square" speech	No
Does China hold assets in crisis area?	Yes	Yes	Yes
Did China show voting congruence with Russia?	Yes	Yes	Yes, including some veto votes
Is the Global South Peer Group Pro-Intervention?	Yes (AU)	Yes (GCC, OIC, LAS) No (AU)	Yes (LAS, GCC) No (OIC)
Is Global South Peer Group Cohesive?	Yes	Yes (GCC, OIC, LAS) No (AU)	No (LAS, GCC, OIC)
Is the Great Power Peer Group Pro-Intervention?	Yes	Yes	Yes
Is the Great Power Peer Group Cohesive?	Yes	Yes	Yes
How Did China Respond to Intervention at the UNSC?	Abstention: ICC (2005, 2008) Yes: Sanctions UNAMID	Yes: ICC Sanctions Abstention: No-Fly Zone	Yes: Humanitarian Corridors Veto: all other proposed measures

interests at stake—whether through economic investments, trade, overseas population; Russian pressure for China to co-vote against intervention; and potential alternatives to intervention were yet to be exhausted. Yet in the case where China's relative material interests were arguably at their lowest—in Syria—China took the harshest line against intervention, casting multiple vetoes instead. Accepting that these are live cases, and holding roughly constant major alternative explanations, gave the neatest test of my theory as possible. Most importantly, these cases have exogenous variation on the independent variable of interest to me—the configuration of status through status triggers and peer groups' ability to affect social influence. These cases together give a clear empirical puzzle, the opportunity to control for confounding factors, multiple tests of my theory's predictions, and the opportunity to source data from which to craft a compelling explanation.

Accepting critique that three cases may appear a small pool in order to understand China's varied response to intervention, I have two replies. First, I examine the *universe of cases*; therefore, dissecting all the possible incidences of China grappling with intervention against the undertones of regime change. Second, each case establishes multiple causal process observations over the period of study—these discrete, non-comparable observations help explicate the link between cause and outcome by giving information about context or causal mechanisms, so as to gain causal inference.[149]

Research Method

I use the congruence method to isolate if the variance in the dependent variable is as predicted by the theory establishing the prospect for a causal relationship.[150] In order to assess whether the relationship between the independent and dependent variables are red herrings or actually causal, and what role intervening variables can play and what the causal processes may be, I use process tracing as a complementary method. Process tracing allows me to ferret out and weigh alternate explanations for the chain of events so as to draw inferences about possible explanations for the cause of events.[151] Taking portions of evidence in each case, I assess to what extent the evidence supports the observable implications of alternate hypotheses against empirical logic tests.[152] Process tracing establishes the order of events and causal mechanisms between the hypothesized catalyst and outcome. Especially relevant for this book, process tracing enables research to go "backward from observed outcomes to potential causes – as well as forward from hypothesized causes to subsequent outcomes."[153]

I use discourse analysis to uncover how conversations, speeches, and bodies of text, can solidify new ideas, practices, and norms by finding the critical moments in the discussion when the language used by Chinese foreign policy actors changes, in order for these actors to participate in the discourse with credibility, authority, and legitimacy. When certain language is "selected against,"[154] it flags how foreign policy elites use different language to establish credibility and legitimacy for China's activities. Moreover, while some qualitative methods seek to understand what social realities mean for actors,[155] discourse analysis probes how these realities were produced, which enables me to understand how China can justify intervention, even in its most extreme form.[156] Two specific forms of discourse analysis are of use here: predicate analysis for the publicly available

THEORY AND EMPIRICAL STRATEGY 59

materials (i.e. speeches and meetings minutes, interview transcripts, and government documents), so as to deconstruct the underlying meanings within each sentence of the discourse,[157] and informal argument analysis[158] to specify the argument's role in the discourse on the contested practice of intervention (e.g. to facilitate deliberation, reframe issues, persuade others etc.), and to consider conflicting arguments against one another. This analysis technique enabled me to identify pre-existing beliefs assumed for making arguments, in contrast to arguments used to uphold or change practices. Informal argument analysis alerts what language is used to denormalize and delegitimize previously supported beliefs, so as to alter the balance of political support for newer ideas, changing terms of the debate.

In order to overcome the problem of infinite regress, I relied upon the use of critical junctures. Critical junctures are "choice points...once an option is selected, it becomes progressively more difficult to return to the initial point when multiple alternatives were still available...after a critical juncture...the range of possible outcomes is narrowed considerably."[159] Therefore, I focus on milestones in which decisions are made that re-route how policy options are formulated, viewed and offered, testing hypotheses at each of these inflection points. However, critical junctures are not limited to grand, public or large-scale events: even "small events and random processes can shape developments during critical junctures, leading to the adoption of options that could not have been predicted by theory."[160] My research must "show how this choice activates key variables that favor certain outcomes over others"[161] (i.e. how other options are dropped from the menu of options).

Chapters 4, 5, and 6 address the case studies on intervention in Darfur, Sudan; Libya; and Syria respectively. These cases combined enable me to make a contingent generalization about how status is reconciled against China's other foreign policy concerns in the context of intervention. The conclusion deals with external validity, sketching cases outside of the case universe, and applying the status-based insights to country cases beyond China.

PART III
CASES

4
Status and Intervention in Darfur, Sudan 2004–2008

Introduction

Sub-state rebellion in the politically and economically marginalized region of Darfur, Sudan became outright conflict against the Khartoum-based government of President Omar al-Bashir in 2002.[1] While Arab and African communities in Darfur have disputed land and resource rights over years, violence took a different turn when rebel groups were willing to counter the government, demanding solutions to longstanding grievances related to underdevelopment in the region. In response, government and *janjaweed* militia forces targeted ethnic groups, using rape, abduction, looting, and a scorched-earth campaign. By the end of 2003, Sudan had closed access to the Darfur region. Conservative estimates put the dead at 130,000 and internally displaced at 1.2 million by mid-2004,[2] and Khartoum was accused of mass atrocities against the peoples of the Darfur region.

The Darfur crisis was inextricably linked to China.[3] China ran a gauntlet of criticisms over its diplomatic, economic, and arms relationship with Sudan,[4] including the linking of the 2008 Beijing Olympic and Paralympic Games[5] to the Darfur crisis under the "Genocide Olympics" moniker. Initially, China rebuffed critics, stating that Sudanese sovereignty should be respected, and that Sudan was responsible for its own domestic affairs. Simply put, as Deputy Foreign Minister Zhou Wenzhong stated in 2004, "business is business" and as China made efforts to "separate politics from business... [the] internal situation in the Sudan is an internal affair."[6] When these measures failed to reduce criticisms of China, Chinese officials took a host of new, bold measures supporting intervention. China wrangled Sudanese consent for the UN-AU Mission in Darfur (UNAMID), the first time that China admitted to securing and enforcing consent.[7] China voted for the peacekeeping mission under Chapter VII, and Chinese engineering units were the first non-African peacekeeping forces to arrive in Darfur. The case also represents the first time that the UN Security Council referred a country case to the International Criminal Court—with China's abstention vote paving the way for the indictment of the sitting head of state, President Omar al-Bashir.

China's efforts to intervene took place against an active public discourse calling for regime change in Sudan, making these innovations all the more curious. The emerging norm of the responsibility to protect shaped debates about intervention in Darfur, with Darfur as the second country case to have the responsibility to protect language applied in a resolution, reminding states of their responsibilities to their populations.[8] Sudanese officials discussed their persistent concerns of being targets for regime change with their Chinese counterparts; President al-Bashir was stunned at China's willingness to intervene in the Darfur crisis, noting "[we] were convinced that China was not, and did not expect, [China] to be an instrument for the American pressure against Sudan."[9] What explains China's response to intervention in the Darfur case?

I argue that China's changing approach to the Darfur crisis, and by extension, its position on UN-sanctioned intervention, is a striking demonstration of status sensitivity. In order to gain status, China was willing to bear a strained relationship with Sudan, with negative implications for Chinese economic investments. The case exhibits both a status trigger and the successful use of social influence from *both* China's Great Power peer group (by way of the P3) and the Global South (primarily by way of the African Union). Resolving the Darfur humanitarian crisis itself was not of intrinsic importance to China; however, the smooth and successful conduct of the Olympic Games was *the* top foreign policy priority for China by 2006.[10] The status trigger of heads of state refusing to join the Games Opening Ceremonies was magnified by the reputational threat of the "Genocide Olympics" campaign, as Chinese officials came to realize the campaign could not be written off as only concerning "so-called Hollywood activists."[11] All of China's peer groups eventually united around a single pro-UN intervention stance, with no major individual state defecting from the respective group. These groups were willing to impose social costs on China for rejecting their preferred positions. Supplemented by a successful US strategy that clarified a UN-led intervention was not a prelude to regime change in Sudan, supporting, and even advocating for intervention became a possible option for China.

The chapter first outlines alternate explanations for China's response to intervention in Darfur, before turning to the discourse regarding Darfur and regime change. Next, the chapter turns to process tracing to show the effects of status in explaining China's response to intervention in Darfur.

Alternate Explanations

Securing Overseas Interests

Critics assert that China's position at the UN Security Council enabled Sudan to continue the violence in Darfur, because China prioritized securing bilateral relations. China and Sudan were close economic partners, with cooperation in their agriculture, communication, energy, infrastructure construction, and water conservancy sectors, and China was Sudan's major international trade partner.[12] By the end of 2003, Chinese investment in Sudan was over $2.7bn, primarily in the oil sector.[13] China purchased two-thirds of Sudanese oil at approximately 400,000 barrels of oil a day in 2007,[14] which was over a 500 percent increase compared to their trade in oil in 2006.[15] Sudan was the main site of China's offshore oil production, crucial to meet the growing petroleum needs of the Chinese economy without subjecting China to fluctuations in the international oil markets.[16] Sudan's oil exports to China went from $1.8bn in 2006 to $4.1bn in 2007 and to $6.3bn in 2008, placing Sudan as China's fifth-largest oil supplier.[17] China engaged in military sales with Sudan. Chinese technology transfers were noted as enabling Sudan to become self-sufficient in its production of small- and medium-sized weapons, used by the Sudanese military and *janjaweed* attacks against civilians.[18]

However, these explanations fall short on a number of counts. First, scholars caution against a popular view that overstates the influence of China on Sudan because of the Sino-Sudanese oil relationship.[19] Research shows that Sudan may not have been as important to the Chinese economy as initially assumed. As Chin-Hao Huang notes, "Sudan's contribution to China's total energy needs is important but not strategic... Sudan's producing oil fields are aging, and its proven oil deposits modest by global standards."[20] Moreover, the bilateral relationship did not always move lockstep during the period under analysis in this chapter. Gaafar Karrar Ahmed writes explicitly about the increasingly tense relationship between Sudan and China during the crisis.[21] Most importantly, explanations that privilege securing China's overseas interests in Sudan fail to elucidate *why* China changed its engagement with the Darfur issue when it did, taking an increasingly tough line *against* Khartoum, and what mechanisms pushed China to modify its approach.

Reputational Concerns

One of the most popular accounts for China's changing response to Darfur was due to the "Genocide Olympics" shaming campaign, mainly associated with the Dream for Darfur advocacy group. As Dream for Darfur does not represent a peer to China, Chinese officials' interests in protecting the Games was strictly a consequentialist calculation: what actions would most expediently negate criticisms from this group?

There are two variants in this "shaming China over Darfur" explanation. First, assessments see China's response to intervention in Darfur simply as the result of the "Genocide Olympics" shaming campaign led by the Dream for Darfur coalition.[22] For example, Hamilton argues: "In an admittedly rare instance, the Olympics, when activists in the West could threaten an image China actually cared about, public shaming had worked."[23] Price notes that Dream for Darfur will be infamous for gathering "under a single banner, much of the accumulated discontent, anxiety, and suspicion about China and human rights."[24] Second, there are those that attribute China's response to the "Spielberg effect" of film director

Steven Spielberg quitting his role as artistic director of the opening ceremonies.[25] For example, analysts went as far to say that "credit goes to Hollywood – Mia Farrow and Steven Spielberg in particular" for changing Chinese activity in Darfur, and that such Hollywood star power "could accomplish what years of diplomacy could not."[26] However, to test the validity of these arguments, further investigation into the timing of the campaign against critical junctures in China's response needs to be done.

Sino-US Relations

An alternative argument put forward is that China's decision to engage in Darfur was at the behest of the United States, the lead state in support of the UNAMID peacekeeping mission.[27] For example, former US Deputy Assistant Secretary of State for East Asian and Pacific Affairs Thomas J. Christensen notes, "Beijing's policy, however, began to change for the better as 2006 progressed, in part due to diplomatic engagement with the United States,"[28] which clarified that the United States had no goal of regime change in Sudan. For example, Christensen asserts that "in early 2007, after a dialogue about the region between the US State Department and the Chinese Foreign Ministry, Beijing agreed to send more than 300 military engineers to Darfur, the first non-African peacekeepers committed to the UN operation."[29] However, while US reassurances may have had an effect, it is unclear *why* these overtures were successful in this case. Further analysis through this chapter lends specificity to alternative explanations of successful US diplomacy in the case of Sino-US relations.

Public Discourse on Darfur and Regime Change

As shown in Graph 4.1, the public discourse on Sudan and regime change reflects the contours of the case study. When the Darfur issue enters the UN Security Council in mid-2004, the public discourse picks up, only to taper as the UN Security Council first favors the "African solution to African problems" strategy. The public discourse drops as the UN Security Council remains in deadlock about the crisis for 2005, but peaks again due to a push for a non-consensual UN peacekeeping effort beginning again in mid-2006.

UN officials reiterated a tough line against Sudan. UN Secretary-General Kofi Annan emphasized that "the international community must be prepared to take swift and appropriate action," specifying that this "may include military action."[30] UN Humanitarian Coordinator Jan Egeland briefed the UN Security Council where he predicted "ethnic cleansing of hundreds of thousands" was possible in the very near future.[31] Reports from the acting High Commissioner for Human

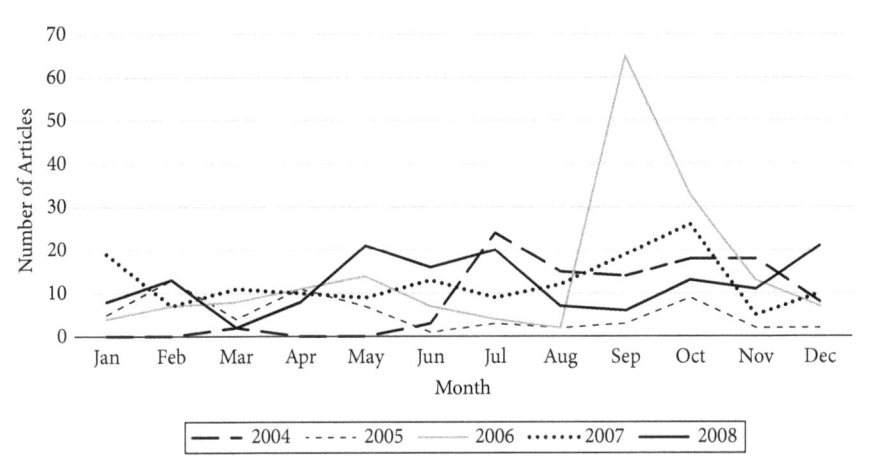

Graph 4.1. Factiva database search of English-language sources regarding "Darfur" and "regime change" within five words, 2004–2008, without duplicates

Rights Bertrand Ramcharan deemed that the violence by the Sudanese government and the *janjaweed* militia in Darfur "may constitute war crimes and/or crimes against humanity."[32] Media op-eds framed the violence as akin to the Rwandan genocide, and called for accountability of Sudan's leaders and the use of tough measures like no-fly zones and the enforcement of humanitarian corridors.[33] Analysts argued that "the time for forceful outside intervention is unmistakably approaching."[34] Observers argued that "regime change alone can end genocide as the domestic security policy of choice in Sudan. And it is the only thing that can avert the deaths of hundreds of thousands in Darfur"[35] and that "the prospect of war crimes charges against General Bashir and his ruling clique [are] brandished."[36]

US policy was clear that Sudan was accountable for the violence,[37] with both Khartoum and the *janjaweed* militia seen as responsible for what the US government termed "genocide."[38] US Secretary of State Colin Powell emphasized at the opening of the crisis on the UN Security Council agenda that "the UN still has options before it... And we do not take any of those options off the table."[39] As the Bush administration did not expressly rule out the use of ground troops, this further underscored the option for the use of all foreign policy tools as necessary.[40] In the same time period, the United Kingdom took a firmer line that a UN Security Council-endorsed no-fly zone was a possibility,[41] and UK Prime Minister Tony Blair asked Whitehall and the Foreign and Commonwealth Office to "draw up plans for possible military intervention in Sudan."[42] Whitehall backed away from the military intervention option a month later,[43] in part due to Sudanese complaints that military intervention would open the door for regime change, but continued to emphasize Khartoum's accountability for the violence in Darfur.[44]

It is no surprise then that throughout the period of the case study, Khartoum held a persistent belief that regime change was a goal of the United States, and that a UN intervention was a tool to achieve this goal.[45] With the contemporaneous examples of US-imposed regime change in Iraq and Afghanistan, Sudan was convinced that regime change in Khartoum was a goal of the UN Security Council due to accusations of mass human rights abuses by the state, and the gathering support for accountability for these mass crimes.[46] Such a belief partly explains Sudanese intransigence to any UN-led intervention.

Sudan's fears about US-led regime change were not entirely unfounded. Contemporary US-Sudan relations alone were rocky at best. Under the Clinton administration, after the 1998 Kenya and Tanzania embassy bombing and the 2000 USS *Cole* attack, the United States steadily ratcheted up pressure on Khartoum. Military retaliation via Operation *Infinite Reach*; the use of sanctions; withdrawal of embassy staff in Khartoum; and a downgrading of diplomatic relations were a prelude to the Clinton administration's endorsement and support for a failed regime change plan executed by a handful of African states.[47] US-Sudanese relations improved from their 1990s nadir, but it was still difficult to shake President al-Bashir's suspicions regarding regime change. The United States supported the Comprehensive Peace Agreement that provided a political solution for the North-South violence in Sudan, but linked the agreement to the ongoing violence in Darfur.[48] The United States made clear that it would not alleviate the sanctions regime while Khartoum's policies were a cause for Darfur's insecurity, and moreover that Sudan would remain blocked from concessionary terms at international financial institutions. Khartoum interpreted this as a "shift of emphasis to Darfur as a revival of America's "regime change agenda" in Darfur."[49] The referral of the Darfur case to the International Criminal Court in 2005 was only seen by Khartoum as a confirmation of its fears. While President al-Bashir signed the 2006 Darfur Peace Agreement, it was with the assurance that the United States would normalize relations with Sudan. When this did not occur and instead the International Criminal Court issued an arrest warrant for President al-Bashir himself, this further stoked Sudanese "paranoia fuelled by the goalpost-shifting pattern on Darfur."[50] As the case study shows, this concern about regime change was communicated to China consistently, contributing to China's initial skepticism regarding intervention.

Sudan's continuing fears of regime change were so strong that it was an uphill battle for the United States to debunk these views, especially against the efforts of public intellectuals advancing the cause of Khartoum's accountability for mass crimes against humanity. US policy documents reflected this attempt at discrediting regime change as Washington's foreign policy goal,[51] along with bilateral diplomatic efforts.

As one senior UN official with responsibility for African Affairs noted: "Sudan absolutely saw UN peacekeeping as a step to oust [President al-Bashir]...which led to all the problems of getting [a peacekeeping mission] access [into Sudan]";[52]

another senior UN Department of Peacekeeping official who worked closely with Sudanese officials to establish the UNAMID mission surmised: "Sudanese officials saw peacekeeping staff as one and the same as [International Criminal Court prosecutor Luis Moreno] Ocampo, out to get [President] al-Bashir thrown out through the ICC."[53]

The following section uses process tracing to complete an historical analysis of the case, identifying the critical junctures in China's response to intervention in Darfur (see Table 4.1).

The Darfur Case
April 2004—August 2006: China Works to Decrease Pressure on Sudan

UN Humanitarian Coordinator in Khartoum Mukesh Kapila called for UN involvement against a systematic campaign of government-led atrocities against civilians,[54] and UN Secretary-General Kofi Annan was "alarmed at the rapidly deteriorating humanitarian situation in the Darfur region of Sudan, and by reports of widespread abuses against civilians, including killings, rape and the burning and looting of entire villages."[55] However, a tipping point for attention to the crisis was not until Humanitarian Coordinator Kapila stated "[this] is ethnic cleansing, this is the world's greatest humanitarian crisis, and I don't know why the world isn't doing more about it," before going on to compare events in Darfur to the beginning phase of the Rwandan genocide.[56] Both US Secretary of State Colin Powell and UN Secretary-General Kofi Annan visited Darfur in late June 2004, officially marking the focus of the United Nations on the Darfur crisis. The US Congress termed the Darfur violence "genocide," and in September 2004 the Bush administration also used the term.[57]

In the opening phase of the Darfur crisis, China stayed within familiar negotiating bounds of stymying efforts for non-consensual intervention, and reducing pressures on Sudan. These efforts included watering down critical presidential statements, rewriting texts to reduce coercive measures, and threatening vetoes to prevent measures from being tabled.[58] At this point, these were acceptable tactics as the African Union remained ambivalent about the use of coercive measures by the United Nations. More importantly, both the P3 and the African Union were still united behind an "African solution for African problems" strategy, relying primarily on an African Union-led force to address insecurity in Darfur. Therefore, backing this AU force initiative was a sign of China's in-status behavior, within the norms of both China's peer groups.

China was successful in diminishing threatened sanctions against Sudan,[59] to simply a consideration of the non-military coercive actions in UN Security Council Resolution 1556.[60] China harnessed skepticism from Russia and a range

Table 4.1. Key UN Security Council Resolutions regarding the Darfur crisis

UN Security Council Resolution	Resolution Intent	China's vote	Votes cast the same as China
1556 July 30, 2004	– called on Sudan to conclude a ceasefire agreement without delay – deployment of international monitors and AU protection force – called on Sudan to disarm *janjaweed* or face sanctions – imposed arms embargo on "non-governmental entities"	Abstention	Pakistan
1564 September 18, 2004	– called for an International Commission of Inquiry on Darfur to investigate rights violations	Abstention	Algeria, Pakistan, and Russia
1590 March 24, 2005	– established the UN Mission in Sudan (UNMIS)	Yes	Unanimous yes vote by UNSC
1591 March 29, 2005	– arms embargo – banned offensive military flights – targeted sanctions	Abstention	Russia and Algeria
1593 March 31, 2005	– referred Darfur to the International Criminal Court	Abstention	Algeria, Brazil, and the United States
1672 April 25, 2006	– sanctions on four Sudanese officials in line with UNSCR 1591	Abstention	Russia and Qatar
1679 May 16, 2006	– called on non-signatories to sign the Darfur Peace Agreement – called for accelerated transition to a UN operation in Darfur – obliged Sudan to permit a UN assessment mission into Darfur	Yes	Unanimous yes vote by UNSC
1706 August 31, 2006	– mandated UNMIS, under Chapter VII, to take over AMIS	Abstention	Russia and Qatar
1769 July 31, 2007	– established the AU-UN Hybrid Mission in Darfur (UNAMID)	Yes	Unanimous yes vote by UNSC

of rotating members at the UN Security Council,[61] in order to reduce the strength of the resolution, ultimately casting an abstention vote with Pakistan. PRC Deputy Permanent Representative Ambassador Zhang Yishan responded that the resolution "was too harsh and would be unhelpful."[62] China also used procedural delays to slow the sanctions committee created by UN Security Council Resolution 1591.[63]

China also threatened veto votes. As the situation in Darfur deteriorated further, the United States, the United Kingdom, Germany, and Romania pushed for an International Commission of Inquiry on Darfur to investigate violations of international humanitarian and human rights law. These efforts produced UN Security Council Resolution 1564,[64] the first time that the UN Security Council had invoked the Convention on the Prevention and Punishment of the Crime of Genocide in a UN Security Council resolution.[65] The draft was revised four times over ten days in order to address concerns about sanctions and fend off a threatened Chinese veto.[66] The final version of UN Security Council Resolution 1564 noted that the Security Council "shall consider" imposing sanctions, and stated that the UN Security Council "welcomes" Sudanese cooperation.[67] Algeria, China, Pakistan, and Russia cast abstention votes, and despite having secured a weaker draft, PRC Ambassador to the United Nations Wang Guangya still cautioned that "The resolution should focus on the Sudanese government's continuing to cooperate rather than the other way around," and reiterated that "[instead] of helping to solve the problem, sanctions may make them even more complicated."[68]

China continued to threaten vetoes through the end of 2004. When the United Kingdom advocated for a referral of Darfur to the International Criminal Court and enforcing an arms embargo, recruiting the United States to co-sponsor three proposals for a resolution to that end, China "announced informally that it would use its veto right if Chinese interests in Sudan came under threat."[69] China continued this hard line with the release of the Report of the International Commission of Inquiry on Darfur, which noted that the Darfur situation was not genocide, but "acts of genocide" – and crimes against humanity were being conducted in Darfur.[70] In response to the possibility of utilizing the sanctions mechanism under UN Security Council Resolution 1564, China "[pledged] to veto any bid to impose an embargo against Khartoum,"[71] formally undermining the credibility of the sanctions threat.

At the end of March 2005, the United Kingdom drafted UN Security Council Resolution 1593, referring Darfur to the International Criminal Court, allowing the Court to act against alleged perpetrators of crimes in Darfur.[72] UN Security Council Resolution 1593 was authorized under Chapter VII, allowing coercive measures for non-compliance.[73] Algeria, Brazil, China, and the United States all abstained. Ambassador Wang Guangya explained China's position as follows: "the perpetrators must be brought to justice. The question before the Council was what was the most appropriate way to do so."[74] With Algeria casting an abstention vote, China was well aware of the limited African support for the International Criminal Court measures. This provided China the opportunity to portray a neutral position, neither blocking nor supporting these efforts in casting its abstention vote.

China's efforts to stymie UN-led intervention were feasible during this period as all of China's status groups prioritized an African Union-led solution to the problem, by way of supporting the African Union Mission in Sudan (AMIS) operation, which deployed to Darfur to monitor the signing of the Humanitarian Ceasefire Agreement.[75] Indeed, as late as June 2005, South African President Thabo Mbeki told US President George W. Bush that it was "critically important that the African continent [deals] with these conflict situations on the continent... We have not asked for anybody outside of the African continent to deploy troops in Darfur. It's an African responsibility and we can do it."[76] The European Union, NATO, and the United Nations supported AMIS.[77] UK Prime Minister Tony Blair stated in Khartoum in October 2004, "I don't think there is any desire on the part of the African Union for outside troops... my very strong understanding is there is not a desire for outside troops from the EU or from Britain to come here."[78]

However, AMIS was a troubled mission from the start, under frequent attack from *janjaweed* militia rebels, with a vast mandate,[79] unclear rules of engagement,[80] circumscribed consent from Sudan,[81] and a serious shortage of manpower and assets.[82] AMIS could not monitor the ceasefire, even with the support of UN Mission in Sudan (UNMIS).[83] AMIS failures were seen in part due to Sudan's willingness to frustrate the operation, and so pressure grew within the African Union to isolate Sudan. At the January 2006 African Union Summit, African countries rejected the Sudanese candidacy for the rotating presidency following the objections of African leaders and human rights watchdogs.[84] With recognition that "African solutions for African problems" was no longer working, in January 2006 the African Union accepted in principle that the UN could have a peacekeeping presence in Darfur. This move marked a key shift in China's peer groups: accepting that there was an independent role for the United Nations meant that there was a change in how peer groups would interpret China's standards of acceptable behavior; supporting efforts for UN peacekeeping was now a sign of a peer group member's good behavior, for example. On March 10, 2006, the African Union confirmed its willingness to transition to a UN-led operation, as long as there was Sudanese consent.[85]

Weeks later, UN Security Council Resolution 1679 passed unanimously, calling for an accelerated transition to a UN operation in Darfur.[86] Regardless, Sudan refused to give consent, blocking the transition to a UN peacekeeping operation. Sudan continued this position, after the authorization of UN Security Council Resolution 1706, calling for a multidimensional peacekeeping operation in August 2006. UN Security Council Resolution 1706 "invited" Sudan to give its consent to the mission's deployment;[87] even with this insertion, Russia, Qatar, and China all abstained from voting.[88] Within hours of the vote being made public, Sudan made it clear it refused consent and that Darfur would become a "graveyard" for peacekeepers.[89] Sudan's rhetoric reflected their "anger" in the resolution's success, especially having "requested China not to allow the resolution to pass, describing it as a threat to the national sovereignty of the country."[90] Sudanese Presidential Adviser Nafie Ali Nafie stated: "Why is China waiting to use the right of veto in the face of unfair resolutions that targets its friends?"[91] Sudan's ire over UN Security Council Resolution 1706 was because these efforts were proof, according to Sudanese Presidential Advisor Mustafa Osman Ismail, of a US policy for "regime change."[92]

August 2006–February 2007: China Voices Opinions About UN Peacekeeping in Darfur

After the failure of launching a peacekeeping mission via UN Security Council Resolution 1706, China shifted to offering vocal support for a UN peacekeeping mission, presenting the first critical juncture in China's approach to Darfur. Chinese Premier Wen Jiabao emphasized that "China is very much concerned about the stability in Darfur...we support the international decision to send in peacekeepers,"[93] and Ambassador Wang Guangya stated "[we] sent a message to [Sudan] that we feel the UN taking over [from AMIS] is a good idea, but it is up to [Khartoum] to agree."[94] Ambassador Wang's comment is key in indicating a shift in China's attitude towards accepting a role for UN peacekeepers. In November 2006 President Hu appealed to Sudanese President al-Bashir in public and in bilateral meetings to more effectively respond to the Darfur crisis.[95]

China and the United States proposed a compromise for a hybrid AU-UN force in mid-November 2006.[96] With input from the UN Security Council and the African Union, Khartoum agreed in principle to phased support for the African Union in Darfur, commonly referred to as the Annan Plan, which would eventually culminate in the hybrid mission. China had persuaded Sudan that there was no hidden agenda in the effort to introduce a stronger peacekeeping force.[97] Interviews reveal that within the closed-door meetings, Ambassador Wang Guangya admonished Sudanese Foreign Minister Lam Akol to accept the proposed joint UN-AU peacekeeping mission in Darfur. Ambassador Wang's reprimands were made in front of other senior UN and foreign officials—not in a private, bilateral *sotto voce* meeting—enabling China to signal its changing position on intervention in Darfur.[98] China had shifted from working against P3-led efforts for UN peacekeeping in Darfur, to one of advocating for a UN-led mission in Darfur, and in so doing, this meeting represented a reset of its policy pathway. Securing a UN mission was the only way forward for China, having now declared its position.

Status pressures and reassurances from China's peer groups explain this shift in China's position. Increased social pressures by African states in response to Sudan's intransigence led to an increasing awareness on the part of Chinese officials that being perceived as Sudan's best advocate was unacceptable to the Global South peer group, represented by the African Union. Chinese officials noted an uptick in meetings concerning the hybrid peacekeeping question with a number of African embassies weighing in, urging Chinese officials to do more "as a friend of Africa."[99] Concurrently, US officials clarified that regime change in Sudan was not a US foreign policy goal. US Special Envoy for Darfur Andrew S. Natsios visited Beijing in January 2007, ahead of President Hu Jintao's return to Africa in February 2007. Special Envoy Natsios focused his efforts on clarifying the US government position on the Darfur question: to avoid state collapse (like in Somalia, a hobby project of China's at the UN Security Council); that the United States was not interested in enforcing regime change (unlike in Iraq), and that "our interests...are solely humanitarian."[100] This same policy position was repeated during multiple meetings between US and Chinese officials in Washington, DC and Beijing.[101] These combined efforts—confirming that China would bear social costs for not acting in support of the African Union position, and clarification that the United States was not targeting Sudan as a site for regime change—made changes in China's position viable, so that China could now support intervention via a UN peacekeeping effort in Darfur.

March 2007–December 2007: China Extracts Sudan's Consent for the AU-UN Peacekeeping Mission

In February 2007, President Hu Jintao visited Sudan for bilateral meetings with President al-Bashir. Visiting Sudan was a last-minute addition to President Hu's African tour,[102] reflecting China's concession that Darfur was becoming a more serious concern for Chinese foreign relations.[103] Sending China's most senior official to Sudan was the second critical juncture in China's stance on Darfur; a strong signal of China's resolve to support a UN peacekeeping mission in Darfur, even at the cost of the relationship with Sudan.[104] In reference to these meetings, Ambassador Wang Guangya stated that "Usually China doesn't send messages, but this time they did...It was a clear strong message the proposal from Kofi Annan [for the AU-UN peacekeeping] is a good one and Sudan has to accept it."[105] China's rhetoric transitioned from giving Sudan agency to give consent to saying that there was no choice but to accept the mission, and that China was no longer willing to oppose the P3 efforts for a UN peacekeeping mission at the UN Security Council.

After accepting a UN peacekeeping mission in principle, Sudan withdrew consent in early March 2007. Sudan was still of the view that the AU-UN force was simply a first step in regime change, akin to the 2003 Iraq War.[106] In the face of increased Sudanese obstinacy, China further distanced its position from Sudan, underscoring that a UN peacekeeping force was a viable and needed solution. China saw that Sudan would first have to accept UN peacekeepers before China could counter threatened sanctions at the UN Security Council, further indicating a cementing of China's position along that of the P3 and the African Union.

In early May 2007, China appointed veteran ambassador Liu Guijin as Special Representative for African Affairs, though his *de facto* focus was on Darfur. As Special Representative Liu noted, serving as a "special envoy for a country, which is thousands of miles far away from China – that is something unprecedented [for China]."[107] Special Representative Liu's appointment meant that China was putting its full effort behind a UN peacekeeping effort. Once appointed, Special Representative Liu completed two trips to Sudan within two months, meeting with representatives from the African Union. China also established multitrack meetings with the European Union and the United States regarding Darfur.[108] Chinese officials noted that these efforts underscored "the readiness of China to cooperate with the international community to stop the violence in Darfur and return stability to the region ... [and] that China and the US share between them a joint vision about Darfur."[109]

China's position was driven by reassurances and an appeal to status concerns. The P3 and the African Union both implored China to use its leverage with Sudan to break the impasse, with increased diplomatic efforts on behalf of the African Union by way of rotating UN Security Council member and regional powerhouse Ghana.[110] US officials continued with earlier efforts to clarify policy goals for Darfur—affirming again that Sudan was not a target of regime change. The Darfur crisis dominated discussions at the US-China Dialogue on Africa in March 2007, and at the June 2007 two-day senior dialogue between US and Chinese senior officials.[111] US officials also used status-based appeals to China: supporting Sudan was putting China counter to the African Union, and increasingly as an outcast in the international community.[112] The focus of US endeavors was not to push material side payments as a means to communicate with China, but offering reassurances that a successful peacekeeping mission would be a signal of China's great power status as China actively brokered global security.[113]

Along with reassurances, China became more sensitive to status pressures, through the rebranding of the 2008 Beijing Olympic Games by way of the "Genocide Olympics" campaign of the Dream for Darfur advocacy group.[114] To be clear, Dream for Darfur was not a peer group for China; dealing with Dream for Darfur was of instrumental purpose for Chinese officials, as a means to reduce criticism and secure the success of the 2008 Olympics. Yet dealing with this reputational threat did not mean that China was immune to status-based pressures. Dream for Darfur's attack on the Beijing Games focused and magnified China's status concerns. Dream for Darfur activists saw "that the [existing Darfur] advocacy was slow moving...just focused on raising the decibel."[115] Dream for Darfur splintered from the greater Darfur activist community, emphasizing their support for the upcoming Olympic Games, but that with accepting the responsibilities of hosting the Games, China had to be held to a higher standard. Because of China's oil and arms relationship with Sudan, China should use its leverage to "insist that Khartoum accept a robust international peacekeeping force to protect defenseless civilians in Darfur."[116] The Dream for Darfur campaign was not about an Olympic boycott, but they did pursue a shaming strategy—where they "took aim at targets that had some stature with China because of the Olympics"—and in so doing, Dream for Darfur diversified targets so as to generate further media coverage.[117]

Dream for Darfur applied pressure on China by comparing the 2008 Olympic Games to the 1936 Berlin Games, challenging the notion of China's "coming-out party"[118] as a great power in world politics.[119] In doing so, the campaign presented a special challenge to China. First, the incendiary label identified the Darfur crisis as genocide—an emotionally-charged term for one of the most abhorrent activities a state can execute. Second, the term targeted China as involved in the Darfur crisis. In tying China to the crisis, the Dream for Darfur coalition linked China to public consciousness and public conscience, presenting a direct threat to the Chinese government narrative of China as a responsible member in international society. As the campaign was solely about Darfur, China could not use domestic policy as a defense (as in the case of China's Tibet activities, for example), nor could China offer statistics to methodically counter critics (as in the case of the environmental impact of the 2008 Games).[120]

Dream for Darfur opened their media campaign in late March 2007, with the "Genocide Games" *Wall Street Journal* op-ed by Hollywood actress and activist Mia Farrow and her son, Ronan Farrow, lambasting China for its relationship with Sudan in natural resources, arms, and other military support.[121] On behalf of Dream for Darfur, they asked China to use its leverage to "insist that Khartoum accept a robust international peacekeeping force to protect defenseless civilians in Darfur."[122] The op-ed compared Steven Spielberg's position as artistic director for the Opening Ceremonies of the Games to Leni Riefenstahl's Nazi propaganda efforts for the 1936 Berlin Olympics. In response, Spielberg's representatives explained that he was "taking steps with China" and repeatedly stated that a formal decision from Spielberg would be forthcoming.[123] Targeting Spielberg was central to the Dream for Darfur strategy to apply pressure on China, as he was a "momentum shaker," and as a "beloved figure in China, with movies on genocide, works on anti-genocide...[this] would be a huge blow to China in the artistic sphere and the Olympic sphere."[124] Within five days of the Farrows' op-ed article, Spielberg responded with a private letter to President Hu, calling on China to "change its policy toward Sudan and pressure the Sudanese government to accept the entrance of United Nations peacekeepers to protect the victims of genocide in Darfur."[125] By the end of July 2007, press reports that Spielberg might be willing to quit his Olympic post[126] caused Chinese officials further concern about the impact of the Genocide Olympics campaign. Dream for Darfur also conceived of a genocide torch relay, that was the centerpiece of the first phase of the campaign, which commenced exactly one year before the Games from the Darfur border, traveling through Rwanda, Armenia, Germany, Bosnia, and Cambodia over a five-month period.[127] China unsuccessfully tried to have the events in Rwanda and Armenia shut down. In Cambodia, China's efforts to block the genocide torch relay developed into a minor media storm.[128]

China responded with two additional diplomatic tactics: first, dismissing the Dream for Darfur group publicly, but meeting with them in private;[129] second, stepping up China's efforts vis-à-vis intervention into Darfur. Chinese officials responded swiftly to the Dream for Darfur criticism:

> We don't think it is appropriate to link the Olympic Games in Beijing with the Darfur issue and we don't think it will be popularly accepted or echoed by people around the world...It is a totally misguided approach for people to link the Darfur issue with the Games and try to tip the balance in their favor in order to enhance their own reputation.[130]

Dream for Darfur's continuing reputational attack on the 2008 Olympics consequently instigated a status trigger for China: representatives of China's status groups were reconsidering their participation in the Opening Ceremonies, and in effect, challenging the notion of granting China status recognition. Chinese officials had a priority on having heads of state and leaders of international organizations at the opening ceremonies of the 2008 Olympics—going as far as taking an unprecedented move of repeatedly extending dozens of invitations via PRC senior officials, as these foreign officials would give prestige and legitimacy of China's event.[131] China then published updates of foreign officials acceptance of these invitations. Therefore, the threat of state leaders—in particular, those from great power states like the United States, the United Kingdom, and France boycotting the opening ceremonies, were another form of social pressure for China. Chinese officials were most concerned that key foreign leaders be present, where the only tangible gain of this effort was to recoup signals of China's status recognition as a member of the great power peer group.

In response to Dream for Darfur advocacy efforts, over 100 members of the US Congress sent a letter to President Hu, ominously warning of a "disaster for China" if the 2008 Olympic Games in Beijing were marred by ongoing accusations of Chinese complicity in the Darfur genocide.[132] As the "Genocide Olympics" campaign picked up pace there were suggestions that there could be a boycott of the highly symbolic Olympic torch lighting opening ceremony. French President

Sarkozy, French Foreign Minister Bernard Kouchner, 2008 French presidential candidates Francois Bayrou and Ségolène Royale and 2008 US presidential candidate Bill Richardson, all threatened to boycott the ceremonies in part due to China's perceived indifference over Darfur.[133] UN Secretary-General Ban Ki-moon declined to attend due to "scheduling conflicts" after being challenged by activists; British Prime Minister Gordon Brown and German Chancellor Angela Merkel also refused to attend.[134] By June 2007, concerns about an international boycott of the Beijing Olympics because of Darfur were very real, with commentators noting public perceptions of China's responsibility in limiting the Darfur crisis.[135]

Facing this status trigger, China pressed on with new efforts to birth the UN peacekeeping mission. Assistant Foreign Minister Zhai Jun was dispatched to Sudan in early April 2007 to bolster Sino-Sudanese relations, while discussing the Darfur issue. Assistant Foreign Minister Zhai toured three refugee camps, "a rare event for a high-ranking official from China,"[136] and in part an effort to explicitly highlight China's humanitarian concerns for Darfur. Upon his return to Beijing, Assistant Foreign Minister Zhai stated bluntly: "I hope the Sudanese government shows further flexibility towards the [Annan] plan... As far as I am concerned, the consultations... have ended."[137] China now saw that Sudan was to accept the proposed hybrid mission. By May 2007, China committed 275 multifunctional engineering soldiers to Darfur, creating a foundation of troop commitments to a forthcoming mission.[138] By "putting the cart before the horse," and making sure other key states were aware of the troop offer, China increased pressures on Sudan to have to actively decline a credible Chinese offer for peacekeeping troops. China's offer stood out, as even after rounds of meetings there were still no credible non-African troop contributions.[139]

China maintained pressure on Sudan, and it is no coincidence that UN Security Council Resolution 1769, unanimously authorizing the UNAMID mission, passed on the last day of China's rotating presidency of the UN Security Council.[140] Ambassador Liu Guijin noted that Sudan's acceptance to allow UN peacekeepers into Darfur "could not be separated" from Chinese efforts.[141] Ambassador Liu likened China to playing the "role of bridge... We have been trying to give advice and to persuade Sudan to be more flexible to accept the UN plan."[142]

By May 2007, there were an increasing number of statements praising China's role in resolving the Darfur peacekeeping impasse. UN Secretary-General Special Envoy for Darfur Jan Eliasson praised China's "positive role" in resolving the Darfur conflict: "the Chinese pushed the Sudanese government to accept the UN so-called heavy support package, another 3,000 peacekeepers to come to Darfur. And they were definitely active on that."[143] US Special Envoy to Sudan Andrew Natsios told a US Senate panel that China's "subtle diplomacy had supplemented, not undermined, the policy of sanctions against Sudan."[144] UK Foreign Secretary Margaret Beckett noted that

[on] Sudan... there has been some criticism of China, but actually China has played really quite a positive role, particularly in the negotiation of the Darfur peace agreement... China, along with all the rest of the international community, very much regrets that that peace agreement has not been honored by the government of Sudan, or indeed necessarily by the rebels.[145]

China dispatched a 315-strong engineering unit for Darfur, with the Chinese contingent as the first peacekeeping contingent to arrive in Sudan at the end of December 2007. At the close of March 2008, besides a formed police unit from Bangladesh, the Chinese forces were the only other deployments to UNAMID. China also committed humanitarian aid and other resources to bolster UNAMID.[146]

January 2008–October 2008: The Olympics Commence and China Hardens Rhetoric Against Sudan

In this phase, China was still sensitive to status pressures, but did not tender any new government initiatives, instead China used harsher rhetoric to alienate Sudan, while emphasizing China's helpful efforts to address the Darfur crisis. As one Chinese official emphasized, having secured consent and deployed to the UNAMID peacekeeping mission, and acquiesced to the International Criminal Court efforts, "What more are we supposed to do?" [147]

Multiple sources of pressure on China increased in this phase: Sudan tempered China's diplomatic successes by announcing in October 2007 that troops from Nepal, Thailand and a handful of Scandinavian countries—all proposed by the United Nations and the African Union—were unacceptable. With press reports of Sudan's foot dragging, and the persistence of the "Genocide Olympics" headlines, Spielberg sent a second letter to President Hu in November 2007—three and a half months after the landmark UN Security Council Resolution 1769, calling upon President Hu to "urge Sudan to accept and rapidly facilitate" the UN peacekeeping force.[148] Concurrently, Dream for Darfur stepped up their efforts to include an international day of action on February 12, 2008, with protests outside multiple PRC embassies and consulates worldwide.[149] During the day of action, eight Nobel peace laureates, over a dozen Olympic athletes, and other public figures, signed an open letter urging China to intensify diplomatic engagement with the Sudanese government to bring peace to Darfur. Dream for Darfur organized events along the official torch relay route in Hong Kong, and partnered with other advocacy groups for events in London, Paris and San Francisco.[150] Dream for Darfur also gave testimony on "Darfur, China and the Olympics" at the US House Committee on Oversight and Government Reform, and worked with the US Mission to the United Nations for an *Arria*-style meeting at the UN Security Council where the group testified in June 2008.[151] With the Olympic Games starting on August 8,

2008, Dream for Darfur also led two other efforts—the Darfur Olympics, a week-long daily webcast from Darfur refugee camps in Chad and also "Switch Over to Darfur," which encouraged viewers to turn off their televisions during official sponsors' promotions during the Olympics telecast. In order to raise attention for these two efforts, Dream for Darfur used a satirical cartoon with a "Gen Gen Genocide" character that was to resemble the official mascots of the Beijing Games.[152] Spielberg also put pressure on China by publicly quitting as artistic director for the Olympic Opening Ceremony in mid-February 2008: "while China's representatives have conveyed to me that they are working to end the terrible tragedy in Darfur, the grim realities of the suffering continue unabated...my conscience will not allow me to continue with business as usual."[153] Press coverage of Spielberg's resignation eclipsed the reporting on the day of international action, stoking Chinese officials' concerns that there would be further reprisals on China.[154]

In response to these increased pressures, Chinese officials used new rhetoric, emphasizing their achievements vis-à-vis Sudan, while distancing themselves from Sudan. Chinese Foreign Ministry officials recast the Spielberg resignation:

> It is understandable if some people do not understand the Chinese government policy on Darfur, but I am afraid that some people may have ulterior motives, and this we cannot accept...China is also concerned about the humanitarian crisis there... we have been playing a positive and constructive role in promoting peace in Darfur... This did not come easily and our efforts have been applauded by the international community.[155]

A few days later, Chinese Ambassador to Sudan Li Chengwen stated that "China helped push forward the Sudanese government, the AU and the UN reaching consensus on the resolution of the hybrid force to Darfur, which did not come easily and our efforts have been applauded by the international community."[156]

China also engaged in a new tactic of ostracizing Sudan—using uncharacteristically colorful language of "massacre" and "disaster" to describe conditions in Darfur. This rhetoric placed China firmly within the "international community," and Ambassador Liu Guijin stated bluntly that "the patience of the international community has started to run out about what is happening in Darfur."[157] In a *volte face* from China's 2004 "business is business" position, Ambassador Liu further elaborated, in perhaps his most candid statement: "the cooperation of China with states such as Sudan does not necessarily mean its approval of offences against human rights there... the Chinese Government does not support any massacre committed by the Sudanese government against its people."[158] Sudan's refusal to accept non-African troops and reports of escalating military activity were preludes to the most direct statement from Ambassador Liu. On March 7, 2008, at a press conference in Beijing, Ambassador Liu called Darfur a "humanitarian disaster"—a departure from the "developmental matter" that China previously labeled the

Darfur crisis.[159] Ambassador Liu put China clearly with members of the international community, as he reiterated that the international community must "speak in one voice" to persuade Sudan to accept the full-fledged hybrid force.[160]

China also faced renewed energies for another intervention pathway, with UN Security Council rotating member Costa Rica leading a campaign to take Sudanese officials to the International Criminal Court. PRC officials' first response was to stonewall the text, coordinating with rotating member Libya and Russia regarding the draft statement. In response, Costa Rican officials decided to reorient their approach towards a UN Security Council Resolution, which would spotlight each state's position by their votes. PRC officials calculated that the United States would dismiss the draft resolution outright—but they had underestimated the strength of the Darfur activist community, which drove the United States to signal at least an abstention vote on the text. Both France and the United Kingdom were in active support of the draft resolution, and besides Libya—a rotating member, but sometimes outcast amongst African states—at this point there was no substantial challenge from African states either. Again, China's status groups had aligned around a particular policy position, with no credible defectors from either group. It was at this point that "the Chinese mission [to the UN]...really panicked."[161] China quickly agreed to sign a presidential statement supporting the International Criminal Court efforts to end impunity in Darfur, and to bring an intransigent Libya into line, in exchange for Costa Rica dropping all efforts on the UN Security Council Resolution. As one Costa Rican official noted, it was "easier [for China] to hide behind the shield of consensus [of a presidential statement] than to vote [individually on a resolution]."[162] In mid-June 2008, the UN Security Council adopted a presidential statement calling upon Sudan "to cooperate fully with the [International Criminal] Court, consistent with resolution 1593 (2005), in order to put an end to impunity for the crimes committed in Darfur."[163]

In July 2008, using UN Security Council Resolution 1593 as the entry point, the International Criminal Court's prosecutor issued an indictment against President al-Bashir with three counts of genocide, five of crimes against humanity, including murder, extermination, forcible transfer, torture and rape, and two of war crimes. The following day, Chinese officials stated their "grave concerns and misgivings" over the move, reminding others that the "International Criminal Court's actions must be beneficial to the stability of the Darfur region and the appropriate settlement of the issue, not the contrary."[164] Despite lobbying to have the case postponed at the International Criminal Court by a year,[165] Chinese Foreign Ministry officials declined to discuss if it would issue a veto, simply stating "China will continue consultation with other members of the UN Security Council but, as for the outcome, [we] don't know."[166] This point became clearer when Assistant Foreign Minister Zhai Jun visited Sudan at the end of August 2008. During Assistant Foreign Minister Zhai's visit to Sudan, Sudan expected a Chinese veto to block the possible arrest warrant.[167] However, Assistant Foreign Minister

Zhai dismissed discussion of a veto "at this stage" when there was no arrest warrant issued, while reiterating Beijing believes that there are "criminal issues [in Darfur] that require resolution."[168] Bilateral discussions with President al-Bashir included

> the Darfur issue, especially the prosecution of the International Criminal Court (ICC) against the Sudanese leader... [Zhai Jun] stressed that China is the friend of the Sudanese people and willing to make joint efforts with the international community including the Sudanese government, other countries in the region, the African Union and the UN to settle related issues at the earliest date possible.[169]

China was unwilling to support Sudan at the cost of its status as a key player in the international community, in line with the great powers and the Global South. After eight months of consideration, the three judges of the International Criminal Court issued an arrest warrant for President al-Bashir on five counts of war crimes and two counts of crimes against humanity, dropping the genocide charges.[170]

Analysis

This chapter argues that there were four phases in Chinese activity on Darfur:

- April 2004—August 2006: China works to decrease pressure on Sudan;
- August 2006—February 2007: China voices opinions about UN peacekeeping in Darfur;
- March 2007—December 2007: China extracts Sudan's consent for the AU-UN peacekeeping mission;
- January 2008—August 2008: the Olympics commence and China only hardens rhetoric against Sudan.

What factors explain China's response to intervention in Darfur? One argument is that China's response was an economically motivated decision, to secure China's overseas investments in Sudan. However, in the run up to the decision to deploy Sino-Sudanese relations became increasingly strained. Sudanese officials document the decline and growing tensions in the Sino-Sudanese relationship during the 2006 through 2008 period, as Sudan became the object of Chinese pressure regarding Darfur.[171] Indeed, China removed Sudan from its preferential investment list in March 2007,[172] at the cost of furthering China's economic role in Sudan.[173] And while this explanation may illuminate China's initial position on UN intervention into Darfur, it cannot elucidate the willingness of China to intervene over time.

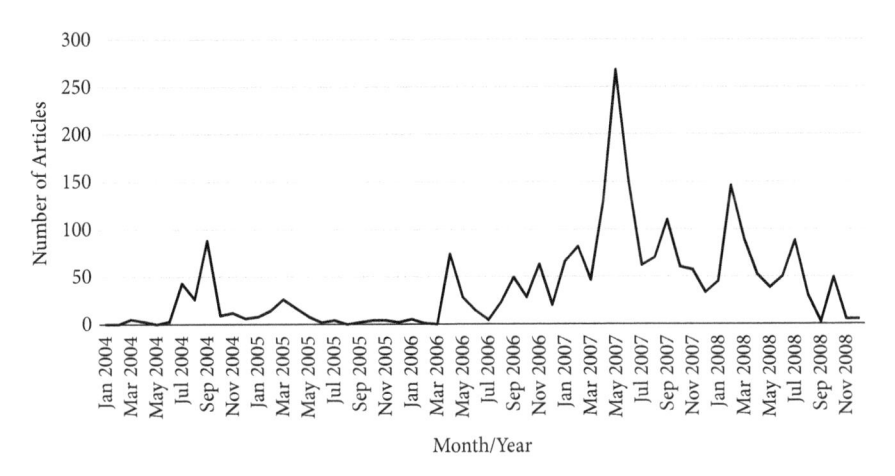

[Graph]

Graph 4.2. Factiva database search of English-language sources regarding "China" and "Darfur" as headline/lead terms, 2004–2008, without duplicates

A second argument emphasizes that China's willingness to support intervention was driven completely by the Dream for Darfur-led reputational attack: if China could gain a reputation for cooperation on intervention matters, then this positive reputation would reduce criticism from both Dream for Darfur and the US Congress as a means to attain a smooth 2008 Olympics.[174] Yet these arguments fall short also. Spikes of reporting linking China and Darfur increased after the Genocide Olympics campaign started at the end of March 2007 (see Graph 4.2). Yet even as Dream for Darfur escalated their shaming campaign in the spring of 2008, and the success of that campaign is partly indicated by the spike in articles in February 2008, China had reached its limit on Chinese policy engagement on peacekeeping, switching to discursive criticism of Sudan instead. Moreover, US Congressional efforts were sporadic, mostly of symbolic value and mainly targeting the United States federal government to find an enforcement solution for Darfur. The threat to withdraw federal funds for US officials to attend the 2008 Olympics was well after China deployed troops to Darfur.[175]

This is not to argue that the Dream for Darfur campaign had no effect on China. As this chapter details, Chinese officials were cognizant and displeased by the Genocide Olympics efforts, which concentrated anti-China criticism "in a way [China has] never before experienced."[176] A more nuanced explanation is to see Dream for Darfur advocacy efforts as amplifying connections between China and Darfur. As the Dream for Darfur campaign continued, a constellation of other actors, including members of the US House of Representatives,[177] Olympic athletes,[178] and other public commentators,[179] made the same demands on China: use China's leverage with Khartoum to end the Darfur genocide, or risk having the 2008 Olympics become a platform to protest China's complicity in the first genocide of the twenty-first century.[180] After Dream for Darfur initiated their campaign, China took increasingly public positions in opposition to Sudan, though China did not produce new policy initiatives. Therefore, though the Dream for Darfur group was important in spotlighting attention on China, analyses that attribute *all* changes in the Chinese approach to the pressure of the Dream for Darfur group or to Steven Spielberg's resignation as artistic director of the Olympic Games, are over-determined arguments on the impact of the campaign. Moreover, these shaming explanations do not illuminate what mechanisms were at play to get China to change its policies—these analyses draw inferences without uncovering causal mechanisms that can illuminate the changes in the Chinese approach.

A third popular argument stresses the importance of constructive relations between China and the United States regarding the Darfur issue.[181] Interviews indicate that Chinese foreign policy elites thought about the Darfur issue as not only an international cooperation issue, but also as an issue in Sino-US relations, elevating the Darfur matter worthy of meetings between Chinese State Councilor Dai Bingguo and US Deputy Secretary of State John Negroponte.[182] The notion that Darfur became important for Sino-US relations can be thought of in two ways. First, interviews with Chinese officials found a consistent Chinese concern that US President Bush would withdraw his attendance at the opening ceremonies in an effort to cause China to "lose face" over Darfur.[183] Second, efforts by the United States, along with those of the United Kingdom and France, urged China to actively engage in addressing the Darfur issue. However, it is unclear in these arguments *why* China may have responded to US overtures when it did, and what mechanisms pushed China to modify its activity regarding the Darfur issue.

Instead, this chapter demonstrates that status is a key causal variable in explaining China's evolving position on intervention in this Darfur case, despite the persistent Sudanese concerns regarding regime change. Though material factors—like reputation-building and securing China's overseas interests—may be necessary preconditions, they alone are insufficient to explain China's calculus. At each of the critical junctures, Chinese officials were receptive to status. Status pressures were successfully transmitted via social influence through the status trigger of attacking the 2008 Olympics via a potential boycott of the opening ceremonies, and peer groups remained unified for a single policy preference, willing to exact social costs on China. Recall that by January 2006, African Union officials were openly acknowledging the need for United Nations support to the AU-led peacekeeping mission. By May 2006, the United Kingdom, France, and the United States had coalesced around the option of deploying a UN peacekeeping mission. Both of these groups of actors are synonymous with the larger peer groups that China wishes to appeal to: the peer group of the African Union (representative of the Global South) and the peer group of the P3 (representative of the great powers).

Turning to the three guides for social influence to establish causality for status, China's commitment to intervention took place in the absence of material side payments. It is often assumed because of the economic and military relationship between China and Sudan, China's deployment to the peacekeeping mission would guarantee a more secure environment for Chinese investment in Sudan. However, simply inserting peacekeeping personnel—even Chinese peacekeeping personnel in Sudan—does not automatically make for a more secure environment from the outset. Internal documentation reveals the well-founded Chinese concerns about deploying their peacekeepers in hostile environment like Darfur—where open fighting was ongoing; insecurity was rife; and consent for the mission from the state and local actors was still fleeting at best.[184] The effect of these conditions on peacekeepers' daily tasks was a real concern for Chinese officials—citing worries about taking fire, returning fire, and dealing with injured Chinese personnel.[185]

Second, China did indeed stress social praise from its peer groups, as illustrated in this chapter. This repetition of recognition from key players of its status groups indicates China's self-consciousness about having status bestowed upon it. Moreover, China's priority on having heads of state attend the opening ceremonies of the 2008 Olympics is again symbolic of China's status recognition as a key player in global politics, with the prestige of these officials adding further legitimacy to this end. This drive for recognition is an inherently status-based argument, since gaining social praise is the end in and of itself.

Third, as it became clear that staying on China's original policy path, and appearing to side with Sudan at all times, would leave China isolated from its peer groups, China's response to intervention began to change. Eventually, China went from stymying to proactively working towards a viable UN peacekeeping operation; and went from acquiescing to an International Criminal Court referral to signaling China's inability in blocking the Court's proceedings on behalf of Sudan. China was disinterested in continually siding with Sudan, at the cost of standing with its peer groups. Understanding this particular aspect of social influence helps explain the success of US diplomacy regarding the UNAMID peacekeeping mission. US diplomats focused their appeals on Chinese diplomats' sense of honor and status, emphasizing that China's support of Sudan would put China at risk of becoming a pariah like the Sudanese, in isolation from its peer groups.

Lastly, to further illuminate the effects of social influence, it is worth using a counterfactual: had there been no status concerns for China, and given that a pro-intervention position was a costly move—having to secure Sudan's consent, while fending off criticism for China's lack of support regarding the International Criminal Court proceedings—China could have simply maintained its original emphasis on respecting Sudanese sovereignty, while downplaying China's role in Darfur. Moreover, addressing material concerns would have been possible by staying within the familiar reach of Chinese policy. However, Chinese officials pursued a different path. In China's response to intervention in Darfur there is evidence that status concerns by way of social influence worked to mediate China's interests.

Conclusion

What insights can we learn about the importance and scope conditions for status in Chinese foreign policy from the Darfur case? One key insight is that status attribution itself was not enough to placate China. Simply hosting the Olympics was unsatisfactory—credit had to be repeatedly given that Beijing was hosting a landmark Games, with just and proper recognition of China's position in the echelon of states. This point speaks to the status literature that emphasizes status attribution as if it is a discrete goal—when perhaps it is best reconsidered along a continuum, where each status-awarding event (securing hosting the Olympic Games) can create a greater drive to secure and reinforce status (having leading heads of states attend the Opening Ceremonies, for example). Such symbolic contact is in line with the emphasis on diplomatic presence and high-level state visits as one measure for status attribution.[186] Acquiring and maintaining status markers in the Darfur case was a considerable preoccupation for China, as these markers "concretize" other states' respect and deference to China.[187]

However, to ultimately secure such status recognition, China itself had to show flexibility in its approach to the intervention parameters at hand and become an active participant in securing intervention into the Darfur conflict. Preconditions made this flexibility feasible, as one Ministry of Foreign Affairs official noted: "Darfur is a soft policy issue for China." In comparison, issues that China has traditionally been shamed over—the Tiananmen Square Incident, for example—were "hard policy issues...things China is sensitive over."[188] Because Darfur was a "soft" issue—a new matter on the policy agenda, not part of a greater discourse of China's failure to comply with "international standards" on human rights, and an issue that occurred overseas—it permitted a level of policy detachment that enabled flexibility in how China engaged the question of a UN peacekeeping mission and an International Criminal Court referral. In comparison to China's rhetoric on the Rwandan genocide or the Srebrenica massacre—where China followed a boilerplate response of obliquely referring to these incidents as "internal issues"—China's labeling of Darfur as a "humanitarian disaster" and willingness to publicly deviate from Sudan's expectations is certainly instructive. The drive to have a smooth Olympic Games was the top foreign policy priority for China, and the desire for this success was enough to magnify social costs of being shunned from China's peer groups. Because of the primacy of the Olympics for Chinese foreign policy, being flexible regarding Darfur was necessary in order to secure a positive environment for the Olympic Games, where China could maximize status markers for its arrival as a great power.

A comparison of the greater context highlights the importance of the remark about Darfur as a "soft" issue. Contemporaneous protests and public criticisms of China for its suppression of anti-Chinese protests in Tibet in March 2008 were met with China's severe disapproval, as documented by China's ostracizing of France and media blackout for the government response in the restive region.[189] This complete inflexibility and dismissal of any criticism was in part due to Tibet being conceived of as a "hard" issue: a well-situated matter on the policy agenda, part of a deep-rooted discourse on China's failure to comply with international standards on human rights, and an issue that took place within Chinese territory.

We can infer from these "hard" issues that China is able to separate reputation from status. Chinese officials were unconcerned about reputation costs due to China's Tibet response, and were willing to bear threatened status losses also.[190] The Darfur case highlights the inverse though: with reinforcing the connection between reputational concerns (i.e. having a good reputation as a means to secure future bargaining outcomes) and social, non-material concerns like status (i.e. accruing status markers is an end in and of itself). The Darfur case study is illustrative of how the transmission of reputational pressures can resonate and magnify status pressures. This is a fine point, speaking to prior works that emphasize how ideational variables, like status, can trump material concerns under certain conditions.[191] The ability of reputation and status to reinforce one another implies then a need to take each of these variables seriously on their own grounds *and* in conjunction with one another, rather than limiting research to a bifurcated approach that emphasizes one at the cost of the other.

In closing, the Darfur case illustrates that status can supersede China's other competing interests regarding intervention. Yet, this is a relatively clean case—China dealt with status pressures from only the P3 and the African Union, which both moved in unison regarding their intervention priorities. In the next case, concerning intervention into the Libya crisis, China dealt with a much more complicated situation; addressing status pressures from the P3 and a series of regional players. This placed China in the position of juggling conflicting peer group priorities and status signals.

5
Status and Intervention in Libya, 2011–2012

Introduction

After revolutions that would topple leaders of Tunisia and Egypt, anti-Gaddafi protests began mid-February 2011 in Benghazi in response to the arrest of a prominent human rights activist.[1] Protests spread through Libya, including to the capital, Tripoli. The Libyan regime's response was swift, with security forces firing on crowds indiscriminately. With the mounting death toll, UN officials noted that the violence could amount to crimes against humanity.[2] The Libyan crisis was immediately framed as a protection issue,[3] and UN Secretary-General Ban Ki-moon reminded Tripoli of its civilian protection responsibilities.[4] By the end of February 2011, diplomatic pressure continued to build on Libya,[5] and the predominant view was that diplomatic measures alone would be insufficient to prevent a massive loss of life.[6] A number of Libyan diplomats defected from their posts, lending credence to the crumbling legitimacy of the regime.[7] In a short window of time, regional groups relevant to the crisis—the League of Arab States, the Organization of Islamic Cooperation, the Gulf Cooperation Council, and the African Union—reprimanded Gaddafi for his actions.

China was in a difficult predicament given the expectation that the UN Security Council should intervene. The responsibility to protect debate intensified to a point that Libya was viewed as the benchmark case for the willingness of the international community to intervene to protect people under attack from their state.[8] A robust public discourse identified Colonel Gaddafi as the source of the mass human rights abuses, leading to calls for Libyan regime change; increasingly, the perception was that resolving the Libyan crisis would be impossible without removing Colonel Gaddafi. Though China initially had a muted position on the anti-Gaddafi protests within Libya,[9] in the space of three weeks, China cast a yes vote for Resolution 1970, the first time that the UN Security Council unanimously referred a case with a sitting head of state to the International Criminal Court, and shortly after, an abstention vote for Resolution 1973 to impose an arms embargo, enforce a no-fly zone over Benghazi, and all necessary measures to ensure protection of civilians. Resolution 1973 is viewed as leading to "decisive alterations to the international framework of law,"[10] as it was the first time that the UN Security Council supported the use of force for explicitly and only humanitarian purposes in opposition to a functioning state.[11] Such a move indicated that the UN Security Council was unafraid to take action on behalf of civilian protection.

Contrary to analysis that dismissed China's actions on Libya as "no big deal,"[12] asserting that Libya was part of China's general trend of permissive action regarding intervention—this case was a turning point for China's role as an arbiter of global security. Indeed, China's support for Resolution 1973 was largely a surprise—many analyses had predicted that China and Russia would cast tandem vetoes of a protection of civilians-centered resolution.[13] Therefore, the central question explored in this chapter is what explains China's position on intervention regarding the Libya crisis?

Understanding how China reconciled its status concerns against other interests is key in explaining its votes in a case that is now regarded as a "benchmark" case of regime change.[14] China already had a heightened sensitivity regarding status— China's standing with its peers within a status community—due to a status trigger: a well-publicized speech by Colonel Gaddafi citing his repression as a parallel to the Tiananmen Square Incident of 1989, where the People's Liberation Army was used to suppress domestic protests calling for political reform. China had increased awareness of its status costs, and became acutely aware of being socially isolated from both of its peer groups if China offered Gaddafi diplomatic cover, as Libya became a pariah in the region and beyond. As China's great power and Global South peer groups sought to ensure Colonel Gaddafi was held accountable for his policies, China perceived the costs were too high to oppose their collective positions and sacrifice China's status.

In a relatively short time, both of China's status groups had coalesced around holding Libya accountable. Representatives of China's great power status at the UN Security Council—the United States, the United Kingdom, and France (informally known as the "P3" due to their permanent status)—strongly advocated for an International Criminal Court referral of the country case. Representatives of China's Global South status—the League of Arab States, the Organization of Islamic Cooperation, the Gulf Cooperation Council—were among the first to support accountability via the International Criminal Court. In showing unanimity in support of a single policy preference, with an implied willingness to socially isolate China, the peer groups successfully used social influence to moderate China's position. Coupled with the status trigger, China's originally preferred position—an abstention vote for Resolution 1970—was deemed impossible due to the potential for social costs. As the intervention debate continued apace, China's great power peer group came out forcefully for a no-fly zone for Benghazi. However, the Global South peer group disagreed on this point: while the three lead Middle East regional groupings advocated a no-fly zone position, the African

Union opposed any military intervention. In the vote for Resolution 1973, China effectively saw itself as avoiding choosing sides and cast an abstention vote regarding the no-fly zone measure, so as to challenge no party in their demands.

However, this is not to say that every time peer groups advocate for intervention that China will move past its initial hesitancy and accede. These peer groups themselves are only sometimes successful in influencing China. In the Libya case, China was responsive to its peer groups for three reasons. First, despite their initial internal debate, the regional organizations and individual states that compose both of China's peer groups had a high degree of cohesion—going as far as calling for a no-fly zone, with no major defectors publicly airing their views as separate from the group. Second, though there was variation in the severity of their reprimand, all the peer groups aligned against Gaddafi, condemning the regime's use of force against Libyan civilians. Third, these peer groups were successful in raising China's concerns of potential public criticism and social isolation for not complying with these groups' advocated policy. Therefore, the case study illustrates the successful use of social influence to isolate status concerns, modifying China's position on intervention.

The chapter first details alternate explanations for China's response to intervention in the Libya crisis. Then I turn to establishing the public discourse on regime change in Libya. Next, the chapter uses process tracing to establish the critical junctures of the case, illustrating how status concerns were recognized and affected determinations made by Chinese officials at key decision points. The chapter closes on the analysis and conclusion.

Alternate Explanations

Defending Overseas Interests

By the time the Libya affair reached the UN Security Council, there was evidence that Colonel Gaddafi was losing control of Libyan domestic security, therefore threatening Chinese national interests. There was growing concern over the safety of the 36,000 Chinese citizens working in Libyan oil, railway, construction, and network development industries. The China National Petroleum Company staff confirmed that their facilities were compromised, as crowds set fire to facilities and attacked workers.[15] Compounding this, the Chinese blogosphere was alive with reports and commentary on the plight of Chinese workers in Libya, as they posted updates on fleeing Libyan violence.[16] China urged Libya to "restore social stability and normalcy as soon as possible and spare no effort to protect the safety of Chinese people, organizations and assets in Libya."[17] China dispatched the PLA Air Force and PLA Navy to support evacuation operations.[18]

Some see China's position on intervention in Libya as logical responses to concerns about defending overseas interests. However, these arguments lack explanatory power, as the UN Security Council efforts were not aimed at stabilizing Colonel Gaddafi's government per se—like brokering a ceasefire, pursuing mediation or dispatching a consensual peacekeeping operation could entail. Instead, the UN Security Council addressed intervention by applying further pressures on Colonel Gaddafi, and challenging the continuity that he offered to Chinese investments. In so doing, China would be taking a much larger risk regarding its Libyan investments in having to work with anti-Gaddafi rebel groups that were already at best ambivalent about China. As it came to light that Chinese firms were supplying arms worth US$200 million to Gaddafi during the arms embargo,[19] rebels reported that these allegations would "make it difficult" to support future Chinese investment.[20] Libyan oil company officials noted they "would be reluctant to do business with Chinese companies" because of China's relationship with Colonel Gaddafi.[21] Moreover, if China was so concerned about defending overseas interests, then one would have expected to see China recognize the National Transition Council at a much earlier interval, rather than as the last permanent UN Security Council member to do so in September 2011.[22] China refused to comment on official recognition of the National Transition Council, even after the June 27 request by the prosecutor of the International Criminal Court for arrest warrants for Gaddafi, his son Saif al-Islam Gaddafi, and head of military intelligence Abdullah al-Senussi—a sign of the increasing pressure on the regime. These data-points imply that drawing a direct connection between China's support for intervention and protecting China's overseas interests is unclear at best.

Diplomatic Practice and Expertise

Adler-Nissen and Pouliot assert that the P3 ability to successfully harness "emergent power"—"the generation and deployment of endogenous resources—social skills and competences"—led to their proposed resolutions coming to fruition at the UN Security Council.[23] P3 diplomatic practices meant that they could out maneuver other UN Security Council members and set the pace and scope of the agenda. Such a view is complemented by the speed at which the Libya affair passed through the UN Security Council. In a matter of weeks—following Colonel Gaddafi's advances against rebel incursions, increasingly indiscriminate tactics and then abrupt removal—the Libyan affair was no longer high on the UN Security Council agenda. As Shi Yinhong observes, Chinese officials had little time to propose and pursue different options in the face of UN Security Council members' pressure on China.[24] Chinese officials were acutely aware of the contagion effect that anti-government protests were having across the Middle East region, and this perceived time pressure may have spurred their interest in engaging,[25] especially as from mid-February 2011 there were unknown Internet sources urging protests for a "jasmine revolution" in China.[26] While there is an argument to be made for P3 diplomatic practice being strengthened by experience and expertise, and that the speed of events compounded impediments of novice rotating members of the UN Security Council, Adler-Nissen and Pouliot's argument cannot explain *China's* votes. Why did China choose a yes vote and an abstention vote for the two landmark resolutions—instead of two abstention votes, for example?

Russian Support

Wuthnow notes that Russia should figure prominently in China's considerations as the only other non-western permanent member of the UN Security Council.[27] Indeed, Russia cast the exact same votes as China regarding both key resolutions. However, it is worth pausing to assess whether the correlation of China's votes with Russia is a causal factor per se. Some assert that the concept of China and Russia as a pair at the UN Security Council is "melting away" with China's increasingly self-directed activity in global politics.[28] If it is the case that the Russian factor was key for China, we would expect affirmative responses from Chinese diplomats to this end; changes in Chinese strategy to occur after coordination with Russia, and public pronouncements emphasizing the relevance of Russia for China. Yet interviews and the case study do not reveal such an emphasis, implying further consideration of this alternate explanation is warranted.

Public Discourse on Libya and Regime Change

The public discourse calling for Libyan regime change was almost immediate, and continued throughout the duration of the Libyan affair at the UN Security Council. Indeed, the connection between Libya and regime change was so strong, that US senior officials actively sought to dismiss the idea that the United States was targeting Gaddafi for removal.[29] Graph 5.1 maps the Libyan regime change discourse—virtually non-existent until the Arab Spring protests—and shows that the public discourse picked up intensity just as the crisis was entering the UN Security Council agenda (see Graph 5.2).

An analysis of the broader public debates reflects these initial data-points, evidencing a phased discussion amongst the United States, the United Kingdom, and France—the powerbrokers if there was to be a case for intervention—regarding targeting Gaddafi due to the Libyan crisis. The United Kingdom pushed for Gaddafi's accountability for his government's abuses and emphasized that the international community would hold Libyan officials culpable.[30] In so doing, the

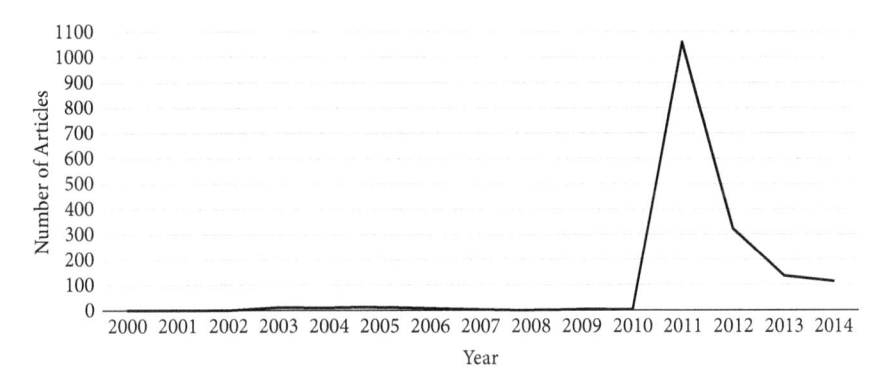

Graph 5.1. Factiva database search of English-language sources regarding "Libya" and "regime change" within five words, 2000–2014, without duplicates

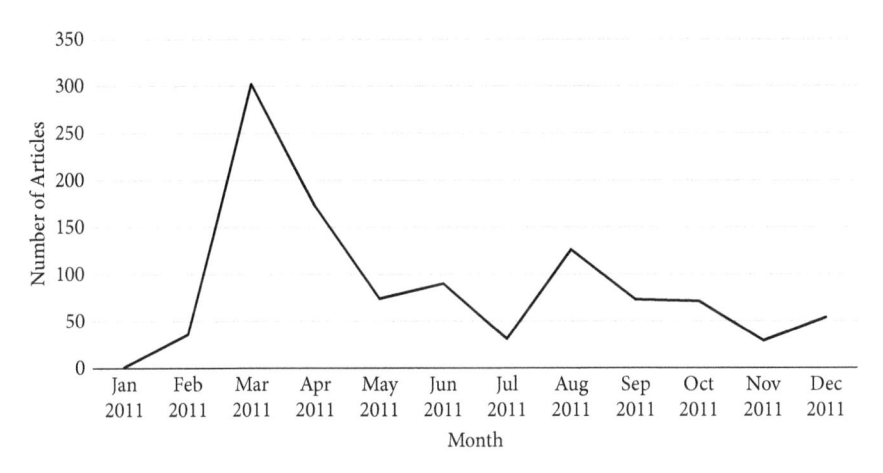

Graph 5.2. Factiva database search of English-language sources regarding "Libya" and "regime change" within five words by month, 2011, without duplicates

United Kingdom was clear that it planned to utilize the United Nations as the venue to implement Libyan accountability. Soon after the United States and France followed suit.[31] The UK position hardened by the end of February 2011, with statements saying that "Colonel Gaddafi's regime must end and he must leave" and that "we do not in any way rule out the use of military assets [to achieve that goal]."[32] These statements continued that Gaddafi's departure was a requirement for Whitehall.[33] France took a similar turn shortly thereafter: "Gaddafi understands that he must go and must leave power,"[34] and officials were direct in their views that by the beginning of March 2011, that France wanted to "increase pressure to bring down Gaddafi and he will fall."[35] Coordination between the United Kingdom and France ensured that there was greater European Union engagement, which again confirmed that "the European Council unanimously requested the departure of Colonel Gaddafi...Mr. Gaddafi is no longer an interlocutor [with Europe], he must go."[36] The United States held the same opinion, with US Secretary of State Hillary Clinton noting towards the end of February 2011: "Muammar Gaddafi has lost the confidence of his people and he should go without further bloodshed and violence."[37] Therefore, by the end of February, the P3 switched to a robust discussion that Gaddafi must depart, citing legal means via Resolution 1970 to facilitate this happening.[38] By early March, the P3 increased the pressure, asserting that "no option [is] off the table so long as the Libyan Government continues to turn its guns on its own people,"[39] and that "the common objectives in Libya must be an immediate end to brutality and violence, the departure of Gaddafi from power as quickly as possible, and a transition that meets the Libyan people's aspirations for freedom."[40]

Members of influential think tanks set an agenda linking the Libya crisis to regime change, reflecting broader discourse, calling for Gaddafi's departure and political reforms for a legitimate and representative government in Libya.[41] There were direct calls to "ensure the ouster of Libyan leader Muammar Gaddafi";[42] predictions that "[this] is the end of the Gaddafi regime"[43] and that "[the] goal is no longer change but regime change,"[44] which was "necessary" and in the interests of the international community,[45] as Gaddafi had finally "lost all remnants of credibility, and it is difficult to see how he could actually rule."[46] Analysts argued for a variety of tools to produce regime change, including the use of targeted sanctions,[47] indefinite embargoes,[48] an International Criminal Court referral,[49] no-drive zones,[50] no-fly zones,[51] armed humanitarian intervention,[52] and even invasion,[53] so as to guarantee regime change in Libya. In so doing, these analysts

Table 5.1. Key UN Security Council Resolutions regarding the Libya crisis

UN Security Council Resolution	Resolution Intent	China's vote	Votes cast the same as China
1970 February 26, 2011	– imposed sanctions on Libya – referred Libya to the International Criminal Court – established the sanctions committee	Yes	Unanimous yes vote
1973 March 17, 2011	– called for all necessary means to protect civilians under threat and enforce arms embargo (excluding an occupation force) – extended no-fly zone – tightened sanctions – established a panel of experts to support UNSCR 1970 sanctions committee	Abstention	Brazil, China, India, Germany, and Russia

linked potential tools of the UN Security Council to producing the dispatch of Gaddafi. Throughout the crisis, the UN Security Council's decisions were taken against a public discourse calling for Libyan regime change (see Table 5.1).

The Libya Case

Mid-February 2011–February 21, 2011: The Libya Crisis Enters the UN Security Council

At the end of February 2011, the predominant opinion was that diplomatic measures were insufficient to prevent a potentially massive loss of life in Libya. Regional organizations relevant to the crisis came out forcefully condemning Colonel Gaddafi's use of force against civilians. The League of Arab States suspended Libya until it halted all violence;[54] the African Union issued a reprimand about Gaddafi's excessive use of force, though it stopped short of dismissing Libya from the Union;[55] and the Organization of Islamic Cooperation issued strongly worded statements against the use of indiscriminate violence against civilians—but also declined to suspend Libya.[56] Each of the regional organizations had a high degree of cohesion amongst their member states, signaling resolve and a commitment by each state member to align against Colonel Gaddafi. Consequently, the UN Security Council issued a statement that condemned the use of force against civilians and called for "steps to address the legitimate demands of the population," while crucially welcoming the decision of the League of Arab States to ostracize Colonel Gaddafi.[57] With all of these regional arrangements applying pressure on Gaddafi, they sent a concerted message that the regime was now an outcast. Such a move set up these organizations to exact social costs on states that were unwilling to isolate Colonel Gaddafi—i.e. to be a friend of Gaddafi's was to also be a potential black sheep to these regional entities.

February 22, 2011–February 25, 2011: China Becomes Acutely Aware of Status in Response to Gaddafi's "Tiananmen" Speech

China faced a unique problem about being seen as pro-Gaddafi after his speech defending his use of force against civilians, with explicit reference to the 1989 Tiananmen Square Incident:

> When Tiananmen Square happened, tanks were sent in to deal with them. It's not a joke. Do whatever it takes to stay united...People in front of tanks were crushed. The unity of China is more important than those people in Tiananmen Square.[58]

Colonel Gaddafi's speech was a status trigger for China. Chinese officials became acutely aware of status concerns, as Colonel Gaddafi had made a comparison to a low-status time in Chinese foreign policy, when China was effectively isolated internationally.[59] The speech was intended to position Colonel Gaddafi as an equal to Chinese leader Deng Xiaoping, and highlight his leadership in exerting control during a serious challenge to government authority. Colonel Gaddafi's speech was also an indirect appeal to Chinese authorities—an attempt to remind them about the importance of state sovereignty over domestic affairs and tip China towards Libya's favor at the UN Security Council. In doing so, Colonel Gaddafi implied that China was a natural partner for his government.

However, the speech had the opposite effect. Chinese officials became well aware of potential social isolation should they show any support for Colonel Gaddafi, and were concerned about "being seen as too close with Gaddafi."[60] The reference to the Tiananmen Square Incident reframed Chinese decision-makers' considerations regarding Libya, encouraging Chinese decision-makers to be sure to clearly distance China from Libya, so as to reduce comparison between the two governments and China's potential isolation from regional organizations.[61] Therefore, the speech represented the first critical juncture in the Libya case, where Chinese officials made an assessment that closely backing Colonel Gaddafi would be potentially too costly for China. Chinese officials were aware that any signals to this effect—tepid public statements regarding the violence or even abstention votes—could be interpreted as being pro-Gaddafi. This meant a reorienting of China's position, away from fence sitting, to a strategy of having to engage with the UN Security Council actions over Libya.

February 26, 2011–March 16, 2011: China Supports an International Criminal Court Referral for Libya

Four days after Gaddafi's speech, the UN Security Council voted on Resolution 1970,[62] which called for sanctions and an International Criminal Court referral to probe whether the state response to Libyan protesters constituted war crimes. Resolution 1970 was submitted by France, the United Kingdom, and Lebanon, with full support from the United States. Exactly how China would signal its stance in relation to Libya was problematic for China, and the Chinese representation was almost "caught off guard"—delaying the vote as the PRC ambassador waited for the final instructions from Beijing.[63] China did indeed cast a yes vote for Resolution 1970, the first time that the UN Security Council would unanimously refer a country case with a sitting head of state to the International Criminal Court. Resolution 1970 therefore represents the second critical juncture of the case. This vote reset China's pathway, as it marked China's formal departure from ambivalence about the violence, and China committed a yes vote for hard interventionist action.

In casting its vote, China explicitly noted that it took into account the positions of various regional groupings.[64] In the face of such unanimous pressure to show resolve against Colonel Gaddafi's actions, and with all the regional organizations blacklisting Libya, even the preferred position of an abstention vote on a coercive resolution could have been interpreted as a reluctance to censure Colonel Gaddafi, especially in light of his Tiananmen Square Incident references in his February 22 speech. Only a yes vote could have sent the firmest signal of China's disapproval for Colonel Gaddafi and resolve to separate comparisons with Gaddafi. In effect, Colonel Gaddafi's speech had the opposite effect of drawing Libya as a parallel for China. Instead, the speech inadvertently tapped the Chinese concern to not return to Beijing's post-Tiananmen isolation.[65] Therefore, despite misgivings about a yes vote, and setting precedent of a referral of live crisis with a sitting head of state at the center of massive human rights abuses, China still perceived an affirmative vote as the only option.[66]

By the end of February, France and the United Kingdom were leading the push to see whether a no-fly zone was feasible.[67] Prime Minister David Cameron announced Whitehall's planning to implement a no-fly zone in order to ensure that this option was available if needed,[68] and contact with NATO planners regarding military options.[69] These efforts were further legitimized with the Interim Council of Benghazi announcing that it was the sole legitimate representative of the Libyan peoples, asking for "the international community [to] fulfill its obligations to protect the Libyan people ... without any direct military intervention on Libyan soil."[70] Middle East regional organizations quickly came out in explicit support of the no-fly zone request: the Gulf Cooperation Council and the League of Arab States both called the UN Security Council to "take all necessary measures to protect civilians including enforcing a no-fly zone over Libya"[71] and the Organization of Islamic Cooperation supported no-fly zone measures also.[72] With this local and regional backing, France, the United Kingdom, and Lebanon introduced a draft resolution regarding a no-fly zone. China blocked the draft on procedural grounds,[73] pushing for further negotiations, explaining that:

> We believe that there are several principles to follow. The first is to respect the sovereignty and territorial integrity of Libya. The second is to push for a peaceful settlement of the current crisis in Libya through dialogue. Third, the UN Security Council should listen to and respect the opinions of the Arabian and African countries.[74]

China was not alone in its conservative stance on the no-fly zone, with other states offering only tepid responses.[75] Russia asked the League of Arab States to reconcile its anti-foreign intervention stance with support for the no-fly zone. The G8 failed to agree on a mutual position on the no-fly zone, and rotating UN Security Council member Germany warned that "[we] do not want to get sucked into a war in North Africa and we would not like to step on a slippery slope."[76]

Most importantly at this interval, the United States showed less enthusiasm for a no-fly zone. While the US Secretary of State Hillary Clinton stressed that "no option [is] off the table,"[77] US Secretary of Defense Robert S. Gates cautioned that a no-fly zone would call for "a big operation in a big country... let's just call a spade a spade... a no-fly zone begins with an attack on Libya to destroy their air defenses."[78] Senior administration officials like Vice President Joseph Biden and National Security Advisor Thomas Donilon lobbied to put full and continued effort behind a diplomatic strategy. Within the United States the public debate over how to respond to the Libya crisis continued.[79] As the pressure increased for action by early March 2011, the Obama administration called for Colonel Gaddafi's departure from office, but avoided stating whether the United States would enforce his departure. President Obama remained committed to reducing the overall US military presence in the Middle East, and was only interested in efforts that would require a military commitment of "days not weeks," where the United States was one of a coalition of states contributing forces.[80] In short, there was still little agreement amongst the P3, let alone the UN Security Council, on how to proceed regarding a no-fly zone over Libya.

In contrast, the African Union issued a statement of its "strong and unequivocal condemnation of the indiscriminate use of force and lethal weapons, whoever it comes from, resulting in the loss of life, both civilian and military, and the transformation of pacific demonstrations into armed rebellion," that the Libyan insecurity was "a serious threat to peace and security in that country and in the region as a whole," while rejecting "any foreign military intervention, whatever its form."[81] In dismissing the no-fly zone, the African Union instead emphasized a political resolution to the conflict, establishing an Ad Hoc High Level Committee of five heads of state dispatched to negotiate a ceasefire, deliver humanitarian assistance, and a peaceful "inclusive transition" to a post-Gaddafi democratically elected government.[82] The African Union saw that South Africa's presence on the Ad Hoc High Level Committee would lead to its liaising with the UN Security Council through its rotating seat. As de Waal notes, in contrast to its position on Tunisia and Egypt, which were viewed as democratic uprisings, the pressures of a Libyan civil war, a disbanding mercenary corps and regional instability led to the African Union's much more conservative view.[83] This point is important as it marked the first official split between the different regional organizations on how to address Libyan violence.[84] Though largely glossed over in the literature,[85] this split highlights that China faced competing policy prescriptions from its Global South peer group.

Not all the regional organizations were internally cohesive either, with a lack of consensus amongst members of the League of Arab States and the African Union. This made the Global South approach to the no-fly zone question more problematic for China to decipher. For example, the League of Arab States no-fly zone resolution highlighted the divisiveness within the group. Though it was ultimately endorsed, only eleven states—half of the League of Arab States membership—were present for the vote. Moreover, it was unclear whether those votes were indeed unanimous as initially understood; Syria and Algeria later registered their opposition.[86] Only Qatar, Jordan, and the United Arab Emirates reiterated endorsement of the no-fly zone, but drew the line at close air support strikes against the regime.[87] The same divisions plagued the African Union—some leaders remained sympathetic to Colonel Gaddafi, like Presidents Yoweri Museveni of Uganda and Robert Mugabe of Zimbabwe; others publicly rejected Colonel Gaddafi like Prime Minister of Ethiopia Meles Zenawi,[88] and Sudan was in flat-out opposition to Colonel Gaddafi and the African Union position, actively participating in supporting the rebellion to lead to his removal.[89] When it came to the UN Security Council vote authorizing the no-fly zone, Gabon, Nigeria, and South Africa—the three African states on the rotating membership of the UN Security Council—voted "yes" for Resolution 1973, in direct opposition to the African Union position.

March 17, 2011–March 19, 2011: China Abstains on a No-Fly Zone Vote over Libya

The United States had held to the line that it was reluctant to push for a harder intervention out of concerns regarding "a new Arab war,"[90] until the morning of March 15, 2011.[91] President Obama pointedly remarked that "[we] can't play the role of Russia or China"[92] in avoiding responsibilities, and that US credibility was on the line if it did not address the eminent attack of civilians.[93] The Obama administration further clarified that any redress of Libya would require broad support and adherence to international law: UN Security Council authorization, political endorsement from regional players and NATO taking on the military lead.[94] This baseline understanding meant that the United States and the United Kingdom were able to build upon earlier discussions on NATO involvement in planning for all possible military operations.[95] Therefore, the United States joined France and the United Kingdom in not only supporting a no-fly zone, but by the end of March 15, the US position was that a no-fly zone itself would be "too little, too late,"[96] as Colonel Gaddafi reported he was within striking distance of killing rebels in their Benghazi stronghold.[97] As US Ambassador to the UN Susan E. Rice explained, "we'd be flying around up in the sky with a great investment of political capital and military assets with zero ability to affect what was going on the ground, which is where the slaughter was taking place."[98]

Therefore, Ambassador Rice led negotiations to "put teeth in this mandate,"[99] looking for "UN support for more than a no-fly zone."[100] What became known as the "no-fly zone plus" emphasized three components: enforcing an arms embargo; imposing a no-fly zone; and the use of all necessary measures to protect civilians and civilian-populated areas. Ultimately, it was the all necessary measures to protect civilians that gave the resolution "teeth." In her eight hours of negotiations with her UN Security Council counterparts, Ambassador Rice pushed for airstrikes against ground, air, and naval assets that threatened civilians; and expanded the legal authority to use force against Colonel Gaddafi's troops and military installations. The United States negotiated for an opening regarding arming rebels, using all necessary measures to protect civilians under threat of attack "notwithstanding" the arms embargo language of Resolution 1970.[101] The United States pushed for a broad international coalition to enforce the mandate, including Arab states. These conditions were expected to trigger a Russian veto.[102] The United States then spent significant effort lobbying other UN Security Council holdouts to support its robust resolution.[103] To be clear, though the US efforts now exceeded the earlier discussions in its robustness, the basis of the draft resolution was still an operative paragraph regarding a no-fly zone.

Colonel Gaddafi made another speech on March 17, 2011, denouncing rebels as "rats"[104] and vowing that his forces "are coming tonight... we will find you in your closets... we will show no mercy and no pity."[105] This speech was the same day as the vote for the UN Security Council to authorize Resolution 1973, calling member states, acting nationally or through regional organizations, to implement a no-fly zone "in order to help protect civilians"[106] and take "all necessary measures... to protect civilians and civilian populated areas under threat of attack," but "excluding a foreign occupation force of any form on any part of the Libyan territory."[107] Resolution 1973 passed with abstentions from Brazil, China, India, Germany, and Russia—all five states asserting that peaceful resolution of the conflict had not been exhausted, neither had questions been answered about the enforcement of the "no-fly zone plus." China explained its vote as such:

> China attaches great importance to the relevant decision by the 22-member Arab League on the establishment of a no-fly zone over Libya, we also attach great importance to the position of African countries and the African Union. In view of this and considering the special circumstance surrounding the situation in Libya, China abstained during the vote on the resolution, Resolution 1973.[108]

While the text of Resolution 1973 clearly went beyond the originally requested no-fly zone, the no-fly zone still formed the backbone of the "no-fly zone plus" text. More importantly, however, interviews reveal that reconciling the respective regional groups' no-fly zone positions dominated Chinese officials concerns regarding Resolution 1973.[109] Chinese officials showed public conformity in "not wanting to choose a side"—therefore voting to abstain—but harbored dissatisfaction privately in having to passively offer acquiescence.[110] Chinese officials were aware that the Russian position had shifted to abstention,[111] and that China would have to dissent alone. Yet China did not actively consider an attempt to block the proposed text—and in permitting the intervention to proceed, this was the third critical juncture of the case.

Although China was "not satisfied, did not agree" with the resolution—China still felt it most appropriate to "not [choose] a stance" as "it wasn't an option" for China to favor any regional group since they pushed for diametrically opposite requests regarding the no-fly zone.[112] China recognized regional groups did not have consensus on how to deal with Libya,[113] but despite serious concerns with no-fly zone authorization, implementation, and future implications of such a measure, China *did not robustly consider a veto option* because of preoccupations with status concerns. The only perceived path of viable action for China was to cast an abstention vote. Though this would permit action to occur, PRC officials reasoned that an abstention vote would enable China to take a non-obtrusive action, showing no favor to the Middle East regional organizations nor the African Union over their respective positions regarding the no-fly zone. PRC officials reasoned that China's abstention was a "neutral" vote.[114] A counterfactual is useful here for clarity: if China was willing to supersede the position of African regional groupings, then Beijing would have voted yes *and* offered enthusiastic justification for its vote. Instead China cast an abstention vote. In order to avoid being isolated from any of its status groups, China cast the only vote *perceived* viable: a middle ground abstention vote. However, in so doing, China acquiesced to having the no-fly zone and all necessary means for protection of civilians go forward.

The P3, NATO, and key Middle Eastern allies like Qatar and Jordan, read Resolution 1973 as permitting a range of military activities so as to enforce a no-fly zone. However, more intervention-resistant states like Russia and China called for a more conservative interpretation of the Resolution. After forty-eight hours of deliberation at the Paris Summit, a coalition of states executed the mandate of Resolution 1973. French aircraft entered Libyan airspace to execute airstrikes to hamper Colonel Gaddafi's advance on rebel-held territories, like Benghazi; and a coalition of states conducted ground target strikes and enforced a naval blockade.[115]

March 20, 2011–October 2011: China Criticizes Enforcement of the No-Fly Zone over Libya

Almost immediately, criticism of the operation commenced, and China's tolerance of UN Security Council Resolution 1973 changed with the implementation of the Resolution. The next day, the PRC Foreign Ministry noted their "serious reservations" about the enforcement actions, noting that China "regrets the military strike against Libya."[116] Within forty-eight hours of the first strikes, the official paper, the *People's Daily* issued a vehement editorial, chastizing the western alliance for its interpretation of Resolution 1973:

> The blood-soaked tempests that Iraq has undergone for eight years and the unspeakable suffering of its people are a mirror and a warning... The military

attacks on Libya are, following on the Afghan and Iraq wars, the third time that some countries have launched armed action against sovereign countries... it should be seen that every time military means are used to address crises, that is a blow to the United Nations Charter and the rules of international relations.[117]

In comparing the coalition's Libyan intervention to the Iraq and Afghanistan Wars, which from the Chinese perspective were unsanctioned escapades of "some countries" military might, the *People's Daily* editorial was an appeal to the members of the Global South, smaller states who fear attack by western powers. In this sense, Chinese officials were drawing a line, clearly marking the interpretation of Resolution 1973 as unacceptable to China and weakening the international system. China later condemned the "arbitrary interpretation" of Resolution 1973 and that these actions went "beyond those mandated by the Council."[118] South Africa also joined in criticism of "the purported implementation of Resolution 1973."[119] The League of Arab States Secretary-General Amr Moussa lamented "[what] is happening in Libya differs from the aim of imposing a no-fly zone, and what we want is the protection of civilians and not the bombardment of more civilians."[120]

In an op-ed in the *China Daily* by Li Qinggong, an official of the China Council for National Security Policy Studies, further chastized the West in the enforcement of the no-fly zone. Li claimed that: "Western countries have long harbored the intention of dethroning Libya's Muammar Gadhafi regime. The recent military strife in the country between government troops and rebels offered an immediate and a rare excuse for Western military intervention," blaming the Libyan crisis on the "political incitement from Western countries."[121] Chinese scholars have also published similar critical appraisals of the no-fly zone enforcement.[122] On March 23, PRC Ministry of Foreign Affairs spokesperson Jiang Yu stated an even sharper position in her regular press briefing calling the no-fly zone enforcement "the abuse of force." Spokesperson Jiang stated:

> China has noted and expresses deep concern over the report of civilian casualties caused by the military actions taken by relevant countries against Libya. Relevant Security Council Resolution was meant to protect civilian safety in Libya. We oppose the abuse of force that can cause more civilian casualties and a bigger humanitarian crisis.[123]

NATO took over enforcement of the no-fly zone on March 25, with a full transfer of operational authority at the end of that month.[124] It it still not a matter of public record when the policy transitioned to one of forcibly removing Gaddafi.[125] With criticism rising, the United States clarified that "[broadening] the military operation to include regime change would be a mistake... Qaddafi needed to leave, to be sure, but his departure was not the objective of the military operation."[126] By the beginning of April, the coalition had grounded the Libyan air force and degraded the command and control for these air systems, aiding rebel groups in establishing control over the east of the country. Yet, despite public protest by President Barack Obama that regime change was not a goal, there was still confusion about political ends and their connection to the use of military means. With the prevention of the imminent attack of Benghazi, the debate reopened about how to best interpret Resolution 1973, which led to NATO to again clarify its goals during its April 14, 2011 foreign ministerial meeting.[127] The same day, Presidents Obama and Sarkozy and Prime Minister Cameron published a joint op-ed article that called for Gaddafi's departure, though not by force.[128] On April 30, 2011, one of Colonel Gaddafi's sons and three of his grandchildren were killed in Tripoli in a NATO strike. The PRC Ministry of Foreign Affairs noted that "[we] express concern over the escalation of conflicts in Libya and ensuing civilian casualties. China always disapproves of any action that goes beyond the authorization of the UN Security Council."[129] Criticisms continued about NATO's shifting objectives, and its simultaneously selective implementation and expansive reinterpretation of the mandate.[130] Chinese officials continued to emphasize that NATO had overstepped their UN Security Council mandate in their no-fly zone; calling for an immediate ceasefire and peaceful political settlement by the relevant parties.[131] Shortly thereafter, US Secretary of Defense Leon E. Panetta noted that "the [US] objective is to do what we can to bring down the regime of Gaddafi."[132] As NATO- and coalition-supported rebels gained control over Libyan territory, Colonel Gaddafi was declared dead on October 20, 2011, during the capture of his hometown, Sirte.

Analysis

This chapter argues that there were five short phases in China's response to the Libya crisis:

- Mid-February 2011–February 21, 2011: the Libya crisis enters the UN Security Council;

- February 22, 2011–February 25, 2011: China becomes acutely aware of status in response to Colonel Gaddafi's "Tiananmen" speech;

- February 26, 2011–March 16, 2011: China supports an International Criminal Court referral for Libya;

- March 17, 2011–March 19, 2011: China abstains on a no-fly zone vote over Libya;

- March 20, 2011—October 2011: China criticizes enforcement of the no-fly zone over Libya.

What factors explain China's response to the Libya crisis? This chapter demonstrates that status was key to China's decisions, and Chinese officials' receptivity to status-based motivations was because of social influence. China's pre-existing status concerns due to Colonel Gaddafi's speech referencing the Tiananmen Square Incident of 1989—a low-status time in China's recent foreign policy history—were accentuated just days before the vote for Resolution 1970. This speech served as a status trigger, and sensitized China's concerns regarding status. Though a yes vote for Resolution 1970 was not China's ideal choice, Chinese officials were well aware that even an abstention vote could have bolstered perceptions that China was an advocate for the Libyan pariah, Colonel Gaddafi. By February 2011, all of China's peer groups—the regional organizations relevant to the crisis (representative of China's Global South status) and the P3 (representative of China's great power status)—had coalesced around supporting sanctions and an International Criminal Court referral of the Libya case entailed in Resolution 1970. With both peer groups coming around to these specific measures, they set the standard that if China was to be a member of either peer group, it too needed to support these efforts. If China offered any support for Libya's intransigence it would be in direct opposition to both its peer groups. Peer groups had united around a single policy option, with no major defectors and were willing to exact social costs on states unwilling to pursue their recommended approach.

However, as pressure continued to build for the imposition of a no-fly zone and a protection of civilians mandate, China recognized the P3 support for the measure, but that the regional organizations could not agree on a policy line—the Middle East groups supporting the call for a no-fly zone, with the African Union rejecting the no-fly zone option. As there was no longer a clear intersubjective normative consensus on good behavior for a peer group member—China "split the difference" per se, voting to abstain. While a tacit acquiescence to intervention, it is key to note that Chinese officials reasoned an abstention vote permitted China to cause the least offence, preventing isolation from any of its peer groups. In either backing Colonel Gaddafi—China's preferred position not only for stability and continuity in relations with the dictatorship, but also in rejecting any attempts of intervention against a public discourse calling for regime change—China would have ended up socially isolated over the short duration of the Libyan crisis at the UN Security Council. Had China been willing to permit the P3 and the Middle East groups, who all favored a baseline no-fly zone, to supersede the position of African regional groupings, then China would have voted yes *and* offered enthusiastic justification for its Resolution 1973 vote.

To further illuminate the effects of social influence, it is worth using a counterfactual: had there been no status concerns for China, and given that votes to apply coercion are costly for China, China could have maintained its original emphasis for a peaceful solution to the crisis, while downplaying China's interests in Libya. Moreover, securing overseas interests and protecting against a reputation as an intervention supporter would have been feasible by staying within the familiar reach of Chinese policy. However, Chinese officials pursued a different path in recognition that their original preferences would have left China isolated from its status groups. In China's shifting approach to Libya, there is evidence that status concerns by way of social influence worked to mediate China's interests.

Moreover, China's two landmark votes took place in the absence of material side payments in two ways. First, China focused on offering support for increasingly heavy measures against Colonel Gaddafi, therefore challenging the stability offered by his regime towards Chinese investments in Libya. If maintaining some form of stability for material side payments was key, one would assume that China would either have committed greater support to Colonel Gaddafi or recognized the National Transition Council of Libya at a much earlier interval—after all, this was to be the group in charge of steering Libyan politics and economy immediately in Colonel Gaddafi's wake. However, by the end of May 2011, China was the only permanent member of the UN Security Council to not have contacted the Libyan interim governing body, instead calling for a peaceful settlement of the issues by the relevant parties. In early June of that year, the PRC Ministry of Foreign Affairs stated that initial discussions with the National Transition Council had taken place.[133] Signaling increasing recognition of the National Transition Council by the end of June 2011, Foreign Minister Yang Jiechi met with not only Libya's special envoy, Foreign Minister Abdul Ati al-Obidi, but also Chairman of the Executive Board of the Libyan Opposition Mahmoud Jibril, calling the National Transition Council an "important dialogue partner," paving the way for Beijing to recognize the National Transition Council on September 12, 2011— well after the rebels had taken the capital by the end of August 2011.[134] These points highlight that these decisions were taken at the cost of material side payments.

Last, China did indeed stress social praise and pressure from its peer groups. In particular, Chinese officials stressed the need to be supportive of their Global South group when explaining votes. This point was emphasized repeatedly during interviews, with Chinese foreign policy elites stressing regional recognition and praise of China's respect for their differing views.[135] Curiously, this desire to resonate with the Global South was so strong that it was the central feature when China explained its vote for Resolution 1973—a sign of China's conviction to being accepted in the peer group, especially when its typical vote explanation language tightly revolves around exceptional conditions of a crisis, respect for sovereignty and territorial integrity, and calls for peaceful resolution to political problems. In regards to the P3, Chinese officials noted that President Obama "had recognized China" in echoing China's principles for intervention, when he invoked the need for UN Security Council authorization and regional player buy-in for action.[136]

Conclusion

This case study illustrates in practice how China reconciles status concerns against other competing interests. In so doing, it implicitly captures China's strategy of shifting to satisficing outcomes when its diplomatic first preferences are deemed to be infeasible. China found means to skillfully reconcile a competing set of pressures from its peers, not all of which agreed on the best means forward in the Libya affair.

However, this is not to say that Chinese officials were immune to the emerging norms of intervention, like accountability for state-led mass violence, especially against a backdrop of credible threats punctuated by Colonel Gaddafi's hate speech. It is more that China's first preference is to avoid engaging proactively in entrenching such norms, especially at the pace demanded in the Libya case. Yet staying within a narrow remit of action—downplaying China's material concerns and calling for a political resolution to the crisis, for example—was quickly dropped by China as it became clearer that these emerging norms of intervention were linked to China's status concerns. To be clear, this is not to say that China acted in response to a deep or even thin commitment to these norms—but more that China's status groups broadly defined awareness of emerging intervention norms translated into status concerns for China, and in turn represented a standard of good behavior for China to comply with. Linking China's status concerns to the emerging intervention norms moved China towards voting for and acquiescing to coercive action in the Libya case.

The Libya case shows that China was able to tolerate interventionist actions, but such acquiescence was followed by swift steps back from the no-fly zone execution. China should not have been surprised that the no-fly zone would start with aerial bombardment of Libyan air defenses. The no-fly zone and its implications were central features of the disagreement amongst western states in the run up to the vote on Resolution 1973. Rather, a way to interpret the Chinese rebuke of NATO activities is to see China appealing to two different groups: an appeal to the West by acquiescing to the P3-led vote, while still appealing to the Global South, maintaining China's credibility in vociferously criticizing the implementation of Resolution 1973. China *tolerated* the no-fly zone policy, then used its acquiescence to underscore Chinese moral opposition in its abstention vote. China's credibility and reputation as a state set apart from the P3 is weakened with votes that bring China closer to liberal states. The implementation of Resolution 1973 also presented China with an opportunity to assert itself as a creative resister, advocating new additions to existing normative structures of "responsibility'—this includes rhetorical action taken in wake of the Syria crisis, where China instigated its "responsible protection" standards.

The case also highlights a broader quandary for China. Having long advocated for UN Security Council authorizations of intervention, with regional backing and some component of local support, these broader conditions "backfired" per se.

Chinese officials were uncomfortable with the decision to support action in Libya, and were conscious of their dissonance with China's self-proclaimed conservative pragmatism regarding mass human rights challenges. Instead of tamping down the potential for intervention, as each of China's individual measures in its normative framework were satisfied, China ostensibly managed to "self-entrap." At this point, it remains too early to see whether or not this process of entrapment is a means to deeper socialization of China into the broadly liberal international order as speculated.[137]

Having established that status can mediate China's other interests regarding intervention, the next chapter deals with the opposite case. In the opening phase of the Syria crisis, status concerns were relegated consistently, indicating that peer groups do not always have the ability to influence China's position.

6
Status and Intervention in Syria, 2011–2015

Introduction

While China was willing to support consensual measures, the Syria case presents a puzzle in that China spent precious vetoes in relatively quick succession—consistently refusing any perceived coercive measures—blocking censure, demands for peace plans compliance, potential sanctions, and an International Criminal Court referral of the Syria case.[1] Given China's record of the absolute lowest number of vetoes across the permanent members of the UN Security Council, the willingness to commit multiple vetoes in a single country case is in and of itself striking. These vetoes become all the more puzzling when considered against the increasing pressure from the P3, regional players, UN official and public intellectuals for the UN Security Council to "do something" against the mounting Syrian death toll and the reporting of the increasingly indiscriminate tactics and measures of the Assad regime. Therefore, the key question guiding this chapter is what explains China's response to the Syria crisis?

I argue that the Syria case presents the "dog that did not bark" per se—where China was able to discount status concerns, accepting some social costs from disassociating with its peer groups, choosing to have its intervention voting ultimately guided by other interests. To be clear though, China was still status conscious: process tracing highlights efforts to reduce status pressures and the logic used to discount social influence. Therefore, the case shows that China's status insensitivity is relative—not absolute (i.e. China is not "immune" to status pressures, proceeding without consideration of status). To make this argument, this chapter details the critical junctures in the Syria case, showing that China could discount social pressures from its peer groups' pro-intervention positions, against other motivations for intervention. Crucially, the case lacks a status trigger for China—at no point did Assad or any of the key players in the case invoke a low-status period for China, nor attack high-status events that China was hosting. Without this trigger to make "a strong connection, with strong feelings to China... [there is] not a direct emotional feeling on this crisis,"[2] meaning that status was not a heightened variable in this case. Moreover, although the P3 coalesced around coercive intervention, with no defections, and steady social opprobrium for China's lack of cooperation, this peer group was not enough to alone apply social influence on China either. As regime change in Libya had been achieved, China was far more cautious regarding P3-led intervention into Syria at the UN Security Council—to the point of largely dismissing P3 critique of China. Regional organizations relevant to the crisis—the League of Arab States, the Organization of Islamic Cooperation, and the Gulf Cooperation Council—represented the Global South peer group. Though these groups had by and large ostracized Assad, PRC officials assessed that these Middle East regional organizations did not unite on a single position supporting draft resolutions; that these groups were plagued by public defections and were incohesive, and thus had limited abilities to exact social costs on China. In part, because these groups could not settle on a group standard of good behavior, attempts to use social influence on China in this particular case were ineffective. Furthermore, China could offset criticism on to Russia, which took the lead in condemning any potential intervention of its Syrian ally. In sharing criticism, China could blunt critiques of its decisions.

Because China could discount status concerns, China actively intervened to ensure that a firm line against non-consensual intervention would be held, and in this case alone China committed three innovations: the use of multiple, successive veto votes; rebranding to delegitimize non-consensual intervention as "regime change"; and engaging in norm shaping of the responsibility to protect regarding the use of force. These three innovations together highlight China's willingness to firmly separate the intervention norm from that of regime change. Unlike in other watershed examples of intervention, the Syria case marks a change in China's approach in its attempt to actively control not only policy outcomes (bringing possible action to a halt via multiple vetoes), but also affect normative discourse and the normative status quo (delegitimizing intervention as back-door "regime change" and projecting China's anti-intervention position as "responsible protection").

The chapter first details alternate explanations for the votes. Then I turn to establishing the public discourse on regime change in Syria. Next, the chapter uses process tracing to establish the critical junctures of the case, illustrating how status concerns were recognized and then discounted by PRC officials at these decision points. The chapter shows that China is willing to support a consensual approach to addressing the Syrian crisis: mediation by the League of Arab States and the UN Special Envoy, a UN monitoring mission, and the political resolution via the Syrian Action Group are all initiatives backed by China. China supplements these multilateral efforts with its own bilateral efforts on diplomacy—with overtures to the Syrian opposition groups and also meeting with delegations from other Middle Eastern states.[3] Chinese-supported measures show a commitment not to push for Assad's resignation or establish a pathway to his departure through coercive measures, and to recognize equal criticism on all parties.

Alternate Explanations

Learning

A number of analysts argue that regime change in Libya produced the veto outcomes for Syria.[4] UN Security Council-authorized resolutions were used as stepping stones for regime change and the removal of Colonel Gaddafi. Therefore, China refuses to endorse coercive intervention into the Syria crisis against a public discourse of regime change out of concern of producing the same result. As one Chinese official noted: "regime change in Libya left [us] with this feeling that... we had been fooled."[5] Moreover, throughout the arc of this particular conflict, China's position has consistently been linked back to the Libya affair. During an initial open debate on protection of civilians in armed conflict, when Syria was introduced to the debate, PRC Ambassador to the United Nations Li Baodong explicitly referenced Libya:

> strengthening the protection of civilians in armed conflict must be done through implementation of Security Council decisions in a comprehensive and strict manner. The original intention of resolutions 1970 (2011) and 1973 (2011) was to put an end to violence... [we] are opposed to any attempt to willfully interpret the resolutions or to take actions that exceed those mandated.[6]

While this argument seems logical—two closely timed crises of the Arab Spring on the UN Security Council agenda must surely impact each other—it is worth some further consideration on three fronts. First, the implication of the "Libya effect" argument is that China only made one critical juncture in the Syria case: i.e. whether to commit the first veto, and once this first veto occurred, that China continued unswervingly down the veto path. This implies that resolutions were rejected *outright*, without consideration of alternate voting options (like an abstention). Second, this view discounts the complications of the Syria case, independent of it following the Libya crisis. Libya is a smaller, relatively ethnically homogenous state, with a leader that had alienated practically every regional player and with no major ally to rest upon. Syria in contrast has a four-times larger population, greater ethnic and religious divisions, and a leader that could call upon Russian support due to Moscow's strategic interests in Syria. Another key difference is the urgency induced in part by Colonel Gaddafi's hate speech, which Assad has largely avoided. These criteria alone make the Syria case relatively more complicated from the beginning. Third, it remains unclear if China's veto response is the result of some type of learning, adaptation, feedback loop or even socialization of China regarding intervention in the context of public discourse for regime change. These distinctions matter as they imply a different pathway to producing the apparently inevitable outcomes for Syria.

Securing Overseas Interests

A popular view is that the vetoes were expected as China shares "economic, security and geopolitical interests, including weapons trade" with Syria, and "protecting the human rights of their own or each other's citizens is not high on their agendas."[7] State-owned enterprise China National Petroleum Corporation owns shares in the two largest Syrian oil firms, and state-owned enterprise Sinochem owns half of the shares in Syrian oil fields. China rounded out the purchases of Syrian crude oil after the European Union's embargo in 2011. In 2011, China was Syria's top trade partner, with exports of over US$2.4 billion shepherded by closer state-to-state coordination through the Syrian-Chinese Business Council. Therefore, the need to reassure Assad and protect national interests present in Syria motivated China's vetoes. If this was the case, then China should be able to disregard status-based arguments completely at the UN Security Council and at other forums, like the UN General Assembly—driven by a sole concern for political continuity as a means to secure China's Syria-based interests.

Russian Support

Another argument put forward is that China has moved "in tandem" with Russia on Syria, as part of a broader strategy to "present a united anti-West alliance to counter international influence by the United States and its allies."[8] Indeed, the two states have cast the same votes in all the resolutions during the time period of study here.[9] Analysis asserts that the Chinese position is due to a causal Russian factor— as Russia commits to a particular vote, China will follow suit. However, it is worth considering the "Russian support" argument on two fronts. First, it is key to determine if China's votes are the result of a causal Russian factor, or out of convenience of using the Russian vote for diplomatic cover. Second, was China's strategy regarding Syria at the UN Security Council only marked by one critical juncture—i.e. follow the first veto and then just continue with veto votes, or was there a reconsideration at each major interval? If the latter was the case, then this implies a weighing and reweighing of the importance of the Russian position for China—indicating that perhaps this factor may not have been as critical as thought.

Public Discourse on Syria and Regime Change

As the Arab Spring spread, protests began in Syria at the end of January 2011. Protesters called for the end of Ba'ath Party rule and the resignation of President Bashar al-Assad. Though the Assad regime initially allowed the protestors small concessions,[10] the government switched to repressive tactics by mid-March 2011. Again, the condemnation for Assad's measures were swift, with the United States and European Union imposing sanctions.[11] Demands for regime change continued even as Assad maintained power through violence.

One crude metric—news articles with the terms "Syria" and "regime change" within five words of each other—shows an active public discourse on Syria and regime change during the duration of the period of study (see Graph 6.1). This news picked up in 2011, averaging almost an article a day, peaking during 2012 (averaging almost two articles a day) and continuing well into 2014 (see Graph 6.2). Such reporting reflects elite discourse.

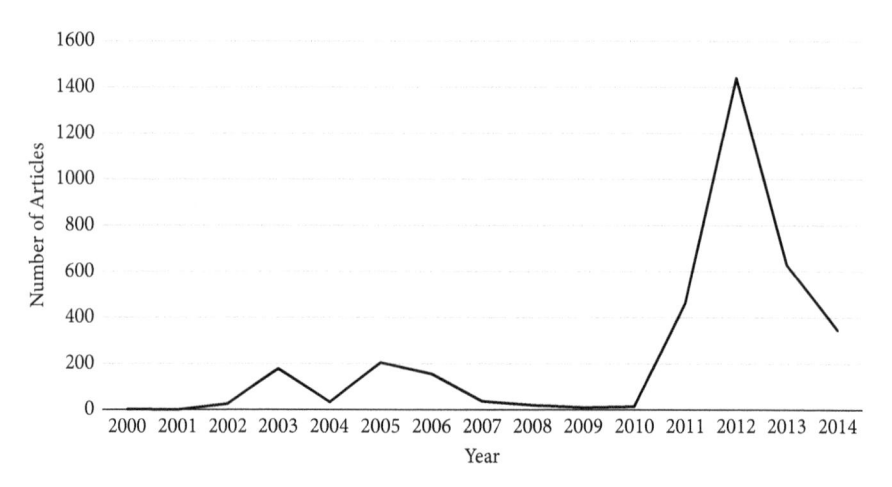

Graph 6.1. Factiva database search of English-language sources regarding "Syria" and "regime change" within five words, 2000–2014, without duplicates

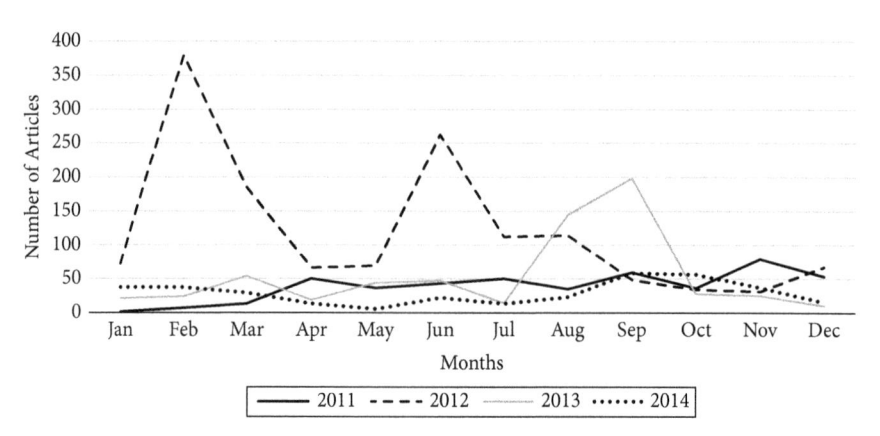

Graph 6.2. Factiva database search of English-language sources regarding "Syria" and "regime change" within five words by month, 2011–2014, without duplicates

France, the United Kingdom, and the United States were actively discussing and advocating for Assad's departure within months of the crisis entering the UN Security Council agenda. By May 2011, President Sarkozy of France came out firmly against Assad, saying "we will not accept that a regime sends the army against peaceful protesters."[12] The United States took a harder line, with President Obama calling for Assad to "lead [political] transition, or get out of the way."[13] By July 2011, the United Kingdom joined the calls for Assad's departure.[14] The P3 coalesced on increasing pressure on Assad with a coordinated, formal call on August 18, 2011 that President Assad must step aside.[15] Through 2012, these states ratcheted up pressure on Assad, establishing that "all options" were available to remove Assad from power. UK Foreign Secretary William Hague stated that "all options should...be on the table."[16] France's Foreign Minister Laurent Fabius reiterated that "we want to move things forward, take down [President Assad] as soon as possible,"[17] emphasizing that "we do not exclude any solution."[18] US Secretary of States John Kerry plainly stated that "there will be consequences" for President Assad, and "should diplomacy fail, the military option is still on the table."[19]

Members of the think-tank community set an agenda linking the Syria crisis to regime change, framing regime change as an inevitable outcome of US and UK foreign policy targeting Syria. For example, commentators at the Council on Foreign Relations noted that Syria represented "the third Arab country [the Obama] administration has targeted for regime change this year,"[20] and more coercive policy was expected "now that Obama has committed the United States to regime change in Damascus."[21] Analysts at Chatham House discussed that "[many] governments, especially in developing countries and former colonies, believe [intervention in Syria] is an excuse for regime change...Britain has called for regime change in Syria before, it funds the Syrian opposition, and has stretched the meaning of previous UN resolutions to justify regime changes in Iraq and Libya."[22] Scholars pointed out "Russian concerns that the ultimate US aim in Syria is coercive regime change."[23] Against this backdrop, experts argued that it was only a matter of time until this political transition would occur,[24] and bipartisan testimony was given at the US Senate Foreign Relations Committee[25] and at the US House of Representatives Committee on Foreign Affairs[26] about the feasibility of regime change. Experts viewed planning for Assad's voluntary departure as naïve,[27] cautioning against the effects of political power vacuum.[28] Instead, a number of commentators called upon the United States to dispatch the regime,[29] sending memoranda to the US President openly calling for "removing Assad [as] a fundamental requirement."[30] There was a healthy lobby calling for regime change as the only viable path forward,[31] going as far as labeling Assad a "'dead man walking'"[32] and emphasizing the array of tools available to achieve such an outcome.[33] Within the policy debate, Syrian regime change was not only for great powers to pursue, but discussed as a goal for the UN Security Council.

Scholars actively debated the importance[34] and irrelevance[35] of the UN Security Council in inducing Assad's departure. Therefore, throughout the crisis, the UN Security Council's decisions were taken against a public discourse on Syrian regime change.

Unique to this case was that Chinese officials at the United Nations and elsewhere utilized the term "regime change" in discourse, serving as an additional confirmation of Chinese recognition of the regime change debate over Syria. Official Chinese mouthpieces used the same framing language. For example, "Zhong Sheng"—a pen name for the "Voice of China"—chided that "a political solution is the only way to resolve the issue of Syria. Some states still do not abandon their intention of changing Syrian regime by external forces."[36] Though Chinese government mouthpieces did not explicitly name states as proponents of regime change, newspapers like the *People's Daily* did come very close, asserting that

> certain Western countries still have not given up on regime change in Syria, and have provided increasing support to rebel forces. Their open discussion of a no-fly zone, along with other irresponsible words and actions, has undermined the solidarity of the Security Council, causing the international community to be unable to reach consensus.... All kinds of indications show that the rumors that certain Western powers are looking outside the framework of the United Nations for a solution to the Syrian crisis are not baseless.[37]

Having established that intervention in Syria took place against a public discourse calling for regime change, the chapter turns to process tracing.

The Syria Case

April 2011–September 2011: China Works to Prevent Censure of Syria

In the opening phase of its Syria activity at the UN Security Council, China mainly spent its efforts trying to prevent censure of Assad. These efforts saw China partnering with Russia, following Moscow's lead in this interval; and efforts at this phase mainly focused on prolonging negotiations, and staving off P3 initiatives with alternate language. At the end of April 2011, the Security Council entered a public debate on Syria, in which China gave a typically neutral statement, calling for "constructive assistance in line with the UN Charter."[38] Indicative of the divisions to come, the UN Security Council failed to even issue a press statement on the conflict at the end of April.[39] When member states came to vote at the UN Human Rights Council about deploying a fact-finding mission, both China and Russia voted no against the non-binding resolution, the first formal signal of their reluctance to intervene in the unfolding conflict.[40] China again repeated that it was focused on promoting "constructive dialogue," and that China "opposed any humiliation of states by naming them," citing that the resolution "would only increase tension in the country and create a dangerous precedent for the region."[41] The fact-finding mission was stillborn, with Syria refusing to permit the mission's entry.[42]

A first attempt at a UN Security Council resolution in June 2011 could not get to vote, with Brazil, South Africa, India, China, and Russia challenging "how Syria should reform itself politically."[43] Russia also pushed to avoid a resolution, instead insisting on a presidential statement regarding the "grave concern at the deteriorating situation in Syria."[44] The UN Security Council continued in disarray. Rotating member Lebanon disassociated itself from the statement shortly thereafter—already indicating the lack of unanimity at the UN Security Council, and proof that there was a Middle East state reluctant to show any pushback on Assad.[45] Talks at the end of August regarding proposed sanctions against members of the government were simply boycotted by China and Russia.[46] The UN Security Council continued on its no vote pattern, discussing a UK-written draft for imposing sanctions, which eventually led to the draft resolution being tabled without a vote. Russia countered with its own draft resolution in September 2011, which also ended without a vote since it was dismissed by the P3 as too weak in its critique of Damascus.

Despite facing a hostile neighborhood and pressures from domestic uprising, Syria could buy time, stalling regional groupings from critique of its repression. After government tanks shelled civilians in Hama, killing over 140 Syrian citizens in one day alone, UN Secretary-General Ban Ki-moon condemned Assad for having "lost all humanity."[47] Yet Syria was not a pariah in the neighborhood, and the disagreements at the UN Security Council reflected debate within the region. Saudi Arabia, Bahrain, and Kuwait recalled their ambassadors from Damascus, registering disgust with Assad's tactics.[48] The Gulf Cooperation Council responded by issuing the first call for Syrian political reforms,[49] later calling for the international community to take measures to enforce protection for Syrian civilians,[50] the only regional group to do so at this point. However, the Organization of Islamic Cooperation and League of Arab States offered no comment. Instead, the League of Arab States made general calls to all states in the region experiencing unrest to refrain from using violence.[51] Therefore, in this phase of China's engagement on the Syria issue there were little consistent status pressures to be addressed. China could offset any critique of its approach by building ties with other skeptical states at the UN Security Council.

October 2011–December 2011: China Hardens its Position, Issuing a Veto Preventing Condemnation and Sanctions for Syria

China's position hardened in early October 2011, when both China and Russia issued their first veto, blocking censure and potential sanctions against Syria in a

French-drafted Resolution, co-introduced by Germany, Portugal, and the United Kingdom (see Table 6.1). The draft resolution sought to condemn "grave and systematic human rights violations" in Syria and aimed to deter President Assad with the threat of sanctions. Even after rounds of negotiations watering down the language, the draft included the call for the UN Security Council "to consider its options, including measures under Article 41 of the Charter of the United Nations."[52] China explained its vote as protecting the norms of international relations, in that actions should comply with the UN Charter, while also respecting the territorial integrity and sovereignty of Syria. China's position was that "sanctions or the threat thereof does not help to resolve the question of Syria," potentially leading to further complications instead.[53]

Pursuing this veto was the first signal that China was willing to prevent intervention. Such a vote was feasible as China had insulated itself not only with Russia's tandem veto, but China had also successfully built an abstention majority of rising powers like Brazil, India, South Africa and the sole Middle East player at the UN Security Council, Lebanon. Building this diplomatic coalition gave China

Table 6.1. Key UN Security Council Resolutions regarding the Syria crisis

UN Security Council Resolution	Resolution Intent	China's vote	Votes cast the same as China
S/2011/612 October 4, 2011	– condemned Syria – could face sanctions if force against civilians continues	Veto	Russia (Brazil, India, Lebanon, South Africa all abstained)
S/2012/77 February 4, 2012	– demanded that all parties in the conflict stop all violence and reprisals – demanded that Syria implement the League of Arab States January 22, 2012 plans without delay	Veto	Russia
2042 April 14, 2012	– deployed Syrian Civil War observer force	Yes	Unanimous yes vote
2043 April 21, 2012	– established UN Supervision Mission in Syria	Yes	Unanimous yes vote
S/2012/538 July 19, 2012	– ten days for Assad to withdraw troops and heavy weapons from populated areas – sanctioned against elites for non-compliance	Veto	Russia (Pakistan and South Africa abstained)
S/2014/348 May 22, 2014	– International Criminal Court referral of the Syria case	Veto	Russia
2165 July 14, 2014	– use of cross-border aid corridors – threats of sanctions	Yes	Unanimous yes vote

credibility in posing the proposed resolution as the expression of only Western-led interests. China framed itself as a member within the international community, emphasizing its interest in pursuing "a positive and constructive role in appropriately resolving the question of Syria."[54] Moreover, Chinese officials reasoned that there was no strong consensus amongst Middle East regional groups regarding President Assad's actions, with no actual condemnation or anti-Assad policy prescriptions. These groups gave China little social pressure, and so China had greater latitude to determine its vote.[55]

Opprobrium was swift. US Ambassador to the UN Susan Rice called the veto a "cheap ruse by those who would rather sell arms to the Syrian regime than stand with the Syrian people," and France's Ambassador to the UN Gérard Araud stated "no veto can give carte blanche to the Syrian parties who have lost full legitimacy in assassinating and killing their people...this veto goes against the sense of history underway in Syria and throughout the region."[56] It was only after the veto that other regional groups started taking a harder line against Syria. Jordan was the first Arab state to call for President Assad's departure and political transition.[57] Turkey stated that President Assad must step down.[58] With these regional players taking the lead, and as violence within Syria increased, with no signs of a peace deal implementation, the League of Arab States suspended Syria in November 2011.[59] To increase the pressure on Damascus, the League of Arab States threatened sanctions and called for individual members to recall their ambassadors. The League of Arab States was clear though that their move did not mean an entry point for military intervention, noting that "no one is talking about a no-fly zone."[60] However, even this group was divided on Syria's suspension, with Iraq casting an abstention vote, and Lebanon and Yemen joining Syria in voting no. At the end of November, the League of Arab States imposed sanctions on Syria (via an investment embargo, an asset freeze, travel ban for senior officials), in response to Syria blocking entry of a League of Arab States ground assessment monitoring team.[61] Again, this was neither a cohesive vote, nor a definitive one; nineteen member states supported the embargo, with three against. Tellingly, League of Arab States officials again emphasized that this was not a measure to enforce regime change, but an effort to push Syria towards compliance with its original peace agreement.[62] In practice, the sanctions against President Assad went unheeded—with Iraq, Jordan, and Lebanon refusing to impose sanctions on their neighbor.

In late December 2011, the League of Arab States dispatched monitors to Syria. Monitors condemned President Assad, bluntly stating "what's happening in Syria is genocide."[63] On January 22, 2012, the League of Arab States passed a resolution calling for President Assad to step down in order to allow for a new unity government, elections and a drafting of a Syrian constitution.[64] Every League state but Lebanon backed this move—a signal of division that Chinese officials took especially seriously as Lebanon sat as a UN Security Council rotating member. The League of Arab States' decision to openly call for President Assad's resignation led to an open debate at the UN Security Council on the Middle East including Syria on its agenda. The Chinese delegation chose not to acknowledge the issue by making no reference to the situation in Syria during Ambassador Li Baodong's remarks.[65] At the end of January 2012, the Gulf Cooperation Council issued a statement that it "unequivocally supports" the League of Arab States' position on Syria.[66]

At this point, Chinese officials recognized they could no longer operate on the assumption of Middle East groups remaining cautious regarding Syria. Yet, Chinese officials were able to discount social pressures because of the League of Arab States' internal disunity, therefore insulating China from status pressures from the group. Chinese officials reasoned that the League of Arab States' position had already proven to be shaky at best: such drastic action as imposing sanctions and suspending a member state requires a unanimous vote, yet these penalties were implemented despite the registered protest of individual members of the regional organization; sanctions were already being breached, and the sole Middle East representative at the UN Security Council rejected the regional organization's stance. Therefore, Chinese officials were able to dismiss the League of Arab States' stance as a guide or standard for the Gulf Cooperation Council also. China's position at the UN Security Council could be shielded from any potential opprobrium, as the "rules and procedures have all been disregarded [by the League of Arab States]...they don't follow their own [rules]."[67]

Yet, China was still aware of status and sought to limit its status concerns in the UN General Assembly, which was becoming increasingly active in light of the UN Security Council deadlock. At the end of November 2011, the UN General Assembly approved two resolutions: calling on Syrian authorities to immediately and fully implement the League of Arab States peace plan,[68] and a resolution condemning the human rights situation in Syria.[69] China cast abstention votes in both cases, and spent considerable efforts leaning on smaller states with close economic and political relationships with Beijing to drop opposition to China's UN General Assembly vote position.[70] As UN General Assembly resolutions are non-binding, Chinese efforts imply a reluctance to be in a minority regarding their voting position.

January 2012–February 2012: China Issues a Second Veto Rejecting Pressures on Assad

By January 2012, both Russia and the P3 had submitted their own individual draft resolutions to the Council.[71] The Western draft was coordinated with several Arab countries, and introduced by Morocco on January 27, 2012.[72] After the first veto, the P3 adjusted tactics, working on "relatively mild texts" that would be a "far cry from the Libya intervention texts... [the] less strident tone... was on purpose."[73] The decision to avoid Chapter VII language was to provide an opportunity for establishing a workaround with China and Russia.[74] Signaling the importance of this vote, both the United States and the United Kingdom dispatched their secretaries of state to the meeting. The draft resolution condemned the violence against the Syrian people, "irrespective of where it comes from," and called upon the Assad regime to implement "without delay" the League of Arab States peace plan.

Keeping both resolutions on the table crystallized the tensions at the UN Security Council. Following reports of over 5,000 civilian deaths, including over 200 people killed in the repeated shelling of Homs, one of the deadliest episodes in the unfolding conflict, China and Russia issued vetoes against the Western-Arab draft resolution. All other states at the UN Security Council, including the only Arab representative, Morocco, voted for the proposed resolution. Morocco emphasized its "great regret and disappointment" that the resolution failed to pass, noting that the Arab states would continue their plans to punish Assad.[75] US Ambassador Susan Rice noted that the United States was "disgusted" and that attempts to right the Syrian conflict was being "held hostage by a couple of members."[76]

China explained its position as follows: that there should be equal attention to "all parties to stop the violence," and though Beijing did "support the good-offices efforts of the Arab League" and "respect the request of the Syrian people for reform," China still felt that the draft resolution was out of sync with China's goals as a Security Council member—namely that the international community "should provide constructive assistance" that still respected "the sovereignty, independence and territorial integrity of Syria."[77] China also tried to further signal that it was not the lead state in this particular case, noting that "China supports the amendments proposed by the Russian Federation" and placing China as part of "the international community... to play a positive and constructive role in the proper settlement of the Syrian issue."[78]

However, despite China's rhetoric, this veto was not a given for China; an abstention vote was considered.[79] Middle East states had attempted to increase pressure on China, literally using a united front of regional ambassadors to "encircle the [PRC Ambassador] at the Council's deliberations before this veto."[80] Pressure from these member states contributed to a hectic environment in the run up to the vote. PRC Ambassador Li Baodong was "in and out of the chambers... to take calls from senior leadership in Beijing about the vote... delaying procedure."[81] This was unusual in China's diplomatic practice. Such actions implied that the vote and its explanation were not decided upon until the last minute, and more importantly for arguments based on Russian support, the coordination with the Russian position was still ongoing, even in chambers.

Ultimately, China judged that the Global South representatives remained split and could discount status pressures on China.[82] For example, the Organization of Islamic Cooperation reiterated it was against the use of foreign military intervention, and only willing to support consensual discussions.[83] In contrast, the League of Arab States increased pressure, with Secretary-General Nabil El-Araby noting that the veto "does not negate that there is clear international support for the resolutions of the Arab League."[84] The League of Arab States reiterated its position that Assad should step down, and called for the Free Syrian Army to form a transitional government.[85] Other regional voices spoke harshly: Saudi Arabia dismissed the veto as "unfavorable," viewing that "the confidence of the world in the United Nations has been shaken"[86] and that China and Russia "had given a green light for the bloodshed to continue."[87] Saudi Arabia made the appeal on behalf of the Gulf Cooperation Council for all states to back the UN General Assembly version of the failed resolution.[88]

Yet, this was not to say that status was of no concern to China. When the UN General Assembly adopted the same resolution less than a fortnight later,[89] China worked hard to apply pressure on smaller states to bring them closer to China's position of voting no.[90] UN General Assembly resolutions are non-binding, and diplomatic resources limited – so to reduce the margin of member states that vote "against" China indicates China's concern about being perceived going against the grain of the majority—i.e. some concern about being isolated from China's status groups. The UN General Assembly cast votes 137 in favor, 12 against and 17 abstaining.[91] Both Russia and China voted against the resolution, which explicitly criticized Syria for "widespread and systematic" violation of human rights, and calling for power transition.[92] No Middle East member state voted against the regime, with only two Middle East states casting abstentions.[93]

March 2012–July 2012: Increased Regional and P3 Pressures, Defiant China Issues a Third Veto

Following the second veto, the divisions amongst the UN Security Council continued, making only consensual, satisficing solutions feasible. Both China and Russia worked to reduce the number of unarmed military observers dispatched to Syria;[94] and shrink the scope and authorities of the UN Supervision Mission in Syria (UNSMIS) peacekeeping team sent to monitor the cessation of violence and support efforts towards the implementation of the Six-Point Plan.[95] Pressure continued to grow on the Assad regime with the International Committee of the Red Cross reporting in early May that killings in Homs and Idlib could qualify Syria as a case of civil war. The UN Security Council could only muster press statements—the least stringent of commentaries, as these statements do not require unanimity before being issued.[96]

At this point, alternative minilateral fora[97] and diplomatic strategies were pursued, including the appointment of former UN Secretary-General Kofi Annan as the Joint Special Envoy of the United Nations and the League of Arab States on the Syrian crisis.[98] Special Envoy Annan worked towards getting support for his Six-Point Peace Plan, which focused on immediate humanitarian outcomes—including a UN supervised ceasefire of all parties; withdrawal of Syrian government forces from cities under siege, and dialogue between Assad and opposition parties towards political reform.[99] Special Envoy Annan's peace plan was purposely disassociated from any regime change discourse—pointedly not calling for Assad's resignation (unlike the positions of the League of Arab States and the Syrian opposition). In so doing, Special Envoy Annan purposely worked closely with both China and Russia, accepting that engaging these two states would be key to the viability of the peace plan.

Regional pressure on Syria escalated. After the US and a number of European embassies closed in Syria, the Gulf Cooperation Council followed suit, with its members pulling their ambassadors from Damascus, and expelling their Syrian envoys,[100] in protest of the "mass slaughter" of civilians in Homs. The League of Arab States attempted to keep pressure on the UN Security Council with meetings at the UN Security Council in the beginning of June 2012 to implement the Six-Point Peace Plan.[101]

However, any potential non-consensual measures were a non-starter for China and Russia. Both countries stepped up their support for Syria, with China taking an unusual approach of explicitly referencing regime change in its speeches at the UN Security Council.[102] The UN Security Council entered three days of intense negotiations at the start of March over a draft resolution introduced by Morocco; ending with no agreement, the draft could not be circulated to the Council for a formal vote. The divisions carried forward into the March 12 high-level debate on the challenges and opportunities in the Middle East, with China spending its allotted time discussing the Syria problem. China was very blunt in emphasizing that China "is against any attempt by external forces to engage in military intervention or push for regime change" and moreover, that "Security Council resolutions must be strictly and comprehensively implemented. No party is to interpret them in any way it wants, let alone take action that exceeds Council mandates."[103] China framed itself as supporting "a constructive role by... Joint Special Envoy Annan in finding a political solution to the Syrian crisis. We support the vigorous efforts by Arab countries and the Arab League in promoting a political settlement in the Syrian crisis."[104]

The delays in implementing the Six-Point Peace Plan due to disrupted ceasefires compounded the debate at the UN Security Council, the sticking point remained on enforcement mechanisms for non-compliance with the peace plan.[105] While the P3 was willing to call for sanctions, China and Russia were against any censure. Failing to get to common agreement, on July 19 the UN

Security Council convened to vote on a draft resolution that called for an extension of the UNSMIS operation, and President Assad to withdraw troops and heavy weapons from populated areas within ten days, or else face sanctions for non-compliance. Drafted by the United Kingdom and co-sponsored by France, Germany, Portugal, and the United States, the resolution was again vetoed by Russia and China, with abstention votes cast by Pakistan and South Africa.[106] China offered its most pointed language after this vote, with a rebuke from Ambassador Li Baodong:

> During consultations on this draft resolution, the sponsoring countries failed to show any political will of cooperation. They adopted a rigid and arrogant approach to the reasonable core concerns of the relevant countries, and refused to make revisions...a few countries have been intent on interfering in other countries' internal affairs, fanning the flame and driving wedges among countries. They are eager to see tumult in the world.[107]

The United Kingdom noted that it was "appalled" and that Russia and China are "failing in their responsibilities as permanent security council members," while explaining that there had been "flexibility on Russia and China's concerns," and criticized Russia and China's "irrational" belief that the Resolution would get "conflict through the backdoor."[108] France was even more direct, noting that "history will prove [Russia and China] wrong, and it will judge them."[109]

Again, China's veto was not a given, with serious consideration for the potential of an abstention given the diplomatic efforts regarding the Six-Point Peace Plan.[110] Since Special Envoy Annan commenced his shuttle diplomacy, a minimum goal was to avoid censure by these two member states, who had already twice proven their willingness to engage in a veto. One means to do this was to divide China and Russia, and apply pressure on China by proving momentum of support for the peace plan, so as to increase the likelihood of China's support for the plan. Special Envoy Annan scheduled his first major international push for the peace plan in the sequence of Cairo, Damascus, Ankara, Doha, Moscow and last, Beijing, in March 2012.[111] This gave momentum for the Six-Point Peace Plan, with news reports that all states[112]—including Damascus and Moscow—had offered support for the proposed terms on March 27, 2012.[113] On that day, Special Envoy Annan met with Prime Minister Wen Jiabao and Vice Foreign Minister Zhang Zhijun, in which these officials underscored China's support for mediation efforts.[114]

Special Envoy Annan requested a ten-day vote delay to ensure sufficient opportunities for the UN Security Council to communicate and commit to a draft.[115] During the delay, UN senior officials ratcheted up their strategy of trying to separate China and Russia, with the goal of convincing China to abstain.[116] Working on the assumption that Russia was more wedded to blocking action than China, Special Envoy Annan continued to appeal to China to consider the option for an abstention vote when facing new draft resolutions.[117] Special Envoy Annan committed last-minute shuttle diplomacy to Moscow, for a joint meeting with President Vladimir Putin and Foreign Minister Sergei Lavrov.[118] UN Secretary-General Ban Ki-Moon traveled to Beijing, in which the Syria crisis was belatedly added to the agenda with President Hu Jintao and Foreign Minister Yang Jiechi, in which UN Secretary-General Ban emphasized unity at the UN Security Council for political dialogue as a means to political transition, and made status-based appeals to China's great power leadership and emphasized mutual interests in supporting healthy multilateralism.[119] Special Envoy Annan's efforts were buttressed by the United States, which emphasized the relevance of Syria as an issue in Sino-US relations.[120]

Ultimately, status appeals from senior figures and critique failed to reshape China's vote. Eleventh-hour coordination between President Putin and President Xi via telephone ultimately contributed to China joining the Russia veto position.[121] On the day of the vote, the Russian diplomatic cadre were "nervous on being separated from China on the potential veto vote"[122]—a response perhaps to how successful UN shuttle diplomacy could have been in producing the possibility of China's abstention vote. However, Chinese suspicions about "sanctions as opening the door for regime change" were not addressed sufficiently, nor countered by status appeals.[123] After emergency meetings in Qatar, on July 22, 2012, the League of Arab States again called on Assad to renounce power in favor of safe exit from Syria.[124] Only at this juncture did the Organization for Islamic Cooperation suspended Syria on August 13, 2012—even then the suspension was contested, with Iranian officials on the record opposing this action,[125] continuing the public divisions amongst Organization for Islamic Cooperation members that riddled the group for the duration of the crisis.[126] Chinese officials saw this as confirmation that the Middle East stance was divided at best, justifying China's ability to discount status pressures and refuse to support the UN-led push.

August 2012–May 2014: Scattering Approaches to the Syria Crisis, China Recommits to Veto

At the end of August, the UN Security Council held a high-level meeting to discuss the humanitarian situation in Syria. At these meetings, China made its most blunt statements yet about possible solutions to the Syria crisis, noting that "China opposes any externally imposed solution aimed at forcing a regime change."[127] China made a virtually identical statement in regards to the UN General Assembly draft resolution that criticized the UN Security Council's failure to act on Syria. China voted against the draft, noting that to "impose a solution from [the] outside will not help defuse the Syrian crisis. China opposes any act of forcing a regime change."[128]

The UN Security Council continued in its deadlock, taking 24 hours to negotiate the issue of a press statement on October 4, 2012 for the shelling of Akcakale in Turkey by Syrian fighters.[129] On October 5, 2012, the UN Security Council condemned attacks in Aleppo via a press statement.[130] Portugal attempted to keep pressure on in the UN Security Council, calling for an *Arria* formula closed-door meeting to meet with the chair of the Human Rights Council's Commission of Inquiry on Syria, Paulo Pinheiro. At the end of October 2012, the UN Security Council issued a press statement supporting the Eid Al-Adha ceasefire as proposed by Special Representative Lakhdar Brahimi.[131] The brokered ceasefire failed and there was a sharp increase in human suffering and increasingly dire reporting on this matter at the Security Council.[132] By mid-January 2013, there were briefings citing as many as 2 million internally displaced persons and 650,000 Syrian refugees, with UN agencies working with hindered access.

When both the opposition and the Syrian state accused each other of using chemical weapons in Ghouta killing 1,300 civilians in August 2013,[133] France took the opportunity to raise the matter at the UN Security Council, which led to the UN Secretary-General Ban announcing efforts to investigate the attack. Upon confirmation from UN investigators that the sarin gas attacks were under Damascus' direction, UN Secretary-General Ban noted the attack to be the "most significant confirmed use of chemical weapons against civilians since Saddam Hussein used them"—proof that Syrian President Bashar al-Assad "has committed many crimes against humanity."[134] However, the UN Security Council could only agree to a press statement condemning the terror attack on a Damascus mosque in late March 2013.[135]

By 2014, estimates had 150,000 dead from the violence. Matters at the UN Security Council came to a head again, when China and Russia issued joint vetoes over a draft resolution calling for a referral of the Syria situation to the International Criminal Court for investigation and possible prosecution of war crimes and crimes against humanity.[136] The call for Syrian accountability was galvanized by Switzerland in January 2013, citing the initial findings of the UN's independent International Commission of Inquiry in 2011,[137] which saw the International Criminal Court as the most appropriate venue to address abuses.[138] On January 14, Switzerland made a push to have Syria referred to the International Criminal Court. Earlier attempts to include mention of the International Criminal Court in draft resolutions was dropped, partly in favor of pursuing other measures on Damascus, and partly out of recognition that China, Russia, and the United States remained cool at best to formal accountability measures.

In organizing the draft resolution, the strategy was to replicate the language of prior successful International Criminal Court referrals, drawing directly from Resolution 1593 on Darfur and Resolution 1973 on Libya. Emphasis on "equal accountability" from all parties was also purposely written in, so as to nullify China's concerns about double standards. Key in this case was getting the United

States' support for the draft, which was feasible once it was ensured that Israel would not come under International Criminal Court prosecution in relation to its occupation of the Golan Heights in Syria.[139] This final measure meant that the P3 could set aside differences about the use of the International Criminal Court in this particular case, and therefore represent a single unified position of the great power peer group.

All other members of the UN Security Council voted for the draft, including "moral authority" states, like rotating member Rwanda that suffered the 1994 genocide, but traditionally remained critical of the International Criminal Court and international war crimes tribunals. The draft resolution was supported by over 100 civil society organizations, and co-sponsored by sixty-five states—including the P3 and UN Security Council rotating members Australia, Chile, Jordan, Lithuania, Luxembourg, and South Korea.[140] UN officials were careful to give equal attention to suspected war criminals on both sides, though the UN Human Rights Commissioner Navi Pillay confirmed that the human rights violations by state security forces far outweighed those of opposition groups. However, there was only lukewarm support from representatives of the Global South group: only Libya and the United Arab Emirates sponsored the resolution,[141] signaling a lack of unanimity in the League, which was reflected in earlier League of Arab States resolutions with oblique references to "fair international trials."[142] No formal statements regarding the proposed referral to the International Criminal Court were released from the Organization of Islamic Cooperation nor the Gulf Cooperation Council. This signaled that the regional organizations themselves could not agree on a single policy position vis-à-vis the draft resolution, or worse, that there was no formal policy position to begin with.

The Chinese Deputy Representative Wang Min made lengthy remarks stressing China's three issues with the draft resolution. First, the resolution ignored the principle of complementarity, which Syrian authorities had addressed in their national preparations to prosecute human rights abuses domestically, therefore negating the use of the International Criminal Court. Second, China, like Russia, favored building trust towards a politically negotiated outcome, before addressing justice issues. Third, China disagreed with the draft resolution being taken to vote so hastily, favoring a longer period of consultation and revisions. Most importantly though was that China confronted its critics, and Deputy Representative Wang called out those states that made "unfounded accusations" and "irresponsible and hypocritical slander" against China. Deputy Representative Wang emphasized that China held an "objective" and "impartial position" as a "responsible member of the international community."[143] With little to no status pressures beyond that of the P3, China maintained its original position of only consensual action to address the Syria crisis.

Condemnation of the vetoes was swift, falling along two themes. A first theme was the critique of the Chinese and Russian complicity in perpetrating the Syrian injustices. For example, US Ambassador to the UN Samantha Power, condemned the veto, and said that the Syrian people "deserve to have history record... those who were willing to raise their hands to deny them a chance at justice." UK Ambassador Mark Lyall Grant remarked that "perpetrators of appalling crimes in Syria may be able to hide behind Russian and Chinese vetoes for now, but they will not be able to evade justice forever." French Ambassador to the United Nations Gerard Araud noted, "Nothing is worse than silence; it is complicity."[144] A second theme were critiques that emphasized the costs of the stalemate for global peace and security, and the functioning of the United Nations:[145] UN Deputy-Secretary-General Jan Eliasson reminded the UN Security Council that "the credibility of this body and of the entire [UN] organization will continue to suffer."[146] UN human rights experts condemned the UN Security Council, saying that further atrocities were to be fuelled by the veto.[147]

The costs of the conflict rose to an estimated 162,000 deaths;[148] with almost half the country's population of 22 million displaced, with close to 3 million refugees by mid-2014.[149] Sensing that China and Russia were "clearly uncomfortable"[150] in casting a veto so quickly after their last, and that Middle East peer group dynamics remained largely unchanged in this period, the P3 presented a unified position in support of some type of humanitarian action. Penholders seized the opportunity to engage Chinese diplomats in discussion on cross-border humanitarian access. Interlocutors emphasized appeals to status and honor: what would it mean for China's position as a great power if China did not exhibit leadership in the face of the burgeoning Syrian humanitarian disaster?[151] Negotiating diplomats were acutely aware of China's concerns about regime change, and offered repeated assurances that Assad was not a target for dispatch.[152] Chinese officials repeatedly stressed that China showed leadership in its crafting of Resolution 2165, as any great power would.[153] Penholders worked in a "purposely cooperative way" to try to find agreement amongst the Council as they negotiated the final draft language over the course of five weeks.[154]

The original draft under Chapter VII permitted the UN to implement cross-border operations in the absence of Syrian consent and included the threat to impose sanctions in the event of non-compliance. China's revisions limited challenges to Syria's consent and deflected criticism from the government for its responsibility in the humanitarian crisis. Added language required both sides of the Syrian conflict to facilitate the entry of humanitarian aid,[155] thereby reinforcing China's views of equal and objective problem-solving efforts. References to the Syrian humanitarian situation as a threat to international peace and security were replaced with threats to only regional peace and security. Chapter VII and even Article 39 references were removed, so there could be no interpretations of the draft as permitting enforcement measures.[156] A crucial correction was to have the cross-border access zones placed in areas no longer under control of Syrian authorities, thereby circumventing the Syrian consent question. As scholars note, in spite of all the popular reporting about Resolution 2165, any "purported encroachment on 'Syrian sovereignty'" was at best "limited":[157] the resolution reaffirmed that primary protection for populations rested on the Syrian state—a key addition advocated for by China. As one official sanguinely noted, with these "corrections made," a "yes vote was obvious" for China, as "there was no need to be so isolated about delivering aid."[158]

Analysis

This chapter argues that there were five phases in Chinese activity in regards to Syria:

- April 2011–September 2011: China works to prevent censure of Assad.
- October 2011–December 2011: China hardens its position, issuing a veto preventing condemnation and sanctions for Syria.
- January 2012–February 2012: China issues a second veto rejecting pressures on Assad.
- March 2012–July 2012: Increased regional and P3 pressures, defiant China issues a third veto.
- August 2012–May 2014: Scattering approaches to the Syria crisis, China recommits to fourth veto.

Understanding the effects of status can illuminate China's response to the Syria crisis. China could discount status as the case presented no status trigger, meaning that China was not sensitized to be particularly concerned about its status. At no point was a high-status event in China part of a smear campaign, nor was a low-status time for China invoked in challenging China. Highlighting this point, one Chinese official noted, "Darfur directly looked forward to the Olympics—therefore the Darfur connection to China was emotional... the Syria problem does not have such strong feelings."[159] Without this status trigger, China was not predisposed to overtly consider status amongst its other competing interests. Two further factors complicated attempts by China's peer groups to invoke status pressures, and I consider each group in turn here.

In regards to the Global South peer group, its representatives included the Gulf Cooperation Council, the League of Arab States and the Organization of Islamic Cooperation—and these individual regional organizations worked independently, providing different policy recommendations in response to the Syria crisis. In so doing, the Global South peer group was therefore incohesive as each regional organization competed for moral authority, with a different stance in addressing the crisis and tolerance level for Assad. As the case study shows, though the Gulf Cooperation Council took the first step in condemning Assad, it was ultimately the League of Arab States that took the harshest stance against Assad. The Organization of Islamic Cooperation took the least interventionist stance of all the groups. Compounding this discrepancy in formal positions was the time lag in this particular case: regional groups took months to work out individual positions, with limited sustained coordination between them.[160] Moreover, regional organizations were plagued by major defections from their individual group stance. For example, Lebanon repeatedly signaled its disagreement with League of Arab States' decisions, providing relief for China as at one point Lebanon was also the sole Middle East rotating member at the UN Security Council. Therefore, Lebanon's defection on the League of Arab States stance was of even more importance. Recall also that the League of Arab States itself was openly divided, passing resolutions with recorded dissenters and with states publicly refusing to enforce draconian measures on Assad. Therefore, the social influence that these regional organizations could execute on China for rejecting their preferred outcomes as a Global South peer was of limited effect. Without a group-agreed-upon intersubjective normative consensus for good behavior, China was able to position itself as a satisficing partial cooperator. China offered the regional organizations support for their more permissive actions, while drawing a firm line at actions that could remotely lead to regime change.

In regards to China's great power peer group, the P3, it also had limited effects on China's response to intervention in this case. China's firm stance that state sovereignty trumps accusations of mass human rights abuses is in clear opposition to the P3 position, which by and large support the spread of liberal democratic norms. While the P3 have decried President Assad's lack of moral authority and legitimacy to rule, China has clearly rejected this position. However, this is not to say that China seeks to "rewrite the rules" regarding intervention,[161] but China does seek to draw a line demarcating UN Security Council-authorized intervention from that of regime change. This was partially because China was suspicious that UN Security Council Resolution 1973, which authorized a no-fly zone effort for Libya, had been abused to unseat Muammar Gaddafi.[162] Therefore, China's cynicism about P3 motives for non-consensual intervention in the Syria case guided its ability to dismiss P3 critique, all the more possible for China in the absence of a status trigger. However, while not entirely dismissing the so-called "Libya effect," the case study sharpens this particular argument. In short, the "Libya effect" implies a single critical juncture: because of the Libyan regime change outcome, China will automatically veto any intervention activities into Syria, and continue to do so. However, the evidence in this case finds multiple critical junctures. Contrary to popular understandings, the four Chinese vetoes were not givens per se. China reconsidered its voting position before each veto, under considerable pressure to assess its preferred stance. At each critical juncture, Chinese officials reweighed possible responses and interests—and the delays before the second and third vetoes remain prime examples of such a period of consideration for China, where we can surmise that alternate votes were considered until the last moment. On a related point, these equivocations before the vetoes again highlights the limitations of the "Russian factor" arguments. Efforts taken by Moscow at the highest levels still left Russian officials unsure of the Chinese position on the day of key votes, implying that coordination with China was a hard-fought process by Russia—arguably until the vote itself occurred. Most recently, Russia has been left to veto solo, a sign of the limitations of this line of reasoning.[163]

Conclusion

What can we infer about the relevance and limitations of status as a variable in Chinese foreign policy from the Syria case? The case highlights how social influence works in guiding China's position—but that social influence itself only works under certain prior conditions: when representatives of the peer groups unite around a particular policy position; when there are no major defections from the articulated policy positions, and when the group can effectively utilize social goods and punishments in relation to China. When these conditions are met, China's behavior—in this case, its response to intervention—can be modified. Yet, the Syria case highlights the limitations of social influence: the Global South, represented by the numerous regional groups, could not satisfy these three conditions—permitting China space to push back on these initiatives. In terms of its Global South peer group, China did not take the decisions at the costs of status per se; instead, Chinese officials reasoned that status costs did not apply to them for the reasons listed throughout the chapter. In the Syria case, China did not waiver from its initial position of preventing any perceived non-consensual measures against Syria, and only sparingly did China explicitly reference criticism from other players—and mostly in order to counter their views on China. The limitations presented by the live case of intervention in Libya guided China's considerations in the Syria case, enabling China to discount the line touted by the great power peer group, the P3. With the Libya case as a prime example, and in the absence of a status trigger to motivate greater sensitivity to status, China could afford to reevaluate P3 pressures at each critical juncture of the case.

However, though status had discounted effects in the Syria case, this was not to say that China was immune to status concerns. When the UN General Assembly adopted the same language from two of the vetoed resolutions of February and July of 2012, China spent significant effort pressuring developing states to join China's "no" position. Since UN General Assembly votes are non-binding, the only significant gain for these energies was to reduce perceptions of China acting as an outlier from its status groups. As diplomatic resources are limited, these efforts highlight that China was cautious about being perceived as opposing a majority and was willing to expend resources to reduce perceptions that China was challenging a majority of states.

China also engaged in new efforts in norm shaping regarding the responsibility to protect, partly in response to concerns about perceptions of its veto votes. China entered a nascent, semi-official concept of "responsible protection" into diplomatic discourse, which reframed China's multiple vetoes against intervention into Syria as fair and responsible. Responsible protection established six criteria for intervention, the key addition was a much narrower interpretation for when non-consensual measures could be used, with a focus on the means-end trade-off when force is used.[164] By asking how intervention can be conducted successfully; pinpointing responsibilities for intervention problems as they occur, and whether these costs were justified, China engaged in the normative discussion over the use of force for humanitarian purposes—an aspect of the responsibility to protect that China had largely avoided.[165] However, China's focus on responsible protection was short-lived, and only for low-level policy discourse.[166] Yet the fact that China tried to gain a foothold in the widening normative discourse appropriating the term "responsible," is significant.[167] This was a first real effort to indicate that China was willing to do more than protest about the casting of China as irresponsible by other states, China was willing to engage in promoting alternative discourses on "responsibility" that emphasizes how China *itself* promotes protection. In so doing, China was still displaying some element of status sensitivity in signaling its position within the international community, supporting norms regarding humanitarianism and civilian protection. Concerns driven from this Syria case was enough to motivate China to no longer be a passive supporter of the responsibility to protect.[168]

Lastly, China introduced a new response during the crisis, delegitimizing attempts at intervention as "regime change." China reaffirmed that it continued to "firmly oppose the use of force to resolve the Syrian issues, as well as practices, such as forcibly pushing for regime change, that violate the purposes and principles of the United Nations Charter and the basic norms that govern international relations."[169] In using such language, and other examples detailed in the chapter, China not only recognized the regime change debate over Syria, but clearly signaled its boundaries regarding intervention. Actions that could now lead to regime change were clearly unacceptable to China, and China rebranded Western discourse, which had framed regime change as a positive goal into an illegitimate activity of a few powerful states against a weaker party. This is remarkable directness for China, which only obliquely referred genocide in Rwanda and ethnic cleansing in Srebrenica as "domestic affairs," and had studiously avoided any reference to "regime change" in the context of the Libya crisis. This new response indicated China's confidence to not only shun the "spoiler" label, but to accuse other states of being complicit in efforts to disrupt peace.

These efforts reflect China's broader diplomatic engagement on countering and shaping international norms. As Zhao Lei notes, there is a "subtle but significant shift in Chinese strategic culture from passively following international norms to actively making them...Chinese leaders [place] an emphasis on "discourse power" and the principle that a great power should constructively set agendas, not just follow the rules set by others."[170] Cyber security, and the nexus of development, security and human rights are other areas that China is actively engaged in projecting norms in line with its own preferences and its interests.[171] Recent official policy guidelines call for active participation in norm shaping, where China should "[vigorously] participate in the formulation of international norms... strengthen our country's discourse power and influence in international legal affairs, use legal methods to safeguard our country's sovereignty, security and development interests."[172] Chinese Foreign Minister Wang Yi reaffirmed China's commitment as an "active builder" of the international normative and legal discourse.[173] In its efforts regarding the Syria crisis, China has played off other states' growing suspicions that attempts to address massive human rights abuses is synonymous with regime change. Russia, India, and Brazil all protested the slide from protection of civilians into favoring the rebel opposition groups during the implementation of UN Security Council Resolution 1973 in Libya.[174] Maximizing these states' skepticism regarding the benefits of non-consensual action in Syria gave China a diplomatic base to counter the promotion of Western liberal standards prioritizing human protection in this case.

PART IV
CONCLUSION

7
Conclusion

Introduction

This book answers two discrete research questions: what explains China's response to intervention at the UN Security Council? And more specifically, how does *status* affect China's position on intervention at the UN Security Council? In order to uncover the answers, the empirical chapters explore the universe of cases where China contended with intervention in its potentially most extreme context, against public calls for regime change. Focusing on 2000 – 2015, these three cases show variance in China's response to intervention—with China pursuing different voting outcomes, various diplomatic maneuvers and changing discursive responses to intervention.

I have argued here that material factors for China's response to intervention are necessary, yet insufficient for a robust explanation. It is key to take into account status to understand China's varied response to intervention at the UN Security Council. I identify the observable implications of status via social influence, which allows us to see status effects at play. Social influence captures China's ability to meet normative standards despite private disquiet: that China's original position will leave it in a dwindling minority—or in the extreme—isolated from its peer groups; that China will emphasize social costs and social opprobrium for its actions, and that China's behavior will be guided without side payments or material gains. In order for status to have maximum effect, two prior conditions have to be met: the presence of a status trigger, which heightens and accentuates pre-existing status concerns; and China's peer groups for intervention—the great powers and the Global South—unify around a single policy position, remain cohesive with no major defector from the group, and are willing to exact social costs for non-compliance with group standards. Indeed, it is the interaction between normative structures and material interests that matters here. Status, through peer groups, transmits normative standards and makes real these intangible guides for legitimate international action. Therefore, this book stands as a corrective to the existing literature on China's response to intervention at the UN Security Council, which is limited by historical period or a lack of theoretical framework to systematically probe China's foreign policy behavior. By thoroughly examining the China case, this book adds to understandings of the workings of the UN Security Council in regards to intervention, in which China is often overlooked entirely.

The empirical cases detail how status pressures work in practice, and show how Chinese officials reconcile China's status dilemma, where China attempts to capture status gains from all of its peer groups. Appreciating the effects of status can better explain China's behavior than conventional material-focused explanations. Chapter 4 details China's changing position on intervention in Sudan in regards to the Darfur crisis. China's diplomatic *volte face* from rejecting any intervention into what it initially termed Sudanese domestic affairs was eventually replaced by *China* pushing for intervention. China actually enforced consent from Sudan for a Chapter VII peacekeeping mission—maintaining pressure on Khartoum to not only accept a UN peacekeeping presence, and also to accept peacekeeping troop offers. Underlining its commitment to intervention, China was the first non-African state to deploy on mission. China acquiesced to sanctions and to an International Criminal Court referral—the first of its kind for a sitting head of state—which ultimately led to the indictment of President Omar al-Bashir. Of key importance in this case was the status trigger presented by the threat of an Olympic opening ceremonies boycott by peer states' leaders—thereby negating legitimacy and other status gain for China—and that both of China's peer groups, represented by the P3 and the African Union, had coalesced around supporting a UN-led effort in Darfur, with no defections and the successful use of social praise and social opprobrium.

Chapter 5 details China's support for intervention in the Libya crisis. Though China initially avoided any call for intervention, instead making appeals for calm and stability, China moved to support and permit intervention in two landmark resolutions: a yes vote for an International Criminal Court referral of the Libya case—the first time that the UN Security Council had been able to do so unanimously in the case of a sitting head of state—and an abstention vote allowing sanctions and enforcement of "no-fly zone plus" over Libyan airspace. Again, status is key to explaining China's position on intervention. When all of China's status groups—represented by the P3 and the various Middle East and African regional players advocated for an International Criminal Court referral, they were able to successfully use status to move China towards a yes vote—especially following the status trigger of Gaddafi's speech making the case for his repression as a parallel to the 1989 Tiananmen Square Incident. Yet, this case highlights a status quandary for China, that its peer groups were split on the appropriate course of action in regards to calls for a no-fly zone. Partly out of concerns regarding status, China *perceived an abstention vote as the only possible option* to satisfy its competing peer group standards of good behavior. In spite of serious reservations about the content of the resolution, China did not consider the veto.

Chapter 6 focuses on China's persistence in preventing any type of nonconsensual intervention in Syria. China broke with its previous diplomatic practice, issuing multiple vetoes in this single country case—blocking sanctions, compliance with peace plans, and referral of the Syria case to the International Criminal Court. China discounted status for a number of reasons: there was the absence of a focal point status trigger; China's Global South peers were disunified in their policy recommendations, with defectors breaking from each Middle East group stance, and with little successful use of social opprobrium against China. China was determined to separate regime change from intervention in this case, and thus China discounted the line touted by the P3. With the Libya case as an ongoing example, and in the absence of a status trigger, China could afford to discount P3 status pressures and appeals at each critical juncture of the case.

A cursory overview of other cases suggests the possibility of extending the application of the theory. For instance, explanations of China's January 2007 veto in the Myanmar case cite a lack of attractive alternatives and low political costs for China's intransigence.[1] China was suspicious of democracy promotion in China's regional sphere of influence, and foreign efforts to promote chaos along its border areas.[2] China and Russia cast tandem vetoes against a draft resolution that urged the military junta to establish measures of "substantive political dialogue" with the opposition National League of Democracy; removing the house arrest for the opposition leader, Aung San Suu Kyi; and to stop attacks against ethnic minorities.[3] By applying status-related insights to this case, I can sharpen existing arguments for this outcome by explaining why and how China justified its veto. China could diffuse status concerns through the ambiguity offered by ASEAN regarding these proposed measures. ASEAN offered conflicting opinions on Myanmar's political conditions in the run up to the vote,[4] and individual ASEAN members were outspoken on Myanmar—though taking a variety of positions;[5] Indonesia, the only ASEAN member at the UN Security Council at the time, viewed Myanmar's issues as domestic matters, "not yet a threat to security in the region, let alone the world."[6] Though the P3 was unified behind the draft resolution, the US strategy in the run up to the vote was to disregard senior-level contact with China, proceeding along the path of accepting the predicted tandem veto.[7] However, this strategy meant forgoing any opportunity to negotiate and make status-based appeals to China. While further confirmation would require research beyond the scope of this book, the sketch here highlights the relevance of understanding status to explain why and how China responds to intervention writ large.

Reflections on Chinese Foreign Policy

Combined, these case findings highlight a range of outcomes regarding status: where China privileges status over other interests, as detailed in the Darfur case and Libya cases to varying extremes—to where China is able to discount status, favoring other interests instead, as detailed in the Syria case. However, while pursuing status may not be China's dominant goal, even in the social environment of the UN Security Council, evidence presented here suggests that China is not status insensitive in these null cases either (i.e. status is wholly rejected as a pursuit by China). As the Syria case highlights in particular, though China may not prioritize status in the first instance, China still used scarce resources to save a modicum of status by reducing peer group opponents to its voting position at the UN General Assembly, and used rhetorical adaptations to present its vetoes as "responsible," while denouncing regime change as illegitimate. China's continuing efforts to this end regarding its fifth and sixth vetoes in the Syria case highlight that China was indeed self-conscious about being pegged as a supporter of the Assad regime at all costs, and the potential isolation this would entail.[8] Such analysis adds a finer distinction to the assumption of an ever-constant priority placed on obtaining status in Chinese foreign policy, and highlights the nuances and trade-offs to obtaining status against other competing foreign policy interests.

We can also draw inferences on the scope conditions for status in Chinese foreign policy. I posit here that a "firewall" of core interests as being impenetrable to ideational pressures, like status, should be reconsidered.[9] The most important core interest is the regime survival and longevity of the Chinese Communist Party. Because PRC diplomats are aware of the United States' "bipartisan fetish for regime change,"[10] and a growing pro-human rights normative discourse, it is assumed that China will not support measures that could result in regime change elsewhere, out of concern for precedent-setting against Chinese Community Party security and longevity at home. However, the Darfur and Libya case studies illustrate two incidences of China being status sensitive in the context of intervention against a public discourse of regime change. More importantly, these cases highlight *how* Chinese officials reappraise interests at the critical junctures in each case—highlighting that core interests and the need to protect core interests are not fixed and pre-existing, but are reconsidered and reconstructed in practice. By taking the three cases in their totality, we can sharpen the scope conditions for status in Chinese foreign policy, using the context of intervention.

If proposed measures lead to *absolute* and *abrupt* regime change, in the context of an intervention, then status will most likely be unable to "breach" the figurative policy firewall. The Libya case highlights this kind of "overnight regime change,"[11] and this is what in effect went too far for China: Colonel Gaddafi's summary execution in the context of a foreign-led use of force by way of the NATO campaign backing rebels gave way to the fundamental alteration of Libya's political institutions. Intervention that *may* lead to a *degree* of regime change by way of the intervention measures imposed, are perhaps acceptable to China. For example, the Darfur intervention featured a status trigger and all of China's peer groups effectively used social influence towards the same policy ends, leading to status to have an effect on China's response in this particular case. Key here is that the intervention measures did not lead to *absolute* and *abrupt* regime change—the arrest warrant for President al-Bashir remains unfulfilled, reflecting waning regional support for the International Criminal Court.[12] This conception of risking regime change in degrees, and not as an absolute outcome, is in line with recent research that conceives of regime change on a continuum: at its most extreme, dictators abruptly fall and political elites and domestic institutions see a complete change at a rapid pace.[13]

The variation in these cases reflects the greater uncertainty about the use of regime change in global politics, and to what extent UN Security Council-authorized intervention should produce that outcome. China's misgivings about regime change are evidently not limited to Sino-US relations,[14] but also affect its views on intervention at the UN Security Council. In part China's response to the Syria crisis reflects views that these invocations of intervention are actually "Trojan horse" attempts at executing regime change, in the knowledge that outright requests for regime change would not be supported by China otherwise.[15] The perception of such ulterior motives limit China's support for intervention. But McMillan and Mickler point out a more cynical problem: "the simple accusation, by critics, that would-be-interveners harbor intentions of regime change may now act as its own Trojan horse, gaining legitimate entry into debates about intervention but then serving to undermine claims for international engagement with contemporary conflicts and masking other ulterior motives served by non-intervention."[16] In an awareness of being tarred with such "ulterior motives" accusations, China has gone one further with rhetorical innovations regarding "responsible protection" and its efforts to delegitimize regime change rhetoric.

These implications matter especially for the UN Security Council and its abilities to concertedly respond to ongoing crises in Yemen, the Democratic Republic of the Congo, Myanmar and beyond, as they suggest another set of viable means to engage China, and that there may be more room to maneuver and negotiate with China than sometimes presumed. Therefore, we can infer that if a goal is to maintain China's steady trajectory of positive engagement with the intervention regime—including those actions that may move towards enforcement—it is key not to use UN Security Council-authorized intervention to deliver absolute and abrupt regime change. Such outcomes only serve to further concerns about the validity of complementary efforts regarding the responsibility to protect or the use of the International Criminal Court, let alone the role of the UN Security Council in regulating global peace and security in the context of a public discourse for regime change. Such disquiet reflects China's focus on the normative underpinnings of global governance, rather than just its concerns with the material basis for its role in international politics. In the Syria case especially, China shows its willingness to contest the definitions of an "appropriate" response to challenges of global order.[17] Evidence suggests recognizing regime change concerns is an important factor in eliciting China's cooperation for intervention into crises beyond those addressing mass abuse. For example, on the matter of nuclear proliferation by the Democratic People's Republic of Korea, when the United States was able to signal a willingness to accept the regime, it helped elicit Chinese support for pressure on Pyongyang in 2006 and 2009.[18] This signaling matters as it clarifies that US policy is not focused on regime change. Analysts infer that clarifying US policy regarding regime change will continue to be key in order to gain China's support to counter proliferation today.[19]

The contested boundaries of regime change and intervention lead some to question whether China is a rising power intent on challenging the US-led liberal international order.[20] China does the yeoman's work of supporting the international system through the United Nations, proving its stakeholder credentials, and therefore has earned the experience and credibility to push for modifications. Whether dispatching the most number of peacekeeping troops compared to the rest of the permanent members combined, or China's increased financial commitments to the UN system, second to only the United States regarding the peacekeeping budget, evidence suggests that China is interested in translating its increased commitments into a willingness to take on policy design and leadership within the UN Secretariat and UN agencies. For example, both China and Russia most recently sought to reduce human rights support as an element of peacekeeping operations, in line with China's skepticism regarding the current conception of human rights, emphasizing cultural and political rights. China was specific in its bargaining tactics, proposing cuts to vacant human rights posts in Mali and the Democratic Republic of the Congo,[21] an extension of China's previous position preventing new human rights posts from being funded, suggesting a toughening Chinese position.[22] Moreover, reports noted China's push to lead the Department of Peacekeeping Operations, thereby heading one of the most important offices for the implementation of intervention.[23]

In this crucial phase of China's rise—where China is expected to "do more" to strengthen global peace and security and has shown a willingness to do so—China *is* contesting the emerging pro-intervention, pro-human-rights-first status quo, but not in ways stereotyped by popular discourse about China's apparently newfound foreign policy "assertiveness."[24] Three cognate concepts in the global peace and security order—regarding the responsibility to protect, the developmental peace, and a "Community for a Shared Future of Mankind"—highlight how China is making a practical push, albeit on the margins, to produce its own norms that limit the intervention regime.

China no longer works as a rejectionist of the responsibility to protect norm,[25] but redefines understandings of its content—reinterpreting sovereignty from a right to a responsibility, bringing the responsibility to protect much more in line with traditional understandings of sovereignty.[26] China uses a complementary, interlocking rhetorical and voting strategy reifying the norms of sovereignty by emphasizing state sovereignty as a means to secure the responsibility to protect.

China advocates for a greater say for regional organizations at the UN Security Council, early warning systems at the state and regional levels,[27] and a redefinition of "timely and decisive response" to mass atrocity crimes as a long-term commitment to protection with the international community supporting individual states.[28] In so doing, China works to fill a gap in the emerging norm; even advocates admit that the initial work on the prevention component of the responsibility to protect was "brief, confused and unoriginal."[29] With these discursive frames, advancement of constitutive norms derived from the prior status quo, and mobilization of support for its preferred solutions with complementary policy initiatives, China is an advocate for the responsibility to protect. China's "norm-brokering approach" is an attempt to modify norms as opposed to reject them outright.[30] The cases here highlight that China instead seeks to limit change to normative structures using updated versions of prior established norms. China's efforts are an attempt to return to an idealized version of a prior status quo, where sovereignty and territorial integrity are respected cornerstones of international affairs.[31]

An emerging concept for China's views on peacebuilding and intervention is in contrast to the promotion of assertive liberal internationalism and its liberal peacebuilding agenda. He Yin calls this the "developmental peace" thesis; while not a concept formally endorsed by China or actors within its aid and development community, the components of developmental peace can be seen in China's foreign policy.[32] Developmental peace sees political and social stability as a prerequisite to development, which itself leads to sustainable peace. The developmental peace approach prioritizes economic development, in contrast to the institution-building emphasis of the liberal peacebuilding agenda. The developmental peace approach includes gifting aid with little to no political conditions, and the state is the central actor, with a limited role for civil society.[33] Another key difference is that the developmental peace approach tempers emphasis on a market-led economy, seeing that states should shape the economy through public investment, the use of state-owned enterprise, and capital flow management. Developmental peace supports states to undertake gradual reforms, based on their individual features, and emphasizes effective governance first—without the human rights-oriented, transparency and good governance-emphasized values of traditional peacebuilding.

China offers new ideas like the "Community for a Shared Future of Mankind," developed as President Xi Jinping's contribution to socialism with Chinese characteristics for a new era,[34] the concept was then added to the PRC Constitution in March 2018. Under a "Community of Shared Future for Mankind," China calls for global governance built on extensive consultation, joint contributions, and benefits shared between parties based on inclusiveness, mutual respect, and win-win cooperation. China positions the "Community for a Shared Future" concept to speak to the UN Charter, with a focus on addressing the new concerns facing a globalized world.[35] It is no surprise then that the United Nations was one of the first venues for President Xi to deliver the concept to an international audience.[36] Other speeches at the United Nations[37] paved the way for China's efforts to integrate the concept into UN General Assembly, UN Security Council and UN Human Rights Council resolutions.[38] These three emerging Chinese concepts together emphasize China's conservative views away from promoting regime change through reaffirming traditional sovereignty, focusing on gradual regime transformation, and emphasizing the rules-based, UN-led international system.

China's new global project, the Belt and Road Initiative, is a manifestation of this more conservative outlook. Launched in 2013, the Belt and Road Initiative sees China spending as much as $1 trillion on projects in approximately seventy countries to link economies from the Baltic to the Pacific.[39] There is no definitive map of where the "belt" and "road" reach as the project is still in its infancy, and interpretations of the Belt and Road Initiative and its potential impact differ. Mainstream views see the Belt and Road as a platform for market-led economic cooperation projects,[40] where China and its partner states focus on building platforms for enterprise to flourish—discrete from China's foreign aid projects and pre-existing peace and security cooperation initiatives.[41] Bilateral and multilateral agreements may drive the Belt and Road Initiative, but the Belt and Road is a platform for markets and enterprise to thrive through greater regional interconnectivity.[42] However, scholars like Li Dongyan see that Belt and Road contains latent peacebuilding potential, especially as President Xi Jinping calls the Initiative a "road for peace."[43] China uses the Belt and Road Initiative for peacebuilding by formally linking Belt and Road with UN agencies, international non-governmental organizations, and civil society groups. For example, China dovetails the Belt and Road with the UN 2030 Agenda for Sustainable Development, the refugee and migration agenda, and the UN peacebuilding agenda. Numerous resolutions specifically list the Belt and Road at both the UN General Assembly[44] and the UN Security Council,[45] and even both the UN Secretary-General Antonio Guterres[46] and UN Secretary-General Ban Ki-Moon lobbied for the success of the Initiative and its peacebuilding components.[47]

However, though China is a leading player in global governance, beginning to offer a narrative for its view on global order that should be situated within the UN framework, China falls short of offering a cohesive alternative model. China's ability to make a practical push limiting intervention requires China to be able to project a consistent normative narrative that addresses solutions for these very difficult cases of mass abuse, and raise support for China's proposed solutions beyond its typical audience of intervention skeptics. Even pro-China advocates admit that challenges remain as "very Chinese concepts," like the "Community for a Shared Future," must successfully be transformed into internationally valued norms.[48] It is feasible that all the criticism associated with the Belt and Road Initiative may induce China to rethink its normative strategy and engagement. For example, the Belt and Road Initiative may spur Chinese strategists to go beyond critique of the current order and aspirational language for a new order, and address thorny issues of how to resolve issues in the field in practice. As Wang Xinsong points out, the Belt and Road Initiative will require China to consider solutions for securing local governance, accountability, anti-corruption, and meaningful local participation in project implementation.[49] In part, China recognizes a window of opportunity presented by the United States' willingness to reduce its presence in multilateral governance. The United States sought budget austerity at the United Nations, providing the opening for China to argue that one appropriate pathway is to reduce peacekeeping funding, for example. China's confidence and ability to lobby are driven, however, by China's robust contributions to a liberal international order, which put China in a position to negotiate based out of field experience and the credibility that comes from that.

Implications for International Relations

Going beyond Chinese foreign policy, I make broader contributions to the International Relations literature through this book. A wider research question here is under what conditions can status motivate cooperation on global security matters? Addressing this question has important implications for the literature on intervention, in that status bridges both rationalist and constructivist approaches. Yet, there is comparatively little systematic treatment of status as a determinant for cooperation, as opposed to the copious materials on status as a cause for conflict. In order to bring this broader research question into sharp relief, I used the critical case of China—a state of crucial importance for the smooth running of global security affairs—most obviously because of its permanent position on the UN Security Council. The findings here indicate that status, under certain conditions, *can* motivate cooperation, even on some of the most contentious issues in global security.

For example, status can be maximized when status appeals are successfully utilized as a component of diplomatic strategy and when status appeals are purposely disconnected from long-standing criticisms of a state's foreign policy. Status appeals can happen in a number of ways: by the peer group themselves effectively utilizing social influence to modify the target's response—primarily in the use of social praise or opprobrium—or by the use of status appeals by peers in specific, closed-door diplomatic negotiations. Recall the use of the honor and status in appeals by US diplomats with their PRC counterparts in the Darfur case. By using these status-based overtures, US officials emphasized that China was no longer able to support Sudan without rejecting its African peer group. These tactics emphasized status, as opposed to hard bargaining about *quid pro quo* trade-offs on diplomatic efforts. Such tactics were effectively amplified when US diplomatic strategy on Darfur reduced public critique of China for its arms sales, human rights record or business practices in Sudan. By focusing on positive gains and social praise for China as opposed to negative critique of China's behavior, US strategy encouraged room for diplomatic maneuvering by China. The Libya case presents a similar finding. When President Obama cited intervention standards that echoed China's principles for intervention, this was taken as a positive sign by Chinese officials, and as recognition of the "correctness" of their views. Without criticizing China publicly at this interval, the US response still left China with the opportunity to lead. Diplomats can also exploit status vulnerability—whether these be status triggers or grouping contentious votes together so as to exploit a state's existing isolation from its peer groups. Evidence from the cases here allow the inference that when *all* peer groups take similar positions, show no defections, and are effectively able to send social costs and benefits, then shifting the policy positions of even the most reluctant states towards cooperation through status is perhaps most feasible. This then implies that a diplomatic strategy that concertedly coordinates efforts across great powers and regional actors would be effective for exploiting status incentives. Further work into the effects of status for global cooperation is a promising research area.

However, the theory presented here may not apply uniformly to all states. Indeed, a working assumption is that states are rational actors in a social context and that states self-identify with a particular peer group to begin with. However, some problematic pariah states, like the DPRK, for example, restrict their international engagement to mostly observer status in regional groups in limited functional areas.[50] Shallow and narrow engagement in international society has ramifications for the use of status-based incentives and pressures in foreign policy beyond the individual state. Deep, iterative and robust membership to a regional institution is symbolic of self-designation as a member of the region and, in turn, regional recognition of such neighborhood membership and self-identification. Without such a link, the ability to utilize status pressures will be limited by the fact that the state is "peerless," as represented by its limited participation in international social life. For each of the empirical cases enclosed here, it was key to establish that the host state was ostracized from their respective regional groups as the context for increased intervention—only after this dismissal had occurred was it credible for regional and great power groups to increase the ante for intervention, utilizing status and social influence against China. However, the DPRK cannot be successfully "cast out" of a regional group per se, as it remains aloof from the majority of regional arrangements. By implication then, pro-intervention players will find the breadth of their status-related levers reduced by DPRK isolationism. Exploring the implications of target states' "thin" or "thick" participation in international society for status will illuminate the scope conditions for my theory.

The status dilemma presented here—how a state seeks to secure recognition from multiple peer groups at once—is generalizable to a wider category of states of rising powers, with differing power structures and regimes from China. Though China may be the only permanent member of the UN Security Council that is a committed member of the Global South, it is certainly not the only state that seeks to secure recognition from multiple peer groups at once. Leading explanations for rising powers' behaviors often emphasize the pursuit of security, and when status is included it is commonly assumed that states seek a unidirectional, upward status (i.e. to hold great power status).[51] However, using the lens of the status dilemma may uncover more robust explanations for rising powers' foreign policy behavior. In order to make this point, I use the example of India[52]—which differs from China in its political, economic, and social dimensions—yet, it is a state that also supports participation in global peace and security institutions as a means to demonstrate its capacity in international affairs.[53] India is also a state recognized as a rising power,[54] but one that remains deeply committed to its position within the Global South.[55]

However, India's behavior in the global peace and security order is at times contradictory. For example, India's efforts regarding the responsibility to protect has puzzled analysts for its inconsistency.[56] India has refused to accept the emerging norm, dismissing it as nothing more than "intrusive monitoring and finger pointing" at other countries;[57] and "a pretext for humanitarian intervention or unilateral action."[58] Yet when India was a rotating UN Security Council member most recently, it supported Resolution 1970 referring the Libyan case to the International Criminal Court under the invocation of the responsibility to protect, and abstained on Resolution 1973 regarding the no-fly zone vote imposition. Despite India's outcry over the implementation of the no-fly zone, India issued yes votes for the first two vetoed draft resolutions regarding intervention into Syria. While it is fair to acknowledge the strategic use of these yes votes in the shadow of suggestions of at least a Russian veto regarding both the drafts,[59] the question remains how India reconciled its status dilemma, and its approach to justifying its great power preferences with its long-standing grievances about non-consensual intervention on behalf of the Global South. Perhaps the use of the status dilemma lens, dissecting India's peer groups and their use of social influence, may be best able to explain India's vacillating stance on the responsibility to protect and its related interventions.

The book captures a different conception of status recognition and significance of status markers, core components to all status-related theories. The literature assumes that status is something a state has or does not have. For example, states have status recognition as being part of a group, and this is conveyed by the allotment of status markers: "positions and protocol symbolizing respect and deference."[60] Rising powers covet status markers like formal state visits, the number of embassies in their capital, and hosting summit meetings and international sporting events, as these indicate community status attribution of their upward mobility.[61] This conception of status markers overlooks that being *in* a peer group requires negotiation and reaffirmation. For example, China went to extremes when hosting the 2008 Olympic Games to maximize its status recognition; simply being awarded the event was not enough. China took the unprecedented step of repeatedly inviting over 100 heads of state and leading international organizations to the Opening Ceremonies, and then publicizing the attendance record.[62] Conceptualizing status markers as non-discrete gains is a research theme worth considering.

Last, the cases detailed here together highlight limitations to arguments regarding "strategic constructivism" or the concept that "mere lip service" can create an opportunity for greater compliance with a norm.[63] Scholars assert that once a state starts to engage in such rhetoric, it can "self-entrap"—even if rhetoric was used for instrumental purposes initially—leading to compliance or possibly even persuasion that the norm itself is just in the long run.[64] However, the Libya case in context of intervention in Syria muddies the argument that such strategic use of rhetoric can produce such outcomes of socialization. The logic behind such scholarship has the unspoken assumption that there may only be one norm to internalize—i.e. that intervention in the face of mass atrocities should be permitted; yet this assumption may not be a sound one to make against the evidence here. Chinese officials took a hard turn against any measure that appeared to be non-consensual—arguably taking another lesson from the Libya case, that the norm of intervention must be kept separate from the norm of regime change. This suggests that it is worth pausing over the assumption that even cheap talk can lead to compliance or a means to socialization. Research should account for choices—strategic or not—over *which* norm can be championed in the process of self-entrapment.

In conclusion, friction still clearly exists as the UN Security Council tries to ascertain why, when and how it should endorse non-consensual intervention. The willingness of UN Security Council members to default on their post-war practice of accommodation, and submit draft resolutions in the full knowledge of an impending veto only hardens divisions. While the UN Security Council is sidelined by disagreement, the global humanitarian system is under record strain. In 2017 alone, 2 billion persons were at poverty and crisis risk, with $27.3 billion in humanitarian aid distributed worldwide.[65] The UN Security Council continues as the forum to address global crises: the five largest recipients of humanitarian aid in 2016 were standard features on the Council's agenda. The disagreement at the UN Security Council on the parameters of intervention has real, ongoing effects: the fall-out from the vetoes over intervention in the Syria crisis has contributed to an estimated 511,000 deaths,[66] and a conflict that cost $2,579 million in humanitarian aid for 2016 alone.

China's willingness to shield autocrats and defy a liberal international order's linear progression on expanding protections for human rights have led critics to dismiss China as such an insurmountable obstacle to action that it should be ignored altogether.[67] However, the conclusion that China is a write-off could not be more wrong-headed. China's response to intervention in these apex cases profiled here imply that China implicitly accepts that some minimal baseline of human rights protection is encapsulated in the right to state sovereignty. It is too shallow to dismiss China as "keeping the world safe for authoritarianism" per se, as this ignores the much larger normative boundaries that China is contesting regarding intervention. Intervention is a costly activity, with foreseeable challenges and unexpected burdens for those involved. The debate at the UN Security Council reflects misgivings about the appropriate boundaries for legitimate international behavior, and what role the UN Security Council has in regulating a host state's affairs. It should be emphasized again that in the cases profiled here, rising powers and established great powers were both concerned about the fine division between intervention and regime change, the costs for intervention, and whether longer-term benefits are generated by such endeavors.[68]

China's rhetoric is too often simplistically viewed as a guise for selfish non-action, rather than as an entry point to discuss valid queries about the nature of non-consensual intervention. Yet China's pushback against the bleeding together of intervention and regime change reflects valid queries about the real humanitarian benefits garnered from militarized action or international legal procedures when resolving conflict. Having China as a productive UN Security Council player, setting policy agendas and working to reinterpret and reapply foundational international relations norms, makes for a smoother functioning of global governance. No major military or social conflict can be mediated multilaterally without at least tacit Chinese cooperation, given China's veto and the sheer size of its economy, territory, and population.[69] Unpacking China's response to intervention is of the utmost importance, and China's re-engagement with negotiating the boundaries of intervention could not be more relevant than now. Future research into the effects of status for intervention, and China's perceptions of the acceptable boundaries for action, will prove fruitful for charting future opportunities for global peace and security cooperation.

APPENDIX

PRC Ambassadors to the United Nations, 1971–2019

Year	Name	Name in Chinese
November 1971—October 1976	Huang Hua	黄 华
May 1977—June 1980	Chen Chu	陈 楚
August 1980—June 1985	Ling Qing	凌 青
August 1985—May 1990	Li Luyue	李鹿野
February 1990—February 1993	Li Daoyu	李道豫
December 1992—May 1995	Li Zhaoxing	李肇星
February 1995—February 2000	Qin Huasun	秦华孙
October 1999—June 2003	Wang Yingfan	王英凡
April 2003—August 2008*	Wang Guangya	王光亚
September 2008—February 2010	Zhang Yesui	张业遂
February 2010—July 2013	Li Baodong	李保东
August 2013—September 2017	Liu Jieyi	刘结一
January 2018—	Ma Zhaoxu	马朝旭

* The UN Security Council meetings records show that the last time that Ambassador Wang Guangya spoke there was on July 31, 2008. The PRC Ministry of Foreign Affairs does not specify which month Ambassador Wang left office.

Source: Ambassadors of China to the United Nations http://www.fmprc.gov.cn/mfa_eng/ziliao_665539/wjrw_665549/3607_665555/3615_665571/t25410.shtml (accessed March 3, 2019).

Endnotes

Introduction

1. For example, see Ministry of Foreign Affairs of the People's Republic of China, "Foreign Ministry Spokesperson Jiang Yu's Remarks on the Death of Gaddafi's Son and Others in NATO's Air Strikes," May 3, 2011, http://www.mfa.gov.cn/eng/xwfw/s2510/2535/t819910.htm (accessed March 3, 2019).
2. Li Qinggong, "Politics behind attacks on Libya," *China Daily*, March 22, 2011.
3. United Nations Security Council, "6826th meeting (S/PV.6826), August 30" (2012). See Permanent Mission of the People's Republic of China to the United Nations, "Explanatory Remarks by Ambassador Wang Min after General Assembly Vote on Draft Resolution on Syria," August 3, 2012, http://www.china-un.org/eng/hyyfy/t958262.htm (accessed March 3, 2019); United Nations General Assembly, "General Assembly, in Resolution, Demands All in Syria 'Immediately and Visibly' Commit to Ending Violence that Secretary-General Says Is Ripping Country Apart (GA/11266/Rev.1), August 3" (2012).
4. Quoting Ambassador Liu Jieyi. United Nations Security Council, "8042nd meeting (S/PV.8042), September 11" (2017). Also see Ambassador Liu's comments in S/PV.8019, 5 August 2017.
5. Courtney J. Fung, "Separating Intervention From Regime Change: China's Diplomatic Innovations at the UN Security Council Regarding the Syria Crisis," *The China Quarterly* (2018).
6. Interview with senior Chinese foreign policy scholar and advisor to the Ministry of Foreign Affairs, Beijing, December 14, 2017. See also Jia Qingguo, "China," in *Humanitarian Intervention: The Evolving Asian Debate*, ed. Koji Watanabe (Tokyo: Japan Center for International Exchange, 2003).
7. Alexander B. Downes and Lindsey A. O'Rourke, "You Can't Always Get What You Want: Why Foreign-Imposed Regime Change Seldom Improves Interstate Relations," *International Security* 41, no. 2 (2016): 43. Foreign-imposed regime change is referred to as simply "regime change" in popular use of the English language.
8. Michael J. Struett, *The Politics of Constructing the International Criminal Court: NGOs, Discourse, and Agency* (New York: Palgrave Macmillan, 2008), 74.
9. Louise Arbour, "For justice and civilians, don't rule out regime change," *The Globe and Mail*, June 26, 2012, http://www.theglobeandmail.com/opinion/for-justice-and-civilians-dont-rule-out-regime-change/article4372211/ (accessed March 3, 2019); Nesam McMillan and David Mickler, "From Sudan to Syria: Locating 'Regime Change' in R2P and the ICC," *Global Responsibility to Protect* 5, no. 3 (2013); Dire Tladi, "Security Council, the use of force and regime change: Libya and Côte d'Ivoire," *South African Yearbook of International Law* 37, no. 1 (2012); Alex J. Bellamy and Paul

D. Williams, "The New Politics of Protection: Côte d'Ivoire, Libya and the Responsibility to Protect," *International Affairs* 87, no. 4 (2011).
10. United Nations Security Council, "Resolution 1593 (2005): Adopted by the Security Council at its 5158th meeting, on 31 March 2005 (S/RES/1593)" (2005). The UN Security Council referred the country case to the International Criminal Court, which then issued indictments against Omar al-Bashir. United Nations Security Council, "Resolution 1970 (2011): Adopted by the Security Council at its 6491st meeting, on 26 February 2011 (S/RES/1970), February 26" (2011). The UN Security Council referred the country case to the International Criminal Court, which then issued indictments against Muammar Gaddafi.
11. Adam Nossiter, "Strikes by U.N. and France Corner Leader of Ivory Coast," *The New York Times*, April 4, 2011; Mark John and Ange Aboa, "Battle rages in Ivory Coast, UN fires on Gbagbo bases," *Reuters*, April 5, 2011; Aislinn Laing, "Ivory Coast: UN and French helicopter gunships attack Laurent Gbagbo residence," *The Telegraph*, April 10, 2011.
12. For a philosophical discussion on the conflation of intervention and regime change, see Cécile Fabre, *Cosmopolitan War*, 1st ed. (Oxford: Oxford University Press, 2012); Nigel Biggar, *In Defence of War* (Oxford: Oxford University Press, 2013); Fernando Tesón and Bas van der Vossen, *Debating Humanitarian Intervention: Should We Try to Save Strangers?* (Oxford: Oxford University Press, 2017); Arthur Isak Applbaum, "Forcing a People to Be Free," *Philosophy & Public Affairs* 35, no. 4 (2007).
13. On consent in the context of intervention, see Neil Fenton, *Understanding the UN Security Council: Coercion or Consent?* (London: Ashgate, 2004); Ian Johnstone, "Managing Consent in Contemporary Peacekeeping Operations," *International Peacekeeping* 18, no. 2 (2011).
14. Definitions of humanitarian intervention do emphasize the use of military force. For example, see Jennifer M. Welsh, "Introduction," in *Humanitarian Intervention and International Relations*, ed. Jennifer M. Welsh (Oxford: Oxford University Press, 2004), 3; J. L. Holzgrefe and Robert O. Keohane, "The humanitarian intervention debate," in *Humanitarian Intervention: Ethical, Legal and Political Dilemmas* (Cambridge: Cambridge University Press, 2004), 18; Thomas G. Weiss, *Humanitarian Intervention: Ideas in Action*, 2nd ed. (Cambridge: Polity Press, 2012); Nicholas J. Wheeler, *Saving Strangers: Humanitarian Intervention in International Society* (Oxford: Oxford University Press, 2002), 2.
15. Though Chapter VI measures that focus on peaceful dispute resolution tools like the use of good offices, negotiation, traditional peacekeeping, monitoring missions are also included in practice.
16. Martha Finnemore, *The Purpose of Intervention: Changing Beliefs about the Use of Force* (Ithaca, NY: Cornell University Press, 2003), 9.
17. R. J. Vincent, *Nonintervention and International Order* (Princeton, NJ: Princeton University Press, 1974), 13.
18. James H. Lebovic and Erik Voeten, "The Politics of Shame: The Condemnation of Country Human Rights Practices in the UNCHR," *International Studies Quarterly* 50, no. 4 (2006); Nicholas J. Wheeler and Tim Dunne, "Good International Citizenship: A Third Way for British Foreign Policy," *International Affairs* 74, no. 4 (1998).

19. Abram Chayes and Antonia Handler Chayes, *The New Sovereignty: Compliance with International Regulatory Agreements* (Cambridge, MA: Harvard University Press, 1995); Thomas M. Franck, *The Power of Legitimacy Among Nations* (New York: Oxford University Press, 1990); Alexander Wendt, *Social Theory of International Politics* (Cambridge: Cambridge University Press, 1999); Wheeler and Dunne, "Good International Citizenship," 1998.
20. See Michal Hirsch Ben-Josef and Jennifer M. Dixon, "Norm Strength and the Norm Life Cycle" (paper presented at the Temple Workshop on International Institutions and Global Governance, Department of Political Science, Temple University, Philadelphia, November 4 2016).
21. International Commission on Intervention and State Sovereignty, "The Responsibility to Protect: Report of the International Commission on Intervention and State Sovereignty" (Ottawa: International Development Research Centre, 2001); United Nations General Assembly, "Implementing the Responsibility to Protect: Report of the Secretary-General (A/63/677), January 12" (2009).
22. Joshua W. Busby, "Bono Made Jesse Helms Cry: Jubilee 2000, Debt Relief, and Moral Action in International Politics," *International Studies Quarterly* 51, no. 2 (2007); Alastair Iain Johnston, *Social States: China in International Institutions, 1980–2000* (Princeton, NJ: Princeton University Press, 2008); Ayşe Zarakol, *After Defeat: How the East Learned to Live with the West* (Cambridge: Cambridge University Press, 2011); Jennifer L. Erickson, *Dangerous Trade: Arms Exports, Human Rights, and International Reputation* (New York: Columbia University Press, 2015).
23. McMillan and Mickler, "From Sudan to Syria," 2013, 286. See also Alex J. Bellamy, "Responsibility to Protect or Trojan Horse? The Crisis in Darfur and Humanitarian Intervention after Iraq," *Ethics & International Affairs* 19, no. 2 (2005).
24. Interview with official from the PRC Mission to the UN, New York, June 11, 2013.
25. Interview with senior Chinese foreign policy scholar and advisor to the Ministry of Foreign Affairs, Beijing, December 14, 2017. Interview with official from the PRC Mission to the UN, New York, June 11, 2013. Interview with Chinese Ministry of Foreign Affairs official, Beijing, December 24, 2008. See also the case studies in this book.
26. For an excellent analysis of discourse, narrative and "causal stories" at the UN Security Council, see Carrie Booth Walling, *All Necessary Measures: The United Nations and Humanitarian Intervention* (Philadephia, PA: University of Pennsylvania Press, 2013).
27. Jennifer Milliken, "The Study of Discourse in International Relations: A Critique of Research and Methods," *European Journal of International Relations* 5, no. 2 (1999): 229.
28. I draw inspiration here from Riikka Kuusisto, "Framing the Wars in the Gulf and in Bosnia: The Rhetorical Definitions of the Western Power Leaders in Action," *Journal of Peace Research* 35, no. 5 (1998); Roxanne Lynn Doty, *Imperial encounters: the politics of representation in North-South relations* (Minneapolis, MN: University of Minnesota Press, 1996).
29. My point echoes Russell A. Burgos, "Origins of Regime Change: 'Ideapolitik' on the Long Road to Baghdad, 1993–2000," *Security Studies* 17, no. 2 (2008): 223. See also, David Dery, "Agenda Setting and Problem Definition," *Policy Studies* 21, no. 1 (2000). I thank participants at workshops at the East Asia Institute (Seoul), Keio University,

Peking University and Seoul National University for spurring this line of thinking during my 2016–17 East Asia Institute research fellowship.
30. I use the shadow analogy like the "shadow of the future" term in the international institutions and negotiations literatures. See James D. Fearon, "Bargaining, Enforcement, and International Cooperation," *International Organization* 52, no. 2 (2003).
31. Interview with senior Chinese foreign policy scholar and advisor to the Ministry of Foreign Affairs, Beijing, December 14, 2017.
32. Legal scholars caution stereotyping UN Security Council deliberations as a closed, inner sanctum of diplomacy. For a discussion of the permeability of the UN Security Council negotiations, see Ian Johnstone, "Security Council Deliberations: The Power of the Better Argument," *European Journal of International Law* 14, no. 3 (2003).
33. For a discussion of the very problem of suspicions about regime change in China's perceptions on UN Security Council Resolutions, see Jason Ralph, "The Responsibility to Protect and the rise of China: Lessons from Australia's role as a 'pragmatic' norm entrepreneur," *International Relations of the Asia-Pacific* 17, no. 1 (2017).
34. Stefan Stähle, "China's Shifting Attitude towards United Nations Peacekeeping Operations," *The China Quarterly* 195 (2008).
35. Kathrin Hille, "China commits combat troops to Mali," *Financial Times*, June 27, 2013.
36. Courtney J. Fung, "China and the Responsibility to Protect: From Opposition to Advocacy," *United States Institute of Peace* 205 (2016); Liu Tiewa, "China and Responsibility to Protect: Maintenance and Change of Its Policy for Intervention," *The Pacific Review* 25, no. 1 (2012); Liu Tiewa and Zhang Haibin, "Debates in China about the responsibility to protect as a developing international norm: a general assessment," *Conflict, Security and Development* 14, no. 4 (2014); Sarah Teitt, "Assessing Polemics, Principles and Practices: China and the Responsibility to Protect," *Global Responsibility to Protect* 1, no. 2 (2009); "The Responsibility to Protect and China's Peacekeeping Policy," *International Peacekeeping* 18, no. 3 (2011), Courtney J. Fung, "Rhetorical Adaptation and International Order-Making: China's Advancement of the Responsibility to Protect." *Cooperation and Conflict* (2019): https://doi.org/10.1177/0010836719858118.
37. Eric Reeves, "Regime Change in Sudan," *The Washington Post*, August 23, 2004.
38. Zalmay Khalilzad, "A regional strategy for democracy in the Middle East," *The Washington Post*, March 15, 2011.
39. Daniel L. Byman, "Finish Him: Why the World Needs to Take Out Bashar al-Assad Now," February 2, 2012, The Brookings Institution, http://www.brookings.edu/research/opinions/2012/02/02-syria-assad-byman (accessed March 3, 2019).
40. Robert O. Keohane and Lisa L. Martin, "The Promise of Institutionalist Theory," *International Security* 20, no. 1 (1995); Chayes and Chayes, *The New Sovereignty*, 1995.
41. Joel Wuthnow, *Chinese Diplomacy and the UN Security Council: Beyond the Veto* (London: Routledge, 2013).
42. Courtney J. Fung, "Global South Solidarity? China, Regional Organisations and Intervention in the Libyan and Syrian Civil Wars," *Third World Quarterly* 37, no. 1 (2016).
43. Ian Hurd, *The UN Security Council, After Anarchy: Legitimacy and Power in the UN Security Council* (Princeton, NJ: Princeton University Press, 2007); Johnston, *Social States*, 2008; Erickson, *Dangerous Trade*, 2015.

44. Treating "states as people" is common in International Relations scholarship, giving states a collective actorhood beyond the sum of their interests. Alexander Wendt, "The state as person in international theory," *Review of International Studies* 30, no. 2 (2004). This anthropomorphizing of the state means that both states and their agents—diplomats, decision-makers, and so forth—can both share status; a point clearly reflected in interviews shared in this manuscript. See also Patrick Thaddeus Jackson, "Hegel's House, or 'People Are States Too'," *Review of International Studies* 30, no. 2 (2004); Erik Ringmar, "On the Ontological Status of the State," *European Journal of International Relations* 2, no. 4 (1996).
45. Jonathan Renshon, *Fighting for Status: Hierarchy and Conflict in World Politics* (Princeton, NJ: Princeton University Press, 2017), 33.
46. Ted Hopf, "The Promise of Constructivism in International Relations Theory," *International Security,* 23, no. 1 (1998).
47. Johnston, *Social States,* 2008; Yong Deng, *China's Struggle for Status: The Realignment of International Relations* (Cambridge: Cambridge University Press, 2008); Manjari Chatterjee Miller, *Wronged by Empire: Post-Imperial Ideology and Foreign Policy in India and China* (Stanford, CA: Stanford University Press, 2013).
48. Chapter 3 details why Russia is not a reference group for China. See also Courtney J. Fung, "What explains China's deployment to UN peacekeeping operations?," *International Relations of the Asia-Pacific* 16, no. 3 (2016); "Global South Solidarity?," 2016.
49. George Modelski, *World Power Concentrations: Typology, Data, Explanatory Framework* (Morristown, NJ: General Learning Press, 1974); Daniel S. Geller and J. David Singer, *Nations at War: A Scientific Study of International Conflict* (Cambridge: Cambridge University Press, 1998).
50. Sheena Chestnut and Alastair Iain Johnston, "Is China Rising?," in *Global Giant: Is China Changing the Rules of the Game?,* ed. Eva Paus, Penelope B. Prime, and Jon Western (New York: Palgrave Macmillan, 2009); Andrew F. Hart and Bruce D. Jones, "How Do Rising Powers Rise?," *Survival: Global Politics and Strategy* 52, no. 6 (2010).
51. Jack S. Levy, *War in the Modern Great Power System, 1495–1975* (Lexington, KY: University of Kentucky Press, 1983); J. David Singer, "Reconstructing the Correlates of War Dataset on Material Capabilities of States, 1816–1985," *International Interactions* 14, no. 2 (1988).
52. Manjari Chatterjee Miller, "The Role of Beliefs in Identifying Rising Powers: Comparing the United States, China, India and Germany," *The Chinese Journal of International Politics* 9, no. 2 (2016). For a discussion of China and status, see Xiaoyu Pu, *Rebranding China: Contested Status Signalling in the Changing Global Order* (Stanford, CA: Stanford University Press, 2019).
53. For a succinct summary of the regime change literature, see Owen, *The Clash of Ideas in World Politics,* 2010.
54. Robert S. Litwak, *Rogue States and U.S. Foreign Policy: Containment after the Cold War* (Washinton D.C.: Woodrow Wilson Center Press, 2000); *Regime Change: U.S. Strategy through the Prism of 9/11* (Washington D.C.: Woodrow Wilson Center Press, 2007); *Outlier States: American Strategies to Change, Contain, or Engage Regimes* (Washington D.C.: Woodrow Wilson Center Press, 2012); Nigel Lo, Barry Hashimoto, and Dan

Reiter, "Ensuring Peace: Foreign-Imposed Regime Change and Postwar Peace Duration, 1914–2001," *International Organization* 62, no. 4 (2008); Anne Sa'adah, "Regime Change: Lessons from Germany on Justice, Institution Building, and Democracy," *Journal of Conflict Resolution* 50, no. 3 (2006); Adam Roberts, "Transformative Military Occupation: Applying the Laws of War and Human Rights," *American Journal of International Law* 100, no. 3 (2006); W. Michael Reisman, "Why Regime Change is (Almost Always) a Bad Idea," *American Journal of International Law* 98, no. 3 (2004). Steven Levitsky and Lucan A. Way, "Linkage versus Leverage. Rethinking the International Dimension of Regime Change," *Comparative Politics* 38, no. 4 (2006); Toby Dodge, "Iraqi Transitions: From Regime Change to State Collapse," *Third World Quarterly* 26, no. 4/5 (2005); Lindsey A. O'Rourke, *Regime Change: America's Covert Cold War* (Ithaca, NY: Cornell University Press, 2018); Daniel L. Byman, "Regime Change in the Middle East: Problems and Prospects," *Political Science Quarterly* 127, no. 1 (2012). A notable exception is Jay Butler, "Responsibility for Regime Change," *Columbia Law Review* 114, no. 3 (2014).
55. Deng, *China's Struggle for Status*, 2008, 8.
56. Shogo Suzuki, "Journey to the West: China Debates Its 'Great Power' Identity," *Millennium* 42, no. 3 (2014): 636.
57. Deng, *China's Struggle for Status*, 2008, 8.
58. Guo Wanchao, *Zhongguo jueqi: yige dongfang daguo de chengzhang zhi dao (Rise of China: The Path to Growth of an Oriental Power)* (Nanchang: Guangxi Renmin Chubanshe, 2004); Yan Xuetong, "The Rise of China and Its Power Status," *Chinese Journal of International Politics* 1, no. 1 (2006).
59. Johnston, *Social States*, 2008; Deng, *China's Struggle for Status*, 2008; Marc Lanteigne, *China and International Institutions: Alternate Paths to Global Power* (London: Routledge, 2005).
60. Such as in the case of China's sole veto against the extension of the UNPREDEP peacekeeping mission in Macedonia in 1996.
61. Jeffrey T. Checkel, "International Institutions and Socialization in Europe: Introduction and Framework," *International Organization* 59, no. 4 (2005).
62. Johnston, *Social States*, 2008, 211.
63. Interview with former head of UN Department of Peacekeeping Operations, September 29, 2009, New York City.
64. Fung, "Global South Solidarity?," 2016.
65. Samuel S. Kim, "The People's Republic of China in the United Nations: A Preliminary Analysis," *World Politics* 26, no. 3 (1974); *China, the United Nations, and World Order* (Princeton: Princeton University Press, 1979); Sally Morphet, "China as a Permanent Member of the Security Council: October 1971 – December 1999," *Security Dialogue*, 31, no. 2 (2000); Nigel Thalakada, "China's Voting Pattern in the Security Council, 1990-1995," in *The Once and Future Security Council*, ed. Bruce Russett (New York: St. Martin's Press, 1997); Wuthnow, *Chinese Diplomacy and the UN Security Council*, 2013; "China and the Processes of Cooperation in UN Security Council Deliberations," *Chinese Journal of International Politics* 3, no. 1 (2010); Jonathan E. Davis, "From Ideology to Pragmatism: China's Position on Humanitarian Intervention in the Post-Cold War Era," *Vanderbilt Journal of Transnational Law* 44, no. 2 (2011); Pang

Zhongying, "China's changing attitude to UN peacekeeping," *International Peacekeeping* 12, no. 1 (2005); Lei Zhao, *Jiangou heping: Zhongguo dui lianheguo waijiao xingweide yanjin (Constructing Peace: The Evolution of China's Diplomatic Behavior Toward the United Nations)* (Beijing: Jiuzhou Chubanshe, 2007); Allen Carlson, "Protecting Sovereignty, Accepting Intervention: The Dilemma of Chinese Foreign Relations in the 1990s" (New York 2002); "Helping to Keep the Peace (Albeit Reluctantly): China's Recent Stance on Sovereignty and Multilateral Intervention," *Pacific Affairs* 77, no. 1 (2004); Susanne Xiao Yang, *Conflicting Understandings, Competing Preferences: China in UN Security Council Decision-making in Relation to Iraq, 1990–2002* (London: Routledge, 2012). The related works on China and peacekeeping include Bates Gill and Chin-hao Huang, "China's Expanding Role in Peacekeeping: Prospects and Policy Implications" (Stockholm 2009); International Crisis Group, "China's Growing Role in UN Peacekeeping" (Beijing/New York/Brussels 2009); Miwa Hirono and Marc Lanteigne, "Introduction: China and UN Peacekeeping," *International Peacekeeping* 18, no. 3 (2011); Fung, "What explains China's deployment to UN peacekeeping operations?," 2016; Courtney J. Richardson, "A Responsible Power? China and the UN Peacekeeping Regime," *International Peacekeeping* 18, no. 3 (2011); Sun Meicen, "A Bigger Bang for a Bigger Buck: What China's Changing Attitude Toward UN Peacekeeping Says About Its Evolving Approach to International Institutions," *Foreign Policy Analysis* 13, no. 2 (2017); Zhao Lei and Gao Xinman, *Zhongguo canyu lianheguo weichi heping xingdong de qianyan wenti (The Cutting-edge Issues of China's Participation in UN Peacekeeping Operations)* (Beijing: Shishi Chubanshe, 2011); Deng Zili and Wang Cuiwen, "Lengzhan hou zhongguo heyi canyu feizhou weihe xingdong (Explaining China's Involvement in UN Peacekeeping Operations since 1989)," *Quarterly Journal of International Politics* 2 (2012); Pang, "China's changing attitude to UN peacekeeping," 2005; Stähle, "China's Shifting Attitude towards United Nations Peacekeeping Operations," 2008; Tang Yongsheng, "Zhongguo yu lianheguo weihe xingdong (China and the UN Peacekeeping Operations)," *World Economics and Politics*, no. 9 (2002).

66. Alexander Thompson, *Channels of Power: The UN Security Council and U.S. Statecraft in Iraq* (Ithaca, NY: Cornell University Press, 2010); David M. Malone, *Decision-Making in the UN Security Council: The Case of Haiti, 1990–1997* (New York: Oxford University Press, 1998); "International Criminal Justice: Just an Expensive Mirage?," *International Journal* 63, no. 3 (2008); Cameron R. Hume, *The United Nations, Iran and Iraq* (Bloomington, IN: Indiana University Press, 1994).

67. Rory Medcalf, "Unselfish giants? Understanding China and India as security providers," *Australian Journal of International Affairs* 66, no. 5 (2012). See also Zhang Huiyu, "Zhongguo canyu lianheguo weihe shuping (A Commentary on China's Participation in the UN Peacekeeping)," *Contemporary International Relations*, no. 2 (2009); Peacekeeping Affairs Office of the Ministry of National Defense of the People's Republic of China, *Mission for Peace' PLA's Participation in UN Peacekeeping Operations* (Beijing: The Great Wall Publishing House, 2009); Miwa Hirono and Xu Manshu, "China's Military Operations Other than War," *The RUSI Journal* 158, no. 6 (2013). Jonathan Holslag, "Embracing Chinese Global Security Ambitions," *The Washington Quarterly* 32, no. 3 (2009).

68. Ann Florini, "Rising Asian Powers and Changing Global Governance," *International Studies Review* 13, no. 1 (2011).
69. Daniel Philpott, *Revolutions in Sovereignty* (Princeton, NJ: Princeton University Press, 2001).
70. Bruce Cronin, "Intervention and the International Community," in *International Intervention: Sovereignty Versus Responsibility*, ed. Michael Keren and Donald A. Sylvan (London: Frank Cass, 2002).
71. Information Office of the State Council of the People's Republic of China, "China's Peaceful Development," September 6, 2011, Beijing: The State Council of the People's Republic of China, http://english.gov.cn/archive/white_paper/2014/09/09/content_281474986284646.htm (accessed March 3, 2019).
72. You Ji, "China's National Security Commission: theory, evolution and operations," *Journal of Contemporary China* 25, no. 98 (2016): 181.
73. For a view from the perspective of international law, see Matthias Vanhullebusch, "Regime Change, the Security Council and China," *Chinese Journal of International Law* 14, no. 4 (2015).
74. For a discussion of regime change as a source of strategic distrust, also see Kenneth Lieberthal and Wang Jisi, "Addressing U.S.-China Strategic Distrust" (Washington D.C., 2012) and Russell Ong, "'Peaceful Evolution,' 'Regime Change' and China's Political Security," *Journal of Contemporary China* 16, no. 53 (2007): 717–27.
75. You, "China's National Security Commission: theory, evolution and operations," 2016, 181; Baoshan Cheng, "Study of Jiang Zemin's thought on National Security strategy," *Military Art Journal*, no. 3 (2004): 28.
76. Thomas J. Christensen, *The China Challenge: Shaping the Choices of a Rising Power* (New York: W.W. Norton & Company, 2015).
77. Miller, *Wronged by Empire*, 2013; Xiaoyu Pu, "Socialisation as a Two-way Process: Emerging Powers and the Diffusion of international Norms," *The Chinese Journal of International Politics* 5, no. 4 (2012); Brantly Womack, "China as a Normative Foreign Policy Actor," in *Who is a Normative Foreign Policy Actor?: The European Union and its Global Partners*, ed. Nathalie Tocci and Daniel S. Hamilton (Brussels: Centre for European Policy Studies, 2008); Zhang Xiaoming, "A Rising China and the Normative Changes in International Society," *East Asia* 28, no. 3 (2011); Rosemary Foot and Rana Siu Inboden, "China's Influence on Asian States during the Creation of the U.N. Human Rights Council: 2005–2007," *Asian Survey* 54, no. 5 (2014); Brian L. Job and Anastasia Shesterinina, "China as a Global Norm-Shaper: Institutionalization and Implementation of the Responsibility to Protect," in *Implementation and World Politics: How International Norms Change Practice*, ed. Alexander Betts and Phil Orchard (Oxford: Oxford University Press, 2014); Rosemary Foot and Andrew Walter, *China, the United States, and Global Order* (Cambridge: Cambridge University Press, 2011).
78. McMillan and Mickler, "From Sudan to Syria," 2013, 285.
79. Associated Press, "China urges Libya to restore social stability," *The Jerusalem Post*, February 22, 2011.
80. Bellamy and Williams, "The New Politics of Protection: Côte d'Ivoire, Libya and the Responsibility to Protect," 2011, 840; Andrew Garwood-Gowers, "Libya and the international community's 'responsibility to protect'," *On Line Opinion: Australia's*

eJournal of Social and Political Debate (2011); Ramesh Thakur, "Libya: The First Stand or the Last Post for the Responsibility to Protect?," *E-International Relations* (2013).

Chapter 1

1. Although none of these operations were justified as solely humanitarian operations, with actions defined by a need to secure self-defense. See Davis, "From Ideology to Pragmatism," 2011. See also Simon Chesterman, *Just War or Just Peace?: Humanitarian Intervention and International Law* (Oxford: Oxford University Press, 2003), 7–44.
2. Kim, *China, the United Nations, and World Order*, 1979, 115.
3. James Traub, "The World According to China," *The New York Times*, September 3, 2006.
4. Kim, *China, the United Nations, and World Order*, 1979; see also Liu Xiaohong, *Chinese Ambassadors: The Rise of Diplomatic Professionalism Since 1949* (Seattle, WA: University of Washington Press, 2001).
5. A total of an additional sixty-five states recognized Beijing and not Taipei by 1979. See Wuthnow, *Chinese Diplomacy and the UN Security Council*, 2013, 18.
6. United Nations Security Council, "Resolution 495 (1981) of 14 December 1981 (S/RES/495)" (1981).
7. Stähle, "China's Shifting Attitude towards United Nations Peacekeeping Operations," 2008.
8. See Pang, "China's changing attitude to UN peacekeeping," 2005; Zhao, *Jiangou heping: Zhongguo dui lianheguo waijiao xingweide yanjin (Constructing Peace: The Evolution of China's Diplomatic Behavior Toward the United Nations)*, 2007, 196–8.
9. Wuthnow, *Chinese Diplomacy and the UN Security Council*, 2013, 20.
10. Barry Naughton, *Growing Out of the Plan: Chinese Economic Reform, 1978–1993* (Cambridge: Cambridge University Press, 1995).
11. Wheeler, *Saving Strangers*, 2002.
12. Michael W. Doyle, Ian Johnstone, and Robert Orr, *Keeping the Peace: Multidimensional UN Operations in Cambodia and El Salvador* (Cambridge: Cambridge University Press, 1997).
13. Roland Paris, "International peacebuilding and the 'mission civilisatrice'," *Review of International Studies* 28, no. 4 (2002).
14. Allen Carlson, *Unifying China, Integrating with the World: Securing Chinese Sovereignty in the Reform Era* (Stanford, CA: Stanford University Press, 2005), 146–83.
15. Morphet, "China as a Permanent Member of the Security Council," 2000.
16. Wu Xinbo, "Four Contradictions Constraining China's Foreign Policy Behavior," *Journal of Contemporary China* 10, no. 27 (2001).
17. The Northern Zone covered three Iraqi provinces under Operation *Provide Comfort* in April 1991 to protect Iraqi Kurds after Saddam Hussein's violent suppression of the Kurdish uprising. The United States dispatched ground troops from April to July 1991 to establish "safe havens" for Kurdish refugees in northern Iraq. The Southern Zone was established in August 1992 in Operation *Southern Watch* to protect Shiites after

Saddam Hussein's repression of their rebellion. The Southern Zone was extended north in 1996, following the use of Iraqi force against Kurdish factions near Irbil, extending through the southern third of the country. This extension was challenged by other participants on the grounds of its humanitarian contribution. For a discussion of the Iraqi no-fly zones as precedent setting in intervention cases, see analysis by Christopher Greenwood, "International Law And The NATO Intervention In Kosovo," *International and Comparative Law Quarterly* 49, no. 4 (2000).

18. United Nations Security Council, "Resolution 688 (1991) of 5 April 1991 (S/RES/688)" (1991). Though the United Kingdom also claimed an emerging principle permitting military intervention to alleviate extreme human suffering. See Christine Gray, "The Use of Force and the International Legal Order," in *International Law*, ed. Malcolm D. Evans (Oxford: Oxford University Press, 2006), 589, 95.

19. United Nations Security Council, "Resolution 688 (1991) of 5 April 1991 (S/RES/688)," 1991.

20. Statement of PRC representative Li Daoyu before the Security Council. United Nations Security Council, "Provisional Verbatim Record of the Two Thousand Nine Hundred and Eighty-Second Meeting (S/PV.2982), April 5" (1991).

21. James Cockayne and David M. Malone, "The Security Council and the 1991 and 2003 Wars in Iraq," in *The United Nations Security Council and War: The Evolution of Thought and Practice Since 1945*, ed. Vaughan Lowe, et al. (Oxford: Oxford University Press, 2008), 384, 93.

22. James Cockayne and David M. Malone, "Creeping Unilateralism: How Operation Provide Comfort and the No-Fly Zones in 1991 and 1992 Paved the Way for the Iraq Crisis of 2003," *Security Dialogue* 37, no. 1 (2006): 133.

23. "Spokesman on U.S. warplane shooting down Iraqi fighter," *Xinhua*, December 28, 1992; "Iraq 'no-fly zone' China 'concerned'; Japan expresses support," *BBC Summary of World Broadcasts/The Monitoring Report*, August 31, 1992. See also "Spokesman on U.S. warplane shooting down Iraqi fighter," 1992.

24. United Nations Security Council, United Nations Security Council, "Letter Dated 30 August 1990 from the Permanent Representatives of Qatar to the United Nations Addressed to the Secretary-General (S/21684), August 30" (1990); The League of Arab States, "The Iraqi Aggression against the State of Kuwait (Res./5037/ES), August 31" (1990); "Compensation due to the State of Kuwait for the Damage Caused by the Iraqi Invasion (Res./5038/ES), August 31" (1990).

25. The Organization of Islamic Conference, "Final Communique of the Annual Meeting of Ministers for Foreign Affairs of the Member States of the Organization of the Islamic Conference, held at United Nations Headquarters New York on 1 October 1990," in *Letter dated 7 March 1991 from the Permanent Representative of Egypt to the United Nations addressed to the Secretary-General: Annex (A/46/113, S/22345)* (United Nations General Assembly and United Nations Security Council, 1990).

26. United Nations Security Council, "Letter Dated 24 August 1990 from the Permanent Representatives of Bahrain, Kuwait, Oman, Qatar, Saudi Arabia and the United Arab Emirates to the United Nations Addressed to the President of the Security Council (S/21639), August 24" (1990).

27. Embassy of the People's Republic of China in the State of Israel, "The Iraq Issue," September 21 2004, http://www.chinaembassy.org.il/eng/zt/dqwt/t159726.htm (accessed March 3, 2019).
28. China voted for Resolution 743, establishing the UN Protection Force (UNPROFOR), a consent-based peacekeeping mission in February 1992, in the, to oversee ceasefire agreements signed at Geneva in late 1991 and Sarajevo in early 1992. United Nations Security Council, "Resolution 743 (1992) of 21 February 1992 (S/RES/743)" (1992); "Provisional Verbatim Record of the Three Thousand and Fifty-Fifth Meeting (S/PV.3055), February 21" (1992).
29. See "Resolution 761 (1992) of 29 June 1992 (S/RES/761)" (1992); "Resolution 762 (1992) of 30 June 1992 (S/RES/762)" (1992); "Resolution 769 (1992): Adopted by the Security Council at its 3104th meeting, on 7 August 1992 (S/RES/769)" (1992); "Resolution 779 (1992): Adopted by the Security Council at its 3118th meeting, on 6 October 1992 (S/RES/779)" (1992). The Prevlaka Peninsula is in Croatia.
30. For example, see United Nations Security Council, "Resolution 770 (1992): Adopted by the Security Council at its 3106th meeting, on 13 August 1992 (S/RES/770)" (1992). China, India and Zimbabwe abstained. United Nations Security Council, "Provisional Verbatim Record of the Three Thousand One Hundred and Sixth Meeting (S/PV.3106), August 13" (1992).
31. Resolution 807 gave Chapter VII authorities to provide for the self-defense of UNPROFOR. United Nations Security Council, "Resolution 807 (1993): Adopted by the Security Council at its 3174th meeting, on 19 February 1993 (S/RES/807)" (1993). United Nations Security Council, "Provisional Verbatim Record of the Three Thousand One Hundred and Ninety-Ninth Meeting (S/PV.3199), April 16" (1993); "Resolution 819 (1993): Adopted by the Security Council at its 3199th meeting, on 16 April 1993 (S/RES/819)" (1993). "Resolution 824 (1993): Adopted by the Security Council at its 3208th meeting, on 6 May 1993 (S/RES/824)" (1993). China insisted that these were "an exceptional case and therefore does not constitute a precedent for future United Nations peacekeeping operations." "Provisional Verbatim Record of the Three Thousand One Hundred and Seventy-Fourth Meeting (S/PV.3174), February 19" (1993). Thereafter, China continued to express reservations about the applicability of Chapter VII to UN peacekeeping operations and to note that Chapter VII's invocation for UNPROFOR operations did not constitute a precedent for future UN peacekeeping missions. For example, see "Provisional Verbatim Record of the Three Thousand One Hundred and Eighty-Ninth Meeting (S/PV.3189), March 30" (1993).
32. China repeatedly demanded respect for sovereignty and territorial integrity during Council debates: S/PV.3200 where China emphasized "the importance of ensuring the sovereignty and territorial integrity of Bosnia and Herzegovina." United Nations Security Council, "Provisional Verbatim Record of the Three Thousand Two Hundredth Meeting (S/PV.3200), April 18" (1993). Similar themes were put forward in "3344th Meeting (S/PV.3344), March 4" (1994); "3356th Meeting (S/PV.3356), March 31" (1994); "3367th Meeting (S/PV.3367), April 21" (1994); "3428th Meeting (S/PV.3428), September 23" (1994); "3454th Meeting (S/PV.3454), November 8" (1994); "3575th Meeting (S/PV.3454), September 8" (1995). See also United Nations

Security Council, "Provisional Verbatim Record of the Three Thousand Two Hundred and Twenty-Eighth Meeting (S/PV.3228), June 4" (1993).
33. United Nations Security Council, "Resolution 781 (1992): Adopted by the Security Council at its 3122nd meeting, on 9 October 1992 (S/RES/781)" (1992).
34. United Nations Security Council, "Resolution 816 (1993): Adopted by the Security Council at its 3191st meeting, on 31 March 1993 (S/RES/816)" (1993). On April 12, NATO commenced Operation *Deny Flight*.
35. U.N. Doc. S/PV.3122, citing the need for "the consent of all relevant parties." See United Nations Security Council, "Provisional Verbatim Record of the Three Thousand and One Hundred and Twenty-Second Meeting (S/PV.3122), October 9" (1992). And in U.N. Doc. S/PV.3191 how the missing consent from the "parties concerned" made China reluctant, "Provisional Verbatim Record of the Three Thousand One Hundred and Ninety-First Meeting (S/PV.3191), March 31" (1993).
36. For a discussion of NATO humanitarian justifications for the intervention by NATO members see Ian Brownlie, *Principles of Public International Law*, 7th ed. (Oxford: Oxford University Press, 2008); Michael J. Matheson, "Justification for the NATO Air Campaign in Kosovo," *Proceedings of the 94th Annual Conference of the American Society of International Law* (2000); Marc Weller, ed. *The Crisis in Kosovo, 1989–1999: From the Dissolution of Yugoslavia to Rambouillet and the Outbreak of Hostilities* (Cambridge: Documents and Analysis, 1999).
37. China stated that: "[M]any countries in the region are multi-ethnic. If the Security Council becomes involved in a dispute without being requested to do so by the countries of the region—or goes even further and unfairly applies pressure on or threatens actions against the Government of the country concerned – it would create a bad precedent and have wider negative implications." United Nations Security Council, "3930th Meeting (S/PV.3930), September 23" (1998).
38. United Nations General Assembly, "Fifty-third Session: 85th plenary meeting (A/53/PV.85), December 9" (1998); United Nations Security Council, "Resolution 1160 (1998): Adopted by the Security Council at its 3868 meeting, on 31 March 1998 (S/RES/1160)" (1998). In the Council meeting on resolution 1160, China emphasized that "Kosovo is an integral part of the territory" of the FRY and that "[t]he question of Kosovo is, in its essence, an internal matter" of the FRY; also finding that China does "not think that the situation in Kosovo endangers regional and international peace and security." See "3868th Meeting (S/PV.3868), March 31" (1998). China cast an abstention vote on resolution 1199 for the same reasons, "Resolution 1199 (1998): Adopted by the Security Council at its 3930th meeting, on 23 September 1998 (S/RES/1199)" (1998). For other Chinese statements calling the situation in Kosovo an internal affair of the FRY, see United Nations General Assembly, "Fifty-second Session: 70th plenary meeting (A/52/PV.70), December 12" (1997); "Fifty-first Session: 82nd plenary meeting (A/51/PV.82), December 12" (1996).
39. China re-emphasized that Resolution 1203 did "not entail any authorization to use force or to threaten to use force against the Federal Republic of Yugoslavia." United Nations Security Council, "Resolution 1203 (1998): Adopted by the Security Council at its 3937th meeting, on 24 October 1998 (S/RES/1203)" (1998).
40. United Nations Security Council,"3968th Meeting (S/PV.3968), January 21" (1999).

41. United Nations Security Council, "3989th Meeting (S/PV.3989), March 26" (1999).
42. Ibid., 9.
43. Wuthnow, *Chinese Diplomacy and the UN Security Council*, 2013, 24.
44. Zhao Lei uses the term "*chaotuode taidu.*" Zhao Lei, "Zhongguo yu Lianheguo: Lilun kuangjia, yanjin moxing fenxi (China and the United Nations: Theoretical Framework and Evolution Model Analysis)," *Xin Yuanjian (New Thinking)* 10 (2007): 60.
45. See United Nations General Assembly and United Nations Security Council, "An Agenda for Peace (A/47/277-S/24111)" (1992).
46. Ibid., paragraph 20.
47. Carlson, "Protecting Sovereignty, Accepting Intervention," 2002, 31–2.
48. Jennifer M. Welsh, "The Security Council and Humanitarian Intervention," in *The United Nations Security Council and War: The Evolution of Thought and Practice Since 1945*, ed. Vaughan Lowe, et al. (Oxford: Oxford University Press, 2008), 535.
49. The Security Council adopted seventeen resolutions regarding Somalia during this interval, all passed unanimously, bar one. Ibid., 538–9. When consent-based peacekeeping failed following the Somali civil war and 1991 coup, the UN turned to Chapter VII. United Nations Security Council, United Nations Security Council, "Resolution 794 (1992): Adopted by the Security Council at its 3145th meeting, on 3 December 1992 (S/RES/794)" (1992).
50. "Provisional Verbatim Record of the Three Thousand One Hundred and Forty-Fifth Meeting (S/PV.3145), December 3" (1992).
51. Ibid.
52. United Nations Security Council, "Resolution 814 (1993): Adopted by the Security Council at its 3188th meeting, on 26 March 1993 (S/RES/814)" (1993).
53. United Nations Security Council, "Provisional Verbatim Record of the Three Thousand One Hundred and Eighty-Eighth Meeting (S/PV.3188), March 26" (1993).
54. Ibid.
55. Ibid. From PRC representative Chen Jian: "It is our understanding that this authorization is based on the needs of the unique situation in Somalia and should not constitute a precedent for United Nations peace-keeping operations."). See also the statement of PRC representative Li Zhaoxing reminder that UNOSOM II's "humanitarian mandate remains unchanged, and the principle of using non-coercive measures should be observed in the performance of that mandate," United Nations Security Council, "3385th Meeting (S/PV.3385), May 31" (1994).
56. United Nations Security Council, "Resolution 827 (1993): Adopted by the Security Council at its 3217th meeting, on 25 May 1993 (S/RES/827)" (1993).
57. See Rachel Murray, "Recent Developments: The Report of the OAU's International Panel of Eminent Personalities to Investigate the 1994 Genocide in Rwanda and the Surrounding Events," *Journal of African Law* 45, no. 1 (2001); George B. N. Ayittey, "The United States of Africa: A Revisit," *The ANNALS of the American Academy of Political and Social Science* 632, no. 1 (2010).
58. Though China was not alone in its abstention; Brazil, New Zealand, Nigeria and Pakistan also abstained on UN Security Council Resolution 929.United Nations Security Council, United Nations Security Council, "Resolution 929 (1994): Adopted by the Security Council at its 3392nd meeting, on 22 June 1994 (S/RES/929)" (1994).

59. In a subsequent reversal of course, the UN Security Council unanimously adopted Resolution 918 in May 1994, expanding the UNAMIR mandate to include the protection of refugees and civilians at risk with the establishment of humanitarian "safe areas." When the UNAMIR force did not materialize, the UN moved to dispatch a French-led force.

    United Nations Security Council, "Resolution 918 (1994): Adopted by the Security Council at its 3377 meeting on 17 May 1994 (S/RES/918)" (1994).
60. "3392nd Meeting (S/PV.3392), June 22" (1994).
61. Ibid.
62. Ibid.
63. Welsh, *"The Security Council and Humanitarian Intervention,"* 2008, supra note 15, 545.
64. United Nations General Assembly and United Nations Security Council, "Supplement to an Agender for Peace: Position Paper of the Secretary-General on the Occasion of the Fiftieth Anniversary of the United Nations (A/50/60-S/1995/1), January 3" (1995).
65. United Nations Security Council, United Nations Security Council, "Resolution 1246 (1999): Adopted by the Security Council at its 4013th meeting, on 11 June 1999 (S/RES/1246)" (1999). Resolution 1246 was adopted unanimously. UNAMET consisted of referendum monitors; civilian police to advise the Indonesian police force, and military liaison officers to advise the Indonesian military. The UNAMET mandate was twice extended. See "Resolution 1257 (1999): Adopted by the Security Council at its 4031st meeting, on 3 August 1999 (S/RES/1257)" (1999); "Resolution 1262 (1999): Adopted by the Security Council at its 4038th meeting, on 27 August 1999 (S/RES/1262)" (1999).
66. United Nations Security Council, "4043rd Meeting (S/PV.4043), September 11" (1999).
67. Key ASEAN players did voice opinions about intervention in East Timor. For example, the Philippines, Vietnam and Singapore all called for action only under the conditions of UNSC endorsement and Indonesian consent; Cambodia and Laos called for strict considerations of Indonesia's sovereignty.
68. Indonesia gave consent under threats to have US military assistance cut; the International Monetary Fund delaying a review of Indonesia's economic climate, potentially impacting the next loan instalment, and the Paris Club of Creditors suspended discussions of debt relief. See Seth Mydans, "Indonesia Says No to Timor Peacekeepers," *The New York Times*, September 8, 1999; "Indonesia Invites a U.N. Force to Timor," *The New York Times*, September 13, 1999; Sander Thoenes, "What made Indonesia accept peacekeepers," *The Christian Science Monitor*, September 14, 1999.
69. "Induced consent" is Welsh's term. See Welsh, *"The Security Council and Humanitarian Intervention,"* 2008, 552.
70. Xi Mi, "A Responsible Decision," *China Daily*, September 15, 1999, 4. ("The outburst of violence in East Timor after its recent vote has somewhat tarnished Indonesia's image... If it does not take prompt action, the next victim will not only be the East Timor people, but also Indonesia's own fundamental interests..... [Jakarta] has now decided to honor a pledge by inviting international peacekeepers to East Timor. This decision, painful as it might be, is rational, respectable and responsible.").
71. United Nations Security Council, "Resolution 1264 (1999): Adopted by the Security Council at its 4045th meeting, on 15 September 1999 (S/RES/1264)" (1999). Resolution

1264 also reaffirmed the sovereignty and territorial integrity of Indonesia. The UN Security Council shortly thereafter established the UN Transitional Administration in East Timor (UNTAET) to establish peace and functioning government services for the East Timorese people via in Resolution 1272. United Nations Security Council, "Resolution 1272 (1999): Adopted by the Security Council at its 4057th meeting, on 25 October 1999 (S/RES/1272)" (1999).
72. Carlson, *Unifying China, Integrating with the World*, 2005, 176.
73. Evan A. Feigenbaum, "China's challenge to Pax Americana," *The Washington Quarterly* 24, no. 3 (2001): 34.
74. United Nations Security Council, "3730th Meeting (S/PV.3730), January 10" (1997).
75. Ibid.
76. The Organization of American States seconded Guatemala's call for the operation; Mexico and other Member States threatened to take the proposed peacekeeping mission to the UN General Assembly for a vote under the Uniting for Peace formula. The Uniting for Peace formula means empowers the General Assembly to act in regards to a threat to peace, breach of peace or an act of aggression in the event of the failure of the UN Security Council to act. For more detail on Uniting for Peace, see United Nations Peacekeeping, "Role of the General Assembly," http://www.un.org/en/peacekeeping/operations/rolega.shtml (accessed March 3, 2019). On the details of MINUGUA, see Paul Lewis, "China Lifts U.N. Veto on Guatemala Monitors," *The New York Times*, January 21, 1997.
77. Diplomats noted that Guatemala agreed to stop pushing for full United Nations status for Taiwan, but that it did not have to withdraw its relations with Taiwan, nor publicly apologize for its invitation to the Taiwanese Foreign Minister. For more detail, see Lewis, "China Lifts U.N. Veto on Guatemala Monitors," 1997.
78. On 25 February 1999, the UN Security Council voted regarding a six-month extension of the UNPREDEP mandate, see United Nations Security Council, "Canada, France, Germany, Italy, Netherlands, Slovenia, United Kingdom of Great Britain and Northern Ireland and United States of America: draft resolution (S/1999/201), February 25" (1999).
79. United Nations Security Council, "Security Council Fails to Extend Mandate of United Nations Preventive Deployment Force in Former Yugoslav Republic of Macedonia (SC/6648), February 25," (1999).
80. Pang Zhongying, "China's changing attitude to UN peacekeeping," 2005, 100. It should be noted, however, that China flatly denied the vote was in any way linked with Taiwan, asserting that peacekeepers were no longer needed in Macedonia as the mandate was fulfilled and China did not consider the situation in Macedonia to represent a threat to international peace and security. For more detail, see "Taiwan criticises China UN veto," *BBC News*, February 26, 1999.
81. For example, see Gabriel Partos, "Analysis: What price Macedonian peace?," *BBC News*, February 25. However, in June 2001, Macedonia approached Beijing about establishing relations with China, signing an agreement regarding recognition of the One China Policy, and leading to its severing of diplomatic relations with Taiwan. For more detail, see Deng Gang, "Macedonian FM Seeks Reestablishing Diplomatic Relations with China," *People's Daily*, June 18, 2001.

166   ENDNOTES

82. United Nations Security Council, "Security Council Fails to Extend Mandate of United Nations Preventive Deployment Force in Former Yugoslav Republic of Macedonia (SC/6648), February 25."
83. Zhao, *Jiangou heping: Zhongguo dui lianheguo waijiao xingweide yanjin (Constructing Peace: The Evolution of China's Diplomatic Behavior Toward the United Nations)*, 2007, 177.
84. Wuthnow, *Chinese Diplomacy and the UN Security Council*, 2013, 23.
85. Table draws from Wuthnow, *Chinese Diplomacy and the UN Security Council*, 26.
86. Juergen Dedring, *The United Nations Security Council in the 1990s: Resurgence and Renewal* (Albany: State University of New York Press, 2008), 115.
87. For a summary, see Wuthnow, *Chinese Diplomacy and the UN Security Council*, 2013, 28.
88. Malone, *Decision-Making in the UN Security Council*, 1998, 63.
89. United Nations Security Council, United Nations Security Council, "Resolution 841: Adopted by the Security Council at its 3238th meeting, on 16 June 1993 (S/RES/841)" (1993).
90. United Nations Security Council, "Provisional Verbatim Record of the Three Thousand Two Hundred and Thirty-Eighth Meeting (S/PV.3238), June 16" (1993).
91. Ibid.
92. Sanctions were established by the Organization of American States in 1991; the exiled Haitian government asked for these sanctions to become "universal and mandatory." See Welsh, *"The Security Council and Humanitarian Intervention,"* 2008, 542. China supported Resolution 875, calling for a naval blockade against Haiti, United Nations Security Council, United Nations Security Council, "Resolution 875 (1993): Adopted by the Security Council at its 3293rd meeting, on 16 October 1993 (S/RES/875)" (1993). repeating that "the unique and exceptional situation" in Haiti, "and in light of the formal request of President Jean-Bertrand Aristide, supported by the Latin American countries and the OAS" that China could vote yes, but stressing that this measure "should not establish a precedent" for intervention. See United Nations Security Council, "Provisional Verbatim Record of the Three Thousand Two Hundred and Ninety-Third Meeting (S/PV.3293), October 16" (1993).
93. United Nations General Assembly and United Nations Security Council, "Identical letters dated 21 August 2000 from the Secretary-General to the President of the General Assembly and the President of the Security Council (A/55/305-S/2000/809)" (2000); United Nations Department of Peacekeeping Operations, "Handbook on United Nations Multidimensional Peacekeeping Operations" (2003); "United Nations Peacekeeping Operations Principles and Guidelines" (2008).
94. Emily Paddon Rhoads, *Taking Sides in Peacekeeping: Impartiality and the Future of the United Nations* (Oxford: Oxford University Press, 2016), 65.
95. United Nations Department of Peacekeeping Operations, "Handbook on United Nations Multidimensional Peacekeeping Operations," 2003, 56.
96. "United Nations Peacekeeping Operations Principles and Guidelines," 2008, 33.
97. Apart from those already mentioned, new missions included UNTAET in Timor Leste, MONUC in the Democratic Republic of the Congo; UNAMSIL in Sierra Leone, UNMIK in Kosovo, UNMIL in Liberia, UNOCI in Côte d'Ivoire, ONUB in Burundi an MINUSTAH in Haiti.

98. High-Level Independent Panel on United Nations Peace Operations, "Uniting Our Strengths for Peace – Politics, Partnership and People" (2015).
99. United Nations Security Council, "Resolution 1542 (2004): Adopted by the Security Council at its 4961st meeting, on 30 April 2004 (S/RES/1542)" (2004).
100. He Yin, "China's Changing Policy on UN Peacekeeping Operations" (Stockholm 2007), 33. Edward Cody, "China Readies Riot Force For Peacekeeping In Haiti," *The Washington Post*, September 29, 2004.
101. Respectively, United Nations Security Council, "Resolution 1264 (1999): Adopted by the Security Council at its 4045th meeting, on 15 September 1999 (S/RES/1264)," 1999; "Resolution 1271 (1999): Adopted by the Security Council at its 4056th meeting, on 22 October 1999 (S/RES/1271)" (1999).
102. "China's peacekeeping forces leave for Liberia," *People's Daily Online*, December 10, 2003.
103. "Chinese Blue Helmets Play Active Role in Africa," *Xinhua*, October 28, 2006.
104. He ,"China's Changing Policy on UN Peacekeeping Operations," 2007, 34.
105. AFP, "China to Send Peacekeeping Troops to the D.R. Congo Next Month," *reliefweb*, February 10, 2003.
106. International Crisis Group, "China's Growing Role in UN Peacekeeping," 2009, 7–8.
107. "China to become 2nd largest contributor to UN peacekeeping budget," *China Daily*, May 30, 2016.
108. UN Peacekeeping, "Contributors to UN Peacekeeping Operations by Country and Post: Police, UN Military Experts on Mission, Staff Officers and Troop," 30 April 2019, https://peacekeeping.un.org/sites/default/files/1-summary_of_contributions.pdf. (accessed May 13, 2019).
109. Countries volunteering troops on mission are reimbursed at the UN standard rate, of approximately US$1,410/soldier/month. See https://peacekeeping.un.org/en/deployment-and-reimbursement.
110. Quoting China's Foreign Minister Wang Yi. Hille, "China commits combat troops to Mali," 2013.
111. Michael Martina and David Brunnstrom, "China's Xi says to commit 8,000 troops for U.N. peacekeeping force," *Reuters*, September 29, 2015.
112. For a discussion of these themes, see Chin-Hao Huang, "Peacekeeping Contributor Profile: The People's Republic of China," April 2017, Providing for Peacekeeping, http://www.providingforpeacekeeping.org/2014/04/03/contributor-profile-china/ (accessed March 3, 2019).
113. Fung, "What explains China's deployment to UN peacekeeping operations?," 2016.
114. Huang Shan, "A decade of China's peacekeeping missions," *China.org.cn*, January 18, 2010. See also Laura Neack, "UN Peace-Keeping: In the Interest of Community or Self?," *Journal of Peace Research* 32, no. 2 (1995); Vincenzo Bove and Leandro Elia, "Supplying peace: Participation in and troop contribution to peacekeeping missions," ibid.48, no. 6 (2011).
115. Richardson, "A Responsible Power?," 2011; Andrews Higgins, "China showcasing its softer side: growing role in U.N. peacekeeping signals desire to project image of benign power," *The Washington Post*, December 2, 2009; Mark Landler and Steven Lee Myers, "U.S. Sees Positive Signs From China on Security Issues," *The New York Times*, April 26, 2012.

116. For a discussion, see Rhoads, *Taking Sides in Peacekeeping*, 2016, 68–9.
117. MONUSCO, UNAMID, UNMIL, UNMISS are all examples of this point.
118. See International Commission on Intervention and State Sovereignty, "The Responsibility to Protect," 2001; UN General Assembly, "Resolution adopted by the General Assembly: World Summit Outcome, A/RES/60/1, 24 October." 2005; United Nations General Assembly, "Implementing the Responsibility to Protect: Report of the Secretary-General (A/63/677), January 12," 2009.
119. Job and Shesterinina, *"China as a Global Norm-Shaper,"* 2014.
120. United Nations Security Council, "5319th meeting (S/PV.5319), December 9" (2005). For analysis, see Teitt, "Assessing Polemics, Principles and Practices," 2009.
121. Interview with Chinese Ministry of Foreign Affairs official, Washington, DC, 1 March 2016.
122. "Veto cover" in the sense that China could co-veto with Russia and share the burden of any criticism, yet China elected not to do this in the case of Resolution 1674 United Nations Security Council, "Resolution 1674 (2006): Adopted by the Security Council at its 5430th meeting, on 28 April 2006 (S/RES/1674)" (2006)., which invoked the responsibility to protect. See Janka Oertel, *China and the United Nations: Chinese UN Policy in the Areas of Peace and Development in the Era of Hu Jintao* (Baden-Baden: Nomos/Bloomsbury, 2015), 177. For analysis, see Fung, "China and the Responsibility to Protect," 2016.
123. Carrie Booth Walling, "The UN Security Council and Its ICC Referral Resolutions: Advancing or Curbing the Justice Norm?" (paper presented at the International Studies Association's 57th Annual Convention, Atlanta, Georgia, March 16–19, 2016).
124. Malone, "International Criminal Justice," 2008.
125. For example, the Convention on the Prevention and Punishment of the Crime of Genocide of 1948, the Convention Against Torture of 1984, amongst other articles of international humanitarian law.
126. Robert Cryer, "Prosecuting the Leaders: Promises, Politics and Pragmatics," *Göttingen Journal of International Law* 1 (2009): 54; Hyeran Jo and Beth A. Simmons, "Can the International Criminal Court Deter Atrocity?," *International Organization* 70, no. 3 (2016).
127. The contemporary mandate is further underscored in Article 58 of the Rome Statute, which permits issuing an arrest warrant when it can prevent additional criminal activities by a defendant. For a discussion of the contemporary jurisdictional mandate issue, see McMillan and Mickler, "From Sudan to Syria," 2013, 298. See also Belinda Cooper, "The Limits of International Justice," *World Policy Journal* 26, no. 3 (2009). Though this is not to say that the International Criminal Court is the only justice mechanism with a contemporary mandate; the International Criminal Tribunal for the former Yugoslavia is another noteworthy example.
128. Alternate pathways include if a state party refers a situation where crimes are alleged to have occurred; or if the prosecutor receives information that crimes have occurred within the Court's jurisdiction and with the authorization of the pretrial chamber of judges. The ICC can exercise jurisdiction when the crimes occur on a signatory state that has ratified the statute, or when the perpetrator has the nationality of a state that has ratified the statute. However, the ICC is "structurally configured" to emphasize

national solutions to these international crimes. McMillan and Mickler, "From Sudan to Syria," 2013, 300. State consent underlines the Court's jurisdiction—and under the principle of complementarity, the ICC has overlapping jurisdiction with national courts—deferring to national courts "unless the State is unwilling or unable genuinely to carry out the investigation or prosecution" (article 17).

129. Two occurrences are studied in detail in the case studies on Darfur and Libya. See United Nations Security Council, "Resolution 1593 (2005): Adopted by the Security Council at its 5158th meeting, on 31 March 2005 (S/RES/1593)," 2005. United Nations Security Council, "Resolution 1970 (2011): Adopted by the Security Council at its 6491st meeting, on 26 February 2011 (S/RES/1970), February 26," 2011.
130. Mark Kersten, "The ICC and Regime Change: Some Thoughts but Mostly Questions," *Justice in Conflict*, January 31, 2013.
131. For a detailed analysis, see Christodoulos Kaoutzanis, "Understanding the United Nations Security Council's Decisions to Initiate Atrocities Investigations" (PhD dissertation, Columbia University, 2016).
132. China and Russia cast vetoes; South Africa also voted no, and Qatar, Indonesia and Congo Republic abstained.
133. China and Russia cast vetoes; Libya and Vietnam voted no, and Indonesia abstained.
134. United Nations Security Council, "5933rd meeting, July 11 (S/PV.5933)" (2008).
135. The UN did not address mass crimes in either of these country cases. For an account on China's approach to these two country cases as nuclear crises at the UN Security Council, see Wuthnow, *Chinese Diplomacy and the UN Security Council*, 2013, 59–94.
136. Jonathan Holslag, "China's True Intentions in Congo," April 19 2010, *Harvard International Review*, http://hir.harvard.edu/article/?a=2604. (accessed March 3, 2019).
137. For details, see United Nations Statistics Division, "UN Comtrade Database," n.d., https://comtrade.un.org/ (accessed March 3, 2019).
138. For an analysis of the "Go Abroad" policy, see Bonnie S. Glaser, "Ensuring the 'Go Abroad' Policy Serves China's Domestic Priorities," *China Brief* 7, no. 5 (2007).

Chapter 2

1. Downes and Monten, "Forced to Be Free?," 2013.
2. O'Rourke, *Regime Change*, 2018.
3. See the review of the regime change literature in Downes and O'Rourke 2016.
4. Lieberthal and Wang, "Addressing U.S.-China Strategic Distrust," 2012.
5. Christensen, *The China Challenge*, 2015.
6. Some degree of ambiguity exists between the two terms for regime change, and they can be used interchangeably in the same publication. As in the English language, this ambiguity reflects the absence of a precise definition of "regime change" and what combination of actions constitutes regime change.
7. These conditions are UN Security Council authorization, host state consent and regional support. China remains consistent in framing its support for enforcement or violations of consent as exceptions due to the case at hand, and not a strict

departure in China's principled position. This framing reflects China's views that the use of force is only acceptable as a last resort; and serves as a blunt instrument to resolve conflict *because* it disregards consent and state sovereignty.

8. Citing Wang Yizhou in Zhang Diyu, "Yizhang foujuepiao de zhengyi (Controversies Around a Veto)," *World Affairs*, no. 5 (2012): 21.
9. Chen Zheng, "China Debates the Non-Interference Principle," *The Chinese Journal of International Politics* 9, no. 3 (2016): 373.
10. Wang Jisi, "China's Search for a Grand Strategy," *Foreign Affairs* 90, no. 2 (2011).
11. Chen, "China Debates the Non-Interference Principle," 2016, 373.
12. Fung, "Separating Intervention From Regime Change," 2018.
13. "*Dangqian, xifang guojia zai Xuliya wenti shang chouchumanzhi, dan shiji yi rijian bei wu jiezhi de tuidong zhengquan gengti de baquan yexin mishi le lizhi.*" Tian Wenlin, "Zai Xu gao zhengquan gengti shi zhanlue duanshi (Promoting Regime Change in Syria is Strategic Shortsightedness)," *People's Daily*, June 11, 2012.
14. "*Xifang ciju de zhenzheng mudi bing bus hi weile suowei de renquan minzhu, er shi youzhe fuza shenyuan de yuanyin. Shouxian, Xuliya juyou zhongyao de diyuan zhenzhi diwei, shi bingjia bizheng de zhanlue yaodi . . . Qici, Asade zhengquan chi fanmei de waijiao zhengce . . . suoyou zhexie dou shi Meiguo yizhi dui Xuliya xian zhenfu jiwei buman, zao jiu xiang dianfu ta, jianli yige qin Xifang de zhengquan, bianyu Xifang geng hao de shentou kongzhi Zhongdong zhe yi zhanlue yao di.*" Liu Junhua, "Cong guojifa shijiao kan Xifang dui Xuliya de ganshe (On the Western Interference in Syria in View of the International Law)," *Nanjing University of Finance and Economics Scholarly Papers* (2012).
15. "*Raner, shi ge liang nian, dang shi guo bu jin meiyou shixian qi yuxiang de zhenzhi wending yu qiangda, jingji fazhan yu fanrong, shehui xianghe yu kaming, faner . . . ge zhong maodun de chongtu jiang gai diqu xingshi dai ru daole renhe ren shixian dou weiceng yuliao dao de dongdang hunluan jingdi . . .*" Yu Ping, "Alabo xuezhe dui 'Alabo Zhichun' de kanfa (Arab Scholar's Views on 'Arab Spring')," *Contemporary World* (2013): 48.
16. "*Xianru fubai he neidou de chouwen zhi zhong . . .*" Zhang Hong, "Wukelan weiji zhong de jiazhi chongtu (Clash of Values Perked up in Crisis-plagued Ukraine)," *Peace and Development* 4 (2015).
17. "*Zhengzhi jushi chixu dongdang*" in relation to the attempted case of regime change in Syria. Wu Ningbo, "Lun 'baohu de zeren' de guojifa kunjing yu chulu (On the Dilemma and Outlet of the International Law of the 'Responsibility to Protect')," *Administration and Law* (2015). See also, Liu Baolai, "2012 nian de zhongdong: liluanfenfen wei jian tian (The Middle East in 2012: Endless Chaos)," *World Affairs*, no. 1 (2013); Liu, "Cong guojifa shijiao kan Xifang dui Xuliya de ganshe (On the Western Interference in Syria in View of the International Law)," 2012.
18. "*Yu ci tongshi, Meiguo zai Libiya he Xuliya deng guo cedong "zhengquan gengti", shi Yisilan jiduan shili huode geng da shengcun kongjian . . .*" Tian Wenlin and Li Gujing, "Meiguo shi guoji zhili moshi dang fansi (wanghai lou) (US-style global governance model should have reflections)," *People's Daily*, November 26, 2014.
19. "*Guangda Alabo guojia yue lai yue renshi dao Zhongguo lichang he zhuzhang de zhengque, renshi dao Zhongguo cai shi zhenzheng wei Alabo guojia liyi zhuoxiang de*

daguo. Yizhi dali ganshe xu shiwu, shizhong mouqiu zhengquan gengdie de xifang guojia zuizhong ye bude buchengren "zhengzhi jiejue shi weiyi chulu", bing kaishile xiangguan de nuli." Zhou Zhou, "Zhuanjia: Zhongguo jiang geng hao de fahui quanhe cutan zuoyong (Experts: China will better perform its functions of mediation)," *People.cn*, March 30, 2016.

20. *"Cong zishen liyi lai jiang, Zhongguo xuyao Zhongdong de nengyuan, xuyao Zhongdong de qinggongye shichang, xuyao laowu shuchu shichang, erqieyou keneng Zhongdong shi Zhongguo de gao jianduanchanpin de shichang, biru daxing jixie shebei, feji, jian chuan deng deng, ruguo zhege di qu xianru zhanluan de hua, bu fuhe Zhongguo de liyi"* Huang Jie, "Zhongdong luanju heshiliao – fang zhuming Zhongdong wenti zhuanjia Yin Gang jiaoshou (When will the Chaos in the Middle East End – an Interview with Professor Yin Gang, and Expert in the Middle East)," *Weishi*, June 15, 2013.

21. Miwa Hirono, "China's Conflict Mediation and the Durability of the Principle of Non-Interference: The Case of Post-2014 Afghanistan," *The China Quarterly*, 1-21, doi:10.1017/S0305741018001753, n.d.; Mathieu Duchâtel, Oliver Bräuner, and Hang Zhou, "Protecting China's Overseas Interests: The Slow Shift away from Non-interference" (Solna, 2014). Liu Hongming and Liu Shuguang, "Dui Fei touzi de zhengzhi fengxia: xin dongxiang yu yindui jianyi (Political Risks of Investment to Africa: New changes and Suggestions on How to Respond)," *Transnational Business* (2012).

22. *Women buneng tongyi dazhe Lianheguo de qihao, xing zhengquan gendie zhi shi.* See online interview with Li Shaoxian, "Xuliya zongli pantao yu zhongdong jushi (The Betrayal of Syria Prime Minister and the Situation in the Middle East)," *People.com.cn*, August 9, 2012. Also see Qian Wenrong, "The Impact of Neo-interventionism on the International Order," *Peace and Development* 1 (2013).

23. For example, see Wang Yusheng, "Zhongguo waijiao de bianyu bubian (The Changes and Consistencies of China's Diplomacy)," *Jiefang Ribao*, October 29, 2012; Wu Xingtang, "Guoji xinshi dongdang duobianxia, Zhongguo waijiao ying jianchi 'sanbu' yuanze (With the Turbulence of the International Situation, China's Diplomacy Should Insist on the 'Three NOs' Principles')," *The Contemporary World*, no. 4 (2012). And see also online commentary like, Lin Bo, "Xifang 'xin ganshe zhuyi' weihai wuqiong (The 'Western Neo-interventionism' is Hazardous)," *CRI online*, February 21, 2012.

24. For example, see Huang, "Zhongdong luanju heshiliao – fang zhuming Zhongdong wenti zhuanjia Yin Gang jiaoshou (When will the Chaos in the Middle East End – an Interview with Professor Yin Gang, and Expert in the Middle East)."

25. Wu, "Lun 'baohu de zeren' de guojifa kunjing yu chulu (On the Dilemma and Outlet of the International Law of the 'Responsibility to Protect')," 2015.

26. See Huang, "Zhongdong luanju heshiliao – fang zhuming Zhongdong wenti zhuanjia Yin Gang jiaoshou (When will the Chaos in the Middle East End – an Interview with Professor Yin Gang, and Expert in the Middle East)." Qu Xing, "Lianheguo xianzhang, baohu de zeren yu xuliya wenti (The UN Charter, the Responsibility to Protect and the Syria Issue)," *International Studies* 12, no. 2 (2012); Yan Xuetong, "Zhongguo foujue Xuliya jueyian de libi (The Pros and Cons of China's Veto on Syria)," February 8 2012, sohu.com, http://yanxuetongvip.blog.sohu.com/203112403.html (accessed March 3, 2019).

27. *"Dui Zhongguo eryan, Wukelan bianju ji E Mei (Ou) zai Wukelan de boyi, qishi yijing chuji dao le Zhongguuo de hexin liyi . . . zhe jiushi . . . dui Zhongguo guojia anquan de*

waiyi xiaoying, qi yingxiang burongxiaoqu, zhide jingti." Zhu Lumin, "Wukelan bianju dui Zhongguo guojia liyi de yingxiang (Impact of Ukraine's Political Upheaval on China's National Interests)," *Pacific Journal* 22, no. 7 (2014).

28. *"Dan ruguo yige tongzhi zhe de xiatai, hushi you benguo renmin de liliang qu tuidong, ershi jiezhu waili, zhege shijie zhixu jiu luan le. Bu ganshe neizheng zhege yuanze yidan bei tupo, ni jiu keyi suyi tiao shijie shang kan bu shunyan de guojia shishi waibu ganshe."* Huang "Zhongdong luanju heshiliao – fang zhuming Zhongdong wenti zhuanjia Yin Gang jiaoshou (When will the Chaos in the Middle East End – an Interview with Professor Yin Gang, and Expert in the Middle East)."
29. Jia, *"China,"* 2003, 25.
30. Bates Gill and James Reilly, "Sovereignty, intervention and peacekeeping: the view from Beijing," *Survival* 42, no. 3 (2000): 42.
31. Wang, "China's Search for a Grand Strategy," 2011.
32. For example, see the statement of Chinese representative, Tang Jiaxuan, United Nations General Assembly, "Fifty-fourth Session: 8th plenary meeting (A/54/PV.8), September 22" (1999).
33. Carlson, "Helping to Keep the Peace (Albeit Reluctantly): China's Recent Stance on Sovereignty and Multilateral Intervention," 2004, 16.
34. For a discussion of regime change vis-à-vis China's political stability, see Duchâtel, Bräuner, and Zhou, "Protecting China's Overseas Interests," 2014, 2.
35. You, "China's National Security Commission: theory, evolution and operations," 2016, 179.
36. Ibid. See also David Lampton, *Following the Leader: Ruling China, from Deng Xiaoping to Xi Jinping* (Berkeley, CA: University of California Press, 2014).
37. You Ji discusses the erosion of the internal and external security concerns in the context of China's National Security Commission. See You, "China's National Security Commission: theory, evolution and operations," 2016.
38. *"Weihu jiben zhidu he guojia anquan, guojia zhuquan he lingtu wanzheng, jingji shehui de chixu wending fazhan."* Translation from Michael D. Swaine, "China's Assertive Behavior—Part One: On 'Core Interests'," *China Leadership Monitor* 34 (2010): 4. See "Shou lun Zhong Mei jingji duihua: chu shang yueqiu wai zhuyao wenti jun yi tan ji (First round of the Sino-U.S Economic Dialogue: All major issues have been discussed apart from going to the Moon)," *China News Online*, July 29, 2009. Also see State Councilor Bingguo Dai, "Closing Remarks for U.S.-China Strategic and Economic Dialogue," July 28, 2009, U.S. State Department, https://2009–2017.state.gov/secretary/20092013clinton/rm/2009a/july/126599.htm (accessed March 3, 2019).
39. You, "China's National Security Commission: theory, evolution and operations," 2016, 181., citing Lieutenant General Cheng Baoshan, "Study of Jiang Zemin's thought on National Security strategy", *Military Art Journal* 3, (2004): 28.
40. Swaine, "China's Assertive Behavior," 2010, 3.
41. Ibid., 4.
42. *"Jue bu dongyao, jue bu tuoxie, jue bu hui rangbu."* For example, Xinhua, "President Hu sets forth guidelines on Taiwan," *China Daily*, March 4, 2005. Commonly referred to as Hu Jintao's so-called "Four Nevers" speech. Ministry of Foreign Affairs of the People's Republic of China, "Hujintoa jiu xin xingshi xia fazhan liangan quanxi ti si dian yijian

(Hu Jintao's four guidelines on cross-strait relations development under a new situation)," March 4, 2005, http://www.fmprc.gov.cn/chn/gxh/tyb/zyxw/t186259.htm (accessed March 3, 2019). For analysis, see Swaine, "China's Assertive Behavior," 2010.
43. Citing Wang Yizhou in Zhang, "Yizhang foujuepiao de zhengyi (Controversies Around a Veto)," 2012, 21.

Chapter 3

1. J. David Singer and Melvin Small, "The Composition and Status Ordering of the International System, 1815–1940," *World Politics* 18, no. 2 (1966).
2. William C. Wohlforth, "Unipolarity, Status Competition, and Great Power War," *World Politics* 61, no. 1 (2009).
3. Scott D. Sagan, "Why Do States Build Nuclear Weapons?: Three Models in Search of a Bomb," *International Security* 21, no. 3 (1996); Samina Ahmed, "Pakistan's Nuclear Weapons Program: Turning Points and Nuclear Choices," *International Security* 23, no. 4 (1999); George Perkovich, *India's Nuclear Bomb: The Impact on Global Proliferation* (Berkeley, CA: University of California Press, 1999); Dong-Joon Jo and Erik Gartzke, "Determinants of Nuclear Weapons Proliferation," *Journal of Conflict Resolution* 51, no. 1 (2007).
4. Barry O'Neill, "Nuclear Weapons and National Prestige" (New Haven, CT: Cowles Foundation, 2006).
5. Charles Glaser, "The flawed case for nuclear disarmament," *Survival* 40, no. 1 (1998).
6. Dana P. Eyre and Mark C. Suchman, "Status, Norms, and the Proliferation of Conventional Weapons: An Institutional Theory Approach," in *The Culture of National Security: Norms and Identity in World Politics*, ed. Peter J. Katzenstein (New York: Columbia University Press, 1996); Lilach Gilady, "Conspicuous Waste in International Relations" (Doctoral Dissertation, Yale University, 2006); Xiaoyu Pu and Randall L. Schweller, "Status Signaling, Multiple Audiences, and China's Blue-Water Naval Ambition," in *Status in World Politics*, ed. T. V. Paul, Deborah Welch Larson, and William C. Wohlforth (New York: Cambridge University Press, 2014).
7. Benjamin de Carvalho and Iver B. Neumann, eds., *Small State Status Seeking: Norway's Quest for International Standing* (Abingdon: Routledge, 2015).
8. Allan Dafoe, Jonathan Renshon, and Paul Huth, "Reputation and Status as Motives for War," *Annual Review of Political Science* 17 (2014): 374. See also Renshon, *Fighting for Status*, 2017, 37–9.
9. Hans J. Morgenthau, *Politics Among Nations: The Struggle for Power and Peace* (New York: Knopf, 1954); Robert Gilpin, *War and Change in World Politics* (New York: Cambridge University Press, 1983).
10. Singer and Small, "The Composition and Status Ordering of the International System, 1815–1940," 1966.
11. John Herz, *Political Realism and Political Idealism* (Chicago, IL: University of Chicago Press, 1951); Deng, *China's Struggle for Status*, 2008.
12. E. H. Carr, *International Relations Since the Peace Treaties* (London: Macmillan and Co., Limited, 1937).

13. Robert H. Frank, *Choosing the Right Pond: Human Behavior and the Quest for Status* (New York: Oxford University Press, 1985); Cecilia L. Ridgeway and Henri A. Walker, "Status Structures," in *Sociological Perspective on Social Psychology*, ed. Karen S. Cook, Gary Alan Fine, and James S. House (Upper Saddle River, NJ: Pearson Education, 1995); Ori Heffetz and Robert H. Frank, "Preferences for Status: Evidence and Economic Implications," in *Handbook of Social Economics*, ed. Jess Benhabib, Matthew O. Jackson, and Alberto Bisin (Amsterdam: North Holland, 2011).
14. Dafoe, Renshon, and Huth, "Reputation and Status as Motives for War," 2014, 374.
15. On the hierarchy of beliefs system, see Renshon, *Fighting for Status*, 2017, 33; O'Neill, "Nuclear Weapons and National Prestige," 2006. Table 3.1 is adapted from Renshon 2017, 39.
16. Jonathan Mercer, *Reputation and International Politics* (Ithaca, NY: Cornell University Press, 1996); Paul K. Huth, *Extended Deterrence and the Prevention of War* (New Haven, CT: Yale University Press, 1988); David Hugh-Jones and Ro'i Zultan, "Reputation and Cooperation in Defense," *Journal of Conflict Resolution* 57, no. 2 (2012); Barbara F. Walter, *Reputation and Civil War: Why Separatist Conflicts Are so Violent*. (New York: Cambridge University Press, 2009); Robert Axelrod, *The Evolution of Cooperation* (New York: Basic Books, 1984); Mark J. C. Crescenzi, Jacob D. Kathman, and Stephen B. Long, "Reputation, History, and War," *Journal of Peace Research* 44, no. 6 (2007).
17. Deborah Welch Larson, "Trust and Missed Opportunities in International Relations," *Political Psychology* 18, no. 3 (1997); Andrew T. Guzman, "A Compliance-Based Theory of International Law," *California Law Review* 90, no. 6 (2002); Anne E. Sartori, "The Might of the Pen: A Reputational Theory of Communication in International Disputes," *International Organization* 56, no. 1 (2002); Robert O. Keohane, *After Hegemony Cooperation and Discord in the World Political Economy* (Princeton, NJ: Princeton University Press, 1984); Michael Tomz, *Reputation and International Cooperation: Sovereign Debt across Three Centuries* (Princeton, NJ: Princeton University Press, 2007).
18. Keohane, *After Hegemony Cooperation and Discord in the World Political Economy*, 1984, 105–6.
19. Erickson, *Dangerous Trade*, 2015, 21.
20. Ibid., 8. Also see J. C. Sharman, *Havens in a Storm: The Struggle for Global Tax Regulation* (Ithaca, NY: Cornell University Press 2006); D. B. Bromley, *Reputation, Image and Impression Management* (Oxford: John Wiley & Sons, 1993).
21. Erickson, *Dangerous Trade*, 2015, 18.
22. Ibid., 7.
23. Scholars note a social dimension to reputation in their works, but do not theorize or explore it. See Busby 2008, Johnston 2008, O'Neill 2006.
24. Renshon operationalizes these peer groups into regional geographic hierarchies and peer groups formed by foreign policy choices (e.g. alliance members), for example. Renshon, *Fighting for Status*, 2017, 44.
25. Dafoe, Renshon, and Huth, "Reputation and Status as Motives for War," 2014, 376.
26. Jamie J. Gruffydd-Jones, "The Impacts of International Pressure with Authoritarian States" (PhD dissertation, Princeton University, 2017). See also Alan M. Wachman, "Does the diplomacy of shame promote human rights in China?," *Third World Quarterly* 22, no. 2 (2001).

27. Renshon, *Fighting for Status*, 2017, 33.
28. See Deborah Welch Larson, T. V. Paul, and William C. Wohlforth, "Status and World Order," in *Status and World Politics*, ed. T. V. Paul, Deborah Welch Larson, and William C. Wohlforth (New York: Cambridge University Press, 2014), 7.
29. Thomas J. Volgy et al., eds., *Major Powers and the Quest for Status in International Politics* (New York: Palgrave/MacMillan, 2011); Deborah Welch Larson and Alexei Shevchenko, "Status Seekers: Chinese and Russian Responses to U.S. Primacy," *International Security* 43, no. 4 (2010); Michelle Murray, "Identity, Insecurity, and Great Power Politics: The Tragedy of German Naval Ambition Before the First World War," *Security Studies* 19, no. 4 (2010); *The Struggle for Recognition in International Relations: Status, Revisionism and Rising Powers* (Oxford: Oxford University Press, 2018).
30. Renshon, *Fighting for Status*, 2017, 33.
31. Joshua Freedman, "Status insecurity and temporality in world politics," *European Journal of International Relations* 22, no. 4 (2015).
32. Fred Hirsch, *Social Limits to Growth* (Cambridge, MA: Harvard University Press, 1976).However, this is not to say that because status is relative that it is zero-sum—status can be a "club good"—i.e. that there can be many members in the same status group or "club" without necessarily diminishing the status of members within the same club. See David A. Lake, "Status, Authority, and the End of the American Century " in *Status in World Politics*, ed. T. V. Paul, Deborah Welch Larson, and William C. Wohlforth (New York: Cambridge University Press, 2014).
33. To be clear, once status forms, though it may be intangible, it can have significant effects on the material environment.
34. Murray Milner, *Status and Sacredness: A General Theory of Status Relations and an Analysis of Indian Culture* (New York: Oxford University Press, 1994), 23–4.
35. See Kenneth N. Waltz, *Theory of International Politics* (Reading, MA: Addison, 1979), 131.
36. Thomas Humphrey Marshall, *Class, Citizenship, and Social Development: Essays* (Westport, CT: Greenwood Press, 1973), 198.
37. Rawi Abdelal et al., "Identity as a Variable," in *Measuring Identity: A Guide for Social Scientists*, ed. Rawi Abdelal, et al. (Cambridge: Cambridge University Press, 2009), 21; Wendt, *Social Theory of International Politics*, 1999.
38. Ridgeway and Walker, *"Status Structures,"* 1995, 281–2.
39. Erickson, *Dangerous Trade*, 2015, 27. See Abraham Tesser and Jennifer Campbell, "Self-Definition: The Impact of the Relative Performance and Similarity of Others," *Social Psychology Quarterly* 43, no. 3 (1980).
40. Wendt, *Social Theory of International Politics*, 1999, 236.
41. Martha Finnemore and Kathryn Sikkink, "International Norm Dynamics and Political Change," *International Organization* 52, no. 4 (1998); Vaughn P. Shannon, "Norms Are What States Make of Them: The Political Psychology of Norm Violation," *International Studies Quarterly* 44, no. 2 (2000); Henri Tajfel, and John C. Turner, "The Social Identity Theory of Intergroup Behavior," in *Psychology of Intergroup Relations*, ed. William G. Austin and Stephen Worchel (Chicago: Nelson-Hall, 1986).
42. Wendt, *Social Theory of International Politics*, 1999, 224.

43. Finnemore, *The Purpose of Intervention: Changing Beliefs about the Use of Force*, 2003; Oded Löwenheim, "'Do Ourselves Credit and Render a Lasting Service to Mankind': British Moral Prestige, Humanitarian Intervention, and the Barbary Pirates," *International Studies Quarterly* 47, no. 1 (2003); Richardson, "A Responsible Power?," 2011.
44. Renshon, 53.
45. These two types of triggers are linked: clearly if China's previous political behavior had not been so high-profile, public, and perceived to convey such unambiguous information, events like the Tiananmen Square" Incident would lack the potential to have the social power as speech acts alone.
46. For a succinct summary on China's post-1989 isolation and China's range of responses, see Harry Harding, "The Impact of Tiananmen on China's Foreign Policy" (Seattle 1990).
47. Though Southeast Asian governments—with the prominent exception of Singapore—did not condemn China, and maintained senior-level bilateral visits.
48. Larson, Paul, and Wohlforth, "Status and World Order," 2014, 10. See also Jonathan Grix and Donna Lee, "Soft Power, Sports Mega-Events and Emerging States: The Lure of the Politics of Attraction," *Global Society* 27, no. 4 (2013); Larson and Shevchenko, "Status Seekers," 2010; Roger Blitz, "Sport Organisers Play High-Stakes Game," *Financial Times*, September 29, 2010; Simon Kuper, "Sport: Developing nations go on offensive for games," *Financial Times,* January 29, 2011.
49. This is not to say that China, or any other host state, can completely control the narratives that develop in response to hosting their event. For a treatment, see Jacques deLisle, "'One World, Different Dreams': The Contest to Define the Beijing Olympics," in *Owning the Olympics: Narratives of the New China*, ed. Monroe E. Price and Daniel Dayan (Ann Arbor, MI: University of Michigan Press, 2008).
50. Scarlett Cornelissen, "The Geopolitics of Global Aspiration: Sport Mega-events and Emerging Powers," *The International Journal of the History of Sport* 27, no. 16–18 (2010): 3008. See also Victor D. Cha, *Beyond the Final Score: The Politics of Sport in Asia* (New York: Columbia University Press, 2009).
51. For analysis of China's Olympic bid efforts and the relevance of securing the 2008 Olympic Games in Beijing, see Xu Guoqi, *Olympic Dreams: China and Sports, 1895–2008* (Cambridge, MA: Harvard University Press, 2008), 225–64.
52. For example, see Victor D. Cha, "Beijing's Olympic-Sized Catch-22," *The Washington Quarterly* 31, no. 3 (2008).
53. Renshon, *Fighting for Status*, 2017, 57.
54. Ibid., 58.
55. Though nuclear weapons can now also emphasize rogue states, and not just great powers, see Glaser, "The flawed case for nuclear disarmament," 1998.; Renshon, *Fighting for Status*, 2017, 59. Pu and Schweller, "Status Signaling, Multiple Audiences," 2014.
56. Johnston, *Social States*, 2008, 79; "Treating International Institutions as Social Environments," *International Studies Quarterly* 45, no. 4 (2001); Li Xiaojun, "Social Rewards and Socialization Effects: An Alternative Explanation for the Motivation Behind China's Participation in International Institutions," *The Chinese Journal of International Politics* 3, no. 3 (2010).

57. Charlan Jeanne Nemeth, "Influence Processes, Problem Solving and Creativity," in *Social Influence: The Ontario Symposium, Volume 5*, ed. Mark P. Zanna, James M. Olson, and C. Peter Herman (Hillsdale, NJ: Lawrence Erlbaum, 1987), 237.
58. Leon Festinger, "An Analysis of Compliant Behavior," in *Group Relations at the Crossroads*, ed. Milbourne Otto Wilson and Muzafer Sherif (New York: Harper & Brothers, 1953).
59. Johnston, "Treating International Institutions as Social Environments," 2001, 499.
60. Ibid.
61. Erik Ringmar, *Identity, Interest and Action: A Cultural Explanation of Sweden's Intervention in Thirty Years War* (Cambridge: Cambridge University Press, 1996); Daniel Seth Markey, "The Prestige Factor in International Relations" (Doctoral Dissertation, Princeton University, 2000).
62. Rosemary Foot, "'Doing some things' in the Xi Jinping era: the United Nations as China's venue of choice," *International Affairs* 90, no. 5 (2014).
63. Kim, *China, the United Nations, and World Order*, 1979; Morphet, "China as a Permanent Member of the Security Council," 2000; Wuthnow, *Chinese Diplomacy and the UN Security Council*, 2013.
64. David L. Bosco, *Five to Rule Them All: The UN Security Council and the Making of the Modern World* (New York: Oxford University Press, 2009).
65. Beverley Loke, "Unpacking the politics of great power responsibility: Nationalist and Maoist China in international order-building," *European Journal of International Relations* (2015); Alison Adcock Kaufman, "The 'Century of Humiliation,' Then and Now: Chinese Perceptions of the International Order," *Pacific Focus* 25, no. 1 (2010).
66. Hurd, *After Anarchy*, 2007. See also Stewart Patrick, "The New 'New Multilateralism': Minilateral Cooperation, but at What Cost?," *Global Summitry* (2015).
67. Foot, "'Doing some things' in the Xi Jinping era," 2014, 1089.
68. Hurd, *After Anarchy*, 2007.
69. For the importance of regular interaction between diplomats for socialization, see Emanuel Adler and Michael N. Barnett, eds., *Security Communities* (New York: Cambridge University Press, 1998); Jeffrey T. Checkel, "Why Comply? Social Learning and European Identity Change," *International Organization* 55, no. 3 (2003); Johnston, *Social States*, 2008.
70. See Erickson, *Dangerous Trade*, 2015, 28–9.
71. Johnston, "Treating International Institutions as Social Environments," 2001.
72. Wheeler and Dunne, "Good International Citizenship," 1998."
73. Shannon, "Norms Are What States Make of Them," 2000, 294. See also Chayes and Chayes, *The New Sovereignty*, 1995; Johnston, *Social States*, 2008.
74. By "Chinese state," I acknowledge that this is a loose term covering Imperial China, post-1911 China, and the modern People's Republic of China. Alison Adcock Kaufman, "In Pursuit of Equality and Respect: China's Diplomacy and the League of Nations," *Modern China* 40, no. 6 (2014); Pichamon Yeophantong, "Governing the World: China's Evolving Conceptions of Responsibility," *Chinese Journal of International Politics* 6, no. 4 (2013); Loke, "Unpacking the politics of great power responsibility," 2015; Suisheng Zhao, "Chinese Intellectuals' Quest for National Greatness and Nationalistic Writing in the 1990s," *The China Quarterly* 152 (1997).

75. Kaufman, "In Pursuit of Equality and Respect," 2014, 33.
76. For a summary and an opposing view see Michael Beckley, "China's Century? Why America's Edge Will Endure," *International Security* 36, no. 3 (2011/2012).
77. Susan L. Shirk, *China: Fragile Superpower* (Oxford: Oxford University Press, 2007).
78. Alastair Iain Johnston, "Is China a Status Quo Power?," *International Security* 27, no. 4 (2003); Barry Buzan, "China in International Society: Is 'Peaceful Rise' Possible?," *Chinese Journal of International Politics* 3, no. 1 (2010): 29–33; Charles Glaser, "Will China's Rise Lead to War? Why Realism Does Not Mean Pessimism," *Foreign Affairs* 72, no. 1 (2011); Yan Xuetong, "From Keeping a Low Profile to Striving for Achievements," *Chinese Journal of International Politics* 7, no. 2 (2014).
79. Jeffrey W. Legro, "What Will China Want: The Future Intention of a Rising Power," *Perspectives on Politics* 5, no. 3 (2007); William A. Callahan, "Chinese Visions of World Order: Post-hegemonic or a New Hegemony?," *International Studies Review* 10, no. 4 (2008).
80. Avery Goldstein, *Rising to the Challenge: China's Grand Strategy and International Security* (Stanford, CA: Stanford University Press, 2005); "First Things First: The Pressing Danger of Crisis Instability in U.S.-China Relations," *International Security* 37, no. 4 (2013); Martin Jacques, *When China Rules the World: The End of the Western World and the Birth of a New Global Order* (New York: Penguin Press, 2009).
81. Miller, "The Role of Beliefs in Identifying Rising Powers," 2016, 10.
82. Vincent Pouliot and Jean-Philippe Therien, "The politics of inclusion: Changing patterns in the governance of international security," *Review of International Studies* 41, no. 2 (2015).
83. Waltz, *Theory of International Politics*, 1979, 198.
84. Martin Wight, *Power Politics* (Leicester: Leicester University Press, 1978); Alfred Zimmern, *The League of Nations and the Rule of Law, 1918–1935* (London: MacMillan and Co., Ltd., 1939).
85. Hedley Bull, *The Anarchical Society: A Study of Order in World Politics* (London: Macmillan, 1977); R. J. Vincent, "Order in International Politics," in *Order and Violence: Hedley Bull and International Relations*, ed. J. D. B. Miller and R. J. Vincent (Oxford: Clarendon Press, 1990).
86. Bull, *The Anarchical Society: A Study of Order in World Politics*, 1977, 196.
87. Loke, "Unpacking the politics of great power responsibility," 2015, 5.
88. Richardson, "A Responsible Power?," 2011; Yong Deng, "China: The Post-Responsible Power," *The Washington Quarterly* 37, no. 4 (2015).
89. Robert B. Zoellick, "Whither China: From Membership to Responsibility?," remarks to the National Committee on United States-China Relations, September 21, 2005, New York https://2001-2009.state.gov/s/d/former/zoellick/rem/53682.htm (accessed March 3, 2019). Though Zoellick is noted to have popularized the responsible China idea within US government circles, prior examples include William H. Perry, "U.S. Strategy: Engage China, Not Contain It," *Defense Issues* 10, no. 109 (1995); Stanley O. Roth, "U.S.-China Relations on the Eve of the Summit: Address at the World Economic Forum" (Hong Kong 1997).
90. Yeophantong, "Governing the World: China's Evolving Conceptions of Responsibility," 2013.

91. For a concise review of the discourse on power and responsibility and the nexus of "responsible power," see Ren Xiao, "The Moral Dimension of Chinese Foreign Policy," in *New Frontiers in China's Foreign Relations*, ed. Allen Carlson and Ren Xiao (New York: Lexington, 2011).
92. Jiang Zemin, "Jiang: Peace and Stability Ensure a Just, Better World," *Beijing Review*, May 12–18, 1997, 11.
93. Li Jie, "The Transition of the International System: From the Perspective of the Theory of Responsibility," *China International Studies* (2007); Ma Zhengang, "China's Responsibility and the 'China Responsibility' Theory," *China International Studies*; Wang Hongying and James N. Rosenau, "China and Global Governance," *Asian Perspective* 33, no. 3 (2009).
94. Yeophantong, "Governing the World: China's Evolving Conceptions of Responsibility," 2013.
95. Xiao Liping, "China: A responsible great power," *Journal of Contemporary China* 10, no. 26 (2001); Xiao Yingrong, "Zhongguo de daguo zeren yu diquzhuyi zhanlue (China's Major Power Responsibilities and Strategy Towards Regionalism)," *World Economics and Politics* 1 (2003).
96. Ma Xiaotian, "The Major Powers and Asian Security: Cooperation or Conflict?" (Singapore 2009).
97. Richardson, "A Responsible Power?," 2011.
98. Levy, *War in the Modern Great Power System*, 1983, 8.
99. Suzuki, "Journey to the West," 2014.
100. Ibid. See also Joseph Kahn, "China, Shy Giant, Shows Signs of Shedding Its False Modesty," *The New York Times*, December 9, 2006; Peng Peng, ed. *Heping jueqi lun: zhongguo chongsu daguo zhi lu (Peaceful Rising Theory: The Path of China Becoming a Great Power)* (Guangdong: Guangdong renmin chubanshe, 2005).
101. Adil Najam, "International Environmental Negotiation: A Strategy for the South," in *Papers on Intenational Environmental Negotiation*, ed. Lawrence E. Susskind, Willian R. Moomaw, and Adil Najam (Cambridge, MA: Program on Negotiation, Harvard Law School, 1993).
102. Lowell Dittmer, "China and the Developing World," in *China, the Developing World, and the New Global Dynamic*, ed. Lowell Dittmer and George T. Yu (Boulder: Lynne Rienner Publishers, 2010); Miller, *Wronged by Empire*, 2013.
103. Liu, "China and Responsibility to Protect," 2012; Teitt, "The Responsibility to Protect and China's Peacekeeping Policy," 2011.
104. Dittmer, "China and the Developing World," 2010.
105. Liselotte Odgaard, *China and Coexistence: Beijing's National Security Strategy for the Twenty-first century* (Washington D.C.: Woodrow Wilson Center Press, 2012); Injoo Sohn, "After Renaissance: China's Multilateral Offensive in the Developing World," *European Journal of International Relations* 18, no. 1 (2012).
106. Dittmer, "China and the Developing World," 2010; Odgaard, *China and Coexistence*, 2012; Sohn, "After Renaissance," 2012; Miller, *Wronged by Empire*, 2013; Dittmer, "China and the Developing World," 2010.
107. Permanent Mission of the People's Republic of China to the United Nations, "Position Paper of the People's Republic of China on the United Nations Reforms," June 7 2005, http://www.china-un.org/eng/chinaandun/zzhgg/t199101.htm (accessed March 3, 2019).

108. United Nations Security Council, "5619th meeting (S/PV.5619), January 12" (2007).
109. United Nations Security Council, "5933rd meeting, July 11 (S/PV.5933)," 2008.
110. Wuthnow, *Chinese Diplomacy and the UN Security Council*, 2013.
111. Pak K. Lee, Gerald Chan, and Lai Ha Chan, "China's 'Realpolitik' Engagement with Myanmar," *China Security* 5, no. 1 (2009): 110.
112. United Nations Security Council, "Letter dated 4 January from the Permanent Representative of China to the United Nations addressed to the Secretary-General (S/2010/9), January 7" (2010).
113. James M. Goldgeier and Michael McFaul, "A tale of two worlds: core and periphery in the post-cold war era," *International Organization* 46, no. 2 (1992); Richard Rosecrance, ed. *The New Great Power Coalition: Toward a World Concert of Nations* (Lanham, MD: Rowman and Littlefield, 2001); Robert Jervis, "Theories of War in an Era of Leading-Power Peace 'Presidential Address, American Political Science Association, 2001'," *The American Political Science Review* 96, no. 1 (2002); Lucian W. Pye, "China: Not Your Typical Superpower," *Problems of Post-Communism* 43, no. 4 (1996); Samuel S. Kim, "China as a Great Power," *Current History* 96, no. 611 (1997); Gilbert Rozman, "China's Quest for Great Power Identity," *Orbis* 43, no. 3 (1999); Larson and Shevchenko, "Status Seekers," 2010.
114. Joseph Y. S. Cheng and Zhang Wankun, "Patterns and Dynamics of China's International Strategic Behavior," in *Chinese Foreign Policy: Pragmatism and Strategic Behavior*, ed. Suisheng Zhao (Armonk, NY: M.E. Sharpe, 2004).
115. Fiona Hill and Bobo Lo, "Putin's Pivot: Why Russia Is Looking East," *Foreign Affairs*, July 31 2013. See also Michael Auslin, "Washington's Chance to Back Up Rhetoric in Asia," *The Wall Street Journal*, April 10, 2014.
116. Alexandr Nemets, "Russia and China: The Mechanics of an Anti-American Alliance," *The Journal of International Security Affairs* 11 (2006).
117. Alexey D. Muraviev, "Comrades in Arms: The Military-Strategic Aspects of China–Russia Relations," *Journal of Asian Security and International Affairs* 1, no. 2 (2014).
118. Bobo Lo, *Axis of Convenience: Moscow, Beijing, and the New Geopolitics* (Washington, D.C.: Brookings Institution Press, 2008).
119. Andrew C. Kuchins, "Russia and the CIS in 2013: Russia's Pivot to Asia," *Asian Survey* 54, no. 1 (2014).
120. Sir Tony Brenton, "Russia and China: An Axis of Insecurity," *Asian Affairs* 44, no. 2 (2013).
121. Sherman W. Garnett, ed. *Rapprochement or Rivalry?: Russia-China Relations in a Changing Asia* (Washington D. C.: Carnegie Endowment for International Peace, 2000).
122. Robert E. Bedeski and Niklas Swanström, eds., *Eurasia's Ascent in Energy and Geopolitics: Rivalry or Partnership for China, Russia, and Central Asia* (London: Routledge, 2012). For an analysis of the lack of consensus on the Sino-Russian relationship, see Alexander Korolev, "Systemic Balancing and Regional Hedging: China–Russia Relations," *The Chinese Journal of International Politics* 9, no. 4 (2016).
123. T. V. Paul, "Soft Balancing in the Age of U.S. Primacy," *International Security* 30, no. 1 (2005); Lo, *Axis of Convenience*, 2008; Brenton, "Russia and China," 2013; Robert A. Pape, "Soft Balancing against the United States," *International Security* 30, no. 1 (2005); Chaka Ferguson, "The Strategic Use of Soft Balancing: The Normative

Dimensions of the Chinese-Russian 'Strategic Partnership'," *Journal of Strategic Studies* 35, no. 2 (2012).
124. For a discussion of this theme, see Bedeski and Swanström, *Eurasia's Ascent in Energy and Geopolitics*.
125. Michael J. Green, "Should America Fear a New Sino-Russian Alliance?," *Foreign Policy*, August 13 2014; Thomas Wright, "China and Russia vs. America: Great-Power Revisionism Is Back," *The National Interest*, April 27, 2015.
126. Jonas Claes, "Protecting Civilians from Mass Atrocities: Meeting the Challenge of R2P Rejectionism," *Global Responsibility to Protect* 4, no. 1 (2012); Patrick Quinton-Brown, "Mapping Dissent: The Responsibility to Protect and Its State Critics," ibid. 5, no. 3 (2013).
127. Andrew C. Kuchins, "Russian Perspective on China: Strategic Ambivalence," in *The Future of China-Russia Relations*, ed. James Bellacqua (Lexington, KY: University of Kentucky Press, 2010).
128. Stefan Wagstyl, Charles Clover, and Geoff Dyer, "China fails to support Kremlin," *Financial Times*, August 29, 2008.
129. China's position of forgoing direct support of Russia in Moscow's maneuvers in the post-Soviet space is yet to be systematically analyzed. For a discussion of this problem, see Alexander Korolev and Vladimir Portyakov, "Navigating in Troubled Waters: System, Unit, and China's Behavior in the Post-Soviet Space" (paper presented at the International Studies Association's 57th Annual Convention, Atlanta, Georgia, March 16–19, 2016).
130. See The Russian Federation and The People's Republic of China, "Russian-Chinese Joint Declaration on a Multipolar World and the Establishment of a New International Order, adopted in Moscow on 23 April 1997" (1997); Peter Ferdinand, "The positions of Russia and China at the UN Security Council in the light of recent crises" (Brussels 2013).
131. Aglaya Snetkov and Marc Lanteigne, "'The Loud Dissenter and its Cautious Partner' – Russia, China, global governance and humanitarian intervention," *International Relations of the Asia-Pacific* 15, no. 1 (2015); See Fu Ying, "How China Sees Russia," *CRI English*, December 18, 2015.
132. Ferdinand, "The positions of Russia and China at the UN Security Council in the light of recent crises," 2013, 4.
133. Lo, *Axis of Convenience*, 2008.
134. Daniel Brumberg and Steven Heydemann, "Global Authoritarians and the Arab Spring: New Challenges for U.S. Diplomacy" (Washington D.C. 2013).
135. Lo, *Axis of Convenience*, 2008, 3.
136. Elizabeth Wishnick, "Sino-Russian Strategic Partnership: View from China," in *China-Russia Relations in the Early 21st Century*, ed. James Bellacqua (Louisville, KY: University of Kentucky Press, 2010).
137. Additional voting outcomes at the UN Security Council include being absent from a vote and being present, but refusing to vote. China has not pursued either voting outcome since the 1980s.
138. Jennifer M. Dixon, "Rhetorical Adaptation and Resistance to International Norms," *Perspectives on Politics* 15, no. 1 (2017).

139. Henry E. Brady and David Collier, eds., *Rethinking Social Inquiry: Diverse Tools, Shared Standards* (Lanham, MD: Rowman & Littlefield Publishers, 2004); Alexander L. George and Andrew Bennett, *Case Studies and Theory Development in the Social Sciences* (Cambridge, MA: MIT Press, 2005).

140. Andrew Bennett, "Process Tracing: A Bayesian Approach," in *The Oxford Handbook of Political Methodology*, ed. Janet M. Box-Steffensmeier, Henry E. Brady, and David Collier (Oxford: Oxford University Press, 2008).

141. The United States utilized Article 51 of the UN Charter, reporting that the United States had "initiated actions in the exercise of its inherent right of individual and collective self-defense following the armed attacks that were carried out against the United States on 11 September 2001." See United Nations Security Council, "Letter dated 2001/10/07 from the Permanent Representative of the United States of America to the United Nations addressed to the President of the Security Council (S/2001/946)" (2001). For analysis, see Thomas M. Franck, "Terrorism and the Rights of Self-Defense," *American Journal of International Law* 95, no. 4 (2001); *Recourse to Force: State Action Against Threats and Armed Attacks* (Cambridge: Cambridge University Press, 2002).

142. See United Nations Security Council, "Resolution 1368 (2001): Adopted by the Security Council at its 4370th meeting, on 12 September 2001 (S/RES/1368)" (2001).

143. Simon Chesterman, "Humanitarian Intervention and Afghanistan," in *Humanitarian Intervention and International Relations*, ed. Jennifer M. Welsh (Oxford: Oxford University Press, 2004), 164. Moreover, the literature on the Afghanistan case as an example of intervention self-consciously explains *why* the case should be included as the United States invoked Article 51 for justification.

144. Michael Byers, "Terrorism, The use of Force and International Law After 11 September," *International and Comparative Law Quarterly* 51, no. 2 (2008).

145. For example, Louis Charbonneau, "U.S. suggests Russia wants 'regime change' in Georgia," *Reuters*, August 10, 2008.

146. Harry Eckstein, "Case studies in political science," in *Handbook of Political Science*, ed. Fred I. Greenstein and Nelson W. Polsby (Reading, MA: Addison-Wesley, 1975), 118. For more detail on most-likely and least-likely cases see George and Bennett, *Case Studies and Theory Development in the Social Sciences*, 2005, 120–3.

147. George and Bennett, *Case Studies and Theory Development in the Social Sciences*, 2005, 121–2.

148. Evan S. Lieberman, "Nested Analysis as a Mixed-Method Strategy for Comparative Research," *American Political Science Review* 99, no. 3 (2005).

149. David Collier, Henry E. Brady, and Jason Seawright, "Sources of Leverage in Causal Inference: Toward an Alternative View of Methodology," in *Rethinking Social Inquiry: Diverse Tools, Shared Standards*, ed. Henry E. Brady and David Collier (Lanham, MD: Rowman & Littlefield Publishers, 2004); See also Henry E. Brady, David Collier, and Jason Seawright, "Toward a Pluralistic Vision of Methodology," *Political Analysis* 14, no. 3 (2006); David Collier, Henry E. Brady, and Jason Seawright, "Outdated Views of Qualitative Methods: Time to Move On," ibid.18, no. 4 (2010). For a dissenting view: Nathaniel Beck, "Causal Process 'Observation': Oxymoron or (Fine) Old Wine," ibid.

150. George and Bennett, *Case Studies and Theory Development in the Social Sciences*, 2005., Ch.9
151. David Collier, "Understanding Process Tracing," *PS: Political Science and Politics* 44, no. 4 (2011).
152. Stephen Van Evera, *Guide to Methods for Students of Political Science* (Ithaca, NY: Cornell University Press, 1997), 31–2.
153. Andrew Bennett, "Process Tracing and Causal Inference," in *Rethinking Social Inquiry: Diverse Tools, Shared Standards*, ed. Henry E. Brady and David Collier (Lanham, MD: Rowman and Littlefield, 2010), 209.
154. Ted Hopf, "Discourse and Content Analysis: Some Fundamental Incompatibilities," *Qualitative Methods Newsletter* (2004): 32.
155. Clifford Geertz, *The Interpretation of Cultures: Selected Essays* (New York: Basic Books, 1973).
156. Cynthia Hardy, Bill Harley, and Nelson Phillips, "Discourse Analysis and Content Analysis: Two Solitudes?," *Qualitative Methods Newsletter* (2004): 19.
157. Jennifer Milliken, "The Study of Discourse in International Relations: A Critique of Research and Methods," *European Journal of International Relations* 5, no. 2 (1999): 232.
158. Neta C. Crawford, "Understanding Discourse: A Method of Ethical Argument Analysis," Qualitative Methods Newsletter 2, no. 1 (2004); Neta C. Crawford, Argument and Change in World Politics: Ethics, Decolonization, and Humanitarian Intervention (Cambridge: Cambridge University Press, 2002).
159. James Mahoney, *The Legacies of Liberalism: Path Dependence and Political Regimes in Central America* (Baltimore, MD: Johns Hopkins University Press, 2001), 7.
160. Ibid.
161. Ibid.

Chapter 4

1. Understandings of what led to the violence vary. See Gerard Prunier, *Darfur: A 21st Century Genocide* (Ithaca, NY: Cornell University Press, 2008); Julie Flint and Alex de Waal, *Darfur: A New History of a Long War* (London: Zed Books, 2008).
2. U.S. Government Accountability Office, "Darfur Crisis: Death Estimates Demonstrate Severity of the Crisis, But Their Accuracy and Credibility Could Be Enhanced (GAO-07-24)," November 9 2006.
3. Popular analyses often assume that China was the ringleader skeptic blocking interventionism. However, it is important to note that other skeptics played an active role in challenging the need for a UN-led intervention. Ambassador of Pakistan to the United Nations Munir Akram noted in a 2006 interview, at the height of the reporting on China's intransigence regarding Darfur, "China was not nearly as active on Darfur as people think. The proposals [to restrict UN Security Council activity vis-à-vis Darfur] came from us or from Algeria." See Traub, "The World According to China," 2006.
4. Jasper Becker, "China fights UN sanctions on Sudan to safeguard oil," *The Independence*, October 15, 2004; Dan Blumenthal, "Unhelpful China," *The Washington Post*,

December 6, 2004; Peter S. Goodman, "China Invests Heavily In Sudan's Oil Industry: Beijing Supplies Arms Used on Villagers," *The Washington Post*, December 23, 2004.
5. Hereafter called the Olympic Games or the Beijing Games.
6. Howard W. French, "China in Africa: All Trade, With No Political Baggage," *The New York Times*, August 8, 2004.
7. Gary J. Bass, "Human Rights Last?," *Foreign Policy*, February 21, 2011.
8. United Nations Security Council, "Resolution 1653 (2006): Adopted by the Security Council at its 5359th meeting, on 27 January 2006 (S/RES/1653)", 2006. For a critique of the responsibility to protect in the Darfur case, see Alex de Waal, "Darfur and the failure of the responsibility to protect," *International Affairs* 83, no. 6 (2007).
9. Gaafar Karrar Ahmed, "The Chinese Stance on the Darfur Conflict" (Johannesburg 2010), 9.
10. Interview with senior Chinese scholar, Beijing, December 24, 2008; interview with Chinese Ministry of Foreign Affairs official covering Sino-US relations, December 26, 2008, interview with senior Chinese scholar, Shanghai, January 5, 2009.
11. Interview with Chinese Ministry of Foreign Affairs official, Beijing, February 2, 2011.
12. Li Anshan, "China and Africa: Policy and Challenges," *China Security* 3, no. 3 (2007).
13. Rangarirai Mlambo, "Africa: China in Africa - a Mutually Beneficial Partnership?," *All Africa*, November 12, 2010.
14. Darren Taylor, "Darfur Crisis Sparks Louder Calls For 2008 Olympics Boycott," *Voice of America*, November 1, 2009.
15. Wang Ying, "China's April Oil Imports From Sudan Rise Sixfold," *Bloomberg*, May 25, 2007.
16. "The China Deals: Trends and Outlook for Chinese Outbound Investment," *HIS Global Insight*, May 22, 2012, 11.
17. Trade figures are from UNComtrade database through a search for import of oil in recent years to China from Sudan. UNComtrade, "Commodity Trade Statistics Database," http://comtrade.un.org/db/ce/ceSearch.aspx?it=oil&rg=1&r=156&p=148&y=recent&px=HS (accessed March 3, 2019).
18. Statement by Eric Reeves. See "Hearing before the Subcommittee on National Security and Foreign Affairs of the Committee on Oversight and Government Reform, House of Representatives, One Hundred Tenth Congress, First session, June 7", (Washington D.C.: House of Representative, Subcommittee on National Security and Foreign Affairs, Committee on Oversight and Government Reform, 2007). China clarified its position on arms sales and that these activities are guided by a focus on the self-defense requirements of the receiving state; causing no damage to the peace, security and stability of concerned regions; and non-interference in the internal affairs of the receiving country. For more detail, see Office of the Commissioner of the Ministry of Foreign Affairs in the Hong Kong Special Administrative Region, "Assistant Foreign Minister Zhai Jun Holds a Briefing for Chinese and Foreign Journalists on the Darfur Issue of Sudan," April 12 2007, http://www.fmcoprc.gov.hk/eng/zgwjsw/t311008.htm (accessed March 3, 2019). China referenced non-Chinese sources to emphasize China's relatively low rank as a small arms trader and its compliance with international arms trade. For example, see Li Shijia and Bai Jie, "PRC Envoy: Not 'Objective' to Accuse China Alone of Arms Sales to Sudan," *Xinhua*, March 7, 2008.

19. Ian Taylor, "The People's Republic of China," in *The International Politics of Mass Atrocities: The Case of Darfur*, ed. David R. Black and Paul D. Williams (New York: Routledge, 2010); Erica S. Downs, "The Fact and Fiction of Sino-African Energy Relations," *China Security* 3, no. 3 (2007); Li Anshan, "China and Africa: Policy and Challenges," 2007.
20. Chin-Hao Huang, "US-China Relations and Darfur," *Fordham International Law Journal* 31, no. 4 (2007): 829. China is not the sole player in the Sudanese energy market—India, Malaysia, Japan, and the United Arab Emirates are all important also.
21. Ahmed, "The Chinese Stance on the Darfur Conflict," 2010.
22. Monroe E. Price and Daniel Dayan, eds., *Owning the Olympics: Narratives of the New China* (Ann Arbor, MI: University of Michigan Press, 2008); Alexandra Cosima Budabin, "Genocide Olympics; The Campaign to pressure China over the Darfur Conflict," *Central European University Political Science Journal* 4, no. 4 (2009).
23. Rebecca Hamilton, *Fighting for Darfur: Public Action and the Struggle to Stop Genocide* (New York: Palgrave Macmillan, 2011), 152.
24. Monroe E. Price, "On Seizing the Olympic Platform," in *Owning the Olympics: Narratives of the New China*, ed. Monroe E. Price and Daniel Dayan (Ann Arbor, MI: University of Michigan Press, 2008), 104.
25. Though it is interesting to note that Spielberg himself was a target of the Dream for Darfur shaming campaign. R. Scott Greathead, "China and the Spielberg Effect," in *China's Great Leap: The Beijing Games and Olympian Human Rights Challenges*, ed. Minky Worden (New York: Seven Stories Press, 2008).
26. Helene Cooper, "Darfur Collides with Olympics, and China Yields," *The New York Times*, April 13, 2007.
27. Price and Dayan, *Owning the Olympics*; Budabin, "Genocide Olympics; The Campaign to pressure China over the Darfur Conflict," 2009; Hamilton, *Fighting for Darfur*, 2011, 152; Sonja Regler, "Struggle over Darfur – the development of Chinese security politics in interaction with the United States" (PhD dissertation, Freedom University of Berlin, 2011).
28. Thomas J. Christensen, "Shaping the Choices of a Rising China: Recent Lessons for the Obama Administration," *The Washington Quarterly* 32, no. 3 (2009): 94.
29. Thomas J. Christensen, "The Advantages of an Assertive China," *Foreign Policy* 90, no. 2 (2011).
30. United Nations Secretary-General Kofi Annan, ""Risk of Genocide Remains Frighteningly Real", Secretary-General Tells Human Rights Commission as He Launches Action Plan to Prevent Genocide (SG/SM/9245-AFR/893-HR/CN/1077)," (2004). However, in this period, even within the UN Secretariat there were conflicting opinions on what to do regarding Darfur. See James Traub, "Unwilling and Unable: The Failed Response to the Atrocities in Darfur" (Brisbane: Global Centre for the Responsibility to Protect, 2010).
31. Jan Egeland, *A Billion Lives: An Eyewitness Report from the Frontlines of Humanity* (New York: Simon & Schuster, 2008), 90.
32. United Nations Commission on Human Rights, "Report of the United Nations High Commission for Human Rights and Follow up to the World Conference on Human Rights: Situation of human rights in Darfur region of the Sudan (E/CN.4/2005/3), May 7" (2004).

33. Roberta A. Cohen, "Sudanese Killings Must be Stopped," *Newsday*, May 21, 2004; Susan E. Rice and Gayle E. Smith, "The Darfur Catastrophe," *The Washington Post*, May 30, 2004; Joe Siegle, "In Sudan's Darfur: Action, Not Just Aid," *The Christian Science Monitor*, June 30, 2004; Richard N. Haass, "Darkness at Darfur," *South China Morning Post*, November 8, 2004.
34. Gareth Evans, "The world should be ready to intervene in Sudan Darfur," *International Herald Tribune*, May 15, 2004.
35. Reeves, "Regime Change in Sudan," 2004.
36. Siegle, "In Sudan's Darfur," 2004.
37. "Khartoum is accountable for the lives that currently hang in the balance due to the humanitarian crisis, and it is the Government's responsibility to see that everything possible is done to save those lives." See the testimony of Charles Snyder, Acting Assistant Secretary of State for African Affairs. Charles Snyder, "Ethnic Cleansing in Darfur: A New Front Opens in Sudan's Bloody War – Testimony Before the House International Relations Committee," May 6, 2004, Washington D.C.: US Department of State, https://2001-2009.state.gov/p/af/rls/rm/32316.htm (accessed March 3, 2019).
38. Colin L. Powell, "The Crisis in Darfur: Testimony Before the Senate Foreign Relations Committee," September 9 2004, Washington D.C.: US Department of State, https://2001-2009.state.gov/secretary/former/powell/remarks/36042.htm (accessed March 3, 2019).
39. Colin L. Powell, "Remarks to the Press with Sudanese Vice President Ali Osman Taha and Sudan People's Liberation Movement Chairman John Garang," January 8 2005, Washington D.C.: US Department of State, https://2001-2009.state.gov/secretary/former/powell/remarks/2005/40461.htm (accessed March 3, 2019).
40. The ambiguity led to other commentators calling for a ruling on the use of US ground troops. See James Phillips, "Pressure Sudan to Halt Oppression in Darfur," October 4, 2004, Washington D.C.: The Heritage Foundation, http://www.heritage.org/research/reports/2004/10/pressure-sudan-to-halt-oppression-in-darfur (accessed March 3, 2019).
41. See Gethin Chamberlain, "Call for no-fly zone as slaughter goes on," *The Scotsman*, June 15, 2004.
42. Ewen MacAskill, "Blair draws up plans to send troops to Sudan," *The Guardian*, July 22, 2004.
43. "Blair drops troops plan as line softens on Darfur," *The Scotsman*, August 25, 2004.
44. Statement of Ambassador Sir Emyr Jones Parry, United Nations Security Council, "5040th meetingn (S/PV.5040), September 18" (2004). See also "5158th meeting (S/PV.5158), March 31" (2005).
45. See Opheera McDoom, "U.S. accused of attempting 'regime change' in Sudan: UN force slated for Darfur," *National Post*, September 5, 2006. For a summary of the Sudanese perceptions of regime change, see M.W. Daly, *Darfur's Sorrow: A History of Destruction and Genocide* (Cambridge: Cambridge University Press, 2007), 308.
46. For a discussion of this matter, see Ahmed, "The Chinese Stance on the Darfur Conflict," 2010. See also Simon Tisdall, "Omar al-Bashir: conflict in Darfur is my responsibility," *The Guardian*, April 20, 2011; Khalid al-Mubarak, "Regime change in Sudan is not the right way to help Darfur," *The Guardian*, July 23, 2010.
47. Andrew S. Natsios, *Sudan, South Sudan, and Darfur: What Everyone Needs to Know* (Oxford: Oxford University Press, 2012).

48. See Snyder, "Ethnic Cleansing in Darfur".
49. Alex de Waal, "Sudanese Stories: Narratives of Grievance, Distrust, and Fatalism in Recurrent Violence," in *Genocidal Nightmares: Narratives of Insecurity and the Logic of Mass Atrocities*, ed. Abdelwahab El-Affendi (New York: Bloomsbury Academic, 2015), 87.
50. Ibid.
51. Ted Dagne, "Sudan: The Crisis in Darfur and Status of the North-South Peace Agreement" (Washington D.C. 2008).
52. Interview with senior UN official, New York, June 9, 2016.
53. Interview with senior UN Department of Peacekeeping official, New York, June 8, 2016.
54. See two of Munesh Kapila's memos here: Frontline, "Mukesh Kapila's Memos To The United Nations," November 20 2007, PBS, http://www.pbs.org/wgbh/pages/frontline/darfur/etc/memo.html (accessed March 3, 2019).
55. Statement attributable to the Spokesman for the Secretary-General on the Situation in Darfur, Sudan. United Nations Secretary-General Kofi Annan, "Secretary-General Alarmed by Deteriorating Humanitarian Situation in Darfur Region of Sudan (SG/SM/9067-AFR/790)," news release, December 9, 2003, http://www.un.org/press/en/2003/sgsm9067.doc.htm.
56. "Mass rape atrocity in west Sudan," *BBC News*, March 19, 2004.
57. Though US Secretary of State Colin Powell emphasized that "no new action is dictated by this [genocide] determination." Steven R. Weisman, "Powell Declares Genocide in Sudan in Bid to Raise Pressure," *The New York Times*, September 9, 2004.
58. Presidential statements are text on a common position taken by the UN Security Council, with negotiations on the text possibly going all the way to the ambassador-level. Though these statements are non-binding and do not require a formal vote, they are read from the chair of the UN Security Council before being entered on the official record. Therefore, presidential statements require unanimity amongst UN Security Council members and no public airing of differences, and can therefore send a message of unity and credibility in a single message from the international community. Presidential statements, unlike press statements (which are also non-binding), remain on the permanent record. Traub notes that Algeria, China, and Pakistan were successful in weakening UN Security Council language to only urging cooperation in its April 2004 presidential statement, for example. See James Traub, *The Best Intentions: Kofi Annan and the UN in the Era of American World Power* (New York: Farrar, Straus and Giroux, 2006), 220.
59. Ibid., 10.
60. United Nations Security Council, "Resolution 1556 (2004): Adopted by the Security Council at its 5015th meeting, on 30 July 2004 (S/RES/1556)" (2004). UN Security Council Resolution 1556 sponsored the deployment of international monitors and an AU protection force, and urged UN member states to support these efforts.
61. Algeria, Angola, Brazil, Pakistan, and the Philippines were all skeptics.
62. "UN Threatens Sudan with Sanctions on Darfur," *China Daily*, July 31, 2004.
63. John Prendergast and David Sullivan, "Irresolution: The UN Security Council on Darfur" (Washington, D.C. 2008), 6. On March 29, 2005, the UN Security Council passed UN Security Council Resolution 1591, which imposed an arms embargo on all

the different actors in Darfur; banned offensive military flights over Darfur, and also put forth targeted sanctions for those in violation of the Comprehensive Peace Agreement. United Nations Security Council, "Resolution 1591 (2005): Adopted by the Security Council at its 5153rd meeting, on 29 March 2005 (S/RES/1591), March 29" (2005). China, Russia and Algeria all abstained from the Resolution.
64. United Nations Security Council, "Resolution 1564 (2004): Adopted by the Security Council at its 5040th meeting, on 18 September 2004 (S/RES/1564)" (2004).
65. Warren Hoge, "UN Threatens Sanctions Against Sudan," *The New York Times*, September 28, 2004.
66. Taylor, "The People's Republic of China," 2010, 181.
67. Hoge, "UN Threatens Sanctions Against Sudan," 2004.
68. Permanent Mission of the People's Republic of China to the United Nations, "Explanatory Remarks by Chinese Permanent Representative Mr. Wang Guangya at Security Council on Sudan Darfur Draft Resolution," September 18, 2004, http://www.china-un.org/eng/hyyfy/t158034.htm (accessed March 3, 2019).
69. Taylor, "The People's Republic of China," 2010, 181.
70. International Commission of Inquiry on Darfur, "Report of the International Commission of Inquiry on Darfur to the United Nations Secretary-General: Pursuant to Security Council Resolution 1564 of 18 September 2004" (2005).
71. Taylor, "The People's Republic of China," 2010, 181.
72. Paul D. Williams, "The United Kingdom," ibid., ed. David R. Black and Paul D. Williams.
73. United Nations Security Council, "Resolution 1593 (2005): Adopted by the Security Council at its 5158th meeting, on 31 March 2005 (S/RES/1593)", 2005.
74. United Nations Security Council, "Security Council Refers Situation in Darfur, Sudan, To Prosecutor of International Criminal Court (SC/8351)," news release, March 31, 2005, http://www.un.org/press/en/2005/sc8351.doc.htm.
75. On April 8, 2004, Sudan, the Sudanese Liberation Movement, the Sudanese Liberation Army and the Justice and Equality Movement all signed the Humanitarian Ceasefire Agreement.
76. Susan E. Rice, "Why Darfur Can't Be Left to Africa," *The Washington Post*, August 7, 2005.
77. The European Union donated €300 million to AMIS; NATO deployed its strategic airlift capabilities to move African units to Darfur, and the United Nations offered guidance on mission structure, seconding military and police advisers, logisticians and other technical personnel.
78. Williams, "The United Kingdom," 2010, 204. This view was echoed by France also, for example, the remarks of Foreign Affairs Minister Michel Barnier: "I believe that the African Union has both the capability and the willingness to manage the crisis among Africans. We encourage, we support African leaders to take responsibility." "France says Africa should take lead in ending Darfur violence," *Sudan Tribune*, July 28, 2004. Some charged enthusiasm for African solutions to these problems as an excuse to avoid Darfur while simultaneously quieting the critics at home. Roberta A. Cohen and William G. O'Neill, "Last stand in Sudan?," *Bulletin of the Atomic Scientists* 62, no. 2 (2006).

79. United Nations Security Council, "Report of the Secretary-General on the Sudan pursuant to paragraph 15 of Security Council resolution 1564 (2004) and paragraphs 6, 13 and 16 of Security Council resolution 1556 (2004) (S/2004/881), November 2" (2004); "Resolution 1590 (2005): Adopted by the Security Council at its 5151st meeting, on 24 March 2005 (S/RES/1590)" (2005).
80. AU Commission Chairman Alpha Oumar Konaré noted in January 2006 that the mandate was "not clearly understood by commanders at all levels." African Union Peace and Security Council, "Report of the Chairperson of the Commission on the Situation in Darfur (The Sudan) [PSC/PR/2(XLV)], January 12" (Addis Ababa: African Union, 2006).
81. Sudan only wanted peacekeepers to use force in self-defense.
82. AMIS troops were supplied from Gambia, Kenya, Nigeria, Rwanda, Senegal, and South Africa; police from Ghana, and observers from Egypt and Libya. AMIS had only 7,000 personnel deployed at the end of 2005, a fraction of the mandated force size. For an analysis on the low deployment levels, see Cristina G. Badescu and Linnea Bergholm, "The African Union," in *The International Politics of Mass Atrocities: The Case of Darfur*, ed. David R. Black and Paul D. Williams (New York: Routledge, 2010).
83. UNMIS was tasked with supporting implementing the Comprehensive Peace Agreement, focusing on humanitarian assistance, promotion of human rights, protection, and support for AMIS.
84. "Decision on AU presidency must take into account Darfurians protection," *Sudan Tribune*, January 21, 2006.
85. Badescu and Bergholm, "The African Union," 2010, 106.
86. United Nations Security Council, "Resolution 1679 (2006): Adopted by the Security Council at its 5439th meeting, on 16 May 2006 (S/RES/1679)" (2006).
87. United Nations Security Council, "Resolution 1706 (2006): Adopted by the Security Council at its 5519th meeting, on 31 August 2006 (S/RES/1706)", 2006.
88. Argentina, Denmark, Greece, and Slovakia were also co-sponsors. See "Security Council Expands Mandate of UN Mission in Sudan to Include Darfur, Adopting Resolution 1706 by Vote of 12 in Favour, with 3 Abstaining (SC/8821)," (2006).
89. P. Parameswaran, "US threatens Sudan after UN resistance," *Independent Media*, August 19, 2006.
90. Ahmed, "The Chinese Stance on the Darfur Conflict," 2010, 8.
91. Ibid.
92. McDoom, "U.S. accused of attempting 'regime change' in Sudan," 2006.
93. "Wen issues warning on Darfur," *Sino Daily*, September 13, 2006.
94. Reuters, "China pushes Sudan to let UN troops into Darfur," *Sudan Tribune*, September 14, 2006.
95. Evan S. Medeiros, "China's International Behavior: Activism, Opportunism, and Diversification" (Santa Monica, CA 2009), 184.
96. Badescu and Bergholm, "The African Union," 2010, 107.
97. Robert F. Worth, "Sudan says it will accept UN-African peace force in Darfur," October 17, 2006; Andrew S. Natsios, "The Escalating Crisis in Darfur: Are There Prospects for Peace?," Hearing before the Committee on Foreign Affairs House of Representatives One Hundred Tenth Congress First Session, February 8, 2007.

98. Interview with senior UN Department of Peacekeeping official, New York, February 11, 2011.
99. Interview with Ministry of Foreign Affairs officials, Beijing, March 11, 2011.
100. Andrew S. Natsios, "Darfur: A 'Plan B' To Stop Genocide?," Hearing before the Committee on Foreign Relations United States Senate One Hundred Tenth Congress First Session, April 11, 2007.
101. Interview with former senior US official via phone, August 17, 2011.
102. Interview with senior African and Middle East Affairs scholar, Beijing, March 10, 2011.
103. Interview with Ministry of Foreign Affairs officials, Beijing, March 11, 2011.
104. Xinhua, "Hu Puts Forward Four-point Principle on Solving Darfur Issue," *People.com.cn*, February 6, 2007.
105. Bloomberg, "China told Sudan to adopt UN's Darfur plan – envoy," *Sudan Tribune*, February 6, 2007.
106. Ahmed, "The Chinese Stance on the Darfur Conflict," 2010, 10.
107. Bass, "Human Rights Last?," 2011, 6.
108. For example, Centre for Chinese Studies of the Stellenbosch University, "Partners in Competition? The EU, Africa and China: A summary of a conference hosted by the EU commission, Brussels, 28th June 2007" (2007); Centre for Foreign Policy Analysis and Chinese Academy of Social Sciences, "Symposium on China-Sudan Relations," July 26, 2007, http://www.cffpa.com/events.php (accessed March 3, 2019).
109. Ahmed, "The Chinese Stance on the Darfur Conflict," 2010, 9.
110. Edith M. Lederer, "Major Powers Want to Encourage Sudan to Accept UN-African Union Force in Darfur," *Associated Press*, March 8, 2007.
111. J. Stephen Morrison, "United States House of Representatives the Subcommittee on Domestic and International Monetary Policy, Trade and Technology," H.R. 180, Darfur Accountability and Divestment Act of 2007, 110th Congress (2007).
112. Interview with former senior US official via telephone, August 17, 2011.
113. Interview with former senior US official via telephone, August 17, 2011.
114. However, this is not to say that Dream for Darfur was the only group that was putting pressure on China about its role in the Darfur crisis. Indeed, as early as 2004, there were already calls on the United States to pressure China to address the Darfur crisis: "Were China to use even a small part of its leverage to call Sudan to account, it would go a long way towards saving lives in Sudan." Quote from Roberta A. Cohen, "Calling on China," *The Washington Post*, August 5, 2004. By 2007, there were groups within the United States, Europe and Australia that were turning their attention to the Chinese role in the Darfur crisis, those these efforts were still largely piecemeal. As Hamilton notes in her detailed analysis of the American activist community, the seeds of a campaign linking China to Darfur already existed: university divestment campaigns often targeted Chinese firms, and there was a smattering of coverage of celebrity George Clooney's visit to Beijing at the end of 2006 to meet with Chinese officials about Darfur. Hamilton, *Fighting for Darfur*, 2011, 137. See Maggie Michael, "George Clooney campaigns in China and Egypt to raise awareness over Darfur conflict," *Associated Press*, December 13, 2006.
115. Interview with Dream for Darfur member via telephone, March 28, 2011.

116. Ronan Farrow and Mia Farrow, "The 'Genocide Olympics'," *The Wall Street Journal*, March 28, 2007.
117. The International Olympic Committee, the United States Olympic Committee, corporate sponsors, the artistic director of the opening ceremonies, athletes, US and UN policymakers all became targets of the campaign, for example.
118. Nicholas Kristof, "China's Genocide Olympics," *The New York Times*, January 24, 2008.
119. Kevin Cullen, "Genocide Games," *The Boston Globe*, March 25, 2007.
120. For an example regarding Beijing's response to critics regarding Tibet see Embassy of the People's Republic of China in United Arab Emirates, "Foreign Ministry Spokesperson Jiang Yu's Remarks on Discussion of Tibet in an Informal Meeting of the EU Foreign Ministers' Council," April 2 2008, http://ae.china-embassy.org/eng/wjbfyrth/t420322.htm (accessed March 3, 2019). For an example of China's response to critics regarding its environmental standards, see Ministry of Foreign Affairs of the People's Republic of China, "Foreign Ministry Spokesperson Qin Gang's Regular Press Conference on March 11, 2008," March 11 2008, http://www.fmprc.gov.cn/eng/xwfw/s2510/t414217.htm (accessed March 3, 2019).
121. Farrow and Farrow, "The 'Genocide Olympics'," 2007. It is also worth noting that having rejected the Farrows' op-ed article, *The New York Times* ended up writing an article about the op-ed—signaling an immediate interest in the story, as did other newspapers that referenced the Farrows' writing.
122. Ibid. Also, from the Dream for Darfur website: "China holds unrivaled influence with the genocidal regime in Sudan. As Beijing prepares to host the 2008 Olympics, join us in urging China to use its leverage to persuade the Sudanese government to allow into Darfur the full protection force outlined by UN Resolution 1769." Dream for Darfur, "Dream for Darfur," 2007, www.dreamfordarfur.org (accessed March 3, 2019).
123. Dream for Darfur final report.
124. Interview with Dream for Darfur senior member via telephone, April 6, 2011. Spielberg was not only a global celebrity linked to the 2008 Olympics, but because he directed the Holocaust film *Schindler's List*, founded the Shoah Foundation Institute at the University of Southern California, and through his philanthropy has given millions to anti-genocide causes—his linkage to the 2008 Olympics was particularly key for the Dream for Darfur coalition.
125. For full text of the Spielberg April 2, 2007 letter to President Hu, see All Things Considered, "Darfur Activists Push Spielberg to Pressure China," *NPR*, July 24, 2007.
126. Russell Goldman, "Spielberg Mulls Quitting Olympics to Pressure Chinese on Darfur," *ABC News*, July 26, 2007.
127. At each torch relay, Dream for Darfur representatives, Darfurian refugees, and genocide survivors lit a torch in commemoration of those who had been killed in genocides.
128. After the Dream for Darfur event permit was revoked by Cambodian authorities, the group still visited Phnom Penh, with international news articles noting that Mia Farrow had faced 100 armed police in riot gear and that the US Ambassador to Cambodia was forbidden to take part in any events. See "Stage set for showdown over Darfur ceremony in Cambodia," *Associated Press*, January 18, 2008; "Observer:

Dream deferred," *Financial Times*, January 18, 2008; "Mia Farrow arrives in Cambodia for banned Darfur protest," *AFP*, January 18, 2008; Ek Madra, "Mia Farrow vows to defy Cambodian Darfur rally ban," *Reuters*, January 19, 2008; Ker Munthit, "Mia Farrow faces off with Cambodian police, blocked from genocide ceremony," *Associated Press*, January 20, 2008.

129. In June 2007, Dream for Darfur met with the New York-based Chinese Deputy Consul General Kuang Weilin and soon after, the Chinese Ambassador to the United States Zhou Wenzhong. Consul Kuang brought "printouts from the [Dream for Darfur] website, each page marked up in hand-written Chinese documenting what Kuang believed to be errors in the campaign's publications," while emphasizing that the "Olympics had nothing to do with Darfur." Hamilton, *Fighting for Darfur*, 2011, 141.

130. Alexa Olesen, "China: Don't link Olympics, Darfur," *Associated Press*, March 29, 2007. For a summary of Chinese officials' public dismissals of Dream for Darfur, see Hamilton, *Fighting for Darfur*, 2011.

131. China continued to publicize the list of heads of states who were attending: Li Zhen, "World Leaders to Attend Beijing Olympic Opening Ceremony," *Epoch Times*, August 7, 2008. Haroon Siddique, "UN chief to miss Olympic opening ceremony," *The Guardian*, April 11, 2008; "Emotion kicks off China's Olympics," *CNN*, August 9, 2008; Jim Yardley, "China's Leaders Try to Impress and Reassure World," *The New York Times*, August 9, 2008; "Head of UN environment agency to attend opening of Olympic Games," August 4, 2008; Ministry of Foreign Affairs of the People's Republic of China, "Hu Jintao Meets with Foreign Leaders to the Opening Ceremony of the Beijing Olympic Games," August 8 2008, http://www.fmprc.gov.cn/mfa_eng/wjb_663304/zzjg_663340/yzs_663350/gjlb_663354/2706_663416/2708_663420/t483123.shtml (accessed March 3, 2019).

132. From the letter: "President Hu, the upcoming 2008 Beijing Olympic Games are going to be an important event for the image of the PRC. Millions of people will visit China, and over a billion people will tune into their radios and televisions to witness the expression of international peace and solidarity, through friendly competition in sports. It would be a disaster for China if the games were to be marred by protests, from concerned individuals and groups, whom will undoubtedly link your government to the continued atrocities in Darfur, if there is no significant improvement in the conditions. Already there are calls to boycott what is increasingly being described as the 2008 'Genocide Olympics.' As Sudan's single largest trading partner, and the main beneficiary of their significant crude oil exports and construction contracts, we urge you to protect your country's image from being irredeemably tarnished, through association with a genocidal regime, for the purposes of economic gains." See Ranking Member Elliot L. Engel (Democrats) of the United States House of Representatives Committee on Foreign Affairs, "Lantos, House Colleagues Send Strong Message to Chinese President, Demand Action on Darfur," May 9, 2007, https://democrats-foreignaffairs.house.gov/news/press-releases/lantos-house-colleagues-send-strong-message-chinese-president-demand-action (accessed March 3, 2019).

133. Yardley, "China's Leaders Try to Impress and Reassure World," 2008; Associated Press, "French presidential candidate calls for Beijing boycott," *ESPN*, March 22, 2007.

For analysis, see Jean-Pierre Cabestan, "China and European Security and Economic Interests: A French Perspective" in *US-China-EU Relations: Managing the New World Order*, ed. Robert S. Ross, Øystein Tunsjø, and Zhang Tuosheng (London: Routledge, 2010).

134. Siddique, "UN chief to miss Olympic opening ceremony," 2008. Instead Ban dispatched his head of the UN environmental agency to participate: UN News Centre, "Head of UN environment agency to attend opening of Olympic Games," 2008.
135. For example, see the commentary of J. Stephen Morrison, Senior Fellow for Africa Studies, Center for Strategic and International Studies, in Darren Taylor, "Pressure Builds On China To Break Darfur Deadlock," *Voice of America*, November 1, 2009.
136. International Crisis Group asserts that "plans were already underway for Assistant Foreign Minister Zhai Jun to visit Sudan when the [Dream for Darfur] campaign...began" "China's Thirst For Oil, Asia Report," (Seoul/Brussels 2008), 27.
137. Consulate General of the People's Republic of China in San Francisco, "Assistant Foreign Minister Zhai Jun Holds a Briefing for Chinese and Foreign Journalists on the Darfur Issue of Sudan," April 12, 2007, http://www.chinaconsulatesf.org/eng/xw/t311008.htm (accessed March 3, 2019).
138. Christensen, "Shaping the Choices of a Rising China," 2009, 94.
139. On June 25, 2007 Vice Foreign Minister Zhang Yesui attended the Paris-based Ministerial Meeting on Darfur, where eighteen countries, who were key donors to Sudan, including China and the Group of Eight industrialized nations, reaffirmed their support for the AU-UN peacekeeping force. However, by the end of the meeting, there was still no firm agreement as to which other countries would contribute soldiers, nor any sign that China had tempered its opposition to imposing sanctions on Sudan. Craig S. Smith, "Little Visible Progress on Darfur at International Conference," *The New York Times*, June 26, 2007. Concurrently, anticipating Bashir's continuing intransigence, the UN Secretariat dispatched the 2007 High Ranking Operational and Technical Advisory Team Mission aimed to supplement the well-established process for generating peacekeeping contributions by introducing an enhanced quality control element to assess whether the potential troop contributing country had requisite capabilities to meet UNAMID challenges. See Marina E. Henke, "Great powers and UN force generation: a case study of UNAMID," *International Peacekeeping* 23, no. 3 (2016).
140. United Nations Security Council, "Resolution 1769 (2007): Adopted by the Security Council at its 5727th meeting, on 31 July 2007 (S/RES/1769)" (2007).
141. Daniel Schearf, "China Takes Credit for Sudan Allowing UN Peacekeepers," *Voice of America*, July 5, 2007.
142. "China Urges Support to Deployment of Peacekeeping Troops in Darfur," *Xinhua*, June 16, 2007.
143. The Altantic Council of the United States Global Leadership Series, "Remarks by Jan Eliasson, UN Special Envoy to Darfur," May 16 2007, www.acus.org/files/070516-Jan%20Eliasson%20-%20transcript.pdf (accessed March 3, 2019).
144. Guy Dinmore and Mark Turner, "US defends China's role in Darfur," *Financial Times*, April 12, 2007.
145. Mure Dickie, "UK minister praises China's role in Darfur," ibid., May 18.

146. Edward Cody, "In China, a Display of Resolve on Darfur," *The Washington Post*, September 16, 2007. Xinhua, "China donates money to help resolve Darfur conflict," *China.org.cn*, March 29, 2008. Yan Liang, "China says linking Olympics with Darfur issue against Olympic Spirit " *Xinhua*, February 14, 2008.
147. Interview with Chinese Ministry of Foreign Affairs official, Beijing, December 24, 2008.
148. Greathead, "China and the Spielberg Effect," 2008, 214.
149. Protest sites included Canberra, London, Paris, Lisbon, Cairo, Accra, Banjul, Lagos, Dakar, and in multiple United States locations, to include Chicago, Houston, Los Angeles, New York, San Francisco, and Washington, DC.
150. China requested to shorten the torch relay stops in San Francisco because of protesters. See "China wants San Francisco Olympic torch's route shortened," *The Times of India*, March 27, 2008. For more detail see, Nora Boustany, "Symbolic Torch Relay Aims to Shine Light on China, Darfur and Death," *The Washington Post*, August 15, 2007. Regarding the Hong Kong-based protests, see Keith Bradsher, "Torch Nears, Posing Test Of Autonomy In Hong Kong," *The New York Times*, April 29, 2008. Min Lee, "Mia Farrow's visit to Hong Kong for critical speech will test Chinese city's freedoms," *Associated Press*, May 1, 2008; Guy Newey, "Farrow arrives in Hong Kong ahead of Olympic torch relay," *AFP*, May 1, 2008; Albert Wong and Joyce Man, "Mia Farrow told to behave for torch relay," *South China Morning Post*, May 2, 2008.
151. *Arria* meetings are essentially open meetings, where concerned states and other actors can exchange their views at the UN Security Council.
152. dream4darfur, "Gengen Genocide," July 7, 2008, YouTube, https://www.youtube.com/watch?v=RhlIM5aa6jc (accessed March 3, 2019).
153. Greathead, "China and the Spielberg Effect," 2008, 215.
154. For example, see Paul Eckert, "Nobel laureates press China over Darfur," *Reuters*, February 12, 2008; Frederick Balfour, "China: Spielberg's Olympics-Sized Snub," *Business Week*, February 13, 2008; James Macintyre, "Spielberg subs Beijing Olympics over Darfur crisis," *The Independent*, February 13, 2008; "Spielberg's Stance on the Olympics Draws Praise," *USA Today*, February 14, 2008.
155. "China Regrets Spielberg Action," *BBC News*, February 14, 2008; Christopher Bodeen and Associated Press, "China says Sudan activists have ulterior motives," *USA Today*, February 14, 2008.
156. Xinhua, "China makes 'unremitting efforts' to resolve crisis in Darfur," *China Daily*, February 16, 2008.
157. Ahmed, "The Chinese Stance on the Darfur Conflict," 2010. note 42. See also "China issues a warning to Sudan over Darfur crisis," *Sudan Tribune*, January 30, 2008.
158. Ahmed, "The Chinese Stance on the Darfur Conflict," 2010, 10. See also Zhang Chun, "Possibility of Cooperation: China and EU in Darfur," *International Review* 52 (2008): 76.
159. Also see chapter 2 for China's comparatively anodyne references to the Rwandan genocide and Srebrenica massacre as "issues" and "matters."
160. Permanent Mission of the People's Republic of China to the United Nations, "China's SR on Darfur Holds a Briefing in Beijing," March 7, 2008, http://www.china-un.org/eng/chinaandun/securitycouncil/regionalhotspots/africa/darfur/t468259.htm (accessed March 3, 2019).

161. Hamilton, *Fighting for Darfur*, 2011, 151.
162. Ibid.
163. United Nations Security Council, "Security Council Urges Sudan's Government to Fully Cooperate with International Ciminal Court 'To Put an End to Impunity for the Crimes Committed in Darfur' (SC/9359)," news release, June 16, 2008, http://www.un.org/press/en/2008/sc9359.doc.htm.
164. Geoff Dyer, "Beijing expresses 'grave concern' over ICC charges," *Financial Times*, July 16, 2008.
165. In the intervening eight months before three judges issued their verdict on the indictment, Sudan, the African Union and the Arab League lobbied the UN Security Council to postpone the case by a year, arguing that sole focus on AU and UN efforts to end the Darfur conflict was needed. Russia and China supported these efforts, but the P3 were unwilling to accept any delays. For analysis, see Hamilton, *Fighting for Darfur*, 2011, 151.
166. Peter Walker and Julian Borger, "China may veto attempt to arrest Sudanese president on genocide charges," *The Guardian*, July 15, 2008.
167. "Sudanese media hail expected China 'veto' to block Bashir arrest warrant," *Sudan Tribune*, September 2, 2008.
168. Ibid.
169. Consulate General of the People's Republic of China in San Francisco, "Special Envoy of the Chinese Government and Assistant Foreign Minister Zhai Jun Visits Sudan Successfully," September 4 2008, http://www.chinaconsulatesf.org/eng/xw/t511195.htm (accessed March 3, 2019).
170. David Charter, "ICC issues war crimes arrest warrant for President al-Bashir of Sudan," *The Times*, March 4, 2009.
171. Ahmed, "The Chinese Stance on the Darfur Conflict," 2010, 9.
172. Sudan Disinvestment UK and Waging Peace, "Matching words with action: how to pressure Sudan to stop its genocidal campaign in Darfur" (2007), 12.
173. Wasil Ali, "China uses economic leverage to pressure Sudan on Darfur – US," *Sudan Tribune*, March 6, 2007.
174. Price and Daniel Dayan, *Owning the Olympics*; Budabin, "Genocide Olympics; The Campaign to pressure China over the Darfur Conflict," 2009; Hamilton, *Fighting for Darfur*, 2011, 152; Regler, "Struggle over Darfur," 2011.
175. In April 2008, HR 5668 was tabled, "Communist Chinese Olympic Accountability Act," proposing to prohibit funding of federal government officials to attend the opening ceremonies in part because of the Chinese ability to influence the Darfur crisis.
176. Sophie Richardson, "Challenges for a "Responsible Power"," in *China's Great Leap: The Beijing Games and Olympian Human Rights Challenges* ed. Minky Worden (New York: Seven Stories Press, 2008), 291.
177. Ranking Member Elliot L. Engel (D) of the United States House of Representatives Committee on Foreign Affairs, "Lantos, House Colleagues Send Strong Message to Chinese President, Demand Action on Darfur."
178. Owen Slot, "Olympians urged to make a stand against China's betrayal of Darfur," *The Times*, August 7, 2007. Tegla Lourope, Kenyan marathon athlete and holder of several long-distance world records, also testified at a US Congress hearing examining a possible boycott of the 2008 Olympics.

179. For example, *The New York Times* columnist Nicholas Kristof.
180. Frank Ching, "China sees tough times as the Games draw near," *New Straits Times*, May 17, 2001; Danna Harman, "Activists press China with 'Genocide Olympics' label," *The Christian Science Monitor*, June 26, 2007.
181. Christensen, "Shaping the Choices of a Rising China," 2009; "The Advantages of an Assertive China," 2011.
182. Reuters, "China, US urge diplomatic solution in Darfur," *Sudan Tribune*, April 10, 2007.
183. Interview with senior Chinese scholar, Beijing, December 24, 2008. Similar points were emphasized in interview with senior Chinese foreign policy researchers, December 29, 2008, interview with Chinese Ministry of Foreign Affairs official covering Sino-US relations, December 26, 2008.
184. Interview with official from the Office of the Military Adviser, UN Department of Peacekeeping, New York, August 29, 2010.
185. "Darfur: Threats to Chinese Engineers will not Delay Remaining Peacekeepers (Wikileaks Cable: 07BEIJING7270_a)," November 29, 2007, https://www.wikileaks.org/plusd/cables/07BEIJING7270_a.html (accessed March 3, 2019).
186. Thomas J. Volgy et al., "Status Considerations in International Politics and the Rise of Regional Powers," in *Status in World Politics*, ed. T. V. Paul, Deborah Welch Larson, and William C. Wohlforth (New York: Cambridge University Press, 2014). See also the use of status attribution in the context of leadership travel in Scott L. Kastner and Phillip C. Saunders, "Is China a Status Quo or Revisionist State? Leadership Travel as an Empirical Indicator of Foreign Policy Priorities," *International Studies Quarterly* 56, no. 1 (2012).
187. Larson, Paul, and Wohlforth, "Status and World Order," 2014, 10.
188. Interview with Chinese Ministry of Foreign Affairs official, Beijing, February 2, 2011.
189. Cabestan, "China and European Security and Economic Interests," 2010.
190. For example, President Sarkozy threatened to boycott the opening ceremonies due to China's response to anti-Chinese protests in Tibet.
191. Ringmar, *Identity, Interest and Action: A Cultural Explanation of Sweden's Intervention in Thirty Years War*, 1996; Johnston, *Social States*, 2008.

Chapter 5

1. I use the spelling Colonel Muammar Gaddafi. Other sources transliterate the spelling differently.
2. United Nations Human Rights Office of the High Commissioner, "Pillay calls for international inquiry into Libyan violence and justice for victims," February 22, 2011; UN Office of the Special Adviser on the Prevention of Genocide, "UN Secretary-General Special Adviser on the Prevention of Genocide, Francis Deng, and Special Adviser on the Responsibility to Protect, Edward Luck, on the Situation in Libya, February 22" (2011).
3. Tim Dunne and Jess Gifkins, "Libya and the state of intervention," *Australian Journal of International Affairs* 65, no. 5 (2011).

4. UN News Centre, "Ban strongly condemns Qadhafi's actions against protesters, calls for punishment," February 23, 2011.
5. United Nations General Assembly, "Resolution adopted by the General Assembly on 1 March 2011: Suspension of the rights of membership of the Libyan Arab Jamahiriya in the Human Rights Council (A/RES/65/265), March 3" (2011).
6. The UN Special Envoy and the AU High-Level Committee had failed to dissuade Gaddafi from using violence and to permit humanitarian aid convoys into beleaguered towns.
7. Libyan ambassadors to Bangladesh, India, Poland, the Arab League, the United Kingdom, the United States, and the United Nations were amongst the first to defect.
8. Edward C. Luck, "The Responsibility to Protect: Growing Pains or Early Promise?," *Ethics & International Affairs* 24, no. 4 (2010); Gareth Evans, "Ending Mass Atrocity Crimes: The Responsibility to Protect Balance Sheet After Libya " July 31 2011, http://www.gevans.org/speeches/speech443.html (accessed March 3, 2019); Aidan Hehir and Robert W. Murray, *Libya, the Responsibility to Protect and the Future of Humanitarian Intervention* (Houndmills, Basingstoke: Palgrave Macmillan, 2013).
9. Associated Press, "China urges Libya to restore social stability," 2011.
10. Lloyd Axworthy, "In Libya, We Move toward a More Humane World," *Globe and Mail*, August 23, 2011.
11. Bellamy and Williams, "The New Politics of Protection: Côte d'Ivoire, Libya and the Responsibility to Protect," 2011; Paul D. Williams, "The Road to Humanitarian War in Libya," *Global Responsibility to Protect* 3, no. 2 (2011): 249.
12. Yun Sun, "China's Acquiescence on UNSCR 1973: No Big Deal," *PacNet 20*, March 31, 2011.
13. Bellamy and Williams, "The New Politics of Protection: Côte d'Ivoire, Libya and the Responsibility to Protect," 2011, 840; Garwood-Gowers, "Libya and the international community's 'responsibility to protect'," 2011; Thakur, "Libya: The First Stand," 2013; Christensen, *The China Challenge*, 2015.
14. For a discussion of the fallout of Libyan regime change see Tom Keating, "The UN Security Council on Libya: Legitimation or Dissimulation?," in *Libya, the Responsibility to Protect and the Future of Humanitarian Intervention*, ed. Aidan Hehir and Robert W. Murray (Basingstoke: Palgrave Macmillan, 2013).
15. Leslie Hook and James Dyer, "Chinese oil interests attacked in Libya," *Financial Times*, February 24, 2011.
16. David Pierson, "Libyan strife exposes China's risks in global quest for oil," *Los Angeles Times*, March 9, 2011.
17. Associated Press, "China urges Libya to restore social stability," 2011.
18. Tan Jie, "PLA Air Force transporters evacuate compatriots from Libya," *PLA Daily*, March 2, 2011; Yao Zibao, "Chinese warship escorts ship evacuating Chinese nationals," ibid., March 3. "Overwhelming majority of Chinese in Libya evacuated: FM," *Xinhua*, March 1, 2011.
19. Michael Wines, "Secret Bid to Arm Qaddafi Sheds Light on Tensions in China Govern," *The New York Times*, September 11, 2011.
20. Steven Sotloff, "China's Libya Problem," *The Diplomat*, 2012.

21. Graeme Smith, "Rift between China, Libya deepens over weapons dealings with Gadhafi," *The Global and Mail*, September 5, 2011.
22. The Chinese Ministry of Foreign Affairs confirmed initial discussions with the National Transition Council in June 2011. "China confirms contact with Libyan opposition leader," *Xinhua*, June 3, 2011.
23. Rebecca Adler-Nissen and Vincent Pouliot, "Power in Practice: Negotiating the International Intervention in Libya," *European Journal of International Relations* (2014): 889.
24. Brian Spegele, "China Takes New Tack in Libya Vote," *The Wall Street Journal*, March 20, 2011.
25. By March 2011, the Arab Spring protests had spread through Tunisia, Algeria, Bahrain, Iran, Egypt, Jordan, Lebanon, Yemen and Syria. For a timeline, see Garry Blight, Sheila Pulham, and Paul Torpey, "Arab Spring: an interactive timeline of Middle East protests," *The Guardian*, January 5, 2012.
26. Andrew Higgins and Keith B. Richburg, "China mulls impact of Mideast uprisings," *The Washington Post*, January 31, 2011.
27. Wuthnow, *Chinese Diplomacy and the UN Security Council*, 2013, 53.
28. Ibid., 156, note 82.
29. US Secretary of State Hillary Clinton stated: "The United Nations Security Council resolution was very broad but explicit about what was legally authorized by the international community...There is nothing in there about getting rid of anybody." See Hillary Clinton, "Transcript: Sec. of State Hillary Clinton Talks With Diane Sawyer About the Situation in Libya," in *ABC News*, ed. Diane Sawyer (2011).
30. Foreign & Commonwealth Office and William Hague, "Foreign Secretary describes situation in Libya as 'deplorable and unacceptable'," February 21 2011, GOV.UK, https://www.gov.uk/government/news/foreign-secretary-describes-situation-in-libya-as-deplorable-and-unacceptable (accessed March 3, 2019). "UK calls for UN action on Libya," February 22, 2011, GOV.UK, https://www.gov.uk/government/news/uk-calls-for-un-action-on-libya (accessed March 1, 2019). Foreign & Commonwealth Office, "Government doing all it can to assist Britons in Libya," February 25 2011, GOV.UK, https://www.gov.uk/government/news/government-doing-all-it-can-to-assist-britons-in-libya (accessed March 1, 2019).
31. Regarding the United States, see Barack Obama, "Remarks by the President on Libya," February 23, 2011, Washington D.C.: Office of the Press Secretary of the White House, https://obamawhitehouse.archives.gov/the-press-office/2011/02/23/remarks-president-libya (accessed March 4, 2019). See Hillary Clinton, "Holding the Qadhafi Government Accountable," February 26, 2011, Washington, D.C.: US Department of State, https://2009-2017.state.gov/secretary/20092013clinton/rm/2011/02/157187.htm (accessed March 4, 2019). Regarding France, see Michele Alliot-Marie, "Minister of State and Minister of Foreign and European Affairs Michele Alliot-Marie's Statement on the situation in Libya," (Paris: France Diplomatie, 2011). See Permanent Representative of France to the United Nations, "Statement by the Permanent Representative of France to the UN to the Human Rights Council Special Session on Libya," February 25, 2011, http://basedoc.diplomatie.gouv.fr/exl-doc/EPI00048723.pdf (accessed March 4, 2019).

32. Foreign & Commonwealth Office, "Prime Minister's statement on Libya," February 28, 2011, GOV.UK, https://www.gov.uk/government/news/prime-minister-s-statement-on-libya (accessed March 1, 2019).
33. Foreign & Commonwealth Office, "Foreign Secretary: British diplomatic team in Benghazi has 'now left Libya'," March 6 2011, GOV.UK, https://www.gov.uk/government/news/foreign-secretary-british-diplomatic-team-in-benghazi-has-now-left-libya (accessed March 1, 2019). "Foreign Secretary calls for an 'immediate stop to the use of armed force against the Libyan people'," March 6 2011, GOV.UK, https://www.gov.uk/government/news/foreign-secretary-calls-for-an-immediate-stop-to-the-use-of-armed-force-against-the-libyan-people (accessed March 1, 2019). Ministry of Defence, "Prime Minister discusses Libya with US President," March 9 2011, GOV.UK, https://www.gov.uk/government/news/prime-minister-discusses-libya-with-us-president (accessed March 1, 2019).
34. France Diplomatie, "Entretien du Premier Ministre "François Fillon, avec "RTL": Extraits (Interview of Prime Minister François Fillion with RTL)," (Paris: France Diplomatie, 2011).
35. France Diplomatie, "Entretien du Ministre d'État, Ministre des Affaires Étrangères et Européennes, Alain Juppé, avec TF1: Extraits (Interview of Foreign Affairs Minister Alain Juppé with TF1)," (2011).
36. France Diplomatie, "Situation en Libye et en Méditerranée Conseil Européen Extraordinaire Conférence de Presse du Président de la République, Nicolas Sarkozy (Press Conference by President Nicolas Sarkozy on the situation in Libya and in the Mediterranean following the Special Session of the European Council)" (2011).
37. Clinton, "Holding the Qadhafi Government Accountable". See also "Briefing on Plane Before Departure for Geneva, Switzerland," February 27, 2011, Washington D.C.: US Department of State, http://www.state.gov/secretary/20092013clinton/rm/2011/02/157200.htm (accessed March 1, 2019).
38. For example, see Barack Obama, David Cameron, and Nicolas Sarkozy, "Libya's Pathway to Peace," *The New York Times*, April 14, 2011.
39. Hillary Rodham Clinton, "Opening Remarks Before the Senate Foreign Relations Committee," March 2 2011, Washington D.C.: US Department of State, http://www.state.gov/secretary/20092013clinton/rm/2011/03/157556.htm (accessed March 1, 2019).
40. Ministry of Defence and Cameron, "Prime Minister discusses Libya with US President".
41. International Crisis Group, "A Ceasefire and Negotiations the Right Way to Resolve the Libya Crisis" (Brussels 2011). The Council on Foreign Relations, op-ed by Elliott Abrams, "Gaddafi's End," *National Review*, February 21, 2011. See Shadi Hamid, "It's Time To Intervene," February 23 2011, The Brookings Institution, https://www.brookings.edu/opinions/its-time-to-intervene/(accessed March 1, 2019). Daniel L. Byman, "Libya's Al Qaeda Problem," February 25 2011, The Brookings Institution, https://www.brookings.edu/opinions/libyas-al-qaeda-problem/ (accessed March 1, 2019).
42. Khalilzad, "A regional strategy for democracy in the Middle East," 2011.
43. Abrams, "Gaddafi's End," 2011. Also see Elliott Abrams and Bernard Gwertzman, "Clashes In Libya – What Is Next?," February 22 2011, Council on Foreign Relations,

http://www.cfr.org/libya/clashes-libya—next/p24185 (accessed March 1, 2019); Ibrahim Fraihat, "The March for Freedom in Libya," February 22 2011, The Brookings Institution, http://www.brookings.edu/blogs/up-front/posts/2011/02/22-libya-sharqieh (accessed March 1, 2019); "Entretien avec Kader A. Abderrahim: Libye: Le système est en train de craquer et de prendre l'eau de toutes parts (Interview with Kader Abderrahim, Research Fellow, 'Libya: The system is cracked and water is coming in from everywhere')," February 24 2011, L'IRIS, http://www.iris-france.org/43137-entretien-avec-kader-a-abderrahim-libye-le-systeme-est-en-train-de-craquer-et-de-prendre-leau-de-toutes-parts/(accessed March 1, 2019); Pascal Boniface, "Vers un massacre en Libye (Towards a Massacre in Libya)," February 23 2011, L'IRIS, http://www.iris-france.org/44201-vers-un-massacre-en-libye/(accessed March 1, 2019).
44. Hamid, "It's Time To Intervene".
45. Byman, "Libya's Al Qaeda Problem".
46. Alison Pargeter, "Libya: An Uncertain Future," February 23, 2011, RUSI, https://rusi.org/commentary/libya-uncertain-future (accessed March 1, 2019).
47. International Crisis Group, "Immediate International Steps Needed to Stop Atrocities in Libya," February 22 2011, https://www.crisisgroup.org/middle-east-north-africa/north-africa/libya/immediate-international-steps-needed-stop-atrocities-libya (accessed March 1, 2019).
48. Sally McNamara, "The Crisis in Libya Exposes a Litany of Failed EU Policies," March 3, 2011, The Heritage Foundation, http://www.heritage.org/research/reports/2011/03/the-crisis-in-libya-exposes-a-litany-of-failed-eu-policies (accessed March 1, 2019).
49. Alman Shaikh, "Libya's Test of the New International Order," February 26, 2011, The Brookings Institution, https://www.brookings.edu/opinions/libyas-test-of-the-new-international-order/ (accessed March 1, 2019); Michael E. O'Hanlon and Paul Wolfowitz, "United States Must Take Lead on Libya," February 26, 2011, The Brookings Institution, http://www.brookings.edu/research/opinions/2011/02/26-libya-ohanlon (accessed March 1, 2019).
50. Michael E. O'Hanlon, "Libya Needs a Multilateral Response," February 25, 2011, The Brookings Institution, http://www.brookings.edu/research/opinions/2011/02/25-libya-ohanlon (accessed March 1, 2019).
51. Anthony Cordesman and Scott Simon, "A Look At Gadhafi "s Fragmented Military," *NPR*, March 5, 2011.
52. Richard M. Dalton, "We must stand ready to intervene in Libya," *The Telegraph*, February 27, 2011.
53. Kenneth M. Pollack, "The Real Military Options in Libya," March 9, 2011, Washington D.C.: The Brookings Institute, https://www.brookings.edu/opinions/the-real-military-options-in-libya/ (accessed March 3, 2019).
54. Roee Nahmias, "Libya suspended from Arab League sessions," *Ynet News*, February 22, 2011.
55. The Peace and Security Council of the African Union, "Communique of the 261st Meeting, PSC/PR/COMM(CCLXI), February 23" (Addis Ababa: The Peace and Security Council of the African Union, 2011).
56. Emily O'Brien and Andrew Sinclair, "The Libyan War: A Diplomatic History" (New York 2011), 6.

57. United Nations Security Council, "Security Council Press Statement on Libya," (2011).
58. Gaddafi labeled dissenters "stray dogs," and also "germs, rats and scumbags." See John-Paul Ford Rojas, "Muammar Gaddafi in his own words," *The Telegraph*, October 20, 2011; John Hudson, "Qaddafi's Most Bizarre Moments in a Bizarre Speech," *The Wire*, February 22, 2011.
59. Interview with senior Chinese foreign policy researcher, Beijing, December 20, 2011. Interview with official from the PRC Mission to the UN, New York, June 11, 2013.
60. Interview with official from the PRC Mission to the UN, New York, June 11, 2013. Similar remarks were made during an interview with senior Chinese foreign policy researcher, Beijing, December 20, 2011 and an interview with an official from the Embassy of France, Beijing, December 22, 2011.
61. Interview with official from the PRC Mission to the UN, New York, June 11, 2013.
62. United Nations Security Council, "Resolution 1970 (2011): Adopted by the Security Council at its 6491st meeting, on 26 February 2011 (S/RES/1970), February 26," 2011.
63. Interview with official from the UK Mission to the UN, New York, June 11, 2013.
64. United Nations Security Council, "6491st meeting (S/PV.6491), February 26" (2011).
65. With the notable exception of ASEAN outreach, China was diplomatically isolated in the aftermath of the Tiananmen Square Incident.
66. Interview with official from the PRC Mission to the UN, New York, June 11, 2013.
67. The Defence Committee of the House of Commons, "Operations in Libya" (London 2012), 18; Foreign & Commonwealth Office and Cameron, "Prime Minister's statement on Libya". France Diplomatie, "Entretien du Premier Ministre François Fillon, avec 'RTL': Extraits (Interview of Prime Minister François Fillion with RTL)."
68. "Cameron: UK working on 'no-fly zone' plan for Libya," *BBC News*, February 28, 2011. For a discussion of the decision-making towards advocating a no-fly zone position, see, The Defence Committee of the House of Commons, The Defence Committee of the House of Commons, "Operations in Libya," 2012, 84.
69. Christopher S. Chivvis, *Toppling Qaddafi: Libya and the Limits of Liberal Intervention* (Cambridge: Cambridge University Press, 2013), 34. David Cameron and Nicolas Sarkozy, "Letter from the PM and President Sarkozy to President Van Rompuy," March 10, 2011, Prime Minister's Office, GOV.UK, https://www.gov.uk/government/news/letter-from-the-pm-and-sarkozy-to-president-van-rompuy (accessed March 1, 2019); Patrick Wintour and Nicholas Watt, "Cameron's War: Why PM Felt Gaddafi Had to Be Stopped," *The Guardian*, October 2, 2011.
70. The Transnational Interim National Council, "Founding Statement of the Interim Transnational National Council (TNC)," March 5, 2011.
71. Samir Salama, "GCC backs no-fly zone to protect civilians in Libya," *GulfNews*, March 9, 2011. See The League of Arab States, "The outcome of the Council of the League of Arab States meeting at the Ministerial level in its extraordinary session on the implications of the current events in Libya and the Arab position (Res. No.: 7630), March 12" (Cairo: Council of the League of Arab States, 2011); Richard Leiby and Muhammad Mansour, "Arab League asks U.N. for no-fly zone over Libya," *The Washington Post*, March 12, 2011.
72. AFP, "OIC chief backs no-fly zone over Libya," *Emirates 24/7 News*, March 8, 2011.

73. Bruce D. Jones, "Libya and the Responsibilities of Power," *Survival* 53, no. 3 (2011): 53; Monitor's Editorial Board, "Libya sanctions: China's new role at the UN," *The Christian Science Monitor*, February 28, 2011.
74. Embassy of the People's Republic of China in the United States, "Foreign Ministry Spokesperson Jiang Yu's Regular Press Conference on March 3, 2011," March 5, 2011, http://www.china-embassy.org/eng/fyrth/t804119.htm (accessed March 3, 2019).
75. Missy Ryan, "No-fly zone for Libya would require attack: Gates," *Reuters*, March 2, 2011; Patrick Donahue and Robert Hutton, "G-8 Split on Libya No-Fly Zone With Russia, Germany Opposed," *Bloomberg*, March 16, 2011.
76. Donahue and Hutton, "G-8 Split on Libya No-Fly Zone With Russia," 2011.
77. Clinton, "Opening Remarks Before the Senate Foreign Relations Committee."
78. David E. Sanger and Thom Shanker, "Gates Warns of Risks of a No-Flight Zone," *The New York Times*, March 2, 2011.
79. Richard N. Haass, "The U.S. Should Keep Out of Libya," *The Wall Street Journal*, March 8, 2011; Anne-Marie Slaughter, "Fiddling While Libya Burns," *The New York Times*, March 13, 2011. Frank Gardner, "Libya: Who is propping up Gaddafi?," *BBC News*, March 2, 2011.
80. Madelene Lindström and Kristina Zetterlund, "Setting the Stage for the Military Intervention in Libya: Decisions Made and their Implications for EU and NATO" (Stockholm 2012), 45.
81. The Peace and Security Council of the African Union, "Communique of the 265th meeting of the Peace and Security Council, PSC/PR/Comm.2(CCLXV), March 10" (Addis Ababa: The Peace and Security Council of the African Union, 2011).
82. The Ad Hoc High Level Committee was composed of the presidents of Mauritania, the Republic of Congo, Mali, South Africa and Uganda—therefore representing all five of Africa's subregions. See Phillip Apuuli Kasaija, "The African Union (AU), the Libya Crisis and the notion of 'African solutions to African problems'," *Journal of Contemporary African Studies* 31, no. 1 (2013).
83. Alex de Waal, "'My Fears, Alas, Were Not Unfounded': Africa's Responses to the Libya Conflict," in *Libya, the Responsibility to Protect and the Future of Humanitarian Intervention*, ed. Aidan Hehir and Robert W. Murray (Basingstoke: Palgrave Macmillan, 2013), 66.
84. For contrasting assessments of the African Union positions on intervention into Libya, see ibid.; Theresa Reinold, "Africa's Emerging Regional Security Culture and the Intervention in Libya," ibid.
85. Aidan Hehir, "The Permanence of Inconsistency: Libya, the Security Council, and the Responsibility to Protect," *International Security* 38, no. 1 (2013).
86. "Arab states seek Libya no-fly zone," *Al Jazerra*, March 13, 2011.
87. "Arab League backs Libya no-fly zone," *BBC News*, March 12, 2011.
88. See AFP, "Possible Diplomatic Opening in Libyan Crisis," *Ma'an News Agency*, July 12, 2011.
89. For a discussion on Sudan's split from the AU regarding the Libya crisis, see de Waal, "My Fears, Alas, Were Not Unfounded," 2013, 73–8.
90. Jo Becker and Scott Shane, "Hillary Clinton, 'Smart Power' and a Dictator's Fall," *The New York Times*, February 27, 2016.

91. For analysis of changes in US policy, see Mark Landler and Dan Bilefsky, "Specter of Rebel Rout Helps Shift U.S. Policy on Libya," *The New York Times*, March 16, 2011; Jo Becker and Scott Shane, "Hillary Clinton, 'Smart Power' and a Dictator's Fall," *The New York* Times, February 27, 2016; Michael Hastings, "Inside Obama's War Room," *Rolling Stone*, October 13, 2011; Colum Lynch, "Amb. Rice: Leading from behind? That's "whacked."," *Foreign Policy*, October 31, 2011.
92. David E. Sanger, *Confront and Conceal: Obama's Secret Wars and Surprising Use of American Power* (New York: Crown Publishers, 2012), 345.
93. Josh Rogin, "How Obama turned on a dime toward war," *Foreign Policy*, March 18, 2011.
94. For coordination amongst the P3 and NATO, see The Defence Committee of the House of Commons, "Operations in Libya," 2012, 19.
95. Office of the Press Secretary of the White House, "Readout of the President's Call with Prime Minister Cameron of the United Kingdom," news release, March 8, 2011.
96. Quoting US officials in Landler and Bilefsky, "Specter of Rebel Rout Helps Shift U.S. Policy on Libya," 2011.
97. "Libya to stop fighting Sun to let protesters surrender," *Al Arabiya News*, March 17, 2011.
98. Lynch, "Amb. Rice: Leading from behind?," 2011.
99. Ibid.
100. Becker and Shane, "Hillary Clinton, 'Smart Power' and a Dictator's Fall," 2016.
101. Laura Trevelyan, "Libya: Coalition divided on arming rebels," *BBC News*, March 29, 2011.
102. Lynch, "Amb. Rice: Leading from behind?," 2011.
103. Jones, "Libya and the Responsibilities of Power," 2011, 54.
104. Becker and Shane, "Hillary Clinton, 'Smart Power' and a Dictator's Fall," 2016.
105. Souhail Karam and Tom Heneghan, "UPDATE 1-Gaddafi tells Benghazi his army is coming tonight," *Reuters*, March 17, 2011.
106. United Nations Security Council, "Resolution 1973 (2011): Adopted by the Security Council at its 6498th meeting, on 17 March 2011 (S/RES/1973)", 2011.
107. Ibid.
108. "'China has serious difficulty with part of the resolution,' envoy says," *Xinhua*, March 18, 2011.
109. Interview with official from the PRC Mission to the UN, New York, June 11, 2013. Interview with official from the PRC Mission to the UN, New York, June 6, 2016. Interview with official from the PRC Embassy to Washington, Washington DC, June 2, 2016.
110. Interview with official from the PRC Mission to the UN, New York, June 11, 2013.
111. Apparently, Qaddafi's March 17, 2011 speech had "helped win over the Russians" bringing them closer to the P3 stance for intervention. Becker and Shane, "Hillary Clinton, 'Smart Power' and a Dictator's Fall," 2016.
112. Interview with official from the PRC Mission to the UN, New York, June 11, 2013.
113. Interview with official from the PRC Mission to the UN, New York, June 11, 2013.
114. Interview with official from the PRC Mission to the UN, New York, June 11, 2013. Interview with official from the PRC Mission to the UN, New York, June 6, 2016.

Interview with official from the PRC Embassy to Washington, Washington DC, June 2, 2016.
115. These states included Belgium, Canada, Denmark, France, Italy, Norway, Spain, Qatar, the United Kingdom, and the United States. NATO eventually came to lead Operation *Unified Protector* to enforce Resolution 1970 and 1973, though airstrikes remained under national authority despite the integrated NATO command structures.
116. "China expresses regret for military strike against Libya," *Xinhua*, March 20, 2011.
117. "Chinese paper condemns Libya air strikes," *China Daily*, March 21, 2011.
118. United Nations Security Council, "6528th meeting (S/PV.6528), May 4" (2011).
119. Ibid.
120. Edward Cody, "Arab League condemns broad bombing campaign in Libya," *The Washington Post*, March 21, 2011.
121. Li Qinggong, "Politics behind attacks on Libya," 2011.
122. For example, see Liu, "China and Responsibility to Protect," 2012.
123. Embassy of the People's Republic of China in the United States, "Foreign Ministry Spokesperson Jiang Yu's Regular Press Conference on March 22, 2011," March 23 2011, http://www.china-embassy.org/eng/fyrth/t809578.htm (accessed March 3, 2019).
124. For a detailed analysis of how NATO came to take on the execution of the Resolution 1973 mandate via Operation *Unified Protector*, see Hylke Dijkstra, *International Organizations and Military Affairs* (New York: Routledge, 2016), 157–77.
125. Micah Zenko, "The Big Lie About the Libyan War," *Foreign Policy*, March 22, 2016.
126. Barack Obama, "Remarks by the President in Address to the Nation on Libya," March 28, 2011, Washington D.C.: Office of the Press Secretary of the White House, https://www.whitehouse.gov/the-press-office/2011/03/28/remarks-president-address-nation-libya (accessed March 1, 2019).
127. NATO would cease military operations under the following conditions: once all attacks and threats of attacks against civilians had ended; the Gaddafi regime had withdrawn all of its military forces from civilian-populated areas that they had already forcibly entered, the Gaddafi regime permitted complete and immediate humanitarian access to all people within Libya that require assistance.
128. Obama, Cameron, and Sarkozy, "Libya's Pathway to Peace," 2011.
129. Ministry of Foreign Affairs of the People's Republic of China, "Foreign Ministry Spokesperson Jiang Yu's Remarks on the Death of Gaddafi's Son and Others in NATO's Air Strikes".
130. Much of the criticisms revolved around whether NATO and other national forces were favoring rebels, and the interpretation of what efforts were permitted to support civilian protection "notwithstanding" the arms embargo of paragraph 9 in Resolution 1970. For a summary, see Micah Zenko, "Libya No-Fly-Zone Is Anything But," *The Atlantic*, July 19, 2011.
131. See, Ministry of Foreign Affairs of the People's Republic of China, "Vice Foreign Minister Zhai Jun Attends the UN Security Council Meeting on Libya," June 16 2011, http://www.china-un.ch/eng/xwdt/t831724.htm (accessed March 3, 2019); Zenko, "Libya No-Fly-Zone Is Anything But," 2011.
132. Jim Garamone, "Panetta Discusses First Week as Defense Secretary," *U.S. Department of Defense*, July 9, 2011.

133. "China confirms contact with Libyan NTC," *China Daily*, June 7, 2011.
134. Tania Branigan, "Libya's NTC gains Chinese recognition," *The Guardian*, September 12, 2011.
135. Interview with official from the PRC Mission to the UN, New York, June 11, 2013. Interview with senior Chinese foreign policy researcher, Beijing, December 20, 2011. Interview with senior Sino-Middle Eastern foreign relations scholar, Hong Kong, March 29, 2016.
136. Interview with official from the PRC Mission to the UN, New York, June 11, 2013. Interview with Chinese official from the PRC Mission to the UN, New York, June 6, 2016.
137. Schweller and Pu, "After Unipolarity," 2011; Thomas Risse and Kathryn Sikkink, "The socialization of international human rights norms into domestic practices: introduction," in *The Power of Human Rights: International Norms and Domestic Change*, ed. Thomas Risse, Stephen C. Ropp, and Kathryn Sikkink (Cambridge: Cambridge University Press, 1999). Fung, "Rhetorical Adaptation and International Order-Making," 2019.

Chapter 6

1. The most recent vetoes by China on December 5, 2016 regarding a ceasefire in Aleppo, Syria, and February 28, 2017 regarding sanctions over chemical weapons use are dealt with in Chapter 7 of this book.
2. Interview with official from the PRC Mission to the UN, New York, June 6, 2016.
3. On February 5, 2012, China invited a delegation from the Syrian National Committee for Democratic Change to meet with Vice Foreign Minister on African and West Asia Zhai Jun. In February 2012, China's Foreign Ministry sent senior delegations to Syria, Egypt, Iran, Israel, Jordan, Palestine, Qatar, and Saudi Arabia.
4. Liu, "Cong guojifa shijiao kan Xifang dui Xuliya de ganshe (On the Western Interference in Syria in View of the International Law)," 2012.
5. Interview with official from the PRC Mission to the UN, New York, June 11, 2013.
6. Statement by Ambassador Li Baodong, see United Nations Security Council, "6531st meeting (S/PV.6531), May 10" (2011).
7. Daniel Kaufmann, "Russia and China Leadership Props Up Syria's Assad," February 6 2012, The Brookings Institution, https://www.brookings.edu/blog/up-front/2012/02/06/russia-and-china-leadership-props-up-syrias-assad/ (accessed March 1, 2019).
8. Bonnie S. Glaser, "How Will China React to a Military Strike on Syria?," September 5, 2013, Centre for Strategic and International Studies, https://www.csis.org/analysis/how-will-china-react-military-strike-syria (accessed March 1, 2019).
9. Russia has cast multiple sole vetoes regarding the Syria crisis since 2016.
10. Such as the release of political prisoners; allowing popular debate etc.
11. "Syria faces more sanctions as EU steps in," *RT*, April 30, 2011; Mark Hosenball and Matt Spetalnick, "U.S. slaps new sanctions on Syria over crackdown," *Reuters*, April 29, 2011.
12. France Diplomatie, "Entretien du Président de la République, Nicolas Sarkozy, avec L'hebdomadaire 'L'Express' (Interview of President Nicolas Sarkozy with L'Express)," 2011.

13. Office of the Press Secretary of the White House, "Remarks by the President on the Middle East and North Africa," news release, May 19, 2011, https://www.whitehouse.gov/the-press-office/2011/05/19/remarks-president-middle-east-and-north-africa (accessed March 1, 2019).
14. Foreign Secretary William Hague called for political reforms or else Assad should "step aside." See Foreign & Commonwealth Office, "Syria: Foreign Secretary comments on situation in Hama," July 5 2011, GOV.UK, https://www.gov.uk/government/news/syria-foreign-secretary-comments-on-situation-in-hama (accessed March 1, 2019).
15. See Macon Phillips, "President Obama: 'The future of Syria must be determined by its people, but President Bashar al-Assad is standing in their way'," August 18 2011, Washington D.C,: The White House, https://www.whitehouse.gov/blog/2011/08/18/president-obama-future-syria-must-be-determined-its-people-president-bashar-al-assad (accessed March 3, 2019); Scott Wilson and Joby Warrick, "Assad must go, Obama says," *The Washington Post*, August 18, 2011. See also "Our three countries believe that President Assad, who is resorting to brutal military force against his own people and who is responsible for the situation, has lost all legitimacy and can no longer claim to lead the country. We call on him to face the reality of the complete rejection of his regime by the Syrian people and to step aside in the best interests of Syria and the unity of its people." France in the United Kingdom, "Syria – Joint statement by Nicolas Sarkozy, President of the Republic, Angela Merkel, Chancellor of Germany, and David Cameron, Prime Minister of the United Kingdom of Great Britain and Northern Ireland," August 18. 2011, http://www.ambafrance-uk.org/French-British-and-German-leaders (accessed March 1, 2019).
16. Foreign & Commonwealth Office, "Foreign Secretary statement to Parliament on the crisis in Syria," June 11 2012, GOV.UK, https://www.gov.uk/government/news/foreign-secretary-statement-to-parliament-on-the-crisis-in-syria (accessed March 1, 2019).
17. France Diplomatie, "Entretien du ministre des Affaires étrangères, M. Laurent Fabius, avec 'France Inter': Extraits, Paris, 29 août 2012 (Foreign Affairs Minister Laurent Fabius' Interview with France Inter)," 2012.
18. France Diplomatie, "Syrie - Entretien du ministre des Affaires étrangères, M. Laurent Fabius, avec 'BFMTV', 'Europe 1', 'RFI', 'France Info', 'RTL' et 'FranceONU TV': New York, 30 août 2012 (Foreign Affairs Minister Laurent Fabius' Interview with BFMTV, Europe 1, RFI, France Info, RTL and FranceONU TV)," 2012.
19. John Kerry, "Remarks With French Foreign Minister Laurent Fabius and U.K. Foreign Secretary William Hague," September 16, 2013, U.S. Department of State, http://www.state.gov/secretary/remarks/2013/09/214266.htm
20. Robert M. Danin, "Calling for Regime Change in Syria," August 18, 2011, Council on Foreign Relations, http://www.cfr.org/syria/calling-regime-change-syria/p25677
21. Martin S. Indyk, "Obama's Belated Syria Hard Line," August 18, 2011, The Brookings Institution, https://www.brookings.edu/opinions/obamas-belated-syria-hard-line/ (accessed March 3, 2019).
22. Jane Kinninmont, "Syria: UK Must Focus on Diplomacy," September 1 2013, Chatham House, https://www.chathamhouse.org/media/comment/view/194051 (accessed March 1, 2019).

23. Samuel Charap and Jeremy Shapiro, "How the US Can Move Russia on Syria," *Al-Monitor*, July 22, 2013.
24. Elliott Abrams, "America Watches As Syria Crumbles," *National Review*, July 18, 2012. See also Michael Doran and Salman Shaikh, "Getting Serious in Syria," July 29 2011, The Brookings Institution, https://www.brookings.edu/articles/getting-serious-in-syria/ (accessed March 1, 2019); Tamara Cofman Wittes et al., "Syria, the U.S., and Arming the Rebels: Assad's Use of Chemical Weapons and Obama's Red Line," June 14, 2013, http://www.brookings.edu/blogs/up-front/posts/2013/06/14-syria-us-arming-rebels-assad-use-chemical-weapons-and-obamas-red-line (accessed March 1, 2019); Michael Doran, "5 truths about Syria," September 3, 2013, Politico, http://www.politico.com/story/2013/09/opinion-michael-doran-5-truth-syria-096178 (accessed March 1, 2019); David Roberts and Michael Stephens, "Bloody days ahead as the Assad regime is decapitated," July 19, 2012, RUSI, https://rusi.org/commentary/bloody-days-ahead-assad-regime-decapitated (accessed March 1, 2019).
25. Tamara Cofman Wittes, "Options for U.S. Policy in Syria," April 19, 2012, The Brookings Institution, http://www.brookings.edu/research/testimony/2012/04/19-syria-wittes (accessed March 1, 2019); Martin S. Indyk, "Next Steps in Syria," August 1, 2012, The Brookings Institution, http://www.brookings.edu/research/testimony/2012/08/01-syria-indyk (accessed March 1, 2019); Jon B. Alterman, "Bad Options and Hard Choices in Syria Policy" (2013).
26. Alterman, "Bad Options and Hard Choices in Syria Policy," 2013.
27. Céline Lussato, "SYRIE. La Russie a-t-elle vraiment la clé de la sortie de secours? (Syria. Does Russia really hold the emergency exit door key?)," *Le Nouvel Obs*, June 1, 2012; Corentin Brustlein et al., "Syrie: l'option militaire reste-t-elle ouverte? (Syria: Does the military option stay open?)" (Paris/Brussels 2013); Henry Boyd, "Henry Boyd: Shades of Hama and Grozny in Homs and Idlib," March 12, 2012, IISS Voices, http://www.iiss.org/en/iiss%20voices/blogsections/2012-6d11/march-2012-bf81/shades-of-hama-and-grozny-8b68 (accessed March 1, 2019).
28. Emile Hokayem, "Syria and its Neighbours," *Survival* 54, no. 2 (2012); Andrew Parasiliti, "It's Time to Engage Iran, Russia on Syria," *Al-Monitor*, July 25, 2012.
29. Michael Doran, "Pursue Regime Change in Syria," January 23, 2014, The Brookings Institution, http://www.brookings.edu/research/papers/2014/01/regime-change-syria-doran (accessed March 1, 2019).
30. Michael Doran and Salman Shaikh, "The Road Beyond Damascus," January 17, 2013, The Brookings Institution, http://www.brookings.edu/research/papers/2013/01/the-road-beyond-damascus (accessed March 1, 2019).
31. Doran, "Pursue Regime Change in Syria."
32. Byman, "Finish Him."
33. For example, emphasizing support for domestic groups to unseat Assad: "Syria's Mutating Conflict" (Damascus/Brussels 2012). See also Andrew Quinn, "With focus on opposition, U.S. races against time on Syria," *Reuters*, December 6, 2012; Jon B. Alterman, "A Tale of Two Crises" (2013). Emphasizing legal tools to unseat Assad: Louise Arbour, "For justice and civilians, don't rule out regime change," *The Globe and Mail*, June 26, 2012; Clark A. Murdock, "What Has Syria Taught Us about

the Right Time to Use Force?," in *2014 Global Forecast: U.S. Security Policy at a Crossroads*, ed. Craig Cohen, Kathleen Hicks, and Josiane Gabel (Washington, DC; Lanham, MD: Center for Strategic and International Studies; and Rowman & Littlefield Publishers, 2013); Steven A. Cook, "It's Time to Think Seriously About Intervening in Syria," *The Atlantic*, January 17, 2012; Robert M. Danin, "Danin: How to help Syria without intervening militarily," *CNN*, January 22, 2012; Meghan L. O'Sullivan, "Sanctions Alone Won't Topple Syria's Assad: Meghan L. O'Sullivan," *Bloomberg*, February 22, 2012. Emphasizing military tools to unseat Assad: Michael Stephens, "Arguments for Military Intervention in Syria," February 8, 2012, RUSI, https://rusi.org/commentary/arguments-military-intervention-syria (accessed March 1, 2019); Michael E. O'Hanlon, "Four Military Options in Syria," August 30, 2011, The Brookings Institution, http://www.brookings.edu/research/opinions/2011/08/30-syria-ohanlon (accessed March 1, 2019). Ed Husain, "We Intervene in Syria at Our Peril," *The Atlantic*, February 1, 2012; James Phillips, "Preparing for a Post-Assad Syria," January 19, 2012, Washington D.C.: The Heritage Foundation, http://www.heritage.org/research/reports/2012/01/us-policy-for-a-post-assad-syria (accessed March 1, 2019).

34. Salman Shaikh, "In Syria, Assad Must Exit the Stage," April 27, 2011, The Brookings Institution, http://www.brookings.edu/research/opinions/2011/04/27-syria-shaikh (accessed March 1, 2019); "As Syria crisis worsens, UN Security Council must act," *The Christian Science Monitor*, December 15, 2011; Jeremy Shapiro and Samuel Charap, "Winning the Peace by Failing in Geneva: How to Work the Syria Negotiations," *Foreign Affairs*, January 9, 2014.

35. Shashank Joshi, "Hama Rules: the resilience of the Syrian Army," August 1 2011, RUSI, https://rusi.org/commentary/hama-rules-resilience-syrian-army (accessed March 1, 2019; Claire Spencer, "The Syrian Conundrum," February 7, 2012, Chatham House, https://www.chathamhouse.org/media/comment/view/182009 (accessed March 1, 2019).

36. Zhong Sheng, "Regime change should not be determined by external forces," *People's Daily*, July 18, 2012.

37. Zhong Sheng, "Be wary of attempt to resolve Syrian crisis outside UN framework," *People's Daily*, August 17, 2012.

38. United Nations Security Council, "6524th meeting (S/PV.6524), April 27" (2011).

39. Neil MacFarquhar, "Push in U.N. for Criticism of Syria Is Rejected," *The New York Times*, April 27, 2011.

40. United Nations Human Rights Council, "Resolution adopted by the Human Rights Council: The current human rights situation in the Syrian Arab Republic in the context of recent events (A/HRC/RES/S-16/1), May 4" (2011).

41. United Nations Human Rights Council, "Human Rights Council passes resolution on Syrian Arab Republic in Special Session," April 29, 2011, http://reliefweb.int/report/syrian-arab-republic/human-rights-council-passes-resolution-syrian-arab-republic-special (accessed March 1, 2019).

42. Thalif Deen, "Russia, China Shield Syria from Possible U.N. Sanctions," *Inter Press Service*, June 9, 2011.

43. What's In Blue, "Draft Resolution on Syria," June 8, 2011, http://www.whatsinblue.org/2011/06/presidential-statement-on-syria.php (accessed March 1, 2019).

44. United Nations Security Council, "Statement by the President of the Security Council (S/PRST/2011/16), August 3" (2011).
45. United Nations Security Council, "Security Council, in Statement, Condemns Syrian Authorities for "Widespread Violations of Human Rights, Use of Force against Civilians' (SC/10352)," (2011).
46. AFP, "Russia, China boycott Syria sanction talks at UN Security Council," *news.com.au*, August 26, 2011.
47. "UN slams Syria's 'loss of humanity'," *ABC News*, August 3, 2011.
48. "Gulf states recall envoys as Syria further isolated," *The Telegraph*, August 8, 2011.
49. "GCC calls for end to violence in Syria," *The National*, August 7, 2011.
50. Global Centre for the Responsibility to Protect, "Timeline of International Response to the Situation in Syria," 2015, http://www.globalr2p.org/media/files/timeline-of-international-response-to-syria-26.pdf (accessed March 1, 2019).
51. MacFarquhar, "Push in U.N. for Criticism of Syria Is Rejected," 2011.
52. United Nations Security Council, "Security Council Fails to Adopt Draft Resolution Condemning Syria's Crackdown on Anti-Government Protestors, Owing to Veto by Russian Federation, China (SC/10403)," (2011).
53. United Nations Security Council, "6627th meeting (S/PV.6627), October 4" (2011).
54. Ibid.
55. Interview with official from the PRC Mission to the UN, New York, June 11, 2013. Interview with official from the PRC Mission to the UN, New York, June 6, 2016.
56. "China and Russia veto UN resolution condemning Syria," *BBC News*, October 5, 2011.
57. Ian Black, "Syria's Assad should step down, says King Abdullah of Jordan," *The Guardian*, November 14, 2011.
58. Jonathon Burch, "Turkey tells Syria's Assad: Step down!," *Reuters*, November 22, 2011.
59. David Batty and Jack Shenker, "Syria suspended from Arab League," *The Guardian*, November 12, 2011.
60. Quoting Qatari Prime Minister Sheikh Hamad bin Jassem bin Jabr Muhammad Al Thani, ibid.
61. For a full text of the League of Arab States Resolution 7442, see The League of Arab States, "Full text of Arab League resolution against Syria," November 28, 2011, Open Briefing, http://www.openbriefing.org/regionaldesks/middleeast/resolution7442/ (accessed March 1, 2019).
62. Neil MacFarquhar and Nada Bakri, "Isolating Syria, Arab League Imposes Broad Sanctions," *The New York Times*, November 27, 2011.
63. "Arab League Observer: Assad Committing Genocide in Syria," *Haaretz*, December 26, 2011. Monitors were gradually withdrawn in the following month as the bloodshed continued, showing the monitoring mission to be of limited use. Saudi Arabia was the first to withdraw its monitors, Bahrain, Kuwait, Oman, Qatar and the United Arab Emirates followed shortly thereafter. See "Saudi Arabia withdraws its monitors from Syria: Arab League calls for power transfer," *Al Arabiya*, January 23, 2012.
64. Yasmine Saleh and Lin Noueihed, "Arab League proposes a new plan for Syrian transition," *Reuters*, January 22, 2012.
65. United Nations Security Council, "6706th meeting (S/PV.6706), January 24" (2012).

210   ENDNOTES

66. Thomas Seibert, "GCC and Turkey stand united on Syria," *The National*, January 30, 2012.
67. Author interview with officials from the PRC Mission to the UN, New York, June 11, 2013. A similar point about League of Arab States voting procedures as "broken" was raised in an interview with senior Sino-Middle East foreign relations scholar, Hong Kong, March 29, 2016.
68. United Nations General Assembly, "Third Committee Approves Resolution Condemning Human Rights Violations in Syria, by Vote of 122 in Favour to 13 Against, with 41 Abstentions (GA/SHC/4033)," (2011).
69. United Nations General Assembly, "Promotion and protection of human rights: human rights situations and reports of special rapporteurs and representatives: Report of the 3rd Committee (A/66/462/Add.3), December 5" (2011); "General Assembly Adopts More Than 60 Resolutions Recommended by Third Committee, Including Text Condemning Grave, Systematic Human Rights Violations in Syria (GA/11198)," (2011).
70. Interview with officials from the UK Mission to the UN, New York, June 11, 2013.
71. On December 15, 2011, Russia called for an emergency UN Security Council meeting, so as to informally discuss its draft resolution regarding events in Syria. Russia inserted harsher language against the regime, noting the "disproportionate use of force by Syrian authorities" and "urging the Syrian government to put an end to suppression of those exercising their rights to freedom of expression, peaceful assembly and association." Despite initial hopes that this draft would lead to UN Security Council consensus for action, as it was the first time that Russia and China recognized that Syria had a role to play in addressing the violence, this draft failed to get to vote. Patrick Worsnip, "Russian draft offers hope of U.N. Syria resolution," *Reuters*, December 15, 2011. "Russia proposes U.N. resolution on Syria; U.S. hopes to work with Moscow on draft," *Al Arabiya*, December 15, 2011.
72. Morocco joined the UN Security Council in January 2012, replacing Lebanon.
73. Interview with Syria desk official from the US Mission to the UN, New York, June 11, 2013.
74. Interview with Middle East section official from the US Mission to the UN, New York, June 11, 2013.
75. Louis Charbonneau and Patrick Worsnip, "Russia, China veto U.N. draft backing Arab plan for Syria," *Reuters*, February 4, 2012.
76. "US 'disgust' as Russia and China veto UN Syria resolution," *BBC News*, February 4, 2012.
77. United Nations Security Council, "6711th meeting (S/PV.6711), February 4" (2012).
78. Ibid.
79. Interview with senior Sino-Middle East foreign relations scholar, Hong Kong, March 29, 2016.
80. Interview with officials from US Mission, New York, June 11, 2013.
81. Interview with official from a rotating member of the UN Security Council, New York, June 11, 2013.
82. Interview with officials from the US Mission to the UN, New York, June 11, 2013. Interview with senior Sino-Middle East foreign relations scholar, Hong Kong, March 29, 2016.

83. "U.N. General Assembly to vote Thursday on Syria: China warns of 'wrong steps'," *Al Arabiya*, February 15, 2012.
84. Sebastian Moffett and Stephen Brown, "Arabs, Turkey criticize veto of Syria resolution," *Reuters*, February 5, 2012; Neil MacFarquhar, "Both Sides Claim Progress as Violence Continues in Syria," *The New York Times*, July 22, 2012.
85. "Arab League calls for transitional government in Syria," *The Telegraph*, July 23, 2012.
86. Reuters, "Saudi king slams veto of UN's Syria move," *ArabianBusiness.com*, February 10, 2012. Rick Gladstone, "In Rare, Blunt Speech, Saudi King Criticizes Syria Vetoes," *The New York Times*, February 10, 2012.
87. United Nations General Assembly, "Top UN Human Rights Official Says Member States "Must Act Now" to Protect Syrian People, as Violent Crackdown Continues, in Briefing to General Assembly (GA/11206), February 13" (2012).
88. Ibid.
89. With the additional clause of asking for special envoy to oversee the Syria issue. UN General Assembly Resolution 66/253 A, February 16, 2012. See press statement: United Nations General Assembly, "General Assembly Adopts Resolution Strongly Condemning 'Widespread and Systematic' Human Rights Violations by Syrian Authorities (GA/11207/Rev.1)," (2012).
90. Interview with officials from the UK Mission, New York, June 11, 2013. Interview with official from a rotating member of the UN Security Council, New York, June 12, 2013.
91. United Nations General Assembly, "General Assembly Adopts Resolution Strongly Condemning "Widespread and Systematic" Human Rights Violations by Syrian Authorities (GA/11207/Rev.1)."
92. States that also voted against the resolution included Bolivia, Belarus, Cuba, Ecuador, Iran, Nicaragua, Democratic People's Republic of Korea, Syria, Venezuela, Zimbabwe.
93. Melissa Bell, "U.N. Syrian resolution: Which countries voted no?," *The Washington Post*, February 16, 2012. Abstention votes within the Middle East region were case by Algeria and Lebanon.
94. United Nations Security Council, "Resolution 2042 (2012): Adopted by the Security Council at its 6751st meeting, on 14 April 2012 (S/RES/2042)" (2012). Essentially, the military observers were to to liaise with parties and report on violence by all parties per the Six-Point Plan.
95. Interview with UN Department of Peacekeeping Operations official, New York, June 12, 2013. "Resolution 2043 (2012): Adopted by the Security Council at its 6756th meeting, on April 21, 2012 (S/RES/2043)" (2012). As these conditions were not met, the mandate expired at the end of its renewal period. "Resolution 2059 (2012): Adopted by the Security Council at its 6812th meeting, on 20 July 2012" (2012).
96. These statements included calling for access for the UN Under-Secretary-General for Humanitarian Affairs and Emergency Relief Coordinator, United Nations Security Council, "Security Council Press Statement on Syria (SC/10564)," (2012).; condemning civilian deaths in terror attacks and government-led operations in el-Houleh, which were confirmed by UN observers – respectively, "Security Council Press Statement on Terrorist Attacks in Damascus (SC/10643)," (2012); "Security Council Press Statement on Attacks in Syria (SC/10658)," (2012).

97. For example, the Syrian Action Group first met in June 2012, composed of senior representatives from the League of Arab States, the United Nations, the European Union, and also the P5, plus key regional players of Iraq, Kuwait, Qatar and Turkey. Russia proposed to expand the Syrian Action Group in February 2013, to add Egypt, Iran and Saudi Arabia as members. Another militareral group, the Friends of Syria Group included core states of the P3, Egypt, Germany, Italy, Jordan, Qatar, Saudi Arabia, Turkey, and the United Arab Emirates, the United Nations, the African Union, the League of Arab States, the European Union, the Gulf Cooperation Council, the Organization of Islamic Cooperation. The Friends of Syria Group called for Assad to give up his presidential power on July 6, 2012, pushing for tougher sanctions and agreeing to offer further aid and support to the Syrian opposition. Members of the Friends of Syria Group. Marc Daou, "'Friends of Syria' push for tougher sanctions," *France 24*, July 7, 2012.

98. United Nations Secretary-General Ban Ki-moon, "Kofi Annan Appointed Joint Special Envoy of United Nations, League of Arab States on Syrian Crisis (SG/SM/14124)," news release, February 23, 2012, http://www.un.org/press/en/2012/sgsm14124.doc.htm (accessed March 1, 2019). See also United Nations General Assembly, "Resolution adopted by the General Assembly on 16 February 2012: The situation in Syrian Arab Republic (A/RES/66/253), February 21" (2012).

99. The contents of the plan are available here: Douglas Hamilton, "Text of Annan's six-point peace plan for Syria," *Reuters*, April 4, 2012.

100. "Syria crisis: Gulf Arab states expel Syrian ambassadors," *BBC News*, February 7, 2012.

101. UN Report (Documents), "Arab League's letter to Security Council on Syria: Act under Chapter 7," June 8, 2012, http://un-report.blogspot.com/2012/06/arab-league-letter-to-security-council.html (accessed March 1, 2019). This move was the outgrowth of an earlier decision based on the League of Arab States Resolution 7507 from June 2, 2012, which not only called upon the UN Security Council to ensure the implementation of the Six-Point Peace Plan, but also called upon the UN Security Council "to take forthwith all the necessary measures to protect Syrian civilians."

102. Zhong, "Regime change should not be determined by external forces," 2012. "Be wary of attempt to resolve Syrian crisis outside UN framework," 2012.

103. United Nations Security Council, United Nations Security Council, "6734th meeting (S.PV/6734), March 12" (2012).

104. A point further underscored by the presidential statement of March 21, 2012, which further supported the Special Envoy's 6-point plan for mediation. See "Statement by the President of the Security Council (S/PRST/2012/6), March 21" (2012). See also "Statement by the President of the Security Council (S/PRST/2012/10), April 5" (2012).

105. As UK Foreign Secretary William Hague stated "We do have a disagreement about the need to enforce or require the implementation" of the peace plan measures. Jim Heintz and Associated Press, "Russia ready to seek consensus in UN on new resolution aimed at ending Syria's civil war," *Vancouver Sun*, July 17, 2012.

106. United Nations Security Council, "Security Council Fails to Adopt Draft Resolution on Syria That Would Have Threatened Sanctions, Due to Negative Votes of China, Russian Federation (SC/10714)," (2012).

107. Permanent Mission of the People's Republic of China to the United Nations, "Explanation of Vote by Ambassador Li Baodong after Vote on Draft Resolution on Syria Tabled by the United Kingdom," July 19 2012, Permanent Mission of the People's Republic of China to the UN, http://www.china-un.org/eng/hyyfy/t953482.htm (accessed March 6, 2019).
108. "Syria crisis: Russia and China veto UN resolution," *The Guardian*, July 19, 2012.
109. Ibid.
110. Interview with senior Sino-Middle East foreign relations scholar, Hong Kong, March 29, 2016.
111. Deputy Special Envoy Nasser al-Kidwa traveled to Istanbul in order to meet with the opposition. See UN News Centre, "UN-Arab League envoy to continue regional consultations on Syrian conflict," March 30, 2012. See also UN Report (Documents), "Kofi Annan's budget, mandate and objectives," April 25, 2012, http://un-report.blogspot.com.au/2012/04/kofi-annans-budget-mandate-and.html (accessed March 1, 2019). In the coming months, Annan included Tehran and Riyadh to his bilateral meeting schedule.
112. For international support of Envoy Annan and the Six-Point Peace Plan, on Qatar, see AFP, "Annan briefs top Qatari officials after Syria trip," *Yahoo News*, March 12, 2012; Shane McGinley, "Kofi Annan contacts Qatar over Syrian crisis," *ArabianBusiness.com*, February 27, 2012. On Egypt, see Edmund Blair, "UN-Arab League Syria envoy Annan seeks political deal," *Reuters*, March 8, 2012. On Turkey, see Republic of Turkey Ministry of Foreign Affairs, "No: 57, 24 February 2012, Press Release Regarding the Appointment of Former UN Secretary-General Kofi Annan as the Joint Special Envoy of the UN and the League of Arab States on the Syrian Crisis," (2012).
113. Palash Ghosh, "Syrian Crisis: Kofi Annan Takes Peace Plan To China," *International Business Times*, March 26, 2012.
114. Embassy of the People's Republic of China in Ireland, "Wen Jiabao Meets with the UN- Arab League Joint Special Envoy Kofi Annan," March 27 2012, http://ie.china-embassy.org/eng/NewsPress/t918582.htm (accessed March 1, 2019).
115. Michelle Nichols, "U.N. Security Council delays Syria vote until Thursday," *Reuters*, July 19, 2012.
116. Interview with official from a rotating member of the UNSC, New York, June 12, 2013. Interview with Syria desk official from the US Mission to the UN, New York, June 11, 2013. Interview with Middle East section official from the US Mission to the UN, New York, June 11, 2013.
117. See earlier diplomatic efforts. Embassy of the People's Republic of China in Ireland, "Wen Jiabao Meets with the UN- Arab League Joint Special Envoy Kofi Annan."
118. Heintz and Associated Press, "Russia ready to seek consensus in UN on new resolution aimed at ending Syria's civil war," 2012.
119. United Nations Secretary-General Ban Ki-moon, "Readout of the Secretary-General's meetings with H.E. Mr. Hu Jintao, President of the People's Republic of China, and H.E. Mr. Yang Jiechi, Foreign Minister of the People's Republic of China," July 18, 2012, https://www.un.org/sg/en/content/sg/readout/2012-07-18/readout-secretary-general%E2%80%99s-meetings-he-mr-hu-jintao-president-people.

120. President Obama and Vice President Biden each discussed the Syria crisis with President Xi Jinping during their individual meetings in February 2012. Dan Robinson, "US Voices Concern about Syria Resolution Veto During Talks with China's VP," *Voice of America*, February 13, 2012.
121. Interview with official from a rotating member of the UNSC, New York, June 12, 2013.
122. Interview with official from a rotating member of the UNSC, New York, June 12, 2013.
123. Interview with senior Chinese foreign policy scholar and advisor to the Ministry of Foreign Affairs, Beijing, December 14, 2017.
124. "Arab League to offer 'safe exit' if Assad resigns," *CNN*, July 22, 2012. This was not the first offer for safe exit, however. Tunisia had offered safe exit for Assad back in February 2012, and journalists noted that Qatar had made informal offers for Assad's safe exit also. Vivienne Walt, "Is Syria's Bashar Assad Going the Way of Muammar Gaddafi?," July 23, 2012.
125. "Organization of Islamic Cooperation suspends Syria's membership," *Al Arabiya*, August 13, 2012.
126. Reuters, "Syria conflict divides OIC summit in Cairo," *Dawn*, February 7, 2013.
127. United Nations Security Council, "6826th meeting (S/PV.6826), August 30," 2012.
128. Permanent Mission of the People's Republic of China to the United Nations, "Explanatory Remarks by Ambassador Wang Min after General Assembly Vote on Draft Resolution on Syria." See also, United Nations General Assembly, "General Assembly, in Resolution, Demands All in Syria 'Immediately and Visibly' Commit to Ending Violence that Secretary-General Says Is Ripping Country Apart (GA/11266/Rev.1), August 3", 2012.
129. United Nations Security Council, "Security Council Press Statement on Shelling of Turkish Town by Syrian Forces (SC/10783)," (2012).
130. United Nations Security Council, "Security Council Press Statement on Terrorist Attacks in Aleppo (SC/10784)," (2012).
131. Lakhdar Brahimi took over as Joint Special Envoy on August 17, 2012, following the resignation of Kofi Annan. United Nations Security Council, "Security Council Press Statement on Ceasefire in Syria (SC/10800)," (2012).
132. See the November 6, 2012 and December 19, 2012 briefing by the Under-Secretary-General for the Department of Political Affairs Jeffrey Feltman; December 17, 2012 briefing from OCHA head Valerie Amos. These senior officials used terms like "the destruction of Syria will be the likely outcome" and saw Syria in terms of "irreversible damage." UN Web TV, "Jeffrey Feltman (DPA) on Syria - Security Council Media Stakeout," November 6, 2012, http://webtv.un.org/media/media-stakeouts/watch/jeffrey-feltman-dpa-on-syria-security-council-media-stakeout/1950949912001 (accessed March 1, 2019); United Nations Security Council, "6894th meeting (S/PV.6894), December 19" (2012); UN Web TV, "Valerie Amos (OCHA) on Syria - Security Council Media Stakeout (17 December 2012)," December 17, 2012, http://webtv.un.org/topics-issues/global-issues/humanitarian-assistance/watch/valerie-amos-ocha-on-syria-security-council-media-stakeout-17-december-2012/2041477549001 (accessed March 1, 2019).

133. "Syrian opposition: 1,300 killed in chemical attack on Ghouta region," *Al Arabiya*, August 21, 2013.
134. Louis Charbonneau and Michelle Nichols, "U.N. confirms sarin used in Syria attack; U.S., UK, France blame Assad," *Reuters*, September 16, 2013.
135. United Nations Security Council, "Security Council Press Statement on Damascus Bombing (SC/10953)," (2013).
136. United Nations Security Council, "Draft Resolution (S/2014/348), May 22" (2014). "Referral of Syria to International Criminal Court Fails as Negative Votes Prevent Security Council from Adopting Draft Resolution (SC/11407)," (2014).
137. United Nations General Assembly and United Nations Security Council, "Letter dated 14 January 2013 from the Chargé d'affaires a.i. of the Permanent Mission of Switzerland to the United Nations addressed to the Secretary-General (A/67/694–S/2013/19), January 16" (2013). Swiss efforts followed calls by High Commissioner for Human Rights Navi Pillay in July 2012 call for an ICC referral; UN News Centre, "UN human rights chief renews call on Security Council to refer Syria to ICC," July 2, 2012. France also tried to pressure Assad after alleged chemical weapons attacks, see Angelique Chrisafis and Julian Borger, "Syria conflict: France to seek tough UN resolution on chemical weapons," *The Guardian*, September 10, 2013. For a leaked draft of the French-drafted resolution, available at https://docs.google.com/file/d/0ByLPNZ-eSjJdX29vd2Y3WlNxQWc/view (accessed March 1, 2019). See Human Rights Watch, "Q&A: Syria and the International Criminal Court," September 17 2013, https://www.hrw.org/news/2013/09/17/qa-syria-and-international-criminal-court (accessed March 1, 2019).
138. Secretary-General Ban supported "the debate triggered by the call of some Member States for the Council to refer the situation in Syria to the International Criminal Court." United Nations Secretary-General Ban Ki-moon, "Secretary-General's remarks to Security Council Open Debate on the Protection of Civilians in Armed Conflict," February 12, 2013, https://www.un.org/sg/en/content/sg/statement/2013-02-12/secretary-generals-remarks-security-council-open-debate-protection (accessed March 1, 2019).
139. Michelle Nichols and Louis Charbonneau, "Russia, China veto U.N. bid to refer Syria to international court," *Reuters*, May 23, 2014.
140. A complete co-sponsors list is as follows: Albania, Andorra, Australia, Belgium, Botswana, Bulgaria, Canada, Central African Republic, Chile, Croatia, Cyprus, Czech Republic, Democratic Republic of the Congo, Denmark, Estonia, Finland, France, Georgia, Germany, Greece, Hungary, Iceland, Ireland, Italy, Ivory Coast, Japan, Jordan, Latvia, Libya, Liechtenstein, Lithuania, Luxembourg, Macedonia, Malta, Marshall Islands, Mexico, Moldova, Monaco, Montenegro, Netherlands, New Zealand, Norway, Panama, Poland, Portugal, Qatar, Romania, Samoa, San Marino, Saudi Arabia, Senegal, Serbia, Seychelles, Slovakia, Slovenia, South Korea, Spain, Sweden, Switzerland, Turkey, UAE, Ukraine, United Kingdom, United States.
141. Smaller Middle East-based human rights group did support the draft resolution. For a full list of supporting civil society organizations, see Human Rights Watch, "Syria: Groups Call for ICC Referral," May 15 2014, https://www.hrw.org/news/2014/05/15/syria-groups-call-icc-referral (accessed March 1, 2019).

142. "Arab ministers hold Syrian gov't responsible for chemical attacks," *Xinhua*, September 2, 2013.
143. Permanent Mission of the People's Republic of China to the United Nations, "Explanatory Remarks by Ambassador Wang Min after Security Council Voting on Draft Resolution on the Referral of the Situation of the Syrian Arab Republic to the International Criminal Court," May 22, 2014, http://www.china-un.org/eng/chinaandun/securitycouncil/regionalhotspots/asia/yz/t1161566.htm (accessed March 1, 2019).
144. United Nations Security Council, "Referral of Syria to International Criminal Court Fails as Negative Votes Prevent Security Council from Adopting Draft Resolution (SC/11407)."
145. The UN Security Council's handling of the Syria crisis was cited by Saudi Arabia in its declining to take up the rotating seat on behalf of the Middle East: "Allowing the ruling regime in Syria to kill and burn its people with chemical weapons while the world stands idly by, without applying deterrent sanctions against the Damascus regime, is also irrefutable evidence and proof of the inability of the Security Council to carry out its duties and responsibilities." See United Nations Security Council, "Letter dated 12 November 2013 from the Permanent Representative of Saudi Arabia to the United Nations addressed to the Secretary-General (A/68/599), November 14" (2013).
146. Nichols and Charbonneau, "Russia, China veto U.N. bid," 2014.
147. United Nations Human Rights Office of the High Commissioner, "Syria: Door remains wide open for further atrocities after lack of referral to the ICC, UN experts warn," May 30, 2014, http://www.ohchr.org/EN/NewsEvents/Pages/DisplayNews.aspx?NewsID=14655&LangID=E (accessed March 1, 2019).
148. Dominic Evans, "At least 162,000 killed in Syria conflict – monitoring group," *Reuters*, May 19, 2014.
149. United Nations Secretary-General Ban Ki-moon, "Secretary-General's address at The Asia Society: 'Crisis in Syria: Civil War, Global Threat'," June 20, 2014, United Nations Secretary-Genera, https://www.un.org/sg/en/content/sg/statement/2014-06-20/secretary-generals-address-asia-society-crisis-syria-civil-war (accessed March 1, 2019).
150. What's in Blue, "Syria: Monday Vote on Draft Resolution on Cross-Border and Cross-Line Humanitarian Access," July 13, 2014, http://www.whatsinblue.org/2014/07/syria-monday-vote-on-draft-resolution-on-cross-border-and-cross-line-humanitarian-access.php (accessed March 1, 2019).
151. Interview with former official of a rotating member of the UN Security Council, New York, June 8, 2016. Interview with official from the PRC Mission to the UN, New York, June 6, 2016.
152. For a discussion of Australia's "pragmatic" negotiating strategy, see Ralph, "The Responsibility to Protect and the rise of China," 2017, 54–5.
153. Interview with official from the PRC Mission to the UN, New York, June 6, 2016. Interview with senior Chinese foreign policy scholar and advisor to the Ministry of Foreign Affairs, Beijing, December 14, 2017.
154. Interview with former official of a rotating member of the UN Security Council, New York, June 8, 2016.

155. This point was repeatedly stressed by Chinese officials, for example see: Ministry of Foreign Affairs of the People's Republic of China, "Foreign Ministry Spokesperson Hong Lei's Remarks on UN Security Council's Adoption of the Resolution on the Humanitarian Issue of Syria," July 15, 2014, http://www.fmprc.gov.cn/mfa_eng/xwfw_665399/s2510_665401/t1174294.shtml (accessed March 1, 2019).
156. Resolution 2165 obliquely mentions that the Council "will take further measures" instead.
157. Nigel Rodley, "R2P and International Law: A Paradigm Shift?," in *The Oxford handbook of the responsibility to protect*, ed. Alex J. Bellamy and Timothy Dunne (Oxford: Oxford University Press, 2016), 201.
158. Interview with senior Chinese foreign policy scholar and advisor to the Ministry of Foreign Affairs, Beijing, December 14, 2017.
159. Interview with official from the PRC Mission to the UN, New York, June 6, 2016.
160. The lack of unity, coordination and speed in the League of Arab States response were cited as issues in interviews by representatives from organization. Interview with representative of the League of Arab States, New York, June 7, 2016. Interview with senior representative of the League of Arab States, New York, June 7, 2016.
161. Gregory Chin and Ramesh Thakur, "Will China Change the Rules of Global Order?," *The Washington Quarterly* 33, no. 4 (2010).
162. Michael D. Swaine, "Chinese Views of the Syrian Conflict," *China Leadership Monitor* 39 (2012); Sun Yun, "Syria: What China Has Learned from its Libya Experience," *Asia Pacific Bulletin* 152 (2012); Adrian Johnson and Saqeb Mueen, "Short War, Long Shadow: The Political and Military Legacies of the 2011 Libya Campaign" (London 2012).
163. For example, Michelle Nichols, "Russia vetoes U.N. demand for end to bombing of Syria's Aleppo," *Reuters*, October 8, 2016.
164. Ruan Zongze, "Responsible protection," *China Daily*, March 15, 2012; "Responsible Protection: Building a Safer World," *China International Studies* 34 (2012).
165. Teitt, "Assessing Polemics, Principles and Practices," 2009; "The Responsibility to Protect and China's Peacekeeping Policy," 2011; Liu, "China and Responsibility to Protect," 2012; Liu and Zhang, "Debates in China about the responsibility to protect," 2014; Fung, "Separating Intervention from Regime Change?" 2018; Fung, "Rhetorical Adaptation and International Order-Making," 2019.
166. For the use of "responsible protection" in official discourse, see "China saying "no" on Syria issue is responsible move: FM Official," *Xinhua*, April 10, 2012; Institute of Strategic and International Studies (ISIS) Malaysia, "China's Strategic Vision and Regional Security in the Asia-Pacific – Remarks by H.E. Ambassador Tong Xiaolong at the 26th Asia-Pacific Roundtable, Kuala Lumpur," May 28, 2012. For a discussion of the responsible protection concept, see Ramesh Thakur, "A Chinese version of 'responsible protection'," *The Japan Times*, November 1, 2013; Andrew Garwood-Gowers, "China's 'Responsible Protection' concept: re-interpreting the Responsibility to Protect (R2P) and military intervention for humanitarian purposes," *Asian Journal of International Law* 6, no. 1 (2016). After 2012, China was instead keen to back Brazil's responsible while protecting initiative.

218   ENDNOTES

167. France and the S5 (the "small five" of Costa Rica, Jordan, Liechtenstein, Singapore, and Switzerland) instigated the "responsibility not to veto" campaign, in the light of the four Syrian vetoes. Permanent Representatives of Costa Rica et al., "Presentation of the S-5 Draft Resolution L.42 on the Improvement of the Working Methods of the Security Council" (2012). Brazil pursued the "responsibility while protecting" concept in 2011, and restarted the responsibility while protecting concept in 2015, see Columbia Global Policy Initiative, *Responsibility while Protecting: Implementation and the Future of the Responsibility to Protect*, ed. Maggie Powers (New York: Columbia Global Policy Initiative, 2015).
168. Fung, "Separating Intervention from Regime Change?" 2018.
169. Permanent Mission of the People's Republic of China to the United Nations, "Statement by Ambassador Li Baodong, Permanent Representative of China to the United Nations, at the Security Council Briefing on the Situation in Syria," January 31, 2012, http://www.china-un.org/eng/hyyfy/t930411.htm (accessed March 1, 2019). Russia also challenged the notion of regime change in the draft resolution, see Steve Gutterman, "Russia won't back U.N. call for Syria's Assad to go," *Reuters*, January 27, 2012.
170. Zhao Lei, "Two Pillars of China's Global Peace Engagement Strategy: UN Peacekeeping and International Peacebuilding," *International Peacekeeping* 18, no. 3 (2011): 352.
171. Respectively, Foot, "'Doing some things' in the Xi Jinping era," 2014; Jon R. Lindsay, "The Impact of China on Cybersecurity: Fiction and Friction," *International Security* 39, no. 3 (2014/15); Foot and Inboden, "China's Influence on Asian States," 2014; Chris Alden and Daniel Large, "On Becoming a Norms Maker: Chinese Foreign Policy, Norms Evolution and the Challenges of Security in Africa," *The China Quarterly* 221 (2015).
172. China Copyright and Media, "CCP Central Committee Decision concerning Some Major Questions in Comprehensively Moving Governing the Country According to the law Forward," October 28, 2014, https://chinacopyrightandmedia.wordpress.com/2014/10/28/ccp-central-committee-decision-concerning-some-major-questions-in-comprehensively-moving-governing-the-country-according-to-the-law-forward/ (accessed March 1, 2019).
173. Wang Yi, "China, a Staunch Defender and Builder of International Rule of Law," *People's Daily*, October 24, 2014.
174. United Nations Security Council, "Resolution 1973 (2011): Adopted by the Security Council at its 6498th meeting, on 17 March 2011 (S/RES/1973)", 2011. For an in-depth discussion, see Spencer Zifcak, "The Responsibility to Protect after Libya and Syria," *Melbourne Journal of International Law* 13, no. 1 (2012). And see also Sarah Brockmeier, Oliver Stuenkel, and Marcos Tourinho, "The Impact of the Libya Intervention Debates on Norms of Protection," *Global Society* 30, no. 1 (2016).

Chapter 7

1. See Wuthnow, *Chinese Diplomacy and the UN Security Council*, 2013, 113–23.
2. Michael Green and Derek Mitchell, "Asia's Forgotten Crisis: A New Approach to Burma," *Foreign Affairs* 86, no. 6 (2007).

3. United Nations Security Council, "United Kingdom of Great Britain and Northern Ireland and United States of America: draft resolution (S/2007/14), January 12" (2007).
4. When ASEAN representatives finally gained access to Myanmar in August 2006, they noted that "[there] is some light at the end of the tunnel [for] reconciliation in Myanmar," and in November 2007, they noted that the military junta had taken "small steps" towards political reform measures. See, respectively: "Philippine Foreign Secretary Optimistic on Burmese Democracy," *BBC Monitoring Asia Pacific*, August 15, 2006; "US to Press for UN Security Council Action on Myanmar," *Japan Economic Newswire*, November 27, 2006.
5. The Philippines supported calls for a UN Security Council briefing on Myanmar's political conditions in December 2005; in August 2006, Indonesia noted that ASEAN could not defend Myanmar unless unless it showed a commitment to greater international interactions, and Malaysia reversed its harsh line against Myanmar in January 2007, affirming a new commitment to stating "Myanmar is not a security threat issue." See, respectively: International Crisis Group, "Burma/Myanmar: After the Crackdown" (Yangon/Jakarta/Brussels 2008), 16. "Indonesia's FM Says Burma to Defend Itself if Brought to UN Security Council," *AFP*, August 23, 2006; "ASEAN Ministers Call for WTO Talks Restart, Say Myanmar No Threat," *Japanese Economic Newswire*, January 11, 2007.
6. "RI Disagrees on Myanmar Draft," *Jakarta Post*, January 6, 2007.
7. See Wuthnow, *Chinese Diplomacy and the UN Security Council*, 2013, 121.
8. China cast vetoes on December 5, 2016 regarding a ceasefire in Aleppo, Syria, and February 28, 2017 regarding sanctions over chemical weapons use.
9. Johnston, *Social States*, 2008, 211.
10. Comments by Thomas J. Christensen, "China's Rise and Challenges for American Security" (paper presented at the 2018 China Research Center Annual Lecture, University of Maryland, March 1, 2018).
11. Christensen, *The China Challenge*, 2015, 322.
12. For example, "AU Chief condemns Bashir warrants," *Al Jazeera*, July 27, 2010; Simon Allison and Daily Maverick, "African revolt threatens international criminal court's legitimacy," *The Guardian*, October 27, 2016. For a discussion, see Dire Tladi, "The African Union and the International Criminal Court: The Battle for the Soul of International Law," *South African Yearbook of International Law* 34 (2009).
13. Byman, "Regime Change in the Middle East," 2012.
14. Christensen, *The China Challenge*, 2015; Lieberthal and Wang, "Addressing U.S.-China Strategic Distrust," 2012.
15. Bellamy, "Responsibility to Protect or Trojan Horse?," 2005.
16. McMillan and Mickler, "From Sudan to Syria," 2013, 286.
17. By "order," I mean the norms and institutions that reflect the interests of the dominant state in the system, the United States. For a discussion of the term, see Naazneen Barma et al., "A World Without the West? Empirical Patterns and Theoretical Implications," *The Chinese Journal of International Politics* 2, no. 4 (2009): 527. For a view of multiple international orders, see Randall L. Schweller, "The Problem of International Order Revisited: A Review Essay," *International Security* 26, no. 1 (2001).

18. For an account, see Wuthnow, *Chinese Diplomacy and the UN Security Council*, 2013, 59–74.
19. Patricia Kim, "How to Persuade China to Squeeze North Korea's Lifeline," *Foreign Policy*, February 27, 2017.
20. Scott L. Kastner, Margaret M. Pearson, and Chad Rector, "Invest, Hold Up, or Accept? China in Multilateral Governance," *Security Studies* 25, no. 1 (2016). G. John Ikenberry, "Liberal Internationalism 3.0: America and the Dilemmas of Liberal World Order," *Perspectives on Politics* 7, no. 1 (2009); Scott L. Kastner, Margaret M. Pearson, and Chad Rector, *China's Strategic Multilateralism: Investing in Global Governance* (Cambridge: Cambridge University Press, 2018).
21. Rick Gladstone, "China and Russia Move to Cut Human Rights Jobs in U.N. Peacekeeping," *The New York Times*, June 27, 2018.
22. Colum Lynch, "Russia and China See in Trump Era a Chance to Roll Back Human Rights Promotion at U.N.," *Foreign Policy*, June 26, 2018.
23. "China Eyes Ending Western Grip on Top U.N. Jobs With Greater Control Over Blue Helmets," *Foreign Policy*, October 2, 2016. See also Murray Brewster and Melissa Kent, "China, Russia aim for key UN peacekeeping positions as Canada prepares deployment," *CBC News*, October 5, 2016.
24. For a critique, see Alastair Iain Johnston, "How New and Assertive Is China's New Assertiveness?," *International Security* 37, no. 4 (2013); Björn Jerdén, "The Assertive China Narrative: Why It Is Wrong and How So Many Still Bought into It," *The Chinese Journal of International Politics* 7, no. 1 (2014); Andrew Scobell and Scott W. Harold, "An "Assertive" China? Insights from Interviews," *Asian Security* 9, no. 2 (2013): 112–13; Michael D. Swaine, "Perceptions of an Assertive China," *China Leadership Monitor* 32 (2010): 2–3.
25. Claes, "Protecting Civilians from Mass Atrocities," 2012, 70.
26. Courtney J. Fung, "Rhetorical Adaptation and International Order-Making: China's Advancement of the Responsibility to Protect." *Cooperation and Conflict* (2019): https://doi.org/10.1177/0010836719858118.
27. Sarah Teitt, "China and the Responsibility to Protect" (Brisbane 2008), 20; United Nations Security Council, "5577th meeting (S/PV.5577), December 4" (2006); "5781st meeting (S/PV.5781), November 20" (2007); "5898th meeting (S/PV.5898), May 27" (2008).
28. United Nations Security Council, "Security Council, in Presidential Statement, Reaffirms Commitment to Protection of Civilians in Armed Conflict, Adopts Updated Aide-Memoire on Issue (SC/9571), January 14" (2009).
29. Alex J. Bellamy, *Responsibility to Protect: The Global Effort to End Mass Atrocities* (Cambridge: Polity, 2009), 52.
30. Nicola P. Contessi, "Multilateralism, Intervention and Norm Contestation: China's Stance on Darfur in the UN Security Council," *Security Dialogue* 41, no. 3 (2010).
31. Sovereignty reflects long-rooted tension between rights and responsibilities. See Luke Glanville, *Sovereignty and the Responsibility to Protect: A New History* (Chicago, IL: University of Chicago Press, 2014).

32. See He Yin, "Lianheguo jianshe heping yu rende anquan baohu (United Nations Peacebuilding and the Protection of Human Security)," *The Journal of International Security Affairs* 32, no. 3 (2014), "Fazhan heping: lianheguo weihe jianhe zhong de zhongguo fangan (Developmental Peace: Chinese Approach to UN Peacekeeping and Peacebuilding)," *The Journal of International Studies* 38, no. 4 (2017). See also Wang Xuejun, "Developmental Peace: Understanding China's Africa Policy in Peace and Security," in Alden C., Alao A., Chun Z., Barber L. (eds) *China and Africa* (London: Palgrave Macmillan, Cham, 2018).
33. Deborah A. Brautigam, *The Dragon's Gift: The Real Story of China in Africa* (Oxford: Oxford University Press, 2009).
34. Xi Jinping, "Secure a Decisive Victory in Building a Moderately Prosperous Society in All Respects and Strive for the Great Success of Socialism with Chinese Characteristics for a New Era," October 18, 2017, Beijing: National Congress of the Communist Party of China, http://www.xinhuanet.com/english/download/Xi_Jinping's_report_at_19th_CPC_National_Congress.pdf (accessed August 30, 2018).
35. Zhang Guihong, "A Community of Shared Future for Mankind" and Implications for the Prevention of Conflict" [unpublished paper], n.d.
36. Xi Jinping, "Working Together to Forge a New Partnership of Win-win Cooperation and Create a Community of Shared Future for Mankind," September 29, 2015, Beijing: Ministry of Foreign Affairs of the People's Republic of China, https://www.fmprc.gov.cn/mfa_eng/wjdt_665385/zyjh_665391/t1305051.shtml (accessed August 30, 2018).
37. Xi Jinping"Work Together to Build a Community of Shared Future for Mankind," January 18 2017, Beijing: Xinhua, http://www.xinhuanet.com/english/2017-01/19/c_135994707.htm (accessed August 30, 2018).
38. United Nations General Assembly, "Resolution adopted by the General Assembly on 4 December 2017: No first placement of weapons in outer space (A/RES/72/27), 11 December" (2017); United Nations Security Council, "Resolution 2344 (2017): Adopted by the Security Council at its 7902nd meeting, on 17 March 2017 (S/RES/2344)" (2017); United Nations General Assembly, "Resolution adopted by the Human Rights Council on 23 March 2017: Question of the realization in all countries of economic, social and cultural rights (A/HRC/RES/34/4), April 6," (2017); United nations Economic and Social Council, "Social dimension of the New Partnership for Africa's Development: Report of the Secretary-General (E/CN.5/2017/2), 22 November" (2016).
39. Ziad Haider, "Can the US Pivot Back to Asia? How Trump Should Respond to China's Belt and Road Initiative," *Foreign Affairs*, May 23, 2017.
40. Li Ziguo, "The Belt and Road Initiative: Achievements, Problems and Ideas," *Eurasian Economy*, no. 4 (2017).
41. Current conceptions of BRI emphasize connectivity in five areas: policy, infrastructure, trade, finance, and people-to-people relations—with infrastructure as the most emphasized component to include projects as diverse as building airports, bridges, communication networks, factories, ports, power grids, roads, bridges, oil and gas pipelines, and ports. See Belt and Road Vision and Actions. For analysis see Nadège Rolland, "China's Belt and Road Initiative: Underwhelming or 'Game-Changer'?," *The Washington Quarterly* 40, no. 1 (2017).

222 ENDNOTES

42. See Ministry of Foreign Affairs of the People's Republic of China, "Joint Communiqué of the Leaders Roundtable of the Belt and Road Forum for International Cooperation," May 16, 2017, https://www.fmprc.gov.cn/mfa_eng/zxxx_662805/t1462012.shtml (accessed August 30, 2018). The Joint Communiqué explicitly puts forward the basic principles, to include "recognizing the role of the market and that of business as key players, while ensuring that the government performs its proper role and highlighting the importance of open, transparent, and non-discriminatory procurement procedures."
43. Speech at the Belt & Road International Forum in May 2017. See Xi Jinping, "Full text of President Xi's speech at opening of Belt and Road forum," *Xinhua*, May 14, 2017.
44. UNGA, "Resolution adopted by the General Assembly on 21 November 2017: 72/10. The situation in Afghanistan", 24 Nov 2017, A/RES/72/10. UNGA, "Resolution adopted by the General Assembly on 17 November 2016: 71/9. The situation in Afghanistan", 6 Dec 2016, A/RES/71/9. UNGA, "Resolution adopted by the General Assembly on 22 December 2016: 71/249. Promotion of interreligious and intercultural dialogue, understanding and cooperation for peace", 20 January 2017, A/RES/71/249. UNGA, "Resolution adopted by the General Assembly on 23 December 2016: 71/252. Follow-up to the Declaration and Programme of Action on a Culture of Peace", 26 January 2017, A/RES/71/252.
45. United Nations Security Council, "Resolution 2274 (2016) Adopted by the Security Council at its 7645th meeting, on 15 March 2016 (S/RES/2274)" (2016); "Resolution 2344 (2017): Adopted by the Security Council at its 7902nd meeting, on 17 March 2017 (S/RES/2344)", 2017.
46. For example, "UN chief: Belt and Road Initiative China's new vision to global development," *CCTV.com*, May 10, 2017; "UN chief calls China pillar of multilateral system", *Xinhua*, April 6, 2018; "President Xi meets UN chief ", *Xinhua*, September 3, 2018.
47. For example, "Interview: China plays active, leading role in global governance - Ban Ki-moon ", *Xinhua*, November 30, 2017.
48. Zhang, "A Community of Shared Future for Mankind" and Implications for the Prevention of Conflict", n.d.
49. Wang Xinsong, "One Belt, One Road's Governance Deficit Problem: How China Can Ensure Transparency and Accountability," *Foreign Affairs*, November 17, 2017.
50. The DPRK is only an observer member of the ASEAN Regional Forum and a member of the Council for Security Cooperation in the Asia Pacific (CSCAP). The DPRK is not a member of most international financial and trade institutions (including the World Bank, International Monetary Fund, Asian Development Bank, Asian Infrastructure Investment Bank, the World Trade Organization, World Customs Organization, and the International Labor Organization). The DPRK is also outside of international institutions addressing arms control and nonproliferation, withdrawing from the Nuclear Non-Proliferation Treaty, and the Organization for the Prohibition for Chemical Weapons, for example.
51. For example, status accommodation is when "higher-status actors acknowledge the state's enhanced responsibilities, privileges, or rights," Larson, Paul, and Wohlforth, "Status and World Order," 2014, 11. The status signaling literature echoes the same assumptions, where the "claim to a particular status," with the goal of modifying or maintaining perceptions of the sender's relative position, is often conceived of as trying

ENDNOTES 223

to signal a higher status. Ibid., 12. Recent literature examines why states covet "small status"—but again this assumes that small status is the only status worth seeking, or that depending on the functional area, a state might prefer small status. See de Carvalho and Neumann, *Small State Status Seeking*.

52. This case sketch is along the lines of a plausibility probe to see whether more detailed efforts for testing are warranted. See George and Bennett, *Case Studies and Theory Development in the Social Sciences*, 2005, 75.

53. India has long been a top troop contributor to UN peacekeeping operations; an advocate for troop contributing countries to have a greater say in mandate design; and has a long-running campaign for representation at the UN Security Council. Respectively, see Dipankar Banerjee, "India," in *Providing Peacekeepers: The Politics, Challenges, and Future of United Nations Peacekeeping Contributions*, ed. Alex J. Bellamy and Paul D. Williams (Oxford: Oxford University Press, 2013); Press Trust of India, "Troop-Contributing Nations Need Greater Say In UN Missions: General Suhag," *NDTV*, May 30, 2016; Manu Bhagavan, "India and the United Nations: Or Things Fall Apart," in *The Oxford Handbook of Indian Foreign Policy*, ed. David M. Malone, C. Raja Mohan, and Srinath Raghavan (New York: Oxford University Press, 2015).

54. Stephen P. Cohen, *India: Emerging Power* (Washington D.C.: Brookings Institution, 2001); David M. Malone, *Does the Elephant Dance? Contemporary Indian Foreign Policy* (New Delhi: Oxford University Press, 2011); Baldev Raj Nayar and T. V. Paul, *India in the World Order: Searching for Major-Power Status* (Cambridge: Cambridge University Press, 2003). For dissenting views, see Aseema Sinha, "Partial accommodation without conflict: India as a rising link power," in *Accommodating Rising Powers: Past, Present, and Future* ed. T. V. Paul (Cambridge: Cambridge University Press, 2016); Miller, "The Role of Beliefs in Identifying Rising Powers," 2016.

55. Primarily through the Group of 77 and the Non-Aligned Movement.

56. For an overview, see Alan Bloomfield, *India and the Responsibility to Protect* (Farnham, Surrey: Ashgate Publishing Limited, 2016).

57. United Nations Security Council, "5225th meeting (S/PV.5225), July 12" (2005).

58. United Nations General Assembly, "Sixty-third session: 99th plenary meeting (A/63/PV.99), July 24" (2009). Similar rhetoric was used a year later, Permanent Mission of India to the United Nations, "Intervention By Ambassador Hardeep Singh Puri Permanent Representative at the Informal Interactive Dialogue of the UN General Assembly on "Early Warning, Assessment and the Responsibility to Protect" on August 9, 2010," August 9 2010, https://www.pminewyork.org/adminpart/uploadpdf/20151ind1716.pdf (accessed January 11, 2017).

59. For detailed process tracing, see Bloomfield, *India and the Responsibility to Protect*, 2016, 145–93.

60. Larson, Paul, and Wohlforth, *"Status and World Order,"* 2014, 10.

61. Volgy et al., *"Status Considerations in International Politics and the Rise of Regional Powers,"* 2014.

62. Li, "World Leaders to Attend Beijing Olympic," 2008.

63. "Strategic constructivism" asserts that actors exploit normative footholds in order to achieve political goals. See Nicolas Jabko, *Playing the Market: A Political Strategy for*

Uniting Europe, 1985–2005 (Ithaca, NY: Cornell University Press, 2006). Richard Price, "Reversing the Gun Sights: Transnational Civil Society Targets Land Mines," *International Organization* 52, no. 3 (1998): 636.

64. Margaret E. Keck and Kathryn Sikkink, *Activists beyond Borders* (Ithaca, NY: Cornell University Press, 1998); Thomas Risse, Stephen C. Ropp, and Kathryn Sikkink, eds., *The Power of Human Rights: International Norms and Domestic Change* (Cambridge: Cambridge University Press, 1999); Thomas Risse, ""Let's Argue!": Communicative Action in World Politics," *International Organization* 54, no. 1 (2000); Beth A. Simmons, *Mobilizing Human Rights: International Law in Domestic Politics* (New York: Cambridge University Press, 2009). Schimmelfennig gives a detailed analysis of the trade-off between strategic calculation and socialization. Frank Schimmelfennig, "Strategic Calculation and International Socialization: Membership Incentives, Party Constellations, and Sustained Compliance in Central and Eastern Europe," *International Organization* 59, no. 4 (2005).

65. The data for the remainder of the paragraph is drawn from Development Initiatives, "Global Humanitarian Assistance Report 2018" (2018), 9.

66. Angus McDowall, "Syrian Observatory says war has killed more than half a million," *Reuters*, March 12, 2018.

67. Olivier Corten, "Human Rights and Collective Security: Is There an Emerging Right of Humanitarian Intervention?," in *Human Rights, Intervention, and the Use of Force*, ed. Philip Alston and Euan Macdonald (Oxford: Oxford University Press, 2008); Michael C. Davis, "The Reluctant Intervenor: The UN Security Council, China's Worldview, and Humanitarian Intervention," in *International Intervention in the Post-Cold War World: Moral Responsibility and Power Politics*, ed. Michael C. Davis, et al. (Armonk, New York: M.E. Sharpe, 2004).

68. Beyond the chapters enclosed, regarding the debate amongst the P3 for intervention in Darfur, see Henke, "Great powers and UN force generation," 2016. Regarding the debate amongst the P3 for intervention in Libya, see Chivvis, *Toppling Qaddafi*, 2013, 31–68. Regarding the debate amongst the P3 for intervention in Syria, see Bloomfield, *India and the Responsibility to Protect*, 2016, 145–94.

69. Observation of Samuel S. Kim, "China in World Politics," in *Does China Matter? A Reassessment—Essays in Memory of Gerald Segal*, ed. Barry Buzan and Rosemary Foot (London: Routledge, 2004), 39.

Bibliography

Abdelal, Rawi, Yoshiko M. Herrera, Alastair Iain Johnston, and Rose McDermot. "Identity as a Variable." In *Measuring Identity: A Guide for Social Scientists*, edited by Rawi Abdelal, Yoshiko M. Herrera, Alastair Iain Johnston, and Rose McDermot, 17–32. Cambridge: Cambridge University Press, 2009.

Abdenur, Adriana Erthal, and Carlos Frederico Pereira da Silva Gama. "Triggering the Norms Cascade: Brazil's Initiatives for Curbing Electronic Espionage." *Global Governance* 21, no. 3 (2015): 455–74.

Abrams, Elliott. "America Watches As Syria Crumbles." *National Review*, July 18, 2012.

Abrams, Elliott. "Gaddafi's End." *National Review*, February 21, 2011.

Abrams, Elliott, and Bernard Gwertzman. "Clashes In Libya – What Is Next?" February 22, 2011, Council on Foreign Relations, http://www.cfr.org/libya/clashes-libya—next/p24185 (accessed March 3, 2019).

Adler-Nissen, Rebecca, and Vincent Pouliot. "Power in Practice: Negotiating the International Intervention in Libya." *European Journal of International Relations* 20, no. 4 (2014): 889–911.

Adler, Emanuel, and Michael N. Barnett, eds. *Security Communities*. New York: Cambridge University Press, 1998.

AFP. "Annan briefs top Qatari officials after Syria trip." *Yahoo News*, March 12, 2012.

AFP. "China to Send Peacekeeping Troops to the D.R. Congo Next Month." *reliefweb*, February 10, 2003.

AFP. "OIC chief backs no-fly zone over Libya." *Emirates 24/7 News*, March 8, 2011.

AFP. "Possible Diplomatic Opening in Libyan Crisis." *Ma'an News Agency*, July 12, 2011.

AFP. "Russia, China boycott Syria sanction talks at UN Security Council." *news.com.au*, August 26, 2011.

AFP. "UN slams Syria's 'loss of humanity'." *ABC News*, August 3, 2011.

African Union Peace and Security Council. "Report of the Chairperson of the Commission on the Situation in Darfur (The Sudan) [PSC/PR/2(XLV)], January 12." Addis Ababa: African Union, 2006.

Ahmed, Gaafar Karrar, "The Chinese Stance on the Darfur Conflict" (Johannesburg: South African Institute of International Affairs, 2010).

Ahmed, Samina. "Pakistan's Nuclear Weapons Program: Turning Points and Nuclear Choices." *International Security* 23, no. 4 (1999): 178–204.

al-Mubarak, Khalid. "Regime change in Sudan is not the right way to help Darfur." *The Guardian*, July 23, 2010.

Alden, Chris, and Daniel Large. "On Becoming a Norms Maker: Chinese Foreign Policy, Norms Evolution and the Challenges of Security in Africa." *The China Quarterly* 221 (March 2015): 123–42.

Ali, Wasil. "China uses economic leverage to pressure Sudan on Darfur – US." *Sudan Tribune*, March 6, 2007.

All Things Considered. "Darfur Activists Push Spielberg to Pressure China." *NPR*, July 24, 2007.

Alliot-Marie, Michele. "Minister of State and Minister of Foreign and European Affairs Michele Alliot-Marie's Statement on the situation in Libya." Paris: France Diplomatie, 2011.

Allison, Simon, and Daily Maverick. "African revolt threatens international criminal court's legitimacy." *The Guardian*, October 27, 2016.

Alterman, Jon B., "Bad Options and Hard Choices in Syria Policy" (Center for Strategic and International Studies, 2013). http://csis.org/files/attachments/ts130605_alterman.pdf (accessed March 3, 2019).

Alterman, Jon B., "A Tale of Two Crises" (Center for Strategic and International Studies, 2013). http://csis.org/files/publication/0413_MENC.pdf (accessed March 3, 2019).

Applbaum, Arthur Isak. "Forcing a People to Be Free." *Philosophy & Public Affairs* 35, no. 4 (2007): 359–400.

"Arab League backs Libya no-fly zone." *BBC News*, March 12, 2011.

"Arab League calls for transitional government in Syria." *The Telegraph*, July 23, 2012.

"Arab League Observer: Assad Committing Genocide in Syria." *Haaretz*, December 26, 2011.

"Arab League to offer 'safe exit' if Assad resigns." *CNN*, July 22, 2012.

"Arab ministers hold Syrian gov't responsible for chemical attacks." *Xinhua*, September 2, 2013.

"Arab states seek Libya no-fly zone." *Al Jazerra*, March 13, 2011.

Arbour, Louise. "For justice and civilians, don't rule out regime change." *The Globe and Mail*, June 26, 2012.

"ASEAN Ministers Call for WTO Talks Restart, Say Myanmar No Threat." *Japanese Economic Newswire*, January 11, 2007.

Associated Press. "China urges Libya to restore social stability." *The Jerusalem Post*, February 22, 2011.

Associated Press. "French presidential candidate calls for Beijing boycott." *ESPN*, March 22, 2007.

"AU Chief condemns Bashir warrants." *Al Jazeera*, July 27, 2010.

Auslin, Michael. "Washington's Chance to Back Up Rhetoric in Asia." *The Wall Street Journal*, April 10, 2014.

Axelrod, Robert. *The Evolution of Cooperation*. New York: Basic Books, 1984.

Axworthy, Lloyd. "In Libya, We Move toward a More Humane World." *Globe and Mail*, August 23, 2011.

Ayittey, George B. N. "The United States of Africa: A Revisit." *The ANNALS of the American Academy of Political and Social Science* 632, no. 1 (2010): 86–102.

Badescu, Cristina G., and Linnea Bergholm. "The African Union." In *The International Politics of Mass Atrocities: The Case of Darfur*, edited by David R. Black and Paul D. Williams, 100–18. New York: Routledge, 2010.

Balfour, Frederick "China: Spielberg's Olympics-Sized Snub." *Business Week*, February 13, 2008.

Banerjee, Dipankar. "India." Chap. 9 In *Providing Peacekeepers: The Politics, Challenges, and Future of United Nations Peacekeeping Contributions*, edited by Alex J. Bellamy and Paul D. Williams, 225–43. Oxford: Oxford University Press, 2013.

Barma, Naazneen, Giacomo Chiozza, Ely Ratner, and Steven Weber. "A World Without the West? Empirical Patterns and Theoretical Implications." *The Chinese Journal of International Politics* 2, no. 4 (2009): 525–44.

Bass, Gary J. "Human Rights Last?" *Foreign Policy*, February 21, 2011.

Batty, David, and Jack Shenker. "Syria suspended from Arab League." *The Guardian*, November 12, 2011.

Beck, Nathaniel. "Causal Process 'Observation': Oxymoron or (Fine) Old Wine." *Political Analysis* 18, no. 4 (2010): 499–505.

Becker, Jasper. "China fights UN sanctions on Sudan to safeguard oil." *The Independence*, October 15, 2004.

Becker, Jo, and Scott Shane. "Hillary Clinton, 'Smart Power' and a Dictator's Fall." *The New York Times*, February 27, 2016.

Beckley, Michael. "China's Century? Why America's Edge Will Endure." *International Security* 36, no. 3 (2011/2012): 41-78.

Bedeski, Robert E., and Niklas Swanström, eds. *Eurasia's Ascent in Energy and Geopolitics: Rivalry or Partnership for China, Russia, and Central Asia*. London: Routledge, 2012.

Bell, Melissa. "U.N. Syrian resolution: Which countries voted no?" *The Washington Post*, February 16, 2012.

Bellamy, Alex J. "Responsibility to Protect or Trojan Horse? The Crisis in Darfur and Humanitarian Intervention after Iraq." *Ethics & International Affairs* 19, no. 2 (2005): 31-54.

Bellamy, Alex J. *Responsibility to Protect: The Global Effort to End Mass Atrocities*. Cambridge: Polity, 2009.

Bellamy, Alex J., and Paul D. Williams. "The New Politics of Protection: Côte d'Ivoire, Libya and the Responsibility to Protect." *International Affairs* 87, no. 4 (2011): 825-50.

Benner, Thorsten, "Brazil as a Norm Entrepreneur: The 'Responsibility While Protecting' Initiative" (Berlin: Global Public Policy Institute, 2013). http://www.gppi.net/fileadmin/user_upload/media/pub/2013/Benner_2013_Working-Paper_Brazil-RWP.pdf (accessed March 3, 2019).

Bennett, Andrew. "Process Tracing and Causal Inference." Chap. 10 In *Rethinking Social Inquiry: Diverse Tools, Shared Standards*, edited by Henry E. Brady and David Collier, 207-19. Lanham, MD: Rowman and Littlefield, 2010.

Bennett, Andrew. "Process Tracing: A Bayesian Approach." Chap. 30 In *The Oxford Handbook of Political Methodology*, edited by Janet M. Box-Steffensmeier, Henry E. Brady, and David Collier, 702-21. Oxford: Oxford University Press, 2008.

Bhagavan, Manu. "India and the United Nations: Or Things Fall Apart." In *The Oxford Handbook of Indian Foreign Policy*, edited by David M. Malone, C. Raja Mohan, and Srinath Raghavan, 596-608. New York: Oxford University Press, 2015.

Biggar, Nigel. *In Defence of War*. Oxford: Oxford University Press, 2013.

Black, Ian. "Syria's Assad should step down, says King Abdullah of Jordan." *The Guardian*, November 14, 2011.

"Blair drops troops plan as line softens on Darfur." *The Scotsman*, August 25, 2004.

Blair, Edmund. "UN-Arab League Syria envoy Annan seeks political deal." *Reuters*, March 8, 2012.

Blight, Garry, Sheila Pulham, and Paul Torpey. "Arab Spring: an interactive timeline of Middle East protests." *The Guardian*, January 5, 2012.

Blitz, Roger. "Sport Organisers Play High-Stakes Game." *Financial Times*, September 29, 2010.

Bloomberg. "China told Sudan to adopt UN's Darfur plan – envoy." *Sudan Tribune*, February 6, 2007.

Bloomfield, Alan. *India and the Responsibility to Protect*. Farnham, Surrey: Ashgate Publishing Limited, 2016.

Blumenthal, Dan. "Unhelpful China." *The Washington Post*, December 6, 2004.

Bodeen, Christopher, and Associated Press. "China says Sudan activists have ulterior motives." *USA Today*, February 14, 2008.

Boniface, Pascal. "Vers un massacre en Libye (Towards a Massacre in Libya)." February 23, 2011, L'IRIS, http://www.iris-france.org/44201-vers-un-massacre-en-libye/ (accessed March 3, 2019).

Bosco, David L. *Five to Rule Them All: The UN Security Council and the Making of the Modern World*. New York: Oxford University Press, 2009.

Boustany, Nora. "Symbolic Torch Relay Aims to Shine Light on China, Darfur and Death." *The Washington Post*, August 15, 2007.

Bove, Vincenzo, and Leandro Elia. "Supplying peace: Participation in and troop contribution to peacekeeping missions." *Journal of Peace Research* 48, no. 6 (2011): 699–714.

Boyd, Henry. "Henry Boyd: Shades of Hama and Grozny in Homs and Idlib." March 12, 2012, IISS Voices, http://www.iiss.org/en/iiss%20voices/blogsections/2012-6d11/march-2012-bf81/shades-of-hama-and-grozny-8b68 (accessed March 3, 2019).

Bradsher, Keith. "Torch Nears, Posing Test Of Autonomy In Hong Kong." *The New York Times*, April 29, 2008.

Brady, Henry E., and David Collier, eds. *Rethinking Social Inquiry: Diverse Tools, Shared Standards*. Lanham, MD: Rowman & Littlefield Publishers, 2004.

Brady, Henry E., David Collier, and Jason Seawright. "Toward a Pluralistic Vision of Methodology." *Political Analysis* 14, no. 3 (2006): 353–68.

Branigan, Tania. "Libya's NTC gains Chinese recognition." *The Guardian*, September 12, 2011.

Brautigam, Deborah A. *The Dragon's Gift: The Real Story of China in Africa*. Oxford: Oxford University Press, 2009.

Brenton, Sir Tony. "Russia and China: An Axis of Insecurity." *Asian Affairs* 44, no. 2 (2013): 231–49.

Brewster, Murray, and Melissa Kent. "China, Russia aim for key UN peacekeeping positions as Canada prepares deployment." *CBC News*, October 5, 2016.

Brockmeier, Sarah, Oliver Stuenkel, and Marcos Tourinho. "The Impact of the Libya Intervention Debates on Norms of Protection." *Global Society* 30, no. 1 (2016): 113–33.

Bromley, D. B. *Reputation, Image and Impression Management*. Oxford: John Wiley & Sons, 1993.

Brownlie, Ian. *Principles of Public International Law*. 7th ed. Oxford: Oxford University Press, 2008.

Brumberg, Daniel, and Steven Heydemann, "Global Authoritarians and the Arab Spring: New Challenges for U.S. Diplomacy" (Washington D.C.: Woodrow Wilson Center and US Institute of Peace and U.S. Institute of Peace, 2013). https://www.wilsoncenter.org/sites/default/files/global_authoritarians_and%20_the_arab_spring_0.pdf (accessed March 3, 2019).

Brustlein, Corentin, Étienne de Durand, Guillaume Garnier, Marc Hecker, and Élie Tenenbaum, "Syrie: l'option militaire reste-t-elle ouverte? (Syria: Does the military option stay open?)" (Paris/Brussels: L'Ifri, 2013). http://www.ifri.org/sites/default/files/atoms/files/notedelifrisyrieloptionmilitaire.pdf (accessed March 3, 2019).

Budabin, Alexandra Cosima. "Genocide Olympics; The Campaign to pressure China over the Darfur Conflict." *Central European University Political Science Journal* 4, no. 4 (2009): 520–65.

Bull, Hedley. *The Anarchical Society: A Study of Order in World Politics*. London: Macmillan, 1977.

Burch, Jonathon. "Turkey tells Syria's Assad: Step down!" *Reuters*, November 22, 2011.

Burgos, Russell A. "Origins of Regime Change: 'Ideapolitik' on the Long Road to Baghdad, 1993–2000." *Security Studies* 17, no. 2 (2008): 221–56.

Busby, Joshua W. "Bono Made Jesse Helms Cry: Jubilee 2000, Debt Relief, and Moral Action in International Politics." *International Studies Quarterly* 51, no. 2 (2007): 247–75.

Butler, Jay. "Responsibility for Regime Change." *Columbia Law Review* 114, no. 3 (2014): 503–81.

Buzan, Barry. "China in International Society: Is 'Peaceful Rise' Possible?" *Chinese Journal of International Politics* 3, no. 1 (2010): 5–36.

Byers, Michael. "Terrorism, The use of Force and International Law After 11 September." *International and Comparative Law Quarterly* 51, no. 2 (2008): 401–14.

Byman, Daniel L. "Finish Him: Why the World Needs to Take Out Bashar al-Assad Now." February 2, 2012, The Brookings Institution, http://www.brookings.edu/research/opinions/2012/02/02-syria-assad-byman (accessed March 3, 2019).

Byman, Daniel L. "Libya's Al Qaeda Problem." February 25, 2011, The Brookings Institution, https://www.brookings.edu/opinions/libyas-al-qaeda-problem/ (accessed March 3, 2019).

Byman, Daniel L. "Regime Change in the Middle East: Problems and Prospects." *Political Science Quarterly* 127, no. 1 (2012): 25–46.

Cabestan, Jean-Pierre. "China and European Security and Economic Interests: A French Perspective." Chap. 7 In *US-China-EU Relations: Managing the New World Order*, edited by Robert S. Ross, Øystein Tunsjø and Zhang Tuosheng, 122–42. London: Routledge, 2010.

Callahan, William A. "Chinese Visions of World Order: Post-hegemonic or a New Hegemony?." *International Studies Review* 10, no. 4 (2008): 749–61.

Cameron, David, and Nicolas Sarkozy. "Letter from the PM and President Sarkozy to President Van Rompuy." March 10, 2011, Prime Minister's Office, GOV.UK, https://www.gov.uk/government/news/letter-from-the-pm-and-president-sarkozy-to-president-van-rompuy (accessed March 3, 2019).

"Cameron: UK working on 'no-fly zone' plan for Libya." *BBC News*, February 28, 2011.

Carlson, Allen. "Helping to Keep the Peace (Albeit Reluctantly): China's Recent Stance on Sovereignty and Multilateral Intervention." *Pacific Affairs* 77, no. 1 (2004): 9–27.

Carlson, Allen. "Protecting Sovereignty, Accepting Intervention: The Dilemma of Chinese Foreign Relations in the 1990s" (New York: National Committee on United States-China Relations, 2002). https://www.ncuscr.org/sites/default/files/page_attachments/Protecting-Sovereignty-Accepting-Intervention.pdf (accessed March 3, 2019).

Carlson, Allen. *Unifying China, Integrating with the World: Securing Chinese Sovereignty in the Reform Era*. Stanford, CA: Stanford University Press, 2005.

Carr, E. H. *International Relations Since the Peace Treaties*. London: Macmillan and Co., Limited, 1937.

Centre for Chinese Studies of the Stellenbosch University, "Partners in Competition? The EU, Africa and China: A summary of a conference hosted by the EU commission, Brussels, 28th June 2007" (2007).

Centre for Foreign Policy Analysis, and Chinese Academy of Social Sciences. "Symposium on China-Sudan Relations." July 26, 2007, http://www.cffpa.com/events.php (accessed March 3, 2019).

Cha, Victor D. "Beijing's Olympic-Sized Catch-22." *The Washington Quarterly* 31, no. 3 (2008): 105–23.

Cha, Victor D. *Beyond the Final Score: The Politics of Sport in Asia*. New York: Columbia University Press, 2009.

Chamberlain, Gethin. "Call for no-fly zone as slaughter goes on." *The Scotsman*, June 15, 2004.

Charap, Samuel, and Jeremy Shapiro. "How the US Can Move Russia on Syria." *Al-Monitor*, July 22, 2013.

Charbonneau, Louis. "U.S. suggests Russia wants 'regime change' in Georgia." *Reuters*, August 10, 2008.

Charbonneau, Louis, and Michelle Nichols. "U.N. confirms sarin used in Syria attack; U.S., UK, France blame Assad." *Reuters*, September 16, 2013.
Charbonneau, Louis, and Patrick Worsnip. "Russia, China veto U.N. draft backing Arab plan for Syria." *Reuters*, February 4, 2012.
Charter, David. "ICC issues war crimes arrest warrant for President al-Bashir of Sudan." *The Times*, March 4, 2009.
Chayes, Abram, and Antonia Handler Chayes. *The New Sovereignty: Compliance with International Regulatory Agreements*. Cambridge, MA: Harvard University Press, 1995.
Checkel, Jeffrey T. "International Institutions and Socialization in Europe: Introduction and Framework." *International Organization* 59, no. 4 (October 2005): 801–26.
Checkel, Jeffrey T. "Why Comply? Social Learning and European Identity Change." *International Organization* 55, no. 3 (2003): 553–88.
Chen, Zheng. "China Debates the Non-Interference Principle." *The Chinese Journal of International Politics* 9, no. 3 (2016): 349–74.
Cheng, Baoshan. "Study of Jiang Zemin's thought on National Security strategy." *Military Art Journal*, no. 3 (2004).
Cheng, Joseph Y. S., and Wankun Zhang. "Patterns and Dynamics of China's International Strategic Behavior." Chap. 10 In *Chinese Foreign Policy: Pragmatism and Strategic Behavior*, edited by Suisheng Zhao, 179–206. Armonk, NY: M.E. Sharpe, 2004.
Chesterman, Simon. "Humanitarian Intervention and Afghanistan." In *Humanitarian Intervention and International Relations*, edited by Jennifer M. Welsh, 163–75. Oxford: Oxford University Press, 2004.
Chesterman, Simon. *Just War or Just Peace?: Humanitarian Intervention and International Law*. Oxford: Oxford University Press, 2003.
Chestnut, Sheena, and Alastair Iain Johnston. "Is China Rising?." Chap. 12 In *Global Giant: Is China Changing the Rules of the Game?*, edited by Eva Paus, Penelope B. Prime and Jon Western, 237–59. New York: Palgrave Macmillan, 2009.
Chin, Gregory, and Ramesh Thakur. "Will China Change the Rules of Global Order?." *The Washington Quarterly* 33, no. 4 (October 2010): 119–38.
"China's peacekeeping forces leave for Liberia." *People's Daily Online*, December 10, 2003.
"China and Russia veto UN resolution condemning Syria." *BBC News*, October 5, 2011.
"China confirms contact with Libyan NTC." *China Daily*, June 7, 2011.
"China confirms contact with Libyan opposition leader." *Xinhua*, June 3, 2011.
China Copyright and Media. "CCP Central Committee Decision concerning Some Major Questions in Comprehensively Moving Governing the Country According to the law Forward." October 28, 2014, https://chinacopyrightandmedia.wordpress.com/2014/10/28/ccp-central-committee-decision-concerning-some-major-questions-in-comprehensively-moving-governing-the-country-according-to-the-law-forward/ (accessed March 3, 2019).
"The China Deals: Trends and Outlook for Chinese Outbound Investment." *HIS Global Insight*, May 22, 2012.
"China expresses regret for military strike against Libya." *Xinhua*, March 20, 2011.
"'China has serious difficulty with part of the resolution,' envoy says." *Xinhua*, March 18, 2011.
"China issues a warning to Sudan over Darfur crisis." *Sudan Tribune*, January 30, 2008.
"China Regrets Spielberg Action." *BBC News*, February 14, 2008.
"China to become 2nd largest contributor to UN peacekeeping budget." *China Daily*, May 30, 2016.
"China Urges Support to Deployment of Peacekeeping Troops in Darfur." *Xinhua*, June 16, 2007.

"China wants San Francisco Olympic torch's route shortened." *The Times of India*, March 27, 2008.
"China's Thirst For Oil, Asia Report," (Seoul/Brussels: International Crisis Group, 2008). https://www.crisisgroup.org/asia/north-east-asia/china/china-s-thirst-oil (accessed March 3, 2019).
"Chinese Blue Helmets Play Active Role in Africa." *Xinhua*, October 28, 2006.
"Chinese paper condemns Libya air strikes." *China Daily*, March 21, 2011.
Ching, Frank. "China sees tough times as the Games draw near." *New Straits Times*, May 17, 2001, 27.
Chivvis, Christopher S. *Toppling Qaddafi: Libya and the Limits of Liberal Intervention*. Cambridge: Cambridge University Press, 2013.
Chrisafis, Angelique, and Julian Borger. "Syria conflict: France to seek tough UN resolution on chemical weapons." *The Guardian*, September 10, 2013.
Christensen, Thomas J. "The Advantages of an Assertive China." *Foreign Policy* 90, no. 2 (March/April 2011): 54–67.
Christensen, Thomas J. *The China Challenge: Shaping the Choices of a Rising Power*. New York: W.W. Norton & Company, 2015.
Christensen, Thomas J. "China's Rise and Challenges for American Security." Paper presented at the 2018 China Research Center Annual Lecture, University of Maryland, March 1, 2018.
Christensen, Thomas J. "Shaping the Choices of a Rising China: Recent Lessons for the Obama Administration." *The Washington Quarterly* 32, no. 3 (2009): 89–104.
Claes, Jonas. "Protecting Civilians from Mass Atrocities: Meeting the Challenge of R2P Rejectionism." *Global Responsibility to Protect* 4, no. 1 (2012): 67–97.
Clinton, Hillary Rodham. "Briefing on Plane Before Departure for Geneva, Switzerland." February 27, 2011, Washington D.C.: U.S. Department of State, http://www.state.gov/secretary/20092013clinton/rm/2011/02/157200.htm (accessed March 3, 2019).
Clinton, Hillary Rodham. "Holding the Qadhafi Government Accountable." February 26, 2011, Washington, D.C.: U.S. Department of State, http://www.state.gov/secretary/20092013clinton/rm/2011/02/157187.htm (accessed March 3, 2019).
Clinton, Hillary Rodham. "Opening Remarks Before the Senate Foreign Relations Committee." March 2, 2011, Washington D.C.: U.S. Department of State, http://www.state.gov/secretary/20092013clinton/rm/2011/03/157556.htm (accessed March 3, 2019).
Clinton, Hillary Rodham. "Transcript: Sec. of State Hillary Clinton Talks With Diane Sawyer About the Situation in Libya." In *ABC News*, edited by Diane Sawyer, 2011.
Cockayne, James, and David M. Malone. "Creeping Unilateralism: How Operation Provide Comfort and the No-Fly Zones in 1991 and 1992 Paved the Way for the Iraq Crisis of 2003." *Security Dialogue* 37, no. 1 (2006): 123–41.
Cockayne, James, and David M. Malone. "The Security Council and the 1991 and 2003 Wars in Iraq." Chap. 17 In *The United Nations Security Council and War: The Evolution of Thought and Practice Since 1945*, edited by Vaughan Lowe, Adam Roberts, Jennifer M. Welsh, and Dominik Zaum, 384–405. Oxford: Oxford University Press, 2008.
Cody, Edward. "Arab League condemns broad bombing campaign in Libya." *The Washington Post*, March 21, 2011.
Cody, Edward. "China Readies Riot Force For Peacekeeping In Haiti." *The Washington Post*, September 29, 2004.
Cody, Edward. "In China, a Display of Resolve on Darfur." *The Washington Post*, September 16, 2007.
Cohen, Roberta A. "Calling on China." *The Washington Post*, August 5, 2004, A18.
Cohen, Roberta A. "Sudanese Killings Must be Stopped." *Newsday*, May 21, 2004.

Cohen, Roberta A., and William G. O'Neill. "Last stand in Sudan?." *Bulletin of the Atomic Scientists* 62, no. 2 (2006): 51–58.
Cohen, Stephen P. *India: Emerging Power*. Washington D.C.: Brookings Institution, 2001.
Collier, David. "Understanding Process Tracing." *PS: Political Science and Politics* 44, no. 4 (2011): 823–30.
Collier, David, Henry E. Brady, and Jason Seawright. "Outdated Views of Qualitative Methods: Time to Move On." *Political Analysis* 18, no. 4 (2010): 506–13.
Collier, David, Henry E. Brady, and Jason Seawright. "Sources of Leverage in Causal Inference: Toward an Alternative View of Methodology." Chap. 13 In *Rethinking Social Inquiry: Diverse Tools, Shared Standards*, edited by Henry E. Brady and David Collier, 229–66. Lanham, MD: Rowman & Littlefield Publishers, 2004.
Columbia Global Policy Initiative. *Responsibility while Protecting: Implementation and the Future of the Responsibility to Protect*. Edited by Maggie Powers.New York: Columbia Global Policy Initiative, 2015.
Consulate General of the People's Republic of China in San Francisco. "Assistant Foreign Minister Zhai Jun Holds a Briefing for Chinese and Foreign Journalists on the Darfur Issue of Sudan." April 12, 2007, http://www.chinaconsulatesf.org/eng/xw/t311008.htm (accessed March 3, 2019).
Consulate General of the People's Republic of China in San Francisco. "Special Envoy of the Chinese Government and Assistant Foreign Minister Zhai Jun Visits Sudan Successfully." September 4, 2008, http://www.chinaconsulatesf.org/eng/xw/t511195.htm (accessed March 3, 2019).
Contessi, Nicola P. "Multilateralism, Intervention and Norm Contestation: China's Stance on Darfur in the UN Security Council." *Security Dialogue* 41, no. 3 (2010): 323–44.
Cook, Steven A. "It's Time to Think Seriously About Intervening in Syria." *The Atlantic*, January 17, 2012.
Cooper, Belinda. "The Limits of International Justice." *World Policy Journal* 26, no. 3 (2009): 91–101.
Cooper, Helene. "Darfur Collides with Olympics, and China Yields." *The New York Times*, April 13, 2007.
Cordesman, Anthony, and Scott Simon. "A Look At Gadhafi's Fragmented Military." *NPR*, March 5, 2011.
Cornelissen, Scarlett. "The Geopolitics of Global Aspiration: Sport Mega-events and Emerging Powers." *The International Journal of the History of Sport* 27, no. 16–18 (2010): 3008–25.
Corten, Olivier. "Human Rights and Collective Security: Is There an Emerging Right of Humanitarian Intervention?." Chap. 3 In *Human Rights, Intervention, and the Use of Force*, edited by Philip Alston and Euan Macdonald, 87–137. Oxford: Oxford University Press, 2008.
Crawford, Neta C. *Argument and Change in World Politics: Ethics, Decolonization, and Humanitarian Intervention*. Cambridge: Cambridge University Press, 2002.
Crawford, Neta C. "Understanding Discourse: A Method of Ethical Argument Analysis." *Qualitative Methods Newsletter* 2, no. 1 (2004): 22–25.
Crescenzi, Mark J. C., Jacob D. Kathman, and Stephen B. Long. "Reputation, History, and War." *Journal of Peace Research* 44, no. 6 (2007): 651–67.
Cronin, Bruce. "Intervention and the International Community." In *International Intervention: Sovereignty Versus Responsibility*, edited by Michael Keren and Donald A. Sylvan. London: Frank Cass, 2002.
Cryer, Robert. "Prosecuting the Leaders: Promises, Politics and Pragmatics." *Göttingen Journal of International Law* 1 (2009): 45–75.

Cullen, Kevin. "Genocide Games." *The Boston Globe*, March 25, 2007.
Dafoe, Allan, Jonathan Renshon, and Paul Huth. "Reputation and Status as Motives for War." *Annual Review of Political Science* 17 (2014): 371–93.
Dagne, Ted, "Sudan: The Crisis in Darfur and Status of the North-South Peace Agreement" (Washington D.C.: United States Congressional Research Service, 2008).
Dai, Bingguo. "Closing Remarks for U.S.-China Strategic and Economic Dialogue." July 28, 2009, U.S. State Department, https://2009-2017.state.gov/secretary/20092013clinton/rm/2009a/july/126599.htm (accessed March 3, 2019).
Dalton, Richard M. "We must stand ready to intervene in Libya." *The Telegraph*, February 27, 2011.
Daly, M.W. *Darfur's Sorrow: A History of Destruction and Genocide*. Cambridge: Cambridge University Press, 2007.
Danin, Robert M. "Calling for Regime Change in Syria." August 18, 2011, Council on Foreign Relations, http://www.cfr.org/syria/calling-regime-change-syria/p25677 (accessed March 3, 2019).
Danin, Robert M. "Danin: How to help Syria without intervening militarily." *CNN*, January 22, 2012.
Daou, Marc. "'Friends of Syria' push for tougher sanctions." *France 24*, July 7, 2012.
Darfur Consortium. "Decision on AU presidency must take into account Darfurians protection." *Sudan Tribune*, January 21, 2006.
"Darfur: Threats to Chinese Engineers will not Delay Remaining Peacekeepers (Wikileaks Cable: 07BEIJING7270_a)." November 29, 2007, https://www.wikileaks.org/plusd/cables/07BEIJING7270_a.html (accessed March 3, 2019).
Davis, Jonathan E. "From Ideology to Pragmatism: China's Position on Humanitarian Intervention in the Post-Cold War Era." *Vanderbilt Journal of Transnational Law* 44, no. 2 (2011): 217–83.
Davis, Michael C. "The Reluctant Intervenor: The UN Security Council, China's Worldview, and Humanitarian Intervention." In *International Intervention in the Post-Cold War World: Moral Responsibility and Power Politics*, edited by Michael C. Davis, Wolfgang Dietrich, Bettina Scholdan, and Dieter Sepp, 241–53. Armonk, New York: M.E. Sharpe, 2004.
de Carvalho, Benjamin, and Iver B. Neumann, eds. *Small State Status Seeking: Norway's Quest for International Standing*. Abingdon: Routledge, 2015.
de Waal, Alex. "Darfur and the failure of the responsibility to protect." *International Affairs* 83, no. 6 (2007): 1039–54.
de Waal, Alex. "'My Fears, Alas, Were Not Unfounded': Africa's Responses to the Libya Conflict." Chap. 4 In *Libya, the Responsibility to Protect and the Future of Humanitarian Intervention*, edited by Aidan Hehir and Robert W. Murray, 58–82. Basingstoke: Palgrave Macmillan, 2013.
de Waal, Alex. "Sudanese Stories: Narratives of Grievance, Distrust, and Fatalism in Recurrent Violence." Chap. 4 In *Genocidal Nightmares: Narratives of Insecurity and the Logic of Mass Atrocities*, edited by Abdelwahab El-Affendi, 73–90. New York: Bloomsbury Academic, 2015.
Dedring, Juergen. *The United Nations Security Council in the 1990s: Resurgence and Renewal*. Albany, NY: State University of New York Press, 2008.
Deen, Thalif. "Russia, China Shield Syria from Possible U.N. Sanctions." *Inter Press Service*, June 9, 2011.
deLisle, Jacques. "'One World, Different Dreams': The Contest to Define the Beijing Olympics." In *Owning the Olympics: Narratives of the New China*, edited by Monroe E. Price and Daniel Dayan, 17–66. Ann Arbor, MI: University of Michigan Press, 2008.

Deng, Gang. "Macedonian FM Seeks Reestablishing Diplomatic Relations with China." *People's Daily*, June 18, 2001.

Deng, Yong. *China's Struggle for Status: The Realignment of International Relations.* Cambridge: Cambridge University Press, 2008.

Deng, Yong. "China: The Post-Responsible Power." *The Washington Quarterly* 37, no. 4 (2015): 117–132.

Deng, Zili, and Cuiwen Wang. "Lengzhan hou zhongguo heyi canyu feizhou weihe xingdong (Explaining China's Involvement in UN Peacekeeping Operations since 1989)." *Quarterly Journal of International Politics* 2 (2012): 1–37.

Dery, David. "Agenda Setting and Problem Definition." *Policy Studies* 21, no. 1 (2000): 37–47.

Development Initiatives. "Global Humanitarian Assistance Report 2016" (2016). www.globalhumanitarianassistance.org/wp-content/ploads/2016/07/GHA-report-2016-full-report.pdf (accessed March 3, 2019).

Development Initiatives. "Global Humanitarian Assistance Report 2018" (2018). http://devinit.org/wp-content/uploads/2018/06/GHA-Report-2018.pdf (accessed March 3, 2019).

Dickie, Mure. "UK minister praises China's role in Darfur." *Financial Times*, May 18, 2007.

Dijkstra, Hylke. *International Organizations and Military Affairs.* New York: Routledge, 2016.

Dinmore, Guy, and Mark Turner. "US defends China's role in Darfur." *Financial Times*, April 12, 2007.

Dittmer, Lowell. "China and the Developing World." Chap. 1 In *China, the Developing World, and the New Global Dynamic*, edited by Lowell Dittmer and George T. Yu, 1–12. Boulder, CO: Lynne Rienner Publishers, 2010.

Dixon, Jennifer M. "Rhetorical Adaptation and Resistance to International Norms." *Perspectives on Politics* 15, no. 1 (March 2017): 83–99.

Dodge, Toby. "Iraqi Transitions: From Regime Change to State Collapse." *Third World Quarterly* 26, no. 4/5 (2005): 705–21.

Donahue, Patrick, and Robert Hutton. "G-8 Split on Libya No-Fly Zone With Russia, Germany Opposed." *Bloomberg*, March 16, 2011.

Doran, Michael. "5 truths about Syria." September 3, 2013, Politico, http://www.politico.com/story/2013/09/opinion-michael-doran-5-truth-syria-096178 (accessed March 3, 2019).

Doran, Michael. "Pursue Regime Change in Syria." January 23, 2014, The Brookings Institution, http://www.brookings.edu/research/papers/2014/01/regime-change-syria-doran (accessed March 3, 2019).

Doran, Michael, and Salman Shaikh. "Getting Serious in Syria." July 29, 2011, The Brookings Institution, https://www.brookings.edu/articles/getting-serious-in-syria/ (accessed March 3, 2019).

Doran, Michael, and Salman Shaikh. "The Road Beyond Damascus." January 17, 2013, The Brookings Institution, http://www.brookings.edu/research/papers/2013/01/the-road-beyond-damascus (accessed March 3, 2019).

Doty, Roxanne Lynn. *Imperial encounters: the politics of representation in North-South relations.* Minneapolis, MN: University of Minnesota Press, 1996.

Downes, Alexander B., and Jonathan Monten. "Forced to Be Free?: Why Foreign-Imposed Regime Change Rarely Leads to Democratization." *International Security* 37, no. 4 (2013): 90–131.

Downes, Alexander B., and Lindsey A. O'Rourke. "You Can't Always Get What You Want: Why Foreign-Imposed Regime Change Seldom Improves Interstate Relations." *International Security* 41, no. 2 (2016): 43–89.

Downs, Erica S. "The Fact and Fiction of Sino-African Energy Relations." *China Security* 3, no. 3 (2007): 42–68.

Doyle, Michael W., Ian Johnstone, and Robert Orr. *Keeping the Peace: Multidimensional UN Operations in Cambodia and El Salvador*. Cambridge: Cambridge University Press, 1997.

dream4darfur. "Gengen Genocide." July 7, 2008, YouTube, https://www.youtube.com/watch?v=RhlIM5aa6jc (accessed March 3, 2019).

Dream for Darfur. "Dream for Darfur." 2007, www.dreamfordarfur.org (accessed March 3, 2019).

Duchâtel, Mathieu, Oliver Bräuner, and Hang Zhou, "Protecting China's Overseas Interests: The Slow Shift away from Non-interference" (Solna: Stockholm International Peace Research Institute, 2014). https://www.sipri.org/sites/default/files/files/PP/SIPRIPP41.pdf (accessed March 3, 2019).

Dunne, Tim, and Jess Gifkins. "Libya and the state of intervention." *Australian Journal of International Affairs* 65, no. 5 (2011): 515–29.

Dyer, Geoff. "Beijing expresses 'grave concern' over ICC charges." *Financial Times*, July 16, 2008.

Eckert, Paul. "Nobel laureates press China over Darfur." *Reuters*, February 12, 2008.

Eckstein, Harry. "Case studies in political science." In *Handbook of Political Science*, edited by Fred I. Greenstein and Nelson W. Polsby, 78–137. Reading, MA: Addison-Wesley, 1975.

Egeland, Jan. *A Billion Lives: An Eyewitness Report from the Frontlines of Humanity*. New York: Simon & Schuster, 2008.

Embassy of the People's Republic of China in Ireland. "Wen Jiabao Meets with the UN-Arab League Joint Special Envoy Kofi Annan." March 27, 2012, http://ie.china-embassy.org/eng/NewsPress/t918582.htm (accessed March 3, 2019).

Embassy of the People's Republic of China in the State of Israel. "The Iraq Issue." September 21, 2004, http://www.chinaembassy.org.il/eng/zt/dqwt/t159726.htm (accessed March 3, 2019).

Embassy of the People's Republic of China in the United States. "Foreign Ministry Spokesperson Jiang Yu's Regular Press Conference on March 3, 2011." March 5, 2011, http://www.china-embassy.org/eng/fyrth/t804119.htm (accessed March 3, 2019).

Embassy of the People's Republic of China in the United States. "Foreign Ministry Spokesperson Jiang Yu's Regular Press Conference on March 22, 2011." March 23, 2011, http://www.china-embassy.org/eng/fyrth/t809578.htm (accessed March 3, 2019).

Embassy of the People's Republic of China in United Arab Emirates. "Foreign Ministry Spokesperson Jiang Yu's Remarks on Discussion of Tibet in an Informal Meeting of the EU Foreign Ministers' Council." April 2, 2008, http://ae.china-embassy.org/eng/wjbfyrth/t420322.htm (accessed March 3, 2019).

"Emotion kicks off China's Olympics." *CNN*, August 9, 2008.

"Entretien avec Kader A. Abderrahim: Libye: Le système est en train de craquer et de prendre l'eau de toutes parts (Interview with Kader Abderrahim, Research Fellow, 'Libya: The system is cracked and water is coming in from everywhere')." February 24, 2011, L'IRIS, http://www.iris-france.org/43137-entretien-avec-kader-a-abderrahim-libye-le-systeme-est-en-train-de-craquer-et-de-prendre-leau-de-toutes-parts/ (accessed March 3, 2019).

Erickson, Jennifer L. *Dangerous Trade: Arms Exports, Human Rights, and International Reputation*. New York: Columbia University Press, 2015.

Evans, Dominic. "At least 162,000 killed in Syria conflict - monitoring group." *Reuters*, May 19, 2014.

Evans, Gareth. "Ending Mass Atrocity Crimes: The Responsibility to Protect Balance Sheet After Libya " July 31, 2011, http://www.gevans.org/speeches/speech443.html (accessed March 3, 2019).

Evans, Gareth. "The world should be ready to intervene in Sudan Darfur." *International Herald Tribune*, May 15, 2004.

Eyre, Dana P., and Mark C. Suchman. "Status, Norms, and the Proliferation of Conventional Weapons: An Institutional Theory Approach." Chap. 3 In *The Culture of National Security: Norms and Identity in World Politics*, edited by Peter J. Katzenstein, 79-113. New York: Columbia University Press, 1996.

Fabre, Cécile. *Cosmopolitan War*. 1st ed. ed. Oxford: Oxford University Press, 2012.

Farrow, Ronan, and Mia Farrow. "The 'Genocide Olympics'." *The Wall Street Journal*, March 28, 2007.

Fearon, James D. "Bargaining, Enforcement, and International Cooperation." *International Organization* 52, no. 2 (2003): 269-305.

Feigenbaum, Evan A. "China's challenge to Pax Americana." *The Washington Quarterly* 24, no. 3 (2001): 31-43.

Fenton, Neil. *Understanding the UN Security Council: Coercion or Consent?* London: Ashgate, 2004.

Ferdinand, Peter, "The positions of Russia and China at the UN Security Council in the light of recent crises" (Brussels: Directorate-General for External Policies, Policy Department, European Union, 2013). http://bookshop.europa.eu/en/the-positions-of-russia-and-china-at-the-un-security-council-in-the-light-of-recent-crises-pbBB3213114/downloads/BB-32-13-114-EN-N/BB3213114ENN_002.pdf?FileName=BB3213114ENN_002.pdf&SKU=BB3213114ENN_PDF&CatalogueNumber=BB-32-13-114-EN-N (accessed March 3, 2019).

Ferguson, Chaka. "The Strategic Use of Soft Balancing: The Normative Dimensions of the Chinese-Russian 'Strategic Partnership'." *Journal of Strategic Studies* 35, no. 2 (2012): 197-222.

Festinger, Leon. "An Analysis of Compliant Behavior." In *Group Relations at the Crossroads*, edited by Milbourne Otto Wilson and Muzafer Sherif, 232-56. New York: Harper & Brothers, 1953.

Finnemore, Martha. *The Purpose of Intervention: Changing Beliefs about the Use of Force*. Ithaca, NY: Cornell University Press, 2003.

Finnemore, Martha, and Kathryn Sikkink. "International Norm Dynamics and Political Change." *International Organization* 52, no. 4 (Autumn 1998): 887-917.

Flint, Julie, and Alex de Waal. *Darfur: A New History of a Long War*. London: Zed Books, 2008.

Florini, Ann. "Rising Asian Powers and Changing Global Governance." *International Studies Review* 13, no. 1 (2011): 24-33.

Foot, Rosemary. "'Doing some things' in the Xi Jinping era: the United Nations as China's venue of choice." *International Affairs* 90, no. 5 (2014): 1085-100.

Foot, Rosemary and Andrew Walter. *China, the United States, and Global Order* (Cambridge: Cambridge University Press, 2011).

Foot, Rosemary, and Rana Siu Inboden. "China's Influence on Asian States during the Creation of the U.N. Human Rights Council: 2005-2007." *Asian Survey* 54, no. 5 (2014): 849-68.

Ford Rojas, John-Paul. "Muammar Gaddafi in his own words." *The Telegraph*, October 20, 2011.

Foreign & Commonwealth Office. "Government doing all it can to assist Britons in Libya." February 25, 2011, GOV.UK, https://www.gov.uk/government/news/government-doing-all-it-can-to-assist-britons-in-libya (accessed March 3, 2019).

Foreign & Commonwealth Office. "Prime Minister's statement on Libya." 28 February, 2011, GOV.UK, https://www.gov.uk/government/news/prime-minister-s-statement-on-libya (accessed March 3, 2019).

Foreign & Commonwealth Office. "Foreign Secretary calls for an 'immediate stop to the use of armed force against the Libyan people'." March 6, 2011, GOV.UK, https://www.gov.uk/government/news/foreign-secretary-calls-for-an-immediate-stop-to-the-use-of-armed-force-against-the-libyan-people (accessed March 3, 2019).

Foreign & Commonwealth Office. "Foreign Secretary describes situation in Libya as 'deplorable and unacceptable'." February 21, 2011, GOV.UK, https://www.gov.uk/government/news/foreign-secretary-describes-situation-in-libya-as-deplorable-and-unacceptable (accessed March 3, 2019).

Foreign & Commonwealth Office. "Foreign Secretary statement to Parliament on the crisis in Syria." June 11, 2012, GOV.UK, https://www.gov.uk/government/news/foreign-secretary-statement-to-parliament-on-the-crisis-in-syria (accessed March 3, 2019).

Foreign & Commonwealth Office. "Foreign Secretary: British diplomatic team in Benghazi has 'now left Libya'." March 6, 2011, GOV.UK, https://www.gov.uk/government/news/foreign-secretary-british-diplomatic-team-in-benghazi-has-now-left-libya (accessed March 3, 2019).

Foreign & Commonwealth Office. "Syria: Foreign Secretary comments on situation in Hama." July 5, 2011, GOV.UK, https://www.gov.uk/government/news/syria-foreign-secretary-comments-on-situation-in-hama (accessed March 3, 2019).

Foreign & Commonwealth Office. "UK calls for UN action on Libya." February 22, 2011, GOV.UK, https://www.gov.uk/government/news/uk-calls-for-un-action-on-libya (accessed March 3, 2019).

Fraihat, Ibrahim. "The March for Freedom in Libya." February 22, 2011, The Brookings Institution, http://www.brookings.edu/blogs/up-front/posts/2011/02/22-libya-sharqieh (accessed March 3, 2019).

France Diplomatie. "Entretien du Ministre d'État, Ministre des Affaires Étrangères et Européennes, Alain Juppé, avec TF1: Extraits (Interview of Foreign Affairs Minister Alain Juppé with TF1)." 2011.

France Diplomatie. "Entretien du ministre des Affaires étrangères, M. Laurent Fabius, avec 'France Inter': Extraits, Paris, 29 août 2012 (Foreign Affairs Minister Laurent Fabius' Interview with France Inter)." 2012.

France Diplomatie. "Entretien du Premier Ministre "François Fillon, avec "RTL": Extraits (Interview of Prime Minister François Fillion with RTL)." Paris: France Diplomatie, 2011.

France Diplomatie. "Entretien du Président de la République, Nicolas Sarkozy, avec L'hebdomadaire "L'Express" (Interview of President Nicolas Sarkozy with L'Express)." 2011.

France Diplomatie. "Situation en Libye et en Méditerranée Conseil Européen Extraordinaire Conférence de Presse du Président de la République, Nicolas Sarkozy (Press Conference by President Nicolas Sarkozy on the situation in Libya and in the Mediterranean following the Special Session of the European Council)." 2011.

France Diplomatie. "Syrie - Entretien du ministre des Affaires étrangères, M. Laurent Fabius, avec 'BFMTV', 'Europe 1', 'RFI', 'France Info', 'RTL' et 'FranceONU TV': New

York, 30 août 2012 (Foreign Affairs Minister Laurent Fabius' Interview with BFMTV, Europe 1, RFI, France Info, RTL and FranceONU TV)." 2012.

France in the United Kingdom. "Syria – Joint statement by Nicolas Sarkozy, President of the Republic, Angela Merkel, Chancellor of Germany, and David Cameron, Prime Minister of the United Kingdom of Great Britain and Northern Ireland." August 18, 2011, http://www.ambafrance-uk.org/French-British-and-German-leaders (accessed March 3, 2019).

"France says Africa should take lead in ending Darfur violence." *Sudan Tribune*, July 28, 2004.

Franck, Thomas M. *The Power of Legitimacy Among Nations*. New York: Oxford University Press, 1990.

Franck, Thomas M. *Recourse to Force: State Action Against Threats and Armed Attacks*. Cambridge: Cambridge University Press, 2002.

Franck, Thomas M. "Terrorism and the Rights of Self-Defense." *American Journal of International Law* 95, no. 4 (2001): 839–43.

Frank, Robert H. *Choosing the Right Pond: Human Behavior and the Quest for Status*. New York: Oxford University Press, 1985.

Fravel, M. Taylor. "China's Attitude Toward UN Peacekeeping Operations Since 1989." *Asian Survey* 36, no. 11 (1996): 1102–21.

Freedman, Joshua. "Status insecurity and temporality in world politics." *European Journal of International Relations* 22, no. 4 (2015): 797–822.

French, Howard W. "China in Africa: All Trade, With No Political Baggage." *The New York Times*, August 8, 2004.

Frontline. "Mukesh Kapila's Memos To The United Nations." November 20, 2007, PBS, http://www.pbs.org/wgbh/pages/frontline/darfur/etc/memo.html (accessed March 3, 2019).

Fu, Ying. "How China Sees Russia." *CRI English*, December 18, 2015.

Fung, Courtney J. "China and the Responsibility to Protect: From Opposition to Advocacy." *United States Institute of Peace* 205 (2016): 1–5.

Fung, Courtney J. "Global South Solidarity? China, Regional Organisations and Intervention in the Libyan and Syrian Civil Wars." *Third World Quarterly* 37, no. 1 (2016): 33–50.

Fung, Courtney J. "What explains China's deployment to UN peacekeeping operations?" *International Relations of the Asia-Pacific* 16, no. 3 (2016): 409–41.

Fung, Courtney J. "Separating Intervention From Regime Change: China's Diplomatic Innovations at the UN Security Council Regarding the Syria Crisis." *The China Quarterly* 235 (2018): 693–712.

Fung, Courtney J. "Rhetorical Adaptation and International Order-Making: China's Advancement of the Responsibility to Protect." *Cooperation and Conflict* (2019): https://doi.org/10.1177/0010836719858118.

Garamone, Jim. "Panetta Discusses First Week as Defense Secretary." *U.S. Department of Defense*, July 9, 2011.

Gardner, Frank. "Libya: Who is propping up Gaddafi?" *BBC News*, March 2, 2011.

Garnett, Sherman W., ed. *Rapprochement or rivalry?: Russia-China relations in a changing Asia*. Washington D.C.: Carnegie Endowment for International Peace, 2000.

Garwood-Gowers, Andrew. "China's 'Responsible Protection' concept: re-interpreting the Responsibility to Protect (R2P) and military intervention for humanitarian purposes." *Asian Journal of International Law* 6, no. 1 (2016): 89–118.

Garwood-Gowers, Andrew. "Libya and the international community's 'responsibility to protect'." *On Line Opinion: Australia's eJournal of Social and Political Debate* (February 25, 2011).

"GCC calls for end to violence in Syria." *The National*, August 7, 2011.

Geertz, Clifford. *The Interpretation of Cultures: Selected Essays*. New York: Basic Books, 1973.

Geller, Daniel S., and J. David Singer. *Nations at War: A Scientific Study of International Conflict*. Cambridge: Cambridge University Press, 1998.

George, Alexander L., and Andrew Bennett. *Case Studies and Theory Development in the Social Sciences*. Cambridge, MA: MIT Press, 2005.

Ghosh, Palash. "Syrian Crisis: Kofi Annan Takes Peace Plan To China." *International Business Times*, March 26, 2012.

Gilady, Lilach. "Conspicuous Waste in International Relations." Doctoral Dissertation, Yale University, 2006.

Gill, Bates, and Chin-hao Huang, "China's Expanding Role in Peacekeeping: Prospects and Policy Implications" (Stockholm: Stockholm International Peace Research Institute, 2009). https://www.sipri.org/publications/2009/sipri-policy-papers/chinas-expanding-role-peacekeeping-prospects-and-policy-implications (accessed March 3, 2019).

Gill, Bates, and James Reilly. "Sovereignty, intervention and peacekeeping: the view from Beijing." *Survival* 42, no. 3 (2000): 41–60.

Gilpin, Robert. *War and Change in World Politics*. New York: Cambridge University Press, 1983.

Gladstone, Rick. "China and Russia Move to Cut Human Rights Jobs in U.N. Peacekeeping." *The New York Times*, June 27, 2018.

Gladstone, Rick. "In Rare, Blunt Speech, Saudi King Criticizes Syria Vetoes." *The New York Times*, February 10, 2012.

Glanville, Luke. *Sovereignty and the Responsibility to Protect: A New History*. Chicago, IL: University of Chicago Press, 2014.

Glaser, Bonnie S. "Ensuring the 'Go Abroad' Policy Serves China's Domestic Priorities." *China Brief* 7, no. 5 (2007).

Glaser, Bonnie S. "How Will China React to a Military Strike on Syria?" September 5, 2013, Centre for Strategic and International Studies, https://www.csis.org/analysis/how-will-china-react-military-strike-syria (accessed March 3, 2019).

Glaser, Charles. "The flawed case for nuclear disarmament." *Survival* 40, no. 1 (1998): 112–28

Glaser, Charles. "Will China's Rise Lead to War? Why Realism Does Not Mean Pessimism." *Foreign Affairs* 72, no. 1 (2011).

Global Centre for the Responsibility to Protect. "Timeline of International Response to the Situation in Syria." 2015, http://www.globalr2p.org/media/files/timeline-of-international-response-to-syria-26.pdf (accessed March 3, 2019).

Goldgeier, James M., and Michael McFaul. "A tale of two worlds: core and periphery in the post-cold war era." *International Organization* 46, no. 2 (1992): 467–91.

Goldman, Russell. "Spielberg Mulls Quitting Olympics to Pressure Chinese on Darfur." *ABC News*, July 26, 2007.

Goldstein, Avery. "First Things First: The Pressing Danger of Crisis Instability in U.S.-China Relations." *International Security* 37, no. 4 (2013): 49–89.

Goldstein, Avery. *Rising to the Challenge: China's Grand Strategy and International Security*. Stanford, CA: Stanford University Press, 2005.

Goodman, Peter S. "China Invests Heavily In Sudan's Oil Industry: Beijing Supplies Arms Used on Villagers." *The Washington Post*, December 23, 2004.

Gray, Christine. "The Use of Force and the International Legal Order." Chap. 20 In *International Law*, edited by Malcolm D. Evans, 589–619. Oxford: Oxford University Press, 2006.

Greathead, R. Scott. "China and the Spielberg Effect." Chap. 15 In *China's Great Leap: The Beijing Games and Olympian Human Rights Challenges*, edited by Minky Worden, 205–21. New York: Seven Stories Press, 2008.

Green, Michael J. "Should America Fear a New Sino-Russian Alliance?" *Foreign Policy*, August 13 2014.

Green, Michael, and Derek Mitchell. "Asia's Forgotten Crisis: A New Approach to Burma." *Foreign Affairs* 86, no. 6 (2007): 147–58.

Greenwood, Christopher. "International Law And The NATO Intervention In Kosovo." *International and Comparative Law Quarterly* 49, no. 4 (2000): 926–34.

Grix, Jonathan, and Donna Lee. "Soft Power, Sports Mega-Events and Emerging States: The Lure of the Politics of Attraction." *Global Society* 27, no. 4 (2013): 521–36.

Gruffydd-Jones, Jamie J. "The Impacts of International Pressure with Authoritarian States." PhD dissertation, Princeton University, 2017.

"Gulf states recall envoys as Syria further isolated." *The Telegraph*, August 8, 2011.

Guo, Wanchao. *Zhongguo jueqi: yige dongfang daguo de chengzhang zhi dao (Rise of China: The Path to Growth of an Eastern Power)*. Nanchang: Guangxi Renmin Chubanshe, 2004.

Gutterman, Steve. "Russia won't back U.N. call for Syria's Assad to go." *Reuters*, January 27, 2012.

Guzman, Andrew T. "A Compliance-Based Theory of International Law." *California Law Review* 90, no. 6 (2002): 1823–87.

Haass, Richard N. "Darkness at Darfur." *South China Morning Post*, November 8, 2004.

Haass, Richard N. "The U.S. Should Keep Out of Libya." *The Wall Street Journal*, March 8, 2011.

Haider, Ziad. "Can the US Pivot Back to Asia? How Trump Should Respond to China's Belt and Road Initiative." *Foreign Affairs*, May 23, 2017.

Hamid, Shadi. "It's Time To Intervene." February 23, 2011, The Brookings Institution, https://www.brookings.edu/opinions/its-time-to-intervene/ (accessed March 3, 2019).

Hamilton, Douglas. "Text of Annan's six-point peace plan for Syria." *Reuters*, April 4, 2012.

Hamilton, Rebecca. *Fighting for Darfur: Public Action and the Struggle to Stop Genocide*. New York: Palgrave Macmillan, 2011.

Harding, Harry, "The Impact of Tiananmen on China's Foreign Policy" (Seattle, WA: The National Bureau of Asian and Soviet Research, 1990).

Hardy, Cynthia, Bill Harley, and Nelson Phillips. "Discourse Analysis and Content Analysis: Two Solitudes?." *Qualitative Methods Newsletter* (Spring 2004): 19–22.

Harman, Danna. "Activists press China with 'Genocide Olympics' label." *The Christian Science Monitor*, June 26, 2007.

Hart, Andrew F., and Bruce D. Jones. "How Do Rising Powers Rise?." *Survival* 52, no. 6 (2010): 63–88.

Hastings, Michael. "Inside Obama's War Room." *Rolling Stone*, October 13, 2011.

He, Yin. "China's Changing Policy on UN Peacekeeping Operations" (Stockholm: Institute for Security and Development Policy, 2007).

He, Yin. "Fazhan heping: lianheguo weihe jianhe zhong de zhongguo fangan (Developmental Peace: Chinese Approach to UN Peacekeeping and Peacebuilding)." *The Journal of International Studies* 38, no. 4 (2017): 10–32.

He, Yin. "Lianheguo jianshe heping yu rende anquan baohu (United Nations Peacebuilding and the Protection of Human Security)." *The Journal of International Security Affairs* 32, no. 3 (2014): 75–91.

"Hearing before the Subcommittee on National Security and Foreign Affairs of the Committee on Oversight and Government Reform, House of Representatives, One Hundred Tenth Congress, First session, June 7." Washington D.C.: House of Representative, Subcommittee on National Security and Foreign Affairs, Committee on Oversight and Government Reform, 2007.

Heffetz, Ori, and Robert H. Frank. "Preferences for Status: Evidence and Economic Implications." In *Handbook of Social Economics*, edited by Jess Benhabib, Matthew O. Jackson, and Alberto Bisin, 69–92. Amsterdam: North Holland, 2011.

Hehir, Aidan. "The Permanence of Inconsistency: Libya, the Security Council, and the Responsibility to Protect." *International Security* 38, no. 1 (2013): 137–59.

Hehir, Aidan, and Robert W. Murray. *Libya, the Responsibility to Protect and the Future of Humanitarian Intervention*. Basingstoke: Palgrave Macmillan, 2013.

Heintz, Jim, and Associated Press. "Russia ready to seek consensus in UN on new resolution aimed at ending Syria's civil war." *Vancouver Sun*, July 17, 2012.

Henke, Marina E. "Great powers and UN force generation: a case study of UNAMID." *International Peacekeeping* 23, no. 3 (2016): 468–92.

Herz, John. *Political Realism and Political Idealism*. Chicago, IL: University of Chicago Press, 1951.

Higgins, Andrew, and Keith B. Richburg. "China mulls impact of Mideast uprisings." *The Washington Post*, January 31, 2011.

Higgins, Andrews. "China showcasing its softer side: growing role in U.N. peacekeeping signals desire to project image of benign power." *The Washington Post*, December 2, 2009.

High-Level Independent Panel on United Nations Peace Operations, "Uniting Our Strengths for Peace – Politics, Partnership and People" (2015). https://peaceoperationsreview.org/wp-content/uploads/2015/08/HIPPO_Report_1_June_2015.pdf (accessed March 3, 2019).

Hill, Fiona, and Bobo Lo. "Putin's Pivot: Why Russia Is Looking East." *Foreign Affairs*, July 31 2013.

Hille, Kathrin. "China commits combat troops to Mali." *Financial Times*, June 27, 2013.

Hirono, Miwa. "China's Conflict Mediation and the Durability of the Principle of Non-Interference: The Case of Post-2014 Afghanistan," *The China Quarterly*, 1–21, doi:10.1017/S0305741018001753, n.d.

Hirono, Miwa, and Marc Lanteigne. "Introduction: China and UN Peacekeeping." *International Peacekeeping* 18, no. 3 (2011): 243–56.

Hirono, Miwa, and Manshu Xu. "China's Military Operations Other than War." *The RUSI Journal* 158, no. 6 (2013): 74–82.

Hirsch Ben-Josef, Michal, and Jennifer M. Dixon. "Norm Strength and the Norm Life Cycle." Paper presented at the Temple Workshop on International Institutions and Global Governance, Department of Political Science, Temple University, Philadelphia, November 4 2016.

Hirsch, Fred. *Social Limits to Growth*. Cambridge, MA: Harvard University Press, 1976.

Hoge, Warren. "UN Threatens Sanctions Against Sudan." *The New York Times*, September 28, 2004.

Hokayem, Emile. "Syria and its Neighbours." *Survival* 54, no. 2 (2012): 7–14.

Holslag, Jonathan. "China's True Intentions in Congo." April 19, 2010, Harvard International Review, http://hir.harvard.edu/article/?a=2604. (accessed March 3, 2019).

Holslag, Jonathan. "Embracing Chinese Global Security Ambitions." *The Washington Quarterly* 32, no. 3 (2009): 105–18.

Holzgrefe, J. L., and Robert O. Keohane. "The humanitarian intervention debate." Chap. 1 In *Humanitarian Intervention: Ethical, Legal and Political Dilemmas*, 15–52. Cambridge: Cambridge University Press, 2004.

Hook, Leslie, and James Dyer. "Chinese oil interests attacked in Libya." *Financial Times*, February 24, 2011.

Hopf, Ted. "Discourse and Content Analysis: Some Fundamental Incompatibilities." *Qualitative Methods Newsletter* (Spring 2004): 31–33.

Hopf, Ted. "The Promise of Constructivism in International Relations Theory." *International Security*, 23, no. 1 (1998): 171–200.

Hosenball, Mark, and Matt Spetalnick. "U.S. slaps new sanctions on Syria over crackdown." *Reuters*, April 29, 2011.

Huang, Chin-Hao. "Peacekeeping Contributor Profile: The People's Republic of China." April, 2017, Providing for Peacekeeping, http://www.providingforpeacekeeping.org/2014/04/03/contributor-profile-china/ (accessed March 3, 2019).

Huang, Chin-Hao. "US-China Relations and Darfur." *Fordham International Law Journal* 31, no. 4 (2007): 826–42.

Huang, Jie. "Zhongdong luanju heshiliao – fang zhuming Zhongdong wenti zhuanjia Yin Gang jiaoshou (When will the Chaos in the Middle East End - an Interview with Professor Yin Gang, and Expert in the Middle East)." *Weishi*, June 15 2013, 88–90.

Huang, Shan. "A decade of China's peacekeeping missions." *China.org.cn*, January 18, 2010.

Hudson, John. "Qaddafi's Most Bizarre Moments in a Bizarre Speech." *The Wire*, February 22, 2011.

Hugh-Jones, David, and Ro'i Zultan. "Reputation and Cooperation in Defense." *Journal of Conflict Resolution* 57, no. 2 (2012): 327–55.

Human Rights Watch. "Q&A: Syria and the International Criminal Court." September 17, 2013, https://www.hrw.org/news/2013/09/17/qa-syria-and-international-criminal-court (accessed March 3, 2019).

Human Rights Watch. "Syria: Groups Call for ICC Referral." May 15, 2014, https://www.hrw.org/news/2014/05/15/syria-groups-call-icc-referral (accessed March 3, 2019).

Hume, Cameron R. *The United Nations, Iran and Iraq*. Bloomington, IN: Indiana University Press, 1994.

Hurd, Ian. *After Anarchy: Legitimacy and Power in the UN Security Council*. Princeton, NJ: Princeton University Press, 2007.

Husain, Ed. "We Intervene in Syria at Our Peril." *The Atlantic*, February 1, 2012.

Huth, Paul K. *Extended Deterrence and the Prevention of War*. New Haven, CT: Yale University Press, 1988.

Ikenberry, G. John. "Liberal Internationalism 3.0: America and the Dilemmas of Liberal World Order." *Perspectives on Politics* 7, no. 1 (2009): 71–87.

"Indonesia's FM Says Burma to Defend Itself if Brought to UN Security Council." *AFP*, August 23, 2006.

Indyk, Martin S. "Next Steps in Syria." August 1, 2012, The Brookings Institution, http://www.brookings.edu/research/testimony/2012/08/01-syria-indyk (accessed March 3, 2019).

Indyk, Martin S. "Obama's Belated Syria Hard Line." August 18, 2011, The Brookings Institution, https://www.brookings.edu/opinions/obamas-belated-syria-hard-line/ (accessed March 3, 2019).

Information Office of the State Council of the People's Republic of China. "China's Peaceful Development." September 6, 2011, Beijing: The State Council of the People's Republic of

China, http://english.gov.cn/archive/white_paper/2014/09/09/content_281474986284646.htm (accessed March 3, 2019).
Institute of Strategic and International Studies (ISIS) Malaysia. "China's Strategic Vision and Regional Security in the Asia-Pacific – Remarks by H.E. Ambassador Tong Xiaolong at the 26th Asia-Pacific Roundtable, Kuala Lumpur." May 28, 2012, http://www.isis.org.my/files/2012/26APR/PS2_Tong_Xiaoling.pdf (accessed March 3, 2019).
International Commission of Inquiry on Darfur, "Report of the International Commission of Inquiry on Darfur to the United Nations Secretary-General: Pursuant to Security Council Resolution 1564 of 18 September 2004" (2005). http://www.un.org/news/dh/sudan/com_inq_darfur.pdf (accessed March 3, 2019).
International Commission on Intervention and State Sovereignty, "The Responsibility to Protect: Report of the International Commission on Intervention and State Sovereignty" (Ottawa: International Development Research Centre, 2001). http://responsibilitytoprotect.org/ICISS%20Report.pdf (accessed March 3, 2019).
International Crisis Group. "Burma/Myanmar: After the Crackdown" (Yangon/Jakarta/Brussels: International Crisis Group, 2008). http://old.crisisgroup.org/en/regions/asia/south-east-asia/myanmar/144-burma-myanmar-after-the-crackdown.html (accessed March 3, 2019).
International Crisis Group. "A Ceasefire and Negotiations the Right Way to Resolve the Libya Crisis" (Brussels: International Crisis Group, 2011). http://old.crisisgroup.org/en/publication-type/media-releases/2011/a-ceasefire-and-negotiations-the-right-way-to-resolve-the-libya-crisis.html (accessed March 3, 2019).
International Crisis Group. "China's Growing Role in UN Peacekeeping" (Beijing/New York/Brussels: International Crisis Group, 2009). https://www.crisisgroup.org/asia/north-east-asia/china/china-s-growing-role-un-peacekeeping (accessed March 3, 2019).
International Crisis Group. "Immediate International Steps Needed to Stop Atrocities in Libya." February 22, 2011, https://www.crisisgroup.org/middle-east-north-africa/north-africa/libya/immediate-international-steps-needed-stop-atrocities-libya (accessed March 3, 2019).
International Crisis Group. "Syria's Mutating Conflict" (Damascus/Brussels: International Crisis Group, 2012). https://www.crisisgroup.org/middle-east-north-africa/eastern-mediterranean/syria/syria-s-mutating-conflict (accessed March 3, 2019).
"Interview: China plays active, leading role in global governance - Ban Ki-moon." *Xinhua*, November 30, 2017.
"Iraq 'no-fly zone' China 'concerned'; Japan expresses support." *BBC Summary of World Broadcasts/The Monitoring Report*, August 31, 1992.
Jabko, Nicolas. *Playing the Market: A Political Strategy for Uniting Europe, 1985–2005*. Ithaca, NY: Cornell University Press, 2006.
Jackson, Patrick Thaddeus. "Hegel's House, or 'People Are States Too'." *Review of International Studies* 30, no. 2 (2004): 281–87.
Jacques, Martin. *When China Rules the World: The End of the Western World and the Birth of a New Global Order*. New York: Penguin Press, 2009.
Jerdén, Björn. "The Assertive China Narrative: Why It Is Wrong and How So Many Still Bought into It." *The Chinese Journal of International Politics* 7, no. 1 (2014): 47–88.
Jervis, Robert. "Theories of War in an Era of Leading-Power Peace 'Presidential Address, American Political Science Association, 2001'." *The American Political Science Review* 96, no. 1 (2002): 1–14.
Jia, Qingguo. "China." Chap. 2 In *Humanitarian Intervention: The Evolving Asian Debate*, edited by Koji Watanabe, 19–32. Tokyo: Japan Center for International Exchange, 2003.

Jiang, Zemin. "Jiang: Peace and Stability Ensure a Just, Better World." *Beijing Review*, May 12–18 1997, 9–11.

Jo, Dong-Joon, and Erik Gartzke. "Determinants of Nuclear Weapons Proliferation." *Journal of Conflict Resolution* 51, no. 1 (2007): 167–94.

Jo, Hyeran, and Beth A. Simmons. "Can the International Criminal Court Deter Atrocity?." *International Organization* 70, no. 3 (2016): 443–75.

Job, Brian L., and Anastasia Shesterinina. "China as a Global Norm-Shaper: Institutionalization and Implementation of the Responsibility to Protect." Chap. 8 In *Implementation and World Politics: How International Norms Change Practice*, edited by Alexander Betts and Phil Orchard, 144–59. Oxford: Oxford University Press, 2014.

John, Mark, and Ange Aboa. "Battle rages in Ivory Coast, UN fires on Gbagbo bases." *Reuters*, April 5, 2011.

Johnson, Adrian and Saqeb Mueen. "Short War, Long Shadow: The Political and Military Legacies of the 2011 Libya Campaign," (London: RUSI, 2012).

Johnston, Alastair Iain. "How New and Assertive Is China's New Assertiveness?." *International Security* 37, no. 4 (2013): 7–48.

Johnston, Alastair Iain. "Is China a Status Quo Power?." *International Security* 27, no. 4 (2003): 5–56.

Johnston, Alastair Iain. *Social States: China in International Institutions, 1980–2000*. Princeton, NJ: Princeton University Press, 2008.

Johnston, Alastair Iain. "Treating International Institutions as Social Environments." *International Studies Quarterly* 45, no. 4 (2001): 487–515.

Johnstone, Ian. "Managing Consent in Contemporary Peacekeeping Operations." *International Peacekeeping* 18, no. 2 (2011): 168–82.

Johnstone, Ian. "Security Council Deliberations: The Power of the Better Argument." *European Journal of International Law* 14, no. 3 (2003): 437–80.

Jones, Bruce D. "Libya and the Responsibilities of Power." *Survival* 53, no. 3 (June–July 2011): 51–60.

Joshi, Shashank. "Hama Rules: the resilience of the Syrian Army." August 1, 2011, RUSI, https://rusi.org/commentary/hama-rules-resilience-syrian-army (accessed March 3, 2019).

Kahn, Joseph. "China, Shy Giant, Shows Signs of Shedding Its False Modesty." *The New York Times*, December 9, 2006.

Kaoutzanis, Christodoulos. "Understanding the United Nations Security Council's Decisions to Initiate Atrocities Investigations." PhD dissertation, Columbia University, 2016.

Karam, Souhail, and Tom Heneghan. "UPDATE 1 – Gaddafi tells Benghazi his army is coming tonight." *Reuters*, March 17, 2011.

Kasaija, Phillip Apuuli. "The African Union (AU), the Libya Crisis and the notion of 'African solutions to African problems'." *Journal of Contemporary African Studies* 31, no. 1 (2013): 117–38.

Kastner, Scott L., Margaret M. Pearson, and Chad Rector. "Invest, Hold Up, or Accept? China in Multilateral Governance." *Security Studies* 25, no. 1 (2016): 142–79.

Kastner, Scott L., Margaret M. Pearson, and Chad Rector, *China's Strategic Multilateralism: Investing in Global Governance* (Cambridge: Cambridge University Press, 2018).

Kastner, Scott L., and Phillip C. Saunders. "Is China a Status Quo or Revisionist State? Leadership Travel as an Empirical Indicator of Foreign Policy Priorities." *International Studies Quarterly* 56, no. 1 (2012): 163–77.

Kaufman, Alison Adcock. "The 'Century of Humiliation,' Then and Now: Chinese Perceptions of the International Order." *Pacific Focus* 25, no. 1 (2010): 1–33.

Kaufman, Alison Adcock. "In Pursuit of Equality and Respect: China's Diplomacy and the League of Nations." *Modern China* 40, no. 6 (2014): 605–38.
Kaufmann, Daniel. "Russia and China Leadership Props Up Syria's Assad." February 6, 2012, The Brookings Institution, https://www.brookings.edu/blog/up-front/2012/02/06/russia-and-china-leadership-props-up-syrias-assad/ (accessed March 3, 2019).
Keating, Tom. "The UN Security Council on Libya: Legitimation or Dissimulation?." Chap. 8 In *Libya, the Responsibility to Protect and the Future of Humanitarian Intervention*, edited by Aidan Hehir and Robert W. Murray, 162–90. Basingstoke: Palgrave Macmillan, 2013.
Keck, Margaret E., and Kathryn Sikkink. *Activists beyond Borders*. Ithaca, NY: Cornell University Press, 1998.
Keohane, Robert O. *After Hegemony Cooperation and Discord in the World Political Economy*. Princeton, NJ: Princeton University Press, 1984.
Keohane, Robert O., and Lisa L. Martin. "The Promise of Institutionalist Theory." *International Security* 20, no. 1 (1995): 39–51.
Kerry, John. "Remarks With French Foreign Minister Laurent Fabius and U.K. Foreign Secretary William Hague." September 16, 2013, U.S. Department of State, http://www.state.gov/secretary/remarks/2013/09/214266.htm (accessed March 3, 2019).
Kersten, Mark. "The ICC and Regime Change: Some Thoughts but Mostly Questions." *Justice in Conflict*, January 31, 2013.
Khalilzad, Zalmay. "A regional strategy for democracy in the Middle East." *The Washington Post*, March 15, 2011.
Kim, Hun Joon. "Will IR Theory with Chinese Characteristics be a Powerful Alternative?." *The Chinese Journal of International Politics* 9, no. 1 (2016): 59–79.
Kim, Patricia. "How to Persuade China to Squeeze North Korea's Lifeline." *Foreign Policy*, February 27, 2017.
Kim, Samuel S. "China as a Great Power." *Current History* 96, no. 611 (1997): 246–51.
Kim, Samuel S. "China in World Politics." Chap. 4 In *Does China Matter? A Reassessment – Essays in Memory of Gerald Segal*, edited by Barry Buzan and Rosemary Foot, 37–53. London: Routledge, 2004.
Kim, Samuel S. *China, the United Nations, and World Order*. Princeton, NJ: Princeton University Press, 1979.
Kim, Samuel S. "The People's Republic of China in the United Nations: A Preliminary Analysis." *World Politics* 26, no. 3 (April 1974): 299–330.
Kinninmont, Jane. "Syria: UK Must Focus on Diplomacy." September 1, 2013, Chatham House, https://www.chathamhouse.org/media/comment/view/194051 (accessed March 3, 2019).
Korolev, Alexander. "Systemic Balancing and Regional Hedging: China–Russia Relations." *The Chinese Journal of International Politics* 9, no. 4 (2016): 375–97.
Korolev, Alexander, and Vladimir Portyakov. "Navigating in Troubled Waters: System, Unit, and China's Behavior in the Post-Soviet Space." Paper presented at the International Studies Association's 57th Annual Convention, Atlanta, Georgia, March 16–19 2016.
Kristof, Nicholas. "China's Genocide Olympics." *The New York Times*, January 24, 2008.
Kuchins, Andrew C. "Russia and the CIS in 2013: Russia's Pivot to Asia." *Asian Survey* 54, no. 1 (2014): 129–37.
Kuchins, Andrew C. "Russian Perspective on China: Strategic Ambivalence." In *The Future of China-Russia Relations*, edited by James Bellacqua, 33–55. Lexington, KY: University of Kentucky Press, 2010.

Kuper, Simon. "Sport: Developing nations go on offensive for games." *Financial Times*, January 29, 2011.

Kuusisto, Riikka. "Framing the Wars in the Gulf and in Bosnia: The Rhetorical Definitions of the Western Power Leaders in Action." *Journal of Peace Research* 35, no. 5 (1998): 603–20.

Laing, Aislinn. "Ivory Coast: UN and French helicopter gunships attack Laurent Gbagbo residence." *The Telegraph*, April 10, 2011.

Lake, David A. "Status, Authority, and the End of the American Century." Chap. 10 In *Status in World Politics*, edited by T. V. Paul, Deborah Welch Larson, and William C. Wohlforth, 246–72. New York: Cambridge University Press, 2014.

Lampton, David. *Following the Leader: Ruling China, from Deng Xiaoping to Xi Jinping*. Berkeley, CA: University of California Press, 2014.

Landler, Mark, and Dan Bilefsky. "Specter of Rebel Rout Helps Shift U.S. Policy on Libya." *The New York Times*, March 16, 2011.

Landler, Mark, and Steven Lee Myers. "U.S. Sees Positive Signs From China on Security Issues." *The New York Times*, April 26, 2012.

Lanteigne, Marc. *China and International Institutions: Alternate Paths to Global Power*. London: Routledge, 2005.

Larson, Deborah Welch. "Trust and Missed Opportunities in International Relations." *Political Psychology* 18, no. 3 (1997): 701–34.

Larson, Deborah Welch, T. V. Paul, and William C. Wohlforth. "Status and World Order." Chap. 1 In *Status and World Politics*, edited by T. V. Paul, Deborah Welch Larson, and William C. Wohlforth, 3–32. New York: Cambridge University Press, 2014.

Larson, Deborah Welch, and Alexei Shevchenko. "Status Seekers: Chinese and Russian Responses to U.S. Primacy." *International Security* 43, no. 4 (Spring 2010): 63–95.

Lebovic, James H., and Erik Voeten. "The Politics of Shame: The Condemnation of Country Human Rights Practices in the UNCHR." *International Studies Quarterly* 50, no. 4 (December 2006): 861–88.

Lederer, Edith M. "Major Powers Want to Encourage Sudan to Accept UN-African Union Force in Darfur." *Associated Press*, March 8, 2007.

Lee, Min. "Mia Farrow's visit to Hong Kong for critical speech will test Chinese city's freedoms." *Associated Press*, May 1, 2008.

Lee, Pak K., Gerald Chan, and Lai Ha Chan. "China's 'Realpolitik' Engagement with Myanmar." *China Security* 5, no. 1 (2009): 101–23.

Legro, Jeffrey W. "What Will China Want: The Future Intention of a Rising Power." *Perspectives on Politics* 5, no. 3 (2007): 515–34.

Leiby, Richard, and Muhammad Mansour. "Arab League asks U.N. for no-fly zone over Libya." *The Washington Post*, March 12, 2011.

Levitsky, Steven, and Lucan A. Way. "Linkage versus Leverage. Rethinking the International Dimension of Regime Change." *Comparative Politics* 38, no. 4 (2006): 379–400.

Levy, Jack S. *War in the Modern Great Power System, 1495–1975*. Lexington, KY: University of Kentucky Press, 1983.

Lewis, Paul "China Lifts U.N. Veto on Guatemala Monitors." *The New York Times*, January 21, 1997.

Li, Anshan. "China and Africa: Policy and Challenges." *China Security* 3, no. 3 (2007): 69–93.

Li, Jie. "The Transition of the International System: From the Perspective of the Theory of Responsibility." *China International Studies* (Winter 2007): 138–58.

Li, Qinggong. "Politics behind attacks on Libya." *China Daily*, March 22, 2011.

Li, Shijia, and Jie Bai. "PRC Envoy: Not 'Objective' to Accuse China Alone of Arms Sales to Sudan." *Xinhua*, March 7, 2008.

Li, Xiaojun. "Social Rewards and Socialization Effects: An Alternative Explanation for the Motivation Behind China's Participation in International Institutions." *The Chinese Journal of International Politics* 3, no. 3 (2010): 347–77.

Li, Zhen. "World Leaders to Attend Beijing Olympic Opening Ceremony." *Epoch Times*, August 7, 2008.

Li, Ziguo. "The Belt and Road Initiative: Achievements, Problems and Ideas." *Eurasian Economy*, no. 4 (2017): 2–18.

"Libya to stop fighting Sun to let protesters surrender." *Al Arabiya News*, March 17, 2011.

Lieberman, Evan S. "Nested Analysis as a Mixed-Method Strategy for Comparative Research." *American Political Science Review* 99, no. 3 (2005): 435–52.

Lieberthal, Kenneth, and Wang Jisi, "Addressing U.S.-China Strategic Distrust" (Washington D.C.: The John L. Thornton China Center at Brookings, 2012). https://www.brookings.edu/wp-content/uploads/2016/06/0330_china_lieberthal.pdf (accessed March 3, 2019).

Lin, Bo. "Xifang 'xin ganshe zhuyi' weihai wuqiong (The 'Western Neo-interventionism' is Hazardous)." *CRI online*, February 21, 2012.

Lindsay, Jon R. "The Impact of China on Cybersecurity: Fiction and Friction." *International Security* 39, no. 3 (Winter 2014/15): 7–47.

Lindström, Madelene, and Kristina Zetterlund, "Setting the Stage for the Military Intervention in Libya: Decisions Made and their Implications for EU and NATO" (Stockholm: Swedish Ministry of Defence, 2012). https://www.foi.se/report-search/pdf?fileName=D%3A%5CReportSearch%5CFiles%5Ce41a7b3e-06c0-4b3b-896f-d32c9fc22465.pdf (accessed March 3, 2019).

Litwak, Robert S. *Outlier States: American Strategies to Change, Contain, or Engage Regime*. Washington D.C.: Woodrow Wilson Center Press, 2012.

Litwak, Robert S. *Regime Change: U.S. Strategy through the Prism of 9/11*. Washington D.C.: Woodrow Wilson Center Press, 2007.

Litwak, Robert S. *Rogue States and U.S. Foreign Policy: Containment after the Cold War*. Washinton D.C.: Woodrow Wilson Center Press, 2000.

Liu, Baolai. "2012 nian de zhongdong: liluanfenfen wei jian tian (The Middle East in 2012: Endless Chaos)." *World Affairs*, no. 1 (January 2013).

Liu, Hongming, and Shuguang Liu. "Dui Fei touzi de zhengzhi fengxia: xin dongxiang yu yindui jianyi (Political Risks of Investment to Africa: New changes and Suggestions on How to Respond)." *Transnational Business* (November 20, 2012): 14–18.

Liu, Junhua "Cong guojifa shijiao kan Xifang dui Xuliya de ganshe (On the Western Interference in Syria in View of the International Law)." *Nanjing University of Finance and Economics Scholarly Papers* (July 20, 2012): 91–6.

Liu, Tiewa. "China and Responsibility to Protect: Maintenance and Change of Its Policy for Intervention." *The Pacific Review* 25, no. 1 (2012): 153–73.

Liu, Tiewa, and Haibin Zhang. "Debates in China about the responsibility to protect as a developing international norm: a general assessment." *Conflict, Security and Development* 14, no. 4 (2014): 403–27.

Liu, Xiaohong. *Chinese Ambassadors: The Rise of Diplomatic Professionalism Since 1949*. Seattle, WA: University of Washington Press, 2001.

Lo, Bobo. *Axis of Convenience: Moscow, Beijing, and the New Geopolitics*. Washington D.C.: Brookings Institution Press, 2008.

Lo, Nigel, Barry Hashimoto, and Dan Reiter. "Ensuring Peace: Foreign-Imposed Regime Change and Postwar Peace Duration, 1914–2001." *International Organization* 62, no. 4 (2008): 717–36.

Loke, Beverley. "Unpacking the politics of great power responsibility: Nationalist and Maoist China in international order-building." *European Journal of International Relations* (2015): 1–25.

Löwenheim, Oded. "'Do Ourselves Credit and Render a Lasting Service to Mankind': British Moral Prestige, Humanitarian Intervention, and the Barbary Pirates." *International Studies Quarterly* 47, no. 1 (2003): 23–48.

Luck, Edward C. "The Responsibility to Protect: Growing Pains or Early Promise?." *Ethics & International Affairs* 24, no. 4 (2010): 349–65.

Lussato, Céline. "SYRIE. La Russie a-t-elle vraiment la clé de la sortie de secours? (Syria. Does Russia really hold the emergency exit door key?)." *Le Nouvel Obs*, June 1, 2012.

Lynch, Colum. "Amb. Rice: Leading from behind? That's 'whacked.'." *Foreign Policy*, October 31, 2011.

Lynch, Colum. "China Eyes Ending Western Grip on Top U.N. Jobs With Greater Control Over Blue Helmets." *Foreign Policy*, October 2, 2016.

Lynch, Colum. "Russia and China See in Trump Era a Chance to Roll Back Human Rights Promotion at U.N." *Foreign Policy*, June 26, 2018.

Ma, Xiaotian, "The Major Powers and Asian Security: Cooperation or Conflict?" (Singapore: Speech at Second Plenary Session of the 8th IISS Asian Security Summit, May 30, 2009).

Ma, Zhengang. "China's Responsibility and the 'China Responsibility' Theory." *China International Studies* (Summer 2007): 5–12.

MacAskill, Ewen. "Blair draws up plans to send troops to Sudan." *The Guardian*, July 22, 2004.

MacFarquhar, Neil. "Both Sides Claim Progress as Violence Continues in Syria." *The New York Times*, July 22, 2012.

MacFarquhar, Neil. "Push in U.N. for Criticism of Syria Is Rejected." *The New York Times*, April 27, 2011.

MacFarquhar, Neil, and Nada Bakri. "Isolating Syria, Arab League Imposes Broad Sanctions." *The New York Times*, November 27, 2011.

Macintyre, James. "Spielberg subs Beijing Olympics over Darfur crisis." *The Independent*, February 13, 2008.

Madra, Ek "Mia Farrow vows to defy Cambodian Darfur rally ban." *Reuters*, January 19, 2008.

Mahoney, James. *The Legacies of Liberalism: Path Dependence and Political Regimes in Central America*. Baltimore, MD: Johns Hopkins University Press, 2001.

Malone, David M. *Decision-Making in the UN Security Council: The Case of Haiti, 1990–1997*. New York: Oxford University Press, 1998.

Malone, David M. *Does the Elephant Dance? Contemporary Indian Foreign Policy*. New Delhi: Oxford University Press, 2011.

Malone, David M. "International Criminal Justice: Just an Expensive Mirage?." *International Journal* 63, no. 3 (2008): 729–41.

Markey, Daniel Seth. "The Prestige Factor in International Relations." Doctoral Dissertation, Princeton University, 2000.

Marshall, Thomas Humphrey. *Class, Citizenship, and Social Development: Essays*. Westport, Conn: Greenwood Press, 1973.

Martina, Michael, and David Brunnstrom. "China's Xi says to commit 8,000 troops for U.N. peacekeeping force." *Reuters*, September 29, 2015.

"Mass rape atrocity in west Sudan." *BBC News*, March 19, 2004.

Matheson, Michael J. "Justification for the NATO Air Campaign in Kosovo." *Proceedings of the 94th Annual Conference of the American Society of International Law* (2000).

McDoom, Opheera. "U.S. accused of attempting 'regime change' in Sudan: UN force slated for Darfur." *National Post [Toronto Edition]*, September 5, 2006, A16.

McDowall, Angus. "Syrian Observatory says war has killed more than half a million." *Reuters*, March 12, 2018.

McGinley, Shane. "Kofi Annan contacts Qatar over Syrian crisis." *ArabianBusiness.com*, February 27, 2012.

McMillan, Nesam, and David Mickler. "From Sudan to Syria: Locating 'Regime Change' in R2P and the ICC." *Global Responsibility to Protect* 5, no. 3 (2013): 283–316.

McNamara, Sally. "The Crisis in Libya Exposes a Litany of Failed EU Policies." March 3, 2011, The Heritage Foundation, http://www.heritage.org/research/reports/2011/03/the-crisis-in-libya-exposes-a-litany-of-failed-eu-policies (accessed March 3, 2019).

Medcalf, Rory. "Unselfish giants? Understanding China and India as security providers." *Australian Journal of International Affairs* 66, no. 5 (2012): 554–66.

Medeiros, Evan S., "China's International Behavior: Activism, Opportunism, and Diversification" (Santa Monica, CA: RAND, 2009). http://www.rand.org/pubs/monographs/MG850.html (accessed March 3, 2019).

Mercer, Jonathan. *Reputation and International Politics*. Ithaca, NY: Cornell University Press, 1996.

"Mia Farrow arrives in Cambodia for banned Darfur protest." *AFP*, January 18, 2008.

Michael, Maggie. "George Clooney campaigns in China and Egypt to raise awareness over Darfur conflict." *Associated Press*, December 13, 2006.

Miller, Manjari Chatterjee. "The Role of Beliefs in Identifying Rising Powers: Comparing the United States, China, India and Germany." *The Chinese Journal of International Politics* 9, no. 2 (2016): 211–38.

Miller, Manjari Chatterjee. *Wronged by Empire: Post-Imperial Ideology and Foreign Policy in India and China*. Stanford, CA: Stanford University Press, 2013.

Milliken, Jennifer. "The Study of Discourse in International Relations: A Critique of Research and Methods." *European Journal of International Relations* 5, no. 2 (1999): 225–54.

Milner, Murray. *Status and Sacredness: A General Theory of Status Relations and an Analysis of Indian Culture*. New York: Oxford University Press, 1994.

Ministry of Defence. "Prime Minister discusses Libya with US President." March 9, 2011, GOV.UK, https://www.gov.uk/government/news/prime-minister-discusses-libya-with-us-president (accessed March 3, 2019).

Ministry of Foreign Affairs of the People's Republic of China. "Foreign Ministry Spokesperson Jiang Yu's Remarks on the Death of Gaddafi's Son and Others in NATO's Air Strikes." May 3, 2011, http://www.mfa.gov.cn/eng/xwfw/s2510/2535/t819910.htm (accessed March 3, 2019).

Ministry of Foreign Affairs of the People's Republic of China. "Foreign Ministry Spokesperson Qin Gang's Regular Press Conference on March 11, 2008." March 11, 2008, http://www.fmprc.gov.cn/eng/xwfw/s2510/t414217.htm (accessed March 3, 2019).

Ministry of Foreign Affairs of the People's Republic of China. "Hu Jintao Meets with Foreign Leaders to the Opening Ceremony of the Beijing Olympic Games." August 8, 2008, http://www.fmprc.gov.cn/mfa_eng/wjb_663304/zzjg_663340/yzs_663350/gjlb_663354/2706_663416/2708_663420/t483123.shtml (accessed March 3, 2019).

Ministry of Foreign Affairs of the People's Republic of China. "Hujintoa jiu xin xingshi xia fazhan liangan quanxi ti si dian yijian (Hu Jintao's four guidelines on cross-strait relations development under a new situation)." March 4, 2005, http://www.fmprc.gov.cn/chn/gxh/tyb/zyxw/t186259.htm (accessed March 3, 2019).

Ministry of Foreign Affairs of the People's Republic of China. "Vice Foreign Minister Zhai Jun Attends the UN Security Council Meeting on Libya." June 16, 2011, http://www.china-un.ch/eng/xwdt/t831724.htm (accessed March 3, 2019).

Ministry of Foreign Affairs of the People's Republic of China. "Foreign Ministry Spokesperson Hong Lei's Remarks on UN Security Council's Adoption of the Resolution on the Humanitarian Issue of Syria." July 15, 2014, http://www.fmprc.gov.cn/mfa_eng/xwfw_665399/s2510_665401/t1174294.shtml (accessed March 3, 2019).

Ministry of Foreign Affairs of the People's Republic of China. "Joint Communiqué of the Leaders Roundtable of the Belt and Road Forum for International Cooperation." May 16, 2017, https://www.fmprc.gov.cn/mfa_eng/zxxx_662805/t1462012.shtml (accessed March 3, 2019).

Mlambo, Rangarirai. "Africa: China in Africa – A Mutually Beneficial Partnership?" *All Africa*, November 12, 2010.

Modelski, George. *World Power Concentrations: Typology, Data, Explanatory Framework*. Morristown, NJ: General Learning Press, 1974.

Moffett, Sebastian, and Stephen Brown. "Arabs, Turkey criticize veto of Syria resolution." *Reuters*, February 5, 2012.

Monitor's Editorial Board. "Libya sanctions: China's new role at the UN." *The Christian Science Monitor*, February 28, 2011.

Morgenthau, Hans J. *Politics Among Nations: The Struggle for Power and Peace*. New York: Knopf, 1954.

Morphet, Sally. "China as a Permanent Member of the Security Council: October 1971 – December 1999." *Security Dialogue*, 31, no. 2 (2000): 151–66.

Morrison, J. Stephen. "United States House of Representatives the Subcommittee on Domestic and International Monetary Policy, Trade and Technology." H.R. 180, Darfur Accountability and Divestment Act of 2007, 110th Congress (2007).

Munthit, Ker. "Mia Farrow faces off with Cambodian police, blocked from genocide ceremony." *Associated Press*, January 20, 2008.

Muraviev, Alexey D. "Comrades in Arms: The Military-Strategic Aspects of China–Russia Relations." *Journal of Asian Security and International Affairs* 1, no. 2 (2014): 163–85.

Murdock, Clark A. "What Has Syria Taught Us about the Right Time to Use Force?." In *2014 Global Forecast: U.S. Security Policy at a Crossroads*, edited by Craig Cohen, Kathleen Hicks, and Josiane Gabel, 13–15. Washington D.C.; Lanham, MD: Center for Strategic and International Studies; and Rowman & Littlefield Publishers, 2013.

Murray, Michelle. "Identity, Insecurity, and Great Power Politics: The Tragedy of German Naval Ambition Before the First World War." *Security Studies* 19, no. 4 (2010): 656–88.

Murray, Michelle. *The Struggle for Recognition in International Relations: Status, Revisionism and Rising Powers*. Oxford: Oxford University Press, 2018.

Murray, Rachel. "Recent Developments: The Report of the OAU's International Panel of Eminent Personalities to Investigate the 1994 Genocide in Rwanda and the Surrounding Events." *Journal of African Law* 45, no. 1 (2001): 123–42.

Mydans, Seth. "Indonesia Invites a U.N. Force to Timor." *The New York Times*, September 13, 1999, A1.

Mydans, Seth. "Indonesia Says No to Timor Peacekeepers." *The New York Times*, September 8, 1999.
Nahmias, Roee. "Libya suspended from Arab League sessions." *Ynet News*, February 22, 2011.
Najam, Adil. "International Environmental Negotiation: A Strategy for the South." In *Papers on Intenational Environmental Negotiation*, edited by Lawrence E. Susskind, Willian R. Moomaw and Adil Najam. Cambridge, MA: Program on Negotiation, Harvard Law School, 1993.
Natsios, Andrew S. "Darfur: A 'Plan B' To Stop Genocide?" Hearing before the Committee on Foreign Relations United States Senate One Hundred Tenth Congress First Session, April 11, 2007.
Natsios, Andrew S."The Escalating Crisis in Darfur: Are There Prospects for Peace?" Hearing before the Committee on Foreign Affairs House of Representatives One Hundred Tenth Congress First Session, February 8, 2007.
Natsios, Andrew S. *Sudan, South Sudan, and Darfur: What Everyone Needs to Know*. Oxford: Oxford University Press, 2012.
Naughton, Barry. *Growing Out of the Plan: Chinese Economic Reform, 1978–1993*. Cambridge: Cambridge University Press, 1995.
Nayar, Baldev Raj, and T. V. Paul. *India in the World Order: Searching for Major-Power Status*. Cambridge: Cambridge University Press, 2003.
Neack, Laura. "UN Peace-Keeping: In the Interest of Community or Self?." *Journal of Peace Research* 32, no. 2 (1995): 181–96.
Nemeth, Charlan Jeanne. "Influence Processes, Problem Solving and Creativity." In *Social Influence: The Ontario Symposium, Volume 5*, edited by Mark P. Zanna, James M. Olson and C. Peter Herman, 237–46. Hillsdale, NJ: Lawrence Erlbaum, 1987.
Nemets, Alexandr. "Russia and China: The Mechanics of an Anti-American Alliance." *The Journal of International Security Affairs* 11 (2006): 83–88.
Newey, Guy. "Farrow arrives in Hong Kong ahead of Olympic torch relay." *AFP*, May 1, 2008.
Nichols, Michelle. "Russia vetoes U.N. demand for end to bombing of Syria's Aleppo." *Reuters*, October 8, 2016.
Nichols, Michelle. "U.N. Security Council delays Syria vote until Thursday." *Reuters*, July 19, 2012.
Nichols, Michelle, and Louis Charbonneau. "Russia, China veto U.N. bid to refer Syria to international court." *Reuters*, May 23, 2014.
Nomikos, William G., Alexander B. Downes, and Jonathan Monten. "Correspondence: Reevaluating Foreign-Imposed Regime Change." *International Security* 38, no. 3 (2013/2014): 184–95.
Nossiter, Adam. "Strikes by U.N. and France Corner Leader of Ivory Coast." *The New York Times*, April 4, 2011.
O'Rourke, Lindsey A. *Regime Change: America's Covert Cold War*. Ithaca, NY: Cornell University Press, 2018.
O'Sullivan, Meghan L. "Sanctions Alone Won't Topple Syria's Assad: Meghan L. O'Sullivan." *Bloomberg*, February 22, 2012.
O'Brien, Emily, and Andrew Sinclair, "The Libyan War: A Diplomatic History" (New York: Center on International Cooperation, New York University, 2011).
O'Hanlon, Michael E. "Four Military Options in Syria." August 30, 2011, The Brookings Institution, http://www.brookings.edu/research/opinions/2011/08/30-syria-ohanlon (accessed March 3, 2019).

O'Hanlon, Michael E. "Libya Needs a Multilateral Response." February 25, 2011, The Brookings Institution, http://www.brookings.edu/research/opinions/2011/02/25-libya-ohanlon (accessed March 3, 2019).

O'Hanlon, Michael E., and Paul Wolfowitz. "United States Must Take Lead on Libya." February 26, 2011, The Brookings Institution, http://www.brookings.edu/research/opinions/2011/02/26-libya-ohanlon (accessed March 3, 2019).

O'Neill, Barry, "Nuclear Weapons and National Prestige" (New Haven, CT: Cowles Foundation for Research in Economics, Yale University, 2006). cowles.yale.edu/sites/default/files/files/pub/d15/d1560.pdf (accessed March 3, 2019).

Obama, Barack, David Cameron, and Nicolas Sarkozy. "Libya's Pathway to Peace." *The New York Times*, April 14, 2011.

"Observer: Dream deferred." *Financial Times*, January 18, 2008.

Odgaard, Liselotte. *China and Coexistence: Beijing's National Security Strategy for the Twenty-first century*. Washington D.C.: Woodrow Wilson Center Press, 2012.

Oertel, Janka. *China and the United Nations: Chinese UN Policy in the Areas of Peace and Development in the Era of Hu Jintao*. Baden-Baden: Nomos/Bloomsbury, 2015.

Office of the Commissioner of the Ministry of Foreign Affairs in the Hong Kong Special Administrative Region. "Assistant Foreign Minister Zhai Jun Holds a Briefing for Chinese and Foreign Journalists on the Darfur Issue of Sudan." April 12, 2007, http://www.fmcoprc.gov.hk/eng/zgwjsw/t311008.htm (accessed March 3, 2019).

Office of the Press Secretary of the White House. "Readout of the President's Call with Prime Minister Cameron of the United Kingdom," news release, March 8, 2011.

Office of the Press Secretary of the White House. "Remarks by the President in Address to the Nation on Libya." March 28, 2011, Washington D.C., https://www.whitehouse.gov/the-press-office/2011/03/28/remarks-president-address-nation-libya (accessed March 3, 2019).

Office of the Press Secretary of the White House. "Remarks by the President on Libya." February 23, 2011, Washington D.C., https://www.whitehouse.gov/the-press-office/2011/02/23/remarks-president-libya (accessed March 3, 2019).

Office of the Press Secretary of the White House. "Remarks by the President on the Middle East and North Africa," news release, May 19, 2011, https://www.whitehouse.gov/the-press-office/2011/05/19/remarks-president-middle-east-and-north-africa (accessed March 3, 2019).

Olesen, Alexa. "China: Don't link Olympics, Darfur." *Associated Press*, March 29, 2007.

"Organization of Islamic Cooperation suspends Syria's membership." *Al Arabiya*, August 13, 2012.

"Overwhelming majority of Chinese in Libya evacuated: FM." *Xinhua*, March 1, 2011.

Owen, John M. *The Clash of Ideas in World Politics: Transnational Networks, States, and Regime Change, 1510–2010*. Princeton, NJ: Princeton University Press, 2010.

Pang, Zhongying. "China's changing attitude to UN peacekeeping." *International Peacekeeping* 12, no. 1 (2005): 87–104.

Pape, Robert A. "Soft Balancing against the United States." *International Security* 30, no. 1 (2005/07/01 2005): 7–45.

Parameswaran, P. "US threatens Sudan after UN resistance." *Independent Media*, August 19, 2006.

Parasiliti, Andrew. "It's Time to Engage Iran, Russia on Syria." *Al-Monitor*, July 25, 2012.

Pargeter, Alison. "Libya: An Uncertain Future." February 23, 2011, RUSI, https://rusi.org/commentary/libya-uncertain-future (accessed March 3, 2019).

Paris, Roland. "International peacebuilding and the 'mission civilisatrice'." *Review of International Studies* 28, no. 4 (2002): 637–56.
Partos, Gabriel. "Analysis: What price Macedonian peace?" *BBC News*, February 25, 1999.
Patrick, Stewart. "The New 'New Multilateralism': Minilateral Cooperation, but at What Cost?." *Global Summitry* (2015): 1–20.
Paul, T. V. "Soft Balancing in the Age of U.S. Primacy." *International Security* 30, no. 1 (2005/07/01 2005): 46–71.
Peacekeeping Affairs Office of the Ministry of National Defense of the People's Republic of China. *Mission for Peace' PLA's Participation in UN Peacekeeping Operations.* Beijing: The Great Wall Publishing House, 2009.
Peng, Peng, ed. *Heping jueqi lun: zhongguo chongsu daguo zhi lu (Peaceful Rising Theory: The Path of China Becoming a Great Power).* Guangdong: Guangdong renmin chubanshe, 2005.
Perkovich, George. *India's Nuclear Bomb: The Impact on Global Proliferation.* Berkeley, CA: University of California Press, 1999.
Permanent Mission of India to the United Nations. "Intervention By Ambassador Hardeep Singh Puri Permanent Representative at the Informal Interactive Dialogue of the UN General Assembly on 'Early Warning, Assessment and the Responsibility to Protect' on August 9, 2010." https://www.pminewyork.org/adminpart/uploadpdf/20151ind1716.pdf (accessed March 3, 2019).
Permanent Mission of the People's Republic of China to the United Nations. "China''s SR on Darfur Holds a Briefing in Beijing." March 7, 2008, http://www.china-un.org/eng/chinaandun/securitycouncil/regionalhotspots/africa/darfur/t468259.htm (accessed March 3, 2019).
Permanent Mission of the People's Republic of China to the United Nations. "Explanation of Vote by Ambassador Li Baodong after Vote on Draft Resolution on Syria Tabled by the United Kingdom." July 19, 2012, Embassy of the People's Republic of China in France, http://wcm.fmprc.gov.cn/preview/ce/cefr/fra/xnyfgk/t953752.htm?randid=0.8791840181675125 (accessed March 3, 2019).
Permanent Mission of the People's Republic of China to the United Nations. "Explanatory Remarks by Ambassador Wang Min after General Assembly Vote on Draft Resolution on Syria." August 3, 2012, http://www.china-un.org/eng/hyyfy/t958262.htm (accessed March 3, 2019).
Permanent Mission of the People's Republic of China to the United Nations. "Explanatory Remarks by Ambassador Wang Min after Security Council Voting on Draft Resolution on the Referral of the Situation of the Syrian Arab Republic to the International Criminal Court." May 22, 2014, http://www.china-un.org/eng/chinaandun/securitycouncil/regionalhotspots/asia/yz/t1161566.htm (accessed March 3, 2019).
Permanent Mission of the People's Republic of China to the United Nations. "Explanatory Remarks by Chinese Permanent Representative Mr. Wang Guangya at Security Council on Sudan Darfur Draft Resolution." September 18, 2004, http://www.china-un.org/eng/hyyfy/t158034.htm (accessed March 3, 2019).
Permanent Mission of the People's Republic of China to the United Nations. "Position Paper of the People's Republic of China on the United Nations Reforms." June 7, 2005, http://www.china-un.org/eng/chinaandun/zzhgg/t199101.htm (accessed March 3, 2019).
Permanent Mission of the People's Republic of China to the United Nations. "Statement by Ambassador Li Baodong, Permanent Representative of China to the United Nations, at the Security Council Briefing on the Situation in Syria." January 31, 2012, http://www.china-un.org/eng/hyyfy/t930411.htm (accessed March 3, 2019).

Permanent Representative of France to the United Nations. "Statement by the Permanent Representative of France to the UN to the Human Rights Council Special Session on Libya." February 25, 2011, http://basedoc.diplomatie.gouv.fr/exl-doc/EPI00048723.pdf (accessed March 3, 2019).

Permanent Representatives of Costa Rica, Jordan, Liechtenstein, Singapore, and Switzerland to the United Nations. "Presentation of the S-5 Draft Resolution L.42 on the Improvement of the Working Methods of the Security Council." 2012.

Perry, William H. "U.S. Strategy: Engage China, Not Contain It." *Defense Issues* 10, no. 109 (October 30, 1995).

"Philippine Foreign Secretary Optimistic on Burmese Democracy." *BBC Monitoring Asia Pacific*, August 15, 2006.

Phillips, James. "Preparing for a Post-Assad Syria." January 19, 2012, Washington D.C.: The Heritage Foundation, http://www.heritage.org/research/reports/2012/01/us-policy-for-a-post-assad-syria (accessed March 3, 2019).

Phillips, James. "Pressure Sudan to Halt Oppression in Darfur." October 4, 2004, Washington D.C.: The Heritage Foundation, http://www.heritage.org/research/reports/2004/10/pressure-sudan-to-halt-oppression-in-darfur (accessed March 3, 2019).

Phillips, Macon. "President Obama: 'The future of Syria must be determined by its people, but President Bashar al-Assad is standing in their way'." August 18, 2011, Washington D. C,: The White House, https://www.whitehouse.gov/blog/2011/08/18/president-obama-future-syria-must-be-determined-its-people-president-bashar-al-assad (accessed March 3, 2019).

Philpott, Daniel. *Revolutions in Sovereignty*. Princeton, NJ: Princeton University Press, 2001.

Pierson, David. "Libyan strife exposes China's risks in global quest for oil." *Los Angeles Times*, March 9, 2011.

Pollack, Kenneth M. "The Real Military Options in Libya." March 9, 2011, Washington D.C.: The Brookings Institute, https://www.brookings.edu/opinions/the-real-military-options-in-libya/ (accessed March 3, 2019).

Pouliot, Vincent, and Jean-Philippe Therien. "The politics of inclusion: Changing patterns in the governance of international security." *Review of International Studies* 41, no. 2 (2015): 211–37.

Powell, Colin L. "The Crisis in Darfur: Testimony Before the Senate Foreign Relations Committee." September 9, 2004, Washington D.C.: U.S. Department of State, https://2001-2009.state.gov/secretary/former/powell/remarks/36042.htm (accessed March 3, 2019).

Powell, Colin L. "Remarks to the Press with Sudanese Vice President Ali Osman Taha and Sudan People's Liberation Movement Chairman John Garang." January 8, 2005, Washington D.C.: U.S. Department of State, https://2001-2009.state.gov/secretary/former/powell/remarks/2005/40461.htm (accessed March 3, 2019).

Prendergast, John, and David Sullivan, "Irresolution: The UN Security Council on Darfur" (Washington, D.C.: Enough Project, 2008). http://www.enoughproject.org/publications/irresolution-un-security-council-darfur (accessed March 3, 2019).

"President Xi meets UN chief." *Xinhua*, September 3, 2018.

Press Trust of India. "Troop-Contributing Nations Need Greater Say In UN Missions: General Suhag." *NDTV*, May 30, 2016.

Price, Monroe E. "On Seizing the Olympic Platform." In *Owning the Olympics: Narratives of the New China*, edited by Monroe E. Price and Daniel Dayan, 86–116. Ann Arbor, MI: University of Michigan Press, 2008.

Price, Monroe E., and Daniel Dayan, eds. *Owning the Olympics: Narratives of the New China*. Ann Arbor, MI: University of Michigan Press, 2008.

Price, Richard. "Reversing the Gun Sights: Transnational Civil Society Targets Land Mines." *International Organization* 52, no. 3 (1998): 613–44.

Prunier, Gerard. *Darfur: A 21st Century Genocide*. Ithaca, NY: Cornell University Press, 2008.

Pu, Xiaoyu. "Socialisation as a Two-way Process: Emerging Powers and the Diffusion of international Norms." *The Chinese Journal of International Politics* 5, no. 4 (Winter 2012): 341–67.

Pu, Xiaoyu. *Rebranding China: Contested Status Signalling in the Changing Global Order* (Stanford: Stanford University Press, 2019).

Pu, Xiaoyu, and Randall L. Schweller. "Status Signaling, Multiple Audiences, and China's Blue-Water Naval Ambition." Chap. 6 In *Status in World Politics*, edited by T. V. Paul, Deborah Welch Larson and William C. Wohlforth, 141–64. New York: Cambridge University Press, 2014.

Pye, Lucian W. "China: Not Your Typical Superpower." *Problems of Post-Communism* 43, no. 4 (1996): 3–15.

Qian, Wenrong "The Impact of Neo-interventionism on the International Order." *Peace and Development* 1 (2013): 23–27.

Qu, Xing. "Lianheguo xianzhang, baohu de zeren yu xuliya wenti (The UN Charter, the Responsibility to Protect and the Syria Issue)." *International Studies* 12, no. 2 (2012): 6–18.

Quinn, Andrew. "With focus on opposition, U.S. races against time on Syria." *Reuters*, December 6, 2012.

Quinton-Brown, Patrick. "Mapping Dissent: The Responsibility to Protect and Its State Critics." *Global Responsibility to Protect* 5, no. 3 (2013): 260–82.

Ralph, Jason. "The Responsibility to Protect and the rise of China: lessons from Australia's role as a 'pragmatic' norm entrepreneur." *International Relations of the Asia-Pacific* 17, no. 1 (2017): 35–65.

Ranking Member Elliot L. Engel (D) of the United States House of Representatives Committee on Foreign Affairs. "Lantos, House Colleagues Send Strong Message to Chinese President, Demand Action on Darfur." May 9, 2007, https://democrats-foreignaffairs.house.gov/news/press-releases/lantos-house-colleagues-send-strong-message-chinese-president-demand-action (accessed March 3, 2019).

Reeves, Eric. "Regime Change in Sudan." *The Washington Post*, August 23, 2004, A15.

Regler, Sonja. "Struggle over Darfur – the development of Chinese security politics in interaction with the United States." PhD dissertation, Freedom University of Berlin, 2011.

Reinold, Theresa. "Africa's Emerging Regional Security Culture and the Intervention in Libya." Chap. 5 In *Libya, the Responsibility to Protect and the Future of Humanitarian Intervention*, edited by Aidan Hehir and Robert W. Murray, 83–109. Basingstoke: Palgrave Macmillan, 2013.

Reisman, W. Michael. "Why Regime Change is (Almost Always) a Bad Idea." *American Journal of International Law* 98, no. 3 (2004): 516–25.

Ren, Xiao. "The Moral Dimension of Chinese Foreign Policy." Chap. 1 In *New Frontiers in China's Foreign Relations*, edited by Allen Carlson and Ren Xiao, 3–24. New York: Lexington, 2011.

Renshon, Jonathan. *Fighting for Status: Hierarchy and Conflict in World Politics*. Princeton, NJ: Princeton University Press, 2017.

Republic of Turkey Ministry of Foreign Affairs. "No: 57, 24 February 2012, Press Release Regarding the Appointment of Former UN Secretary-General Kofi Annan as the Joint Special Envoy of the UN and the League of Arab States on the Syrian Crisis." 2012.
Reuters. "China pushes Sudan to let UN troops into Darfur." *Sudan Tribune*, September 14, 2006.
Reuters. "China, US urge diplomatic solution in Darfur." *Sudan Tribune*, April 10, 2007.
Reuters. "Saudi king slams veto of UN's Syria move." *ArabianBusiness.com*, February 10, 2012.
Reuters. "Syria conflict divides OIC summit in Cairo." *Dawn*, February 7, 2013.
Rhoads, Emily Paddon. *Taking Sides in Peacekeeping: Impartiality and the Future of the United Nations*. Oxford: Oxford University Press, 2016.
"RI Disagrees on Myanmar Draft." *Jakarta Post*, January 6, 2007.
Rice, Susan E. "Why Darfur Can't Be Left to Africa." *The Washington Post*, August 7, 2005.
Rice, Susan E., and Gayle E. Smith. "The Darfur Catastrophe." *The Washington Post*, May 30, 2004.
Richardson, Courtney J. "A Responsible Power? China and the UN Peacekeeping Regime." *International Peacekeeping* 18, no. 3 (2011): 286-97.
Richardson, Sophie. "Challenges for a 'Responsible Power'." Chap. 22 In *China's Great Leap: The Beijing Games and Olympian Human Rights Challenges* edited by Minky Worden, 283-95. New York: Seven Stories Press, 2008.
Ridgeway, Cecilia L., and Henri A. Walker. "Status Structures." In *Sociological Perspective on Social Psychology*, edited by Karen S. Cook, Gary Alan Fine, and James S. House, 281-310. Upper Saddle River, NJ: Pearson Education, 1995.
Ringmar, Erik. *Identity, Interest and Action: A Cultural Explanation of Sweden's Intervention in Thirty Years War*. Cambridge: Cambridge University Press, 1996.
Ringmar, Erik. "On the Ontological Status of the State." *European Journal of International Relations* 2, no. 4 (1996): 439-66.
Risse, Thomas. "'Let's Argue!': Communicative Action in World Politics." *International Organization* 54, no. 1 (2000): 1-39.
Risse, Thomas, Stephen C. Ropp, and Kathryn Sikkink, eds. *The Power of Human Rights: International Norms and Domestic Change*. Cambridge: Cambridge University Press, 1999.
Risse, Thomas, and Kathryn Sikkink. "The socialization of international human rights norms into domestic practices: introduction." Chap. 1 In *The Power of Human Rights: International Norms and Domestic Change*, edited by Thomas Risse, Stephen C. Ropp, and Kathryn Sikkink, 1-38. Cambridge: Cambridge University Press, 1999.
Roberts, Adam. "Transformative Military Occupation: Applying the Laws of War and Human Rights." *American Journal of International Law* 100, no. 3 (2006): 580-622.
Roberts, David, and Michael Stephens. "Bloody days ahead as the Assad regime is decapitated." July 19, 2012, RUSI, https://rusi.org/commentary/bloody-days-ahead-assad-regime-decapitated (accessed March 3, 2019).
Robinson, Dan. "US Voices Concern about Syria Resolution Veto During Talks with China's VP." *Voice of America*, February 13, 2012.
Rodley, Nigel. "R2P and International Law: A Paradigm Shift?." Chap. 11 In *The Oxford handbook of the responsibility to protect*, edited by Alex J. Bellamy and Timothy Dunne, 186-207. Oxford: Oxford University Press, 2016.
Rogin, Josh. "How Obama turned on a dime toward war." *Foreign Policy*, March 18, 2011.
Rolland, Nadège. "China's Belt and Road Initiative: Underwhelming or 'Game-Changer'?." *The Washington Quarterly* 40, no. 1 (2017): 127-42.
Rosecrance, Richard, ed. *The New Great Power Coalition: Toward a World Concert of Nations*. Lanham, MD: Rowman and Littlefield, 2001.

BIBLIOGRAPHY 257

Roth, Stanley O., "U.S.-China Relations on the Eve of the Summit: Address at the World Economic Forum" (Hong Kong: 1997).
Rozman, Gilbert. "China's Quest for Great Power Identity." *Orbis* 43, no. 3 (1999): 383–402.
Ruan, Zongze. "Responsible protection." *China Daily*, March 15, 2012.
Ruan, Zongze. "Responsible Protection: Building a Safer World." *China International Studies* 34 (2012).
"Russia proposes U.N. resolution on Syria; U.S. hopes to work with Moscow on draft." *Al Arabiya*, December 15, 2011.
Ryan, Missy. "No-fly zone for Libya would require attack: Gates." *Reuters*, March 2, 2011.
Sa'adah, Anne. "Regime Change: Lessons from Germany on Justice, Institution Building, and Democracy." *Journal of Conflict Resolution* 50, no. 3 (2006): 303–23.
Sagan, Scott D. "Why Do States Build Nuclear Weapons?: Three Models in Search of a Bomb." *International Security* 21, no. 3 (1996): 54–86.
Salama, Samir. "GCC backs no-fly zone to protect civilians in Libya." *GulfNews*, March 9, 2011.
Saleh, Yasmine, and Lin Noueihed. "Arab League proposes a new plan for Syrian transition." *Reuters*, January 22, 2012.
Sanger, David E. *Confront and Conceal: Obama's Secret Wars and Surprising Use of American Power*. New York: Crown Publishers, 2012.
Sanger, David E., and Thom Shanker. "Gates Warns of Risks of a No-Flight Zone." *The New York Times*, March 2, 2011.
Sartori, Anne E. "The Might of the Pen: A Reputational Theory of Communication in International Disputes." *International Organization* 56, no. 1 (2002): 121–49.
"Saudi Arabia withdraws its monitors from Syria: Arab League calls for power transfer." *Al Arabiya*, January 23, 2012.
Schearf, Daniel. "China Takes Credit for Sudan Allowing UN Peacekeepers." *Voice of America*, July 5, 2007.
Schimmelfennig, Frank. "Strategic Calculation and International Socialization: Membership Incentives, Party Constellations, and Sustained Compliance in Central and Eastern Europe." *International Organization* 59, no. 4 (2005): 827–60.
Schweller, Randall L. "The Problem of International Order Revisited: A Review Essay." *International Security* 26, no. 1 (2001): 161–86.
Schweller, Randall L., and Xiaoyu Pu. "After Unipolarity: China's Visions of International Order in an Era of U.S. Decline." *International Security* 36, no. 1 (Summer 2011): 41–72.
Scobell, Andrew, and Scott W. Harold. "An 'Assertive' China? Insights from Interviews." *Asian Security* 9, no. 2 (2013): 111–31.
Seibert, Thomas. "GCC and Turkey stand united on Syria." *The National*, January 30, 2012.
Shaikh, Alman. "Libya's Test of the New International Order." February 26, 2011, The Brookings Institution, https://www.brookings.edu/opinions/libyas-test-of-the-new-international-order/ (accessed March 3, 2019).
Shaikh, Salman. "As Syria crisis worsens, UN Security Council must act." *The Christian Science Monitor*, December 15, 2011.
Shaikh, Salman. "In Syria, Assad Must Exit the Stage." April 27, 2011, The Brookings Institution, http://www.brookings.edu/research/opinions/2011/04/27-syria-shaikh (accessed March 3, 2019).
Shannon, Vaughn P. "Norms Are What States Make of Them: The Political Psychology of Norm Violation." *International Studies Quarterly* 44, no. 2 (2000): 293–316
Shapiro, Jeremy, and Samuel Charap. "Winning the Peace by Failing in Geneva: How to Work the Syria Negotiations." *Foreign Affairs*, January 9, 2014.

Sharman, J. C. *Havens in a Storm: The Struggle for Global Tax Regulation*. Ithaca: Cornell University Press 2006.

Shirk, Susan L. *China: Fragile Superpower*. Oxford: Oxford University Press, 2007.

"Shou lun Zhong Mei jingji duihua: chu shang yueqiu wai zhuyao wenti jun yi tan ji (First round of the Sino-U.S Economic Dialogue: All major issues have been discussed apart from going to the Moon)." *China News Online*, July 29, 2009.

Siddique, Haroon. "UN chief to miss Olympic opening ceremony." *The Guardian*, April 11, 2008.

Siegle, Joe. "In Sudan's Darfur: Action, Not Just Aid." *The Christian Science Monitor*, June 30, 2004.

Simmons, Beth A. *Mobilizing Human Rights: International Law in Domestic Politics*. New York: Cambridge University Press, 2009.

Singer, J. David. "Reconstructing the Correlates of War Dataset on Material Capabilities of States, 1816–1985." *International Interactions* 14, no. 2 (1988): 115–32.

Singer, J. David, and Melvin Small. "The Composition and Status Ordering of the International System, 1815–1940." *World Politics* 18, no. 2 (1966): 236–82.

Sinha, Aseema. "Partial accommodation without conflict: India as a rising link power." In *Accommodating Rising Powers: Past, Present, and Future* edited by T. V. Paul, 222–45. Cambridge: Cambridge University Press, 2016.

Slaughter, Anne-Marie. "Fiddling While Libya Burns." *The New York Times*, March 13, 2011.

Slot, Owen. "Olympians urged to make a stand against China's betrayal of Darfur." *The Times*, August 7, 2007.

Smith, Craig S. "Little Visible Progress on Darfur at International Conference." *The New York Times*, June 26, 2007.

Smith, Graeme. "Rift between China, Libya deepens over weapons dealings with Gadhafi." *The Global and Mail*, September 5, 2011.

Snetkov, Aglaya, and Marc Lanteigne. "'The Loud Dissenter and its Cautious Partner' - Russia, China, global governance and humanitarian intervention." *International Relations of the Asia-Pacific* 15, no. 1 (2015): 113–46.

Snyder, Charles. "Ethnic Cleansing in Darfur: A New Front Opens in Sudan's Bloody War - Testimony Before the House International Relations Committee." May 6, 2004, Washington D.C.: U.S. Department of State, https://2001-2009.state.gov/p/af/rls/rm/32316.htm (accessed March 3, 2019).

Sohn, Injoo. "After Renaissance: China's Multilateral Offensive in the Developing World." *European Journal of International Relations* 18, no. 1 (2012): 77–101.

Sotloff, Steven. "China's Libya Problem." *The Diplomat*, 2012.

Spegele, Brian. "China Takes New Tack in Libya Vote." *The Wall Street Journal*, March 20, 2011.

Spencer, Claire. "The Syrian Conundrum." February 7, 2012, Chatham House, https://www.chathamhouse.org/media/comment/view/182009 (accessed March 3, 2019).

"Spielberg's Stance on the Olympics Draws Praise." *USA Today*, February 14, 2008.

"Spokesman on U.S. warplane shooting down Iraqi fighter." *Xinhua*, December 28, 1992.

"Stage set for showdown over Darfur ceremony in Cambodia." *Associated Press*, January 18, 2008.

Stähle, Stefan. "China's Shifting Attitude towards United Nations Peacekeeping Operations." *The China Quarterly* 195 (September 2008): 631–55.

Stephens, Michael. "Arguments for Military Intervention in Syria." February 8, 2012, RUSI, https://rusi.org/commentary/arguments-military-intervention-syria (accessed March 3, 2019).

Struett, Michael J. *The Politics of Constructing the International Criminal Court: NGOs, Discourse, and Agency*. New York: Palgrave Macmillan, 2008.

Sudan Disinvestment UK, "Matching words with action: How to pressure Sudan to stop its genocidal campaign in Darfur." *Waging Peace* (2007).

"Sudanese media hail expected China 'veto' to block Bashir arrest warrant." *Sudan Tribune*, September 2, 2008.

Sun, Meicen. "A Bigger Bang for a Bigger Buck: What China's Changing Attitude Toward UN Peacekeeping Says About Its Evolving Approach to International Institutions." *Foreign Policy Analysis* 13, no. 2 (2017): 338–60.

Sun, Yun. "China's Acquiescence on UNSCR 1973: No Big Deal." *PacNet* 20, March 31, 2011.

Sun, Yun. "Syria: What China Has Learned from its Libya Experience." *Asia Pacific Bulletin* 152 (February 27 2012).

Suzuki, Shogo. "Journey to the West: China Debates Its 'Great Power' Identity." *Millennium* 42, no. 3 (2014): 632–50.

Swaine, Michael D. "China's Assertive Behavior—Part One: On 'Core Interests'." *China Leadership Monitor* 34 (2010).

Swaine, Michael D. "Chinese Views of the Syrian Conflict." *China Leadership Monitor* 39 (2012).

Swaine, Michael D. "Perceptions of an Assertive China." *China Leadership Monitor* 32 (2010): 1–19.

"Syria crisis: Gulf Arab states expel Syrian ambassadors." *BBC News*, February 7, 2012.

"Syria crisis: Russia and China veto UN resolution." *The Guardian*, July 19, 2012.

"Syria faces more sanctions as EU steps in." *RT*, April 30, 2011.

"Syrian opposition: 1,300 killed in chemical attack on Ghouta region." *Al Arabiya*, August 21, 2013.

"Taiwan criticises China UN veto." *BBC News*, February 26, 1999.

Tajfel, Henri, and John C. Turner. "The Social Identity Theory of Intergroup Behavior." In *Psychology of Intergroup Relations*, edited by William G. Austin and Stephen Worchel, 7–24. Chicago, IL: Nelson-Hall, 1986.

Tan, Jie. "PLA Air Force transporters evacuate compatriots from Libya." *PLA Daily*, March 2, 2011.

Tang, Yongsheng. "Zhongguo yu lianheguo weihe xingdong (China and the UN Peacekeeping Operations)." *World Economics and Politics*, no. 9 (2002): 39–44.

Taylor, Darren. "Darfur Crisis Sparks Louder Calls For 2008 Olympics Boycott." *Voice of America*, November 1, 2009.

Taylor, Darren. "Pressure Builds On China To Break Darfur Deadlock." *Voice of America*, November 1, 2009.

Taylor, Ian. "The People's Republic of China." In *The International Politics of Mass Atrocities: The Case of Darfur*, edited by David R. Black and Paul D. Williams, 176–94. New York: Routledge, 2010.

Teitt, Sarah. "Assessing Polemics, Principles and Practices: China and the Responsibility to Protect." *Global Responsibility to Protect* 1, no. 2 (2009): 208–36.

Teitt, Sarah. "China and the Responsibility to Protect" (Brisbane: Asia-Pacific Centre for the Responsibility to Protect, 2008). https://r2pasiapacific.org/filething/get/1284/China%20and%20R2P%20Dec%202008.pdf

Teitt, Sarah. "The Responsibility to Protect and China's Peacekeeping Policy." *International Peacekeeping* 18, no. 3 (2011): 298–312.

Tesón, Fernando, and Bas van der Vossen. *Debating Humanitarian Intervention: Should We Try to Save Strangers?* Oxford: Oxford University Press, 2017.

Tesser, Abraham, and Jennifer Campbell. "Self-Definition: The Impact of the Relative Performance and Similarity of Others." *Social Psychology Quarterly* 43, no. 3 (1980): 341–47.

Thakur, Ramesh. "A Chinese version of 'responsible protection'." *The Japan Times*, November 1, 2013.

Thakur, Ramesh. Libya: The First Stand or the Last Post for the Responsibility to Protect?." *E-International Relations* (March 13 2013).

Thalakada, Nigel. "China's Voting Pattern in the Security Council, 1990-1995." In *The Once and Future Security Council*, edited by Bruce Russett, 83–118. New York: St. Martin's Press, 1997.

The Altantic Council of the United States Global Leadership Series. "Remarks by Jan Eliasson, UN Special Envoy to Darfur." May 16, 2007, www.acus.org/files/070516-Jan%20Eliasson%20-%20transcript.pdf (accessed March 3, 2019).

The Defence Committee of the House of Commons, "Operations in Libya" (London: The House of Commons, 2012). http://www.publications.parliament.uk/pa/cm201012/cmselect/cmdfence/950/950.pdf (accessed March 3, 2019).

The League of Arab States. "Compensation due to the State of Kuwait for the Damage Caused by the Iraqi Invasion (Res./5038/ES), August 31." 1990.

The League of Arab States. "Full text of Arab League resolution against Syria." November 28, 2011, Open Briefing, http://www.openbriefing.org/regionaldesks/middleeast/resolution7442/ (accessed March 3, 2019).

The League of Arab States. "The Iraqi Aggression against the State of Kuwait (Res./ 5037/ES), August 31." 1990.

The League of Arab States. "The outcome of the Council of the League of Arab States meeting at the Ministerial level in its extraordinary session on the implications of the current events in Libya and the Arab position (Res. No.: 7630), March 12." Cairo: Council of the League of Arab States, 2011.

The Organization of Islamic Conference. "Final Communiqué of the Annual Meeting of Ministers for Foreign Affairs of the Member States of the Organization of the Islamic Conference, held at United Nations Headquarters New York on 1 October 1990." In *Letter dated 7 March 1991 from the Permanent Representative of Egypt to the United Nations addressed to the Secretary-General: Annex (A/46/113, S/22345)*: United Nations General Assembly and United Nations Security Council, 1990.

The Peace and Security Council of the African Union. "Communiqué of the 261st Meeting, PSC/PR/COMM(CCLXI), February 23." Addis Ababa: The Peace and Security Council of the African Union, 2011.

The Peace and Security Council of the African Union. "Communiqué of the 265th meeting of the Peace and Security Council, PSC/PR/Comm.2(CCLXV), March 10." Addis Ababa: The Peace and Security Council of the African Union, 2011.

The Russian Federation, and The People's Republic of China. "Russian-Chinese Joint Declaration on a Multipolar World and the Establishment of a New International Order, adopted in Moscow on 23 April 1997." 1997.

The Transnational Interim National Council. "Founding Statement of the Interim Transnational National Council (TNC)." 5 March 2011, 2011.

Thoenes, Sander. "What made Indonesia accept peacekeepers." *The Christian Science Monitor*, September 14, 1999.

Thompson, Alexander. *Channels of Power: The UN Security Council and U.S. Statecraft in Iraq*. Ithaca, NY: Cornell University Press, 2010.

Tian, Wenlin. "Zai Xu gao zhengquan gengti shi zhanlue duanshi (Promoting Regime Change in Syria is Strategic Shortsightedness)." *People's Daily*, June 11, 2012.

Tian, Wenlin, and Gujing Li. "Meiguo shi guoji zhili moshi dang fansi (wanghai lou) (US-style global governance model should have reflections)." *People's Daily*, November 26, 2014, 1.

Tisdall, Simon. "Omar al-Bashir: conflict in Darfur is my responsibility." *The Guardian*, April 20, 2011.

Tladi, Dire. "The African Union and the International Criminal Court: The Battle for the Soul of International Law." *South African Yearbook of International Law* 34 (2009): 57–69.

Tladi, Dire. "Security Council, the use of force and regime change: Libya and Cote d'Ivoire." *South African Yearbook of International Law* 37, no. 1 (2012): 22–45.

Tomz, Michael. *Reputation and International Cooperation: Sovereign Debt across Three Centuries*. Princeton, NJ: Princeton University Press, 2007.

Traub, James. *The Best Intentions: Kofi Annan and the UN in the Era of American World Power*. New York: Farrar, Straus and Giroux, 2006.

Traub, James. "Unwilling and Unable: The Failed Response to the Atrocities in Darfur" (Brisbane: Global Centre for the Responsibility to Protect, 2010). http://www.globalr2p.org/media/files/unwilling-and-unable-the-failed-response-to-the-atrocities-in-darfur.pdf (accessed March 3, 2019).

Traub, James. "The World According to China." *The New York Times*, September 3, 2006.

Trevelyan, Laura. "Libya: Coalition divided on arming rebels." *BBC News*, March 29, 2011.

"U.N. General Assembly to vote Thursday on Syria: China warns of 'wrong steps'." *Al Arabiya*, February 15, 2012.

U.S. Government Accountability Office. "Darfur Crisis: Death Estimates Demonstrate Severity of the Crisis, But Their Accuracy and Credibility Could Be Enhanced (GAO-07-24)." November 9, 2006.

"UN chief calls China pillar of multilateral system." *Xinhua*, April 6, 2018.

"UN chief: Belt and Road Initiative China's new vision to global development." *CCTV.com*, May 10, 2017.

UN News Centre. "Ban strongly condemns Qadhafi's actions against protesters, calls for punishment." February 23, 2011.

UN News Centre. "Head of UN environment agency to attend opening of Olympic Games." August 4, 2008.

UN News Centre. "UN-Arab League envoy to continue regional consultations on Syrian conflict." March 30, 2012.

UN News Centre. "UN human rights chief renews call on Security Council to refer Syria to ICC." July 2, 2012.

UN Office of the Special Adviser on the Prevention of Genocide. "UN Secretary-General Special Adviser on the Prevention of Genocide, Francis Deng, and Special Adviser on the Responsibility to Protect, Edward Luck, on the Situation in Libya, February 22." 2011.

UN Report (Documents). "Arab League's letter to Security Council on Syria: Act under Chapter 7." June 8, 2012, http://un-report.blogspot.com/2012/06/arab-league-letter-to-security-council.html (accessed March 3, 2019).

UN Report (Documents). "Kofi Annan's budget, mandate and objectives." April 25, 2012, http://un-report.blogspot.com.au/2012/04/kofi-annans-budget-mandate-and.html (accessed March 3, 2019).

"UN Threatens Sudan with Sanctions on Darfur." *China Daily*, July 31, 2004.

UN Web TV. "Jeffrey Feltman (DPA) on Syria - Security Council Media Stakeout." November 6, 2012, http://webtv.un.org/media/media-stakeouts/watch/jeffrey-feltman-dpa-on-syria-security-council-media-stakeout/1950949912001 (accessed March 3, 2019).

UN Web TV. "Valerie Amos (OCHA) on Syria - Security Council Media Stakeout (17 December 2012)." December 17, 2012, http://webtv.un.org/topics-issues/global-issues/humanitarian-assistance/watch/valerie-amos-ocha-on-syria-security-council-media-stakeout-17-december-2012/2041477549001 (accessed March 3, 2019).

UNComtrade. "Commodity Trade Statistics Database." http://comtrade.un.org/db/ce/ceSearch.aspx?it=oil&rg=1&r=156&p=148&y=recent&px=HS (accessed March 3, 2019).

United Nations Commission on Human Rights. "Report of the United Nations High Commission for Human Rights and Followup to the World Conference on Human Rights: Situation of human rights in Darfur region of the Sudan (E/CN.4/2005/3), May 7." 2004.

United Nations Department of Peacekeeping Operations. "Handbook on United Nations Multidimensional Peacekeeping Operations." 2003.

United Nations Department of Peacekeeping Operations. "Role of the General Assembly." http://www.un.org/en/peacekeeping/operations/rolega.shtml (accessed March 3, 2019).

United Nations Department of Peacekeeping Operations. "United Nations Peacekeeping Operations Principles and Guidelines." 2008.

United Nations Economic and Social Council. "Social dimension of the New Partnership for Africa's Development: Report of the Secretary-General (E/CN.5/2017/2), 22 November." 2016.

United Nations General Assembly. "Fifty-first Session: 82nd plenary meeting (A/51/PV.82), December 12." 1996.

United Nations General Assembly. "Fifty-fourth Session: 8th plenary meeting (A/54/PV.8), September 22." 1999.

United Nations General Assembly. "Fifty-second Session: 70th plenary meeting (A/52/PV.70), December 12." 1997.

United Nations General Assembly. "Fifty-third Session: 85th plenary meeting (A/53/PV.85), December 9." 1998.

United Nations General Assembly. "General Assembly Adopts More Than 60 Resolutions Recommended by Third Committee, Including Text Condemning Grave, Systematic Human Rights Violations in Syria (GA/11198)." 2011.

United Nations General Assembly. "General Assembly Adopts Resolution Strongly Condemning 'Widespread and Systematic' Human Rights Violations by Syrian Authorities (GA/11207/Rev.1)." 2012.

United Nations General Assembly. "General Assembly, in Resolution, Demands All in Syria 'Immediately and Visibly' Commit to Ending Violence that Secretary-General Says Is Ripping Country Apart (GA/11266/Rev.1), August 3." 2012.

United Nations General Assembly. "Implementing the Responsibility to Protect: Report of the Secretary-General (A/63/677), January 12." 2009.

United Nations General Assembly. "Promotion and protection of human rights: human rights situations and reports of special rapporteurs and representatives: Report of the 3rd Committee (A/66/462/Add.3), December 5." 2011.

United Nations General Assembly. "Resolution adopted by the General Assembly on 1 March 2011: Suspension of the rights of membership of the Libyan Arab Jamahiriya in the Human Rights Council (A/RES/65/265), March 3." 2011.

United Nations General Assembly. "Resolution adopted by the General Assembly on 4 December 2017: No first placement of weapons in outer space (A/RES/72/27), 11 December." 2017.

United Nations General Assembly. "Resolution adopted by the General Assembly on 16 February 2012: The situation in Syrian Arab Republic (A/RES/66/253), February 21." 2012.
UN General Assembly. "Resolution adopted by the General Assembly on 16 September 2005: World Summit Outcome, A/RES/60/1, 24 October." 2005.
United Nations General Assembly. "Resolution adopted by the Human Rights Council on 23 March 2017: Question of the realization in all countries of economic, social and cultural rights (A/HRC/RES/34/4), April 6." (2017).
United Nations General Assembly. "Sixty-third session: 99th plenary meeting (A/63/PV.99), July 24." 2009.
United Nations General Assembly. "Third Committee Approves Resolution Condemning Human Rights Violations in Syria, by Vote of 122 in Favour to 13 Against, with 41 Abstentions (GA/SHC/4033)." 2011.
United Nations General Assembly. "Top UN Human Rights Official Says Member States 'Must Act Now' to Protect Syrian People, as Violent Crackdown Continues, in Briefing to General Assembly (GA/11206), February 13." 2012.
United Nations General Assembly, and United Nations Security Council. "An Agenda for Peace (A/47/277-S/24111)." 1992.
United Nations General Assembly, and United Nations Security Council. "Identical letters dated 21 August 2000 from the Secretary-General to the President of the General Assembly and the President of the Security Council (A/55/305-S/2000/809)." 2000.
United Nations General Assembly, and United Nations Security Council. "Letter dated 14 January 2013 from the Chargé d'affaires a.i. of the Permanent Mission of Switzerland to the United Nations addressed to the Secretary-General (A/67/694–S/2013/19), January 16." 2013.
United Nations General Assembly, and United Nations Security Council. "Supplement to an Agender for Peace: Position Paper of the Secretary-General on the Occasion of the Fiftieth Anniversary of the United Nations (A/50/60-S/1995/1), January 3." 1995.
United Nations Human Rights Council. "Human Rights Council passes resolution on Syrian Arab Republic in Special Session." April 29, 2011, http://reliefweb.int/report/syrian-arab-republic/human-rights-council-passes-resolution-syrian-arab-republic-special (accessed March 3, 2019).
United Nations Human Rights Council. "Resolution adopted by the Human Rights Council: The current human rights situation in the Syrian Arab Republic in the context of recent events (A/HRC/RES/S-16/1), May 4." 2011.
United Nations Human Rights Office of the High Commissioner. "Pillay calls for international inquiry into Libyan violence and justice for victims." February 22, 2011.
United Nations Human Rights Office of the High Commissioner. "Syria: Door remains wide open for further atrocities after lack of referral to the ICC, UN experts warn." May 30, 2014, http://www.ohchr.org/EN/NewsEvents/Pages/DisplayNews.aspx?NewsID=14655&LangID=E (accessed March 3, 2019).
United Nations Secretary-General Ban Ki-moon. "Kofi Annan Appointed Joint Special Envoy of United Nations, League of Arab States on Syrian Crisis (SG/SM/14124)," news release, February 23, 2012, http://www.un.org/press/en/2012/sgsm14124.doc.htm (March 3, 2019).
United Nations Secretary-General Ban Ki-moon. "Readout of the Secretary-General's meetings with H.E. Mr. Hu Jintao, President of the People's Republic of China, and H.E. Mr. Yang Jiechi, Foreign Minister of the People's Republic of China." July 18, 2012, https://www.un.org/sg/en/content/sg/readout/2012-07-18/readout-secretary-

general%E2%80%99s-meetings-he-mr-hu-jintao-president-people (accessed March 3, 2019).
United Nations Secretary-General Ban Ki-moon. "Secretary-General's address at The Asia Society: 'Crisis in Syria: Civil War, Global Threat'." June 20, 2014, United Nations Secretary-Genera, https://www.un.org/sg/en/content/sg/statement/2014-06-20/secretary-generals-address-asia-society-crisis-syria-civil-war (accessed March 3, 2019).
United Nations Secretary-General Ban Ki-moon. "Secretary-General's remarks to Security Council Open Debate on the Protection of Civilians in Armed Conflict." February 12, 2013, https://www.un.org/sg/en/content/sg/statement/2013-02-12/secretary-generals-remarks-security-council-open-debate-protection (accessed March 3, 2019).
United Nations Secretary-General Kofi Annan. "'Risk of Genocide Remains Frighteningly Real', Secretary-General Tells Human Rights Commission as He Launches Action Plan to Prevent Genocide (SG/SM/9245-AFR/893-HR/CN/1077)." 2004.
United Nations Secretary-General Kofi Annan. "Secretary-General Alarmed by Deteriorating Humanitarian Situation in Darfur Region of Sudan (SG/SM/9067-AFR/790)," news release, December 9, 2003, http://www.un.org/press/en/2003/sgsm9067.doc.htm (March 3, 2019).
United Nations Security Council. "3344th Meeting (S/PV.3344), March 4." 1994.
United Nations Security Council. "3356th Meeting (S/PV.3356), March 31." 1994.
United Nations Security Council. "3367th Meeting (S/PV.3367), April 21." 1994.
United Nations Security Council. "3385th Meeting (S/PV.3385), May 31." 1994.
United Nations Security Council. "3392nd Meeting (S/PV.3392), June 22." 1994.
United Nations Security Council. "3428th Meeting (S/PV.3428), September 23." 1994.
United Nations Security Council. "3454th Meeting (S/PV.3454), November 8." 1994.
United Nations Security Council. "3575th Meeting (S/PV.3454), September 8." 1995.
United Nations Security Council. "3730th Meeting (S/PV.3730), January 10." 1997.
United Nations Security Council. "3868th Meeting (S/PV.3868), March 31." 1998.
United Nations Security Council. "3930th Meeting (S/PV.3930), September 23." 1998.
United Nations Security Council. "3968th Meeting (S/PV.3968), January 21." 1999.
United Nations Security Council. "3989th Meeting (S/PV.3989), March 26." 1999.
United Nations Security Council. "4043rd Meeting (S/PV.4043), September 11." 1999.
United Nations Security Council. "5040th meetingn (S/PV.5040), September 18." 2004.
United Nations Security Council. "5158th meeting (S/PV.5158), March 31." 2005.
United Nations Security Council. "5225th meeting (S/PV.5225), July 12." 2005.
United Nations Security Council. "5319th meeting (S/PV.5319), December 9." 2005.
United Nations Security Council. "5577th meeting (S/PV.5577), December 4." 2006.
United Nations Security Council. "5619th meeting (S/PV.5619), January 12." 2007.
United Nations Security Council. "5781st meeting (S/PV.5781), November 20." 2007.
United Nations Security Council. "5898th meeting (S/PV.5898), May 27." 2008.
United Nations Security Council. "5933rd meeting, July 11 (S/PV.5933)." 2008.
United Nations Security Council. "6491st meeting (S/PV.6491), February 26." 2011.
United Nations Security Council. "6524th meeting (S/PV.6524), April 27." 2011.
United Nations Security Council. "6528th meeting (S/PV.6528), May 4." 2011.
United Nations Security Council. "6531st meeting (S/PV.6531), May 10." 2011.
United Nations Security Council. "6627th meeting (S/PV.6627), October 4." 2011.
United Nations Security Council. "6706th meeting (S/PV.6706), January 24." 2012.
United Nations Security Council. "6711th meeting (S/PV.6711), February 4." 2012.
United Nations Security Council. "6734th meeting (S.PV/6734), March 12." 2012.
United Nations Security Council. "6826th meeting (S/PV.6826), August 30." 2012.

United Nations Security Council. "6894th meeting (S/PV.6894), December 19." 2012.
United Nations Security Council. "8042nd meeting (S/PV.8042), September 11." 2017.
United Nations Security Council. "Canada, France, Germany, Italy, Netherlands, Slovenia, United Kingdom of Great Britain and Northern Ireland and United States of America: draft resolution (S/1999/201), February 25." 1999.
United Nations Security Council. "Draft Resolution (S/2014/348), May 22." 2014.
United Nations Security Council. "Letter dated 4 January from the Permanent Representative of China to the United Nations addressed to the Secretary-General (S/2010/9), January 7." 2010.
United Nations Security Council. "Letter dated 12 November 2013 from the Permanent Representative of Saudi Arabia to the United Nations addressed to the Secretary-General (A/68/599), November 14." 2013.
United Nations Security Council. "Letter Dated 24 August 1990 from the Permanent Representatives of Bahrain, Kuwait, Oman, Qatar, Saudi Arabia and the United Arab Emirates to the United Nations Addressed to the President of the Security Council (S/21639), August 24." 1990.
United Nations Security Council. "Letter Dated 30 August 1990 from the Permanent Representatives of Qatar to the United Nations Addressed to the Secretary-General (S/21684), August 30." 1990.
United Nations Security Council. "Letter dated 2001/10/07 from the Permanent Representative of the United States of America to the United Nations addressed to the President of the Security Council (S/2001/946)." 2001.
United Nations Security Council. "Provisional Verbatim Record of the Three Thousand and Fifty-Fifth Meeting (S/PV.3055), February 21." 1992.
United Nations Security Council. "Provisional Verbatim Record of the Three Thousand and One Hundred and Twenty-Second Meeting (S/PV.3122), October 9." 1992.
United Nations Security Council. "Provisional Verbatim Record of the Three Thousand One Hundred and Eighty-Eighth Meeting (S/PV.3188), March 26." 1993.
United Nations Security Council. "Provisional Verbatim Record of the Three Thousand One Hundred and Eighty-Ninth Meeting (S/PV.3189), March 30." 1993.
United Nations Security Council. "Provisional Verbatim Record of the Three Thousand One Hundred and Forty-Fifth Meeting (S/PV.3145), December 3." 1992.
United Nations Security Council. "Provisional Verbatim Record of the Three Thousand One Hundred and Ninety-First Meeting (S/PV.3191), March 31." 1993.
United Nations Security Council. "Provisional Verbatim Record of the Three Thousand One Hundred and Ninety-Ninth Meeting (S/PV.3199), April 16." 1993.
United Nations Security Council. "Provisional Verbatim Record of the Three Thousand One Hundred and Seventy-Fourth Meeting (S/PV.3174), February 19." 1993.
United Nations Security Council. "Provisional Verbatim Record of the Three Thousand One Hundred and Sixth Meeting (S/PV.3106), August 13." 1992.
United Nations Security Council. "Provisional Verbatim Record of the Three Thousand Two Hundred and Ninety-Third Meeting (S/PV.3293), October 16." 1993.
United Nations Security Council. "Provisional Verbatim Record of the Three Thousand Two Hundred and Thirty-Eighth Meeting (S/PV.3238), June 16." 1993.
United Nations Security Council. "Provisional Verbatim Record of the Three Thousand Two Hundred and Twenty-Eighth Meeting (S/PV.3228), June 4." 1993.
United Nations Security Council. "Provisional Verbatim Record of the Three Thousand Two Hundredth Meeting (S/PV.3200), April 18." 1993.

United Nations Security Council. "Provisional Verbatim Record of the Two Thousand Nine Hundred and Eighty-Second Meeting (S/PV.2982), April 5." 1991.

United Nations Security Council. "Referral of Syria to International Criminal Court Fails as Negative Votes Prevent Security Council from Adopting Draft Resolution (SC/11407)." 2014.

United Nations Security Council. "Report of the Secretary-General on the Sudan pursuant to paragraph 15 of Security Council resolution 1564 (2004) and paragraphs 6, 13 and 16 of Security Council resolution 1556 (2004) (S/2004/881), November 2." 2004.

United Nations Security Council. "Resolution 495 (1981) of 14 December 1981 (S/RES/495)." 1981.

United Nations Security Council. "Resolution 688 (1991) of 5 April 1991 (S/RES/688)." 1991.

United Nations Security Council. "Resolution 743 (1992) of 21 February 1992 (S/RES/743)." 1992.

United Nations Security Council. "Resolution 761 (1992) of 29 June 1992 (S/RES/761)." 1992.

United Nations Security Council. United Nations Security Council. "Resolution 762 (1992) of 30 June 1992 (S/RES/762)." 1992.

United Nations Security Council. "Resolution 769 (1992): Adopted by the Security Council at its 3104th meeting, on 7 August 1992 (S/RES/769)." 1992.

United Nations Security Council. "Resolution 770 (1992): Adopted by the Security Council at its 3106th meeting, on 13 August 1992 (S/RES/770)." 1992.

United Nations Security Council. "Resolution 779 (1992): Adopted by the Security Council at its 3118th meeting, on 6 October 1992 (S/RES/779)." 1992.

United Nations Security Council. "Resolution 781 (1992): Adopted by the Security Council at its 3122nd meeting, on 9 October 1992 (S/RES/781)." 1992.

United Nations Security Council. "Resolution 794 (1992): Adopted by the Security Council at its 3145th meeting, on 3 December 1992 (S/RES/794)." 1992.

United Nations Security Council. "Resolution 807 (1993): Adopted by the Security Council at its 3174th meeting, on 19 February 1993 (S/RES/807)." 1993.

United Nations Security Council. "Resolution 814 (1993): Adopted by the Security Council at its 3188th meeting, on 26 March 1993 (S/RES/814)." 1993.

United Nations Security Council. "Resolution 816 (1993): Adopted by the Security Council at its 3191st meeting, on 31 March 1993 (S/RES/816)." 1993.

United Nations Security Council. "Resolution 819 (1993): Adopted by the Security Council at its 3199th meeting, on 16 April 1993 (S/RES/819)." 1993.

United Nations Security Council. "Resolution 824 (1993): Adopted by the Security Council at its 3208th meeting, on 6 May 1993 (S/RES/824)." 1993.

United Nations Security Council. "Resolution 827 (1993): Adopted by the Security Council at its 3217th meeting, on 25 May 1993 (S/RES/827)." 1993.

United Nations Security Council. "Resolution 841: Adopted by the Security Council at its 3238th meeting, on 16 June 1993 (S/RES/841)." 1993.

United Nations Security Council. "Resolution 875 (1993): Adopted by the Security Council at its 3293rd meeting, on 16 October 1993 (S/RES/875)." 1993.

United Nations Security Council. "Resolution 918 (1994): Adopted by the Security Council at its 3377 meeting on 17 May 1994 (S/RES/918)." 1994.

United Nations Security Council. "Resolution 929 (1994): Adopted by the Security Council at its 3392nd meeting, on 22 June 1994 (S/RES/929)." 1994.

BIBLIOGRAPHY 267

United Nations Security Council. "Resolution 1160 (1998): Adopted by the Security Council at its 3868 meeting, on 31 March 1998 (S/RES/1160)." 1998.

United Nations Security Council. "Resolution 1199 (1998): Adopted by the Security Council at its 3930th meeting, on 23 September 1998 (S/RES/1199)." 1998.

United Nations Security Council. "Resolution 1203 (1998): Adopted by the Security Council at its 3937th meeting, on 24 October 1998 (S/RES/1203)." 1998.

United Nations Security Council. "Resolution 1246 (1999): Adopted by the Security Council at its 4013th meeting, on 11 June 1999 (S/RES/1246)." 1999.

United Nations Security Council. "Resolution 1257 (1999): Adopted by the Security Council at its 4031st meeting, on 3 August 1999 (S/RES/1257)." 1999.

United Nations Security Council. "Resolution 1262 (1999): Adopted by the Security Council at its 4038th meeting, on 27 August 1999 (S/RES/1262)." 1999.

United Nations Security Council. "Resolution 1264 (1999): Adopted by the Security Council at its 4045th meeting, on 15 September 1999 (S/RES/1264)." 1999.

United Nations Security Council. "Resolution 1271 (1999): Adopted by the Security Council at its 4056th meeting, on 22 October 1999 (S/RES/1271)." 1999.

United Nations Security Council. "Resolution 1272 (1999): Adopted by the Security Council at its 4057th meeting, on 25 October 1999 (S/RES/1272)." 1999.

United Nations Security Council. "Resolution 1368 (2001): Adopted by the Security Council at its 4370th meeting, on 12 September 2001 (S/RES/1368)." 2001.

United Nations Security Council. "Resolution 1542 (2004): Adopted by the Security Council at its 4961st meeting, on 30 April 2004 (S/RES/1542)." 2004.

United Nations Security Council. "Resolution 1556 (2004): Adopted by the Security Council at its 5015th meeting, on 30 July 2004 (S/RES/1556)." 2004.

United Nations Security Council. "Resolution 1564 (2004): Adopted by the Security Council at its 5040th meeting, on 18 September 2004 (S/RES/1564)." 2004.

United Nations Security Council. "Resolution 1590 (2005): Adopted by the Security Council at its 5151st meeting, on 24 March 2005 (S/RES/1590)." 2005.

United Nations Security Council. "Resolution 1591 (2005): Adopted by the Security Council at its 5153rd meeting, on 29 March 2005 (S/RES/1591), March 29." 2005.

United Nations Security Council. "Resolution 1593 (2005): Adopted by the Security Council at its 5158th meeting, on 31 March 2005 (S/RES/1593)." 2005.

United Nations Security Council. "Resolution 1653 (2006): Adopted by the Security Council at its 5359th meeting, on 27 January 2006 (S/RES/1653)." 2006.

United Nations Security Council. "Resolution 1674 (2006): Adopted by the Security Council at its 5430th meeting, on 28 April 2006 (S/RES/1674)." 2006.

United Nations Security Council. "Resolution 1679 (2006): Adopted by the Security Council at its 5439th meeting, on 16 May 2006 (S/RES/1679)." 2006.

United Nations Security Council. "Resolution 1706 (2006): Adopted by the Security Council at its 5519th meeting, on 31 August 2006 (S/RES/1706)." 2006.

United Nations Security Council. "Resolution 1769 (2007): Adopted by the Security Council at its 5727th meeting, on 31 July 2007 (S/RES/1769)." 2007.

United Nations Security Council. "Resolution 1970 (2011): Adopted by the Security Council at its 6491st meeting, on 26 February 2011 (S/RES/1970), February 26." 2011.

United Nations Security Council. "Resolution 1973 (2011): Adopted by the Security Council at its 6498th meeting, on 17 March 2011 (S/RES/1973)." 2011.

United Nations Security Council. "Resolution 2042 (2012): Adopted by the Security Council at its 6751st meeting, on 14 April 2012 (S/RES/2042)." 2012.

268   BIBLIOGRAPHY

United Nations Security Council. "Resolution 2043 (2012): Adopted by the Security Council at its 6756th meeting, on 21 April 2012 (S/RES/2043)." 2012.
United Nations Security Council. "Resolution 2059 (2012): Adopted by the Security Council at its 6812th meeting, on 20 July 2012." 2012.
United Nations Security Council. "Resolution 2274 (2016) Adopted by the Security Council at its 7645th meeting, on 15 March 2016 (S/RES/2274)." 2016.
United Nations Security Council. "Resolution 2344 (2017): Adopted by the Security Council at its 7902nd meeting, on 17 March 2017 (S/RES/2344)." 2017.
United Nations Security Council. "Security Council Expands Mandate of UN Mission in Sudan to Include Darfur, Adopting Resolution 1706 by Vote of 12 in Favour, with 3 Abstaining (SC/8821)." 2006.
United Nations Security Council. "Security Council Fails to Adopt Draft Resolution Condemning Syria's Crackdown on Anti-Government Protestors, Owing to Veto by Russian Federation, China (SC/10403)." 2011.
United Nations Security Council. "Security Council Fails to Adopt Draft Resolution on Syria That Would Have Threatened Sanctions, Due to Negative Votes of China, Russian Federation (SC/10714)." 2012.
United Nations Security Council. "Security Council Fails to Extend Mandate of United Nations Preventive Deployment Force in Former Yugoslav Republic of Macedonia (SC/6648), February 25." 1999.
United Nations Security Council. "Security Council Press Statement on Attacks in Syria (SC/10658)." 2012.
United Nations Security Council. "Security Council Press Statement on Ceasefire in Syria (SC/10800)." 2012.
United Nations Security Council. "Security Council Press Statement on Damascus Bombing (SC/10953)." 2013.
United Nations Security Council. "Security Council Press Statement on Libya." 2011.
United Nations Security Council. "Security Council Press Statement on Shelling of Turkish Town by Syrian Forces (SC/10783)." 2012.
United Nations Security Council. "Security Council Press Statement on Syria (SC/10564)." 2012.
United Nations Security Council. "Security Council Press Statement on Terrorist Attacks in Aleppo (SC/10784)." 2012.
United Nations Security Council. "Security Council Press Statement on Terrorist Attacks in Damascus (SC/10643)." 2012.
United Nations Security Council. "Security Council Refers Situation in Darfur, Sudan, To Prosecutor of International Criminal Court (SC/8351)," news release, March 31, 2005, http://www.un.org/press/en/2005/sc8351.doc.htm (accessed March 3, 2019).
United Nations Security Council. "Security Council Urges Sudan's Government to Fully Cooperate with International Ciminal Court 'To Put an End to Impunity for the Crimes Committed in Darfur' (SC/9359)," news release, June 16, 2008, http://www.un.org/press/en/2008/sc9359.doc.htm (accessed March 3, 2019).
United Nations Security Council. "Security Council, in Presidential Statement, Reaffirms Commitment to Protection of Civilians in Armed Conflict, Adopts Updated Aide-Memoire on Issue (SC/9571), January 14." 2009.
United Nations Security Council. "Security Council, in Statement, Condemns Syrian Authorities for 'Widespread Violations of Human Rights, Use of Force against Civilians' (SC/10352)." 2011.

United Nations Security Council. "Statement by the President of the Security Council (S/PRST/2011/16), August 3." 2011.
United Nations Security Council. "Statement by the President of the Security Council (S/PRST/2012/6), March 21." 2012.
United Nations Security Council. "Statement by the President of the Security Council (S/PRST/2012/10), April 5." 2012.
United Nations Security Council. "United Kingdom of Great Britain and Northern Ireland and United States of America: draft resolution (S/2007/14), January 12." 2007.
United Nations Statistics Division. "UN Comtrade Database." n.d., https://comtrade.un.org/ (accessed March 3, 2019).
"Updated French Draft Resolution on Chemical Weapons in Syria." September 13, 2013, https://docs.google.com/file/d/0ByLPNZ-eSjJdX29vd2Y3WlNxQWc/view (accessed March 3, 2019).
"US 'disgust' as Russia and China veto UN Syria resolution." *BBC News*, February 4, 2012.
"US to Press for UN Security Council Action on Myanmar." *Japan Economic Newswire*, November 27, 2006.
Van Evera, Stephen. *Guide to Methods for Students of Political Science*. Ithaca, NY: Cornell University Press, 1997.
Vanhullebusch, Matthias. "Regime Change, the Security Council and China." *Chinese Journal of International Law* 14, no. 4 (2015): 665-707.
Vincent, R. J. *Nonintervention and International Order*. Princeton, NJ: Princeton University Press, 1974.
Vincent, R. J. "Order in International Politics." In *Order and Violence: Hedley Bull and International Relations*, edited by J. D. B. Miller and R. J. Vincent. Oxford: Clarendon Press, 1990.
Volgy, Thomas J., Renato Corbetta, Keith A. Grant, and Ryan G. Baird, eds. *Major Powers and the Quest for Status in International Politics*. New York: Palgrave/MacMillan, 2011.
Volgy, Thomas J., Renato Corbetta, J. Patrick Rhamey, Ryan G. Baird, and Keith Grant. "Status Considerations in International Politics and the Rise of Regional Powers." Chap. 3 In *Status in World Politics*, edited by T. V. Paul, Deborah Welch Larson, and William C. Wohlforth, 58-84. New York: Cambridge University Press, 2014.
Wagstyl, Stefan, Charles Clover, and Geoff Dyer. "China fails to support Kremlin." *Financial Times*, August 29, 2008.
Walker, Peter, and Julian Borger. "China may veto attempt to arrest Sudanese president on genocide charges." *The Guardian*, July 15, 2008.
Walling, Carrie Booth. *All Necessary Measures: The United Nations and Humanitarian Intervention*. Philadephia, PA: University of Pennsylvania Press, 2013.
Walling, Carrie Booth. "The UN Security Council and Its ICC Referral Resolutions: Advancing or Curbing the Justice Norm?" Paper presented at the International Studies Association's 57th Annual Convention, Atlanta, Georgia, March 16-19 2016.
Walt, Vivienne. "Is Syria's Bashar Assad Going the Way of Muammar Gaddafi?," July 23, 2012.
Walter, Barbara F. *Reputation and Civil War: Why Separatist Conflicts Are so Violent*. New York: Cambridge University Press, 2009.
Waltz, Kenneth N. *Theory of International Politics*. Reading, MA: Addison, 1979.
Wang, Hongying, and James N. Rosenau. "China and Global Governance." *Asian Perspective* 33, no. 3 (2009): 5-39.
Wang, Jisi. "China's Search for a Grand Strategy." *Foreign Affairs* 90, no. 2 (2011): 69-79.

Wang, Xinsong. "One Belt, One Road's Governance Deficit Problem: How China Can Ensure Transparency and Accountability." *Foreign Affairs* 96, no. 6, November 17, 2017.
Wang Xuejun, "Developmental Peace: Understanding China's Africa Policy in Peace and Security," in Alden C., Alao A., Chun Z., Barber L. (eds) *China and Africa* (London: Palgrave Macmillan, Cham, 2018).
Wang, Yi. "China, a Staunch Defender and Builder of International Rule of Law." *People's Daily*, October 24, 2014.
Wang, Ying. "China's April Oil Imports From Sudan Rise Sixfold." *Bloomberg*, May 25, 2007.
Wang, Yusheng. "Zhongguo waijiao de bianyu bubian (The Changes and Consistencies of China's Diplomacy)." *Jiefang Ribao*, October 29, 2012.
Weisman, Steven R. "Powell Declares Genocide in Sudan in Bid to Raise Pressure." *The New York Times*, September 9, 2004.
Weiss, Thomas G. *Humanitarian Intervention: Ideas in Action*. 2nd ed. Cambridge: Polity Press, 2012.
Weller, Marc, ed. *The Crisis in Kosovo, 1989-1999: from the dissolution of Yugoslavia to Rambouillet and the outbreak of hostilities*. Cambridge: Documents and Analysis, 1999.
Welsh, Jennifer M. "Introduction." Chap. 1 In *Humanitarian Intervention and International Relations*, edited by Jennifer M. Welsh, 1-8. Oxford: Oxford University Press, 2004.
Welsh, Jennifer M. "The Security Council and Humanitarian Intervention." Chap. 24 In *The United Nations Security Council and War: The Evolution of Thought and Practice Since 1945*, edited by Vaughan Lowe, Adam Roberts, Jennifer M. Welsh, and Dominik Zaum, 535-62. Oxford: Oxford University Press, 2008.
"Wen issues warning on Darfur." *Sino Daily*, September 13, 2006.
Wendt, Alexander. *Social Theory of International Politics*. Cambridge: Cambridge University Press, 1999.
Wendt, Alexander. "The state as person in international theory." *Review of International Studies* 30, no. 2 (2004): 289-316.
What's In Blue. "Draft Resolution on Syria." June 8, 2011, http://www.whatsinblue.org/2011/06/presidential-statement-on-syria.php (accessed March 3, 2019).
What's In Blue. "Syria: Monday Vote on Draft Resolution on Cross-Border and Cross-Line Humanitarian Access." July 13, 2014, http://www.whatsinblue.org/2014/07/syria-monday-vote-on-draft-resolution-on-cross-border-and-cross-line-humanitarian-access.php (accessed March 3, 2019).
Wheeler, Nicholas J. *Saving Strangers: Humanitarian Intervention in International Society*. Oxford: Oxford University Press, 2002.
Wheeler, Nicholas J., and Tim Dunne. "Good International Citizenship: A Third Way for British Foreign Policy." *International Affairs* 74, no. 4 (1998): 847-70.
Wight, Martin. *Power Politics*. Leicester: Leicester University Press, 1978.
Williams, Paul D. "The Road to Humanitarian War in Libya." *Global Responsibility to Protect* 3, no. 2 (2011): 248-59.
Williams, Paul D. "The United Kingdom." In *The International Politics of Mass Atrocities: The Case of Darfur*, edited by David R. Black and Paul D. Williams, 195-212. New York: Routledge, 2010.
Wilson, Scott, and Joby Warrick. "Assad must go, Obama says." *The Washington Post*, August 18, 2011.
Wines, Michael. "Secret Bid to Arm Qaddafi Sheds Light on Tensions in China Govern." *The New York Times*, September 11, 2011.

Wintour, Patrick, and Nicholas Watt. "Cameron's War: Why PM Felt Gaddafi Had to Be Stopped." *The Guardian*, October 2, 2011.

Wishnick, Elizabeth. "Sino-Russian Strategic Partnership: View from China." In *China-Russia Relations in the Early 21st Century*, edited by James Bellacqua. Louisville, KY: University of Kentucky Press, 2010.

Wittes, Tamara Cofman. "Options for U.S. Policy in Syria." April 19, 2012, The Brookings Institution, http://www.brookings.edu/research/testimony/2012/04/19-syria-wittes (accessed March 3, 2019).

Wittes, Tamara Cofman, Michael Doran, Daniel L. Byman, Shadi Hamid, and Bruce Riedel. "Syria, the U.S., and Arming the Rebels: Assad's Use of Chemical Weapons and Obama's Red Line." June 14, 2013, http://www.brookings.edu/blogs/up-front/posts/2013/06/14-syria-us-arming-rebels-assad-use-chemical-weapons-and-obamas-red-line (accessed March 3, 2019).

Wohlforth, William C. "Unipolarity, Status Competition, and Great Power War." *World Politics* 61, no. 1 (2009): 28–57.

Womack, Brantly. "China as a Normative Foreign Policy Actor." Chap. 6 In *Who is a Normative Foreign Policy Actor?: The European Union and its Global Partners*, edited by Nathalie Tocci and Daniel S. Hamilton, 265–99. Brussels: Centre for European Policy Studies, 2008.

Wong, Albert, and Joyce Man. "Mia Farrow told to behave for torch relay." *South China Morning Post*, May 2, 2008.

Worsnip, Patrick. "Russian draft offers hope of U.N. Syria resolution." *Reuters*, December 15, 2011.

Worth, Robert F. "Sudan says it will accept UN-African peace force in Darfur." October 17, 2006.

Wright, Thomas. "China and Russia vs. America: Great-Power Revisionism Is Back." *The National Interest*, April 27 2015.

Wu, Ningbo. "Lun 'baohu de zeren' de guojifa kunjing yu chulu (On the Dilemma and Outlet of the International Law of the 'Responsibility to Protect')." *Administration and Law*, no. 4 (2015): 123–9.

Wu, Xinbo. "Four Contradictions Constraining China's Foreign Policy Behavior." *Journal of Contemporary China* 10, no. 27 (2001): 293–301.

Wu, Xingtang. "Guoji xinshi dongdang duobianxia, Zhongguo waijiao ying jianchi 'sanbu' yuanze (With the Turbulence of the International Situation, China's Diplomacy Should Insist on the 'Three NOs' Principles')." *The Contemporary World*, no. 4 (2012).

Wuthnow, Joel. "China and the Processes of Cooperation in UN Security Council Deliberations." *Chinese Journal of International Politics* 3, no. 1 (2010): 55–77.

Wuthnow, Joel. *Chinese Diplomacy and the UN Security Council: Beyond the Veto*. London: Routledge, 2013.

Xi, Jinping. "Full text of President Xi's speech at opening of Belt and Road forum." *Xinhua*, May 14, 2017.

Xi, Jinping. "Secure a Decisive Victory in Building a Moderately Prosperous Society in All Respects and Strive for the Great Success of Socialism with Chinese Characteristics for a New Era." October 18, 2017, Beijing: National Congress of the Communist Party of China, http://www.xinhuanet.com/english/download/Xi_Jinping's_report_at_19th_CPC_National_Congress.pdf (accessed March 3, 2019).

Xi, Jinping. "Work Together to Build a Community of Shared Future for Mankind." January 18, 2017, Beijing: Xinhua, http://www.xinhuanet.com/english/2017-01/19/c_135994707.htm (accessed March 3, 2019).

Xi, Jinping. "Working Together to Forge a New Partnership of Win-win Cooperation and Create a Community of Shared Future for Mankind." September 29, 2015, Beijing: Ministry of Foreign Affairs of the People's Republic of China, https://www.fmprc.gov.cn/mfa_eng/wjdt_665385/zyjh_665391/t1305051.shtml (accessed March 3, 2019).

Xi, Mi. "A Responsible Decision." *China Daily*, September 15, 1999, 4.

Xia, Liping. "China: A responsible great power." *Journal of Contemporary China* 10, no. 26 (2001): 17–25.

Xiao, Yingrong. "Zhongguo de daguo zeren yu diquzhuyi zhanlue (China's Major Power Responsibilities and Strategy Towards Regionalism)." *Shijie jingji yu zhengzhi (World Economics and Politics)* 1 (2003): 46–51.

Xinhua. "China donates money to help resolve Darfur conflict." *China.org.cn*, March 29, 2008.

Xinhua. "China makes 'unremitting efforts' to resolve crisis in Darfur." *China Daily*, February 16, 2008.

Xinhua. "China saying 'no' on Syria issue is responsible move: FM Official." *Xinhua*, April 10, 2012.

Xinhua. "Hu Puts Forward Four-point Principle on Solving Darfur Issue." *People.com.cn*, February 6, 2007.

Xinhua. "President Hu sets forth guidelines on Taiwan." *China Daily*, March 4, 2005.

Xu, Guoqi. *Olympic Dreams: China and Sports, 1895–2008*. Cambridge, MA: Harvard University Press, 2008.

"Xuliya zongli pantao yu zhongdong jushi (The Betrayal of Syria Prime Minister and the Situation in the Middle East)." *People.com.cn*, August 9, 2012.

Yan, Liang. "China says linking Olympics with Darfur issue against Olympic Spirit " *Xinhua*, February 14, 2008.

Yan, Xuetong. "From Keeping a Low Profile to Striving for Achievements." *Chinese Journal of International Politics* 7, no. 2 (2014): 153–84.

Yan, Xuetong. "The Rise of China and Its Power Status." *Chinese Journal of International Politics* 1, no. 1 (2006): 5–33.

Yan, Xuetong. "Zhongguo foujue Xuliya jueyian de libi (The Pros and Cons of China's Veto on Syria)." February 8, 2012, sohu.com, http://yanxuetongvip.blog.sohu.com/203112403.html (accessed March 3, 2019).

Yang, Susanne Xiao. *Conflicting Understandings, Competing Preferences: China in UN Security Council Decision-making in Relation to Iraq, 1990–2002*. London: Routledge, 2012.

Yao, Zibao. "Chinese warship escorts ship evacuating Chinese nationals." *PLA Daily*, March 3, 2011.

Yardley, Jim. "China's Leaders Try to Impress and Reassure World." *The New York Times*, August 9, 2008.

Yeophantong, Pichamon. "Governing the World: China's Evolving Conceptions of Responsibility." *Chinese Journal of International Politics* 6, no. 4 (2013): 329–64.

You, Ji. "China's National Security Commission: theory, evolution and operations." *Journal of Contemporary China* 25, no. 98 (2016): 178–96.

Yu, Ping. "Alabo xuezhe dui 'Alabozhichun' de kanfa (Arab Scholar's Views on 'Arab Spring')." *Contemporary World* (March 2013): 48–50.

Zarakol, Ayşe. *After Defeat: How the East Learned to Live with the West*. Cambridge: Cambridge University Press, 2011.

Zenko, Micah. "The Big Lie About the Libyan War." *Foreign Policy*, March 22, 2016.

Zenko, Micah. "Libya No-Fly-Zone Is Anything But." *The Atlantic*, July 19, 2011.

Zhang, Chun. "Possibility of Cooperation: China and EU in Darfur." *International Review* 52 (2008): 55–82.

Zhang, Diyu. "Yizhang foujuepiao de zhengyi (Controversies Around a Veto)." *World Affairs*, no. 5 (2012): 21–24.
Zhang, Guihong. "A Community of Shared Future for Mankind" and Implications for the Prevention of Conflict" [unpublished paper], n.d.
Zhang, Hong. "Wukelan weiji zhong de jiazhi chongtu (Clash of Values Perked up in Crisis-plagued Ukraine)." *Peace and Development* 4 (2015): 88–99.
Zhang, Huiyu. "Zhongguo canyu lianheguo weihe shuping (A Commentary on China's Participation in the UN Peacekeeping)." *Contemporary International Relations*, no. 2 (2009): 51–7.
Zhang, Xiaoming. "A Rising China and the Normative Changes in International Society." *East Asia* 28, no. 3 (2011): 235–46.
Zhao, Lei. *Jiangou heping: Zhongguo dui lianheguo waijiao xingweide yanjin (Constructing Peace: The Evolution of China's Diplomatic Behavior Toward the United Nations)*. Beijing: Jiuzhou Chubanshe, 2007.
Zhao, Lei. "Two Pillars of China's Global Peace Engagement Strategy: UN Peacekeeping and International Peacebuilding." *International Peacekeeping* 18, no. 3 (2011): 344–62.
Zhao, Lei. "Zhongguo yu Lianheguo: Lilun kuangjia, yanjin moxing fenxi (China and the United Nations: Theoretical Framework and Evolution Model Analysis)." *New Thinking* 10 (2007).
Zhao, Lei, and Xinman Gao. *Zhongguo canyu lianheguo weichi heping xingdong de qianyan wenti (The Cutting-edge Issues of China's Participation in UN Peacekeeping Operations)*. Beijing: Shishi Chubanshe, 2011.
Zhao, Suisheng. "Chinese Intellectuals' Quest for National Greatness and Nationalistic Writing in the 1990s." *The China Quarterly* 152 (1997): 725–45.
Zhong, Sheng. "Be wary of attempt to resolve Syrian crisis outside UN framework." *People's Daily*, August 17, 2012.
Zhong, Sheng. "Regime change should not be determined by external forces." *People's Daily*, July 18, 2012.
Zhou, Zhou. "Zhuanjia: Zhongguo jiang geng hao de fahui quanhe cutan zuoyong (Experts: China will better perform its functions of mediation)." *People.cn*, March 30, 2016.
Zhu, Lumin. "Wukelan bianju dui Zhongguo guojia liyi de yingxiang (Impact of Ukraine's Political Upheaval on China's National Interests)." *Pacific Journal* 22, no. 7 (2014): 30–8.
Zifcak, Spencer. "The Responsibility to Protect after Libya and Syria." *Melbourne Journal of International Law* 13, no. 1 (2012): 60–96.
Zimmern, Alfred. *The League of Nations and the Rule of Law, 1918–1935*. London: MacMillan, 1939.
Zoellick, Robert B. "Whither China: From Membership to Responsibility?," remarks to the National Committee on United States-China Relations, September 21, 2005, New York, https://2001-2009.state.gov/s/d/former/zoellick/rem/53682.htm (accessed March 3, 2019).

Index

Note: Figures and tables are indicated by an italic '*f*' and '*t*', respectively, following the page number.

abstention 10, 15–16, 19, 23*t*, 51–3
  on Bosnia 18
  on Cambodia 22
  on Democratic People's Republic of Korea (DPRK) 22
  on Eritrea 26–7
  on Iraq (1991) 17–18
  on Libya 4, 8, 11, 57*t*, 88–92, 94*t*, 96–7, 100–1, 103–4, 136, 145
  on Rwanda 20
  on Sudan 4, 10, 57*t*, 63, 69–73, 70*t*, 81
  on Syria 4, 110, 116–23, 116*t*
accountability 1–2, 4, 47, 66–8, 89–90, 92–4, 106, 124–5, 142–3
Ad Hoc High Level Committee 98
ad hoc tribunals 26, 125
Afghanistan 55, 68
Afghanistan War 101–2
African Union (AU) 10–11, 24–5, 47, 50–1, 69, 72–5, 79–80, 82, 84, 87–8, 95, 98–101, 104, 188n.78, 195n.166, 202n.84, *see* Global South; peer groups; regional organizations
  peer group 64, 74, 84, 89–90, 136
Akol, Lam 73
al Senussi, Abdalla 90–1
al-Assad, Bashar 3–4, 11, 31, 108–24, 116*t*, 126–9, 137–8, *see* Syria
Albania 18–19
al-Bashir, Omar 10, 26, 63–4, 66–9, 73–4, 81–2, 136, 138–9, *see* Sudan
Algeria 70*t*, 71–2, 98–9
al-Obidi, Abdul Ati 105
Ankara, Turkey 122, *see* Turkey
Annan, Kofi 21–2, 66–7, 69, 73–4, 78, 121–3, 214n.131
Arab countries 32, 97, 99–100, 113–14, 117–19, 121, *see* Middle East
Arab Spring 29–32, 92, 110–12, 198n.25
Araud, Gerard 117, 125–6
Armenia 77
arms embargo 23*t*, 26–7, 70*t*, 71, 88–91, 94*t*, 99–100, 187n.63, 197n.10, 204n.130, 222n.50, *see* sanctions
arms sale 26–7, 63, 75–7, 90–1, 111, 117, 143–4, 184n.18, 197n.10

Arria formula meeting 47, 79–80, 124, 194n.152
asset freeze 22, 117, *see* sanctions
Association of Southeast Asian Nations (ASEAN) 50–1, 137, 164n.68, 201n.65, 219nn.4–5, *see* Global South; peer groups; regional organizations
Aung San Suu Kyi 137
Australia 20–1, 125, 190n.114, 195n.177, 217n.155

Bahrain 115
Baltic states 142
Ban, Ki-moon 77–8, 88, 115, 122–4, 142
Bangladesh 15–16, 79
Beckett, Margaret 78
Beijing Olympic Games (2008) 10, 43–4, 63–6, 75–80, 82–6, 127, 136, 145–6, 191nn.122,124, 192n.129
Belt and Road Initiative (BRI) 142–3, 221n.41
Benghazi, Libya 88–90, 99, 101–3, *see* Libya
Biden, Joseph 98, 214n.120
Blair, Tony 67, 72
Bosnia 18, 23*t*, 76–7
Bosnia-Herzegovina 23*t*
Brahimi, Lakhdar 22–4, 124, 214n.131
Brazil 70*t*, 71–2, 94*t*, 100, 115–17, 116*t*, 218nn.169–70
Brown, Gordon 77–8
Burma *see* Myanmar
Bush, George W. 67, 69, 72, 84

Cairo, Egypt 122, *see* Egypt
Cambodia 15–16, 23*t*, 76–7, 164n.68, 191n.128
Cameron, David 97, 102–3
ceasefire 72, 98, 102–3, 121–2, 124, 205nn.1, 9, 219n.8
  agreement 20, 70*t*, 72, 90–1, 161n.29, 188n.75
censure 11, 26–7, 97, 108, 114–16, 121–2, 127
Chile 125
China
  approach of intervention 15, 17, 24, 86, 105, 143–4
  China's rise 8–9, 31, 39–40, 48–9, 140, *see* rising powers
  core interests 1, 7–10, 33–4, 138
  discourse of intervention 31, 53–4

China (cont.)
  regime change precedent-setting 1, 8–10, 33, 138
  rejection of regime change 31, 33–5, 104
  responsible protection 106, 109, 130, 139, 218n.169
China National Petroleum Corporation 90, 111
Chinese Communist Party (CCP) 1, 8–9, 33–4
  regime survival 8–9, 138
Chinese People's Liberation Army (PLA) 89–90
civil war 20–1, 98, 116t, 120, 163n.50
Clinton, Bill 68
Clinton, Hillary Rodham 92–4, 98, 198n.29
coercive intervention 2, 108–10, *see* humanitarian intervention; non-consensual intervention
coercive measures 69–72, 106, 108–9
collective goods *see* social goods
  human rights 2
  non-proliferation 2
consensual measures 108, 125
Costa Rica 81
Côte d'Ivoire 2, 26–7
crimes against humanity 25–6, 66–8, 71, 81–2, 88, 124
critical juncture 10, 59, 65–6, 69, 73–4, 84, 90, 96, 100, 108–11, 128–9, 136–8

Dai, Bingguo 84
Damascus, Syria 113–15, 117, 121–2, 124, *see* Syria
Darfur, Sudan 3–4, 10, 24, 56, 57t, 59, 63–9, 67f, 70t, 71–87, 83f, 124–5, 127, 136–9, 143–4, 169n.132, 184n.5, 185n.30, 187n.63, 188n.78, 190n.114, 191n.122, 192n.132, 193n.140, 195n.166, 224n.68, *see* Sudan
Darfur Peace Agreement (2006) 68, 70t, 79
  International Commission of Inquiry on Darfur 70t, 71
democracy 16–17, 31
  promotion 51–3, 137
Democratic People's Republic of Korea (DPRK) 1, 22, 23t, 26–7, 29–31, 55, 139–40, 144, 211n.92, 222n.50
Democratic Republic of the Congo (DRC) 26–7, 139–40
Deng, Xiaoping 96
developing states 24–5, 33–4, 113–14, 129–30, *see* Global South
  status 5, 41, 43, *see* status
developmental peace 140–1
Diaoyu Islands 33

diplomacy 2, 34, 43–4, 47, 49, 54–5, 65–6, 78–80, 85, 89, 106, 111, 113, 116–17, 122–3, 129–30, 154n.32
diplomatic efforts 47, 53–4, 66, 68, 75, 79–80, 86, 91–2, 109, 119, 122, 136–7
diplomatic maneuvering 53–4, 135
diplomatic measures 9, 47, 88, 95
diplomatic relations 7–8, 24, 52–3, 63, 66, 68, 130–1
diplomatic strategy 77, 98, 121, 143–4
  gunboat diplomacy 33–4
Doha, Qatar 122, *see* Qatar
Donilon, Thomas 98
Dream for Darfur 65–6, 75–80, 83–4, 185n.25, 190n.114, 191nn.124, 127–8, 192nn.129–30, 193n.137, *see* Genocide Olympics

East Timor 19–21, 164n.68
Egeland, Jan 66–7
Egypt 29, 88, 98, 189n.82, 198n.25, 205n.3, 212n.97, 213n.112
El-Araby, Nabil 120
Eliasson, Jan 125–6
Eritrea 26–7
Ethiopia 23t, 98–9
ethnic cleansing 1–2, 18, 25–6
  Darfur 66–7, 69
  Srebrenica 130
Europe 33, 92–4, 121, 190n.114, 195n.177
European Council 92–4
European Union (EU) 72, 75, 92–4, 111–12, 212n.97

Fabius, Laurent 113–14
Farrow, Ronan 76–7
Farrow, Mia 65–6, 76–7, 191n.128
Federal Republic of Yugoslavia (FRY) 18–19, 23t, 26, 162n.40
Five Principles of Peaceful Coexistence 3–4, 34–5, 48–9
foreign aid 141–2
France 5, 20, 31, 49–50, 77–8, 81, 84, 87, 89–90, 92–4, 96–7, 99, 101, 113, 115–17, 121–2, 124–6, 139–40, 164n.60, 188n.78, 204n.115, 206n.15, 215n.137, 218n.170, *see* P3 (the United States, United Kingdom, and France); great powers; peer groups

Gabon 98–9
Gaddafi, Muammar 1–4, 8, 11, 40t, 88–106, 110, 128–9, 136, 138–9, 152n.10, 196n.1, 197n.6, 201n.58, 203n.111, 204n.127, *see* Libya
Gates, Robert S. 98
Gbagbo, Laurent 26–7

genocide 1–4, 20, 25–6, 67, 69, 71, 76–84, 117–18, 168n.128, 191nn.124, 127
  acts of genocide 71
  Rwanda 66–7, 69, 86, 125, 130, 194n.160
Genocide Olympics 10, 57*t*, 63–6, 75–80, 83–4, 192n.132, *see* Beijing Olympic Games (2008), *see* Darfur
Georgia 29–31, 51–2, 55–6
Germany 71, 76–8, 94*t*, 97, 100, 115–16, 121–2
Ghana 75, 189n.82
global governance 8–9, 11–12, 48, 50–1, 140–3, 147
Global South 5–7, 48–50, 82, 84, 102, 105–6, 120, 129, 145, *see* African Union (AU); Association of Southeast Asian Nations (ASEAN); Gulf Cooperation Council (GCC); League of Arab States (LAS); Middle East; Non-Aligned Movement (NAM); Organization of Islamic Cooperation (OIC); peer groups; regional organizations
  approach 98–9
  leader 25
  peer group 10–11, 47, 50–1, 57*t*, 64, 74, 89–90, 98, 108–9, 125, 127–9, 135–7
  status 89–90, 104
great powers 7, 17, 47–50, 52–3, 76–7, 82, 84, 113–14, 122–3, 126, 130–1, 143–7, 177n.57, *see* P3 (the United States, United Kingdom, and France); peer groups
  definition 48
  peer group 10–11, 47, 49–50, 57*t*, 64, 77, 89–90, 124–5, 128–9, 135–6
  recognition 7, 48
  responsibilities 46, 48–9
  status 5–7, 25, 39, 41, 43, 48–9, 75, 86, 89–90, 104, 145
  status-quo 48
Guatemala 21, 165nn.77–8
Gulf Cooperation Council (GCC) 17–18, 40*t*, 88–90, 97, 108–9, 115, 117–18, 120–1, 125, 127–8, *see* Global South; Middle East; peer groups; regional organizations
  peer group 11, 57*t*, 104, 127–8
Gulf of Aden 49
Guterres, Antonio 142

Hague, William 113, 206n.14, 212n.105
Haiti 22, 166n.92
hierarchy 39, 41–2, 49, 174nn.15, 25
honor 10, 39–41, 40*t*, 85, 126, 143–4
host state consent 2–4, 15, 17–20, 27–8, 50, 169n.131, 170n.8
Hu, Jintao 73–4, 76–80, 122–3, 192n.132

human rights 2, 9, 18–21, 31, 53, 65–6, 80–1, 88, 111, 118, 130–1, 138, 140, 143–4, 146–7
  experts 125–6
  international standards 41, 86–7
  law 71
  watchdogs 72
human rights abuse 2–4, 8–9, 16–18, 26–7, 49–51, 56–8, 68, 88–9, 97, 115–16, 120, 125, 128–31
human rights challenges 106–7
humanitarian aid 49, 79, 126–7, 146, 197n.6
humanitarian corridors 57*t*, 66–7, 116*t*
humanitarian crisis 17–18, 50–1, 64, 69, 80, 102, 126–7, 186n.37
humanitarian intervention 2, 18–21, 55, 145, *see* non-consensual intervention
  armed 94–5
humanitarianism 17–18, 32–3, 88–9, 130
  norms 130
Hussein, Saddam 124, 160n.18

identity 4–5, 40–3, 45–6
India 15–16, 33, 94*t*, 100, 115–17, 116*t*, 130–1, 145
Indian Ocean 27, 49
Indonesia 20–1, 137, 164n.66, 68–9
International Atomic Energy Agency 22
international community 25–8, 40–2, 48, 66–7, 75, 80–2, 88–9, 92–5, 97, 114–17, 119, 124, 140–1, 144, 187n.58, 198n.29
  legitimate players 42
  norms 42
  recognized member 44
  responsible member 2, 76, 125
  social standing 47
International Criminal Court (ICC) 2, 26, 57*t*, 68–9, 89–90, 94–5, 125, 139–40, 169nn.130–1
  and Libya 1–4, 8, 11, 88–91, 94*t*, 96, 103–4, 136, 145, 152n.10
  and Sudan 1–4, 10, 63, 68–9, 70*t*, 71–2, 79, 81–2, 85–6, 136, 138–9
  and Syria 11, 108, 116*t*, 124–5, 136–7, 215nn.138, 140
international peace and security 7, 22, 26–7, 31, 46, 125–6, 139–40, 142, 145, 147
  threats to 1–2, 8–9, 17–19, 50–1, 98, 126–7, 139–40, 162n.39, 165n.81, 184n.18
international responsibilities 2, 48–9
investment 16, 32, 43–4, 56–8, 117, 141
  in Libya 4, 90–1, 105
  in Sudan 64–5, 82, 85
Iran 17–18, 26–7, 29–31, 55–6, 123, 198n.25, 205n.3, 212n.97

Iraq 17–18, 23t, 29–31, 55–6, 68, 74, 101–2, 113–14, 117
Iraq War (1990) 17–18, 160n.18
Iraq War (2003) 51–2, 74–5, 101–2
Ismail, Mustafa Osman 72–3
Israel 15–16, 55–6, 124–5, 205n.3

janjaweed 63–7, 70t, 72, see Sudan
Japan 24–5, 29–31, 185n.20
Jiang, Yu 102
Jiang, Zemin 48–9
Jibril, Mahmoud 105
Jordan 98–9, 101, 117, 119, 198n.25, 205n.3, 218n.170

Kapila, Mukesh 69
Kenya 68, 189n.82, 196n.179
Kerry, John 113
Khartoum, Sudan 10, 65, 67–9, 71–3, 75–7, 79, 83–4, 136, 186n.37, see Sudan
Korean War 17
Kosovo 18–21, 23t, 162n.39, 166n.97
Kosovo War (1999) 51–2
Kouchner, Bernard 77–8
Kuwait 115, 209n.63

Lavrov, Sergei 122–3
League of Arab States (LAS) 17–18, 40t, 47, 88–90, 95, 97–100, 102, 109, 115, 116t, 117–21, 123–5, 127–8, 195n.166, 210n.67, 217n.163, see Global South; Middle East; peer groups; regional organizations
    peer group 11, 108–9, 127–8
Lebanon 96–7, 115, 116t, 117–18, 127–8, 198n.25, 210n.72
Li, Baodong 117–19, 121–2
Li, Chengwen 80
Libya 1–4, 8, 10–11, 23t, 27, 29–32, 56, 57t, 59, 81, 87–94, 93f, 94t, 95–110, 113–14, 118–19, 124–5, 128–30, 136–9, 143–6, 169n.132, 189n.82, 197n.10, 204n.127
Libya effect 110, 128–9, see Libya
Lithuania 125
Liu, Guijin 75, 78, 80–1
Luxembourg 125
Lyall Grant, Mark 125–6

Macedonia 21–2, 166–7nn.81–2
Mali 24–5, 140
mass atrocities 2, 10, 26, 63, 69, 125–6, 140–1, 146, 192n.132, see human rights abuse
massacre
    Darfur 80–1
    Srebrenica 86, 194n.160

material interests 6–7, 27, 56–8, 135–6
Mbeki, Thabo 72
Merkel, Angela 77–8
Middle East 11, 32, 43, 52–3, 91–2, 98, 101, 109, 115–21, 123, 127–8, 136–7, 216n.147, see Global South; Gulf Cooperation Council (GCC); League of Arab States (LAS); Organization of Islamic Cooperation (OIC); peer groups; regional organizations
    peer group 126, 136–7
    regional organizations 11, 43, 89–90, 97, 101, 104, 108–9, 116–18
military intervention 17, 67, 89–90, 97–8, 102, 117, 120–1, see non-consensual intervention
    Kosovo Force (KFOR) 18–19
military operation 99, 102–3, 204n.127
    United Task Force (UNITAF) 19–20
Moreno, Luis 68–9
Morocco 118–19, 121, 210n.72
Moscow, Russia 110, 114–15, 122–3, 128–9, 181n.133
Moussa, Amr 102
Mugabe, Robert 26–7, 98–9
Museveni, Yoweri 98–9
Myanmar 26–7, 50–2, 137, 139–40, 219nn.4–5

Nafie, Nafie Ali 72–3
national interests 3–4, 22, 32, 52, 90, 111
national reunification 8–9
national security 8–9, 26–7, 33–4, 48, 50–1, 98, 102
National Transition Council 90–1, 105, 198n.22, see Libya
Natsios, Andrew S. 74, 78
Negroponte, John 84
Nepal 79–80
Nigeria 98–9, 189n.82
no vote 56–8
    Syria 114–15, 120, 123, 211n.92
no-drive zone 94–5
no-fly zone 1–4, 8, 11, 17–18, 57t, 66–7, 88–90, 94–5, 94t, 97–104, 106, 114, 117, 128–9, 136, 145, 160n.18
Non-Aligned Movement (NAM) 15–16, 50, 223n.55, see Global South; peer groups
non-consensual intervention 2, 8–9, 25, 29, 69, 109, 128–9, 136–7, 145–7, see humanitarian intervention
    definition 2
    examples 15–16
non-consensual measures 121, 129–30
non-interference principle 20, 27–8, 33, 184n.18

INDEX 279

non-proliferation 2
Non-Proliferation Treaty 22, 23*t*, 39, 222n.50
norm entrepreneur 9
norms 2, 7–8, 22–6, 42, 47, 49, 51, 53, 58–9, 69, 106, 109, 128–31, 140–3, 146
  accountability 1–2, 4, *see* accountability
  international relations 17–18, 115–16, 130, 147
  international system 49–50
  intervention 11–12, 106, 109, 146
  norm shaping 109, 130
  protection of civilians 1–2, 25–6, 130, *see* protection of civilians
  responsibility to protect 1–2, 25–6, 63–4, 109, 140–1, 145, *see* responsibility to protect
  sovereignty 17, 140–1, *see* sovereignty
North Atlantic Treaty Organization (NATO) 18–19, 23*t*, 51–2, 72, 97, 99, 101–3, 106, 138–9, 162nn.35, 37, 188n.77, 203n.94, 204nn.115,124,127,130
nuclear proliferation 39, 55, 139–40
nuclear weapons 26–7, 39, 44, 177n.57

Obama, Barack 98–9, 102–3, 105, 113–14, 143–4, 214n.120
One China Policy 21–2, 166n.82
Organization for African Unity 20
Organization of Islamic Cooperation (OIC) 57*t*, 88–90, 97, 115, 120, 125, 127–8, *see* Global South; Middle East; peer groups; regional organizations
  peer group 11, 49, 108–9, 127–8

P3 (the United States, United Kingdom, and France) 5, 10–11, 17–18, 24, 49–52, 69, 73–5, 87, 89–94, 98, 101, 104–6, 108–9, 113–15, 118–19, 121–2, 124–9, 136–7, 146–7, 195n.166, 203nn.94, 111, *see* great powers; peer groups
peer group 49–50, 64, 84, 104, 128–9, 136
Pacific states 142
Pakistan 15–16, 49, 69–71, 70*t*, 116*t*, 121–2, 184n.5, 187nn.58, 61
Panetta, Leon E. 102–3
Paris Summit 101
peace plan
  Syria 11, 57*t*, 108, 118–19, 121–2, 136–7, 211n.94, 212nn.101, 105, 213n.112
peacekeeping 2, 8–10, 16–17, 19–25, 49, 63, 66, 68–9, 72–80, 82–6, 130–1, 136, 140, 142–3, 163nn.50, 56, 165n.77, 167n.109, 193n.140
  African Union Mission in Sudan (AMIS) 70*t*, 72–3, 188n.77, 189nn.82–3
  High-level Independent Panel on Peace Operations (HIPPO) 24

International Force in East Timor (INTERFET) 20–1, 24
UN Assistance Mission in Rwanda (UNAMIR) 20, 164n.60
UN Interim Force in Lebanon (UNIFIL) 24
UN Mission for East Timor (UNAMET) 20–1, 164n.66
UN Mission in Sudan (UNMIS) 24, 70*t*, 72, 189n.83
UN Organization Mission in the Democratic Republic of Congo (MONUC) 24, 166n.97
UN Peacekeeping Force in Cyprus (UNFICYP) 16
UN Preventative Deployment Force (UNPREDEP) 21, 156n.60
UN Protection Force (UNPROFOR) 18, 161nn.29, 32
UN Supervision Mission in Syria (UNSMIS) 116*t*, 120–2
UN Verification Mission in Guatemala (MINUGUA) 21, 165n.77
UN–AU Hybrid Mission in Darfur (UNAMID) 24, 57*t*, 63, 66, 68–9, 70*t*, 78–9, 85, 168n.119, 193n.140
United Nations Mission in Liberia (UNMIL) 24, 166n.97, 168n.119
United Nations Operation in Somalia II (UNOSOM II) 19–20, 163n.56
United Nations Stabilization Mission in Haiti (MINUSTAH) 24, 166n.97
United Nations Transitional Administration in East Timor (UNTAET) 24, 165n.72, 166n.97
  norms 22–4
peace enforcement 1–4, 19
peace operation 2–4, 16–17, 19–20, 22–5, 72–3, 85, 90–1, 140, 161n.32, 163n.56, 223n.53
peacebuilding 19, 141–2
peacekeepers 16–17, 19–20, 22–4, 164n.71, 165n.81
peacemaking 16–17
peer groups 4–12, 15–16, 27–8, 41–7, 49–52, 56–8, 57*t*, 64, 69, 72, 74–7, 81, 84–7, 89–90, 98, 101, 104–9, 120, 124–30, 135–9, 143–6, 174n.25, 175n.33, *see* African Union (AU); Association of Southeast Asian Nations (ASEAN); Global South; great powers; Gulf Cooperation Council (GCC); League of Arab States (LAS); Middle East; Non-Aligned Movement (NAM);Organization of Islamic Cooperation (OIC); P3 (the United States, United Kingdom, and France)
  defection 5, 43, 45, 64, 81, 90, 104, 127–9, 135–7, 143–4

peer groups (*cont.*)
  definition 41
  expectations 43, 47
  good behavior 4–7, 41–3, 45–7, 69, 72, 104, 106, 108–9, 125–6, 136
  interaction 45
  isolation 43–4, 46, 85, 89, 101, 104–5, 120, 135–6, 143–4
  leader 16, 42, 136
  normative consensus 43, 45–6, 104, 127–8
  norms 69
  recognition 42, 46, 77, 85, 105
  social costs 11
peer states 52–3, 155n.48, *see* Russia
Pillay, Navi 125, 215n.137
Pinheiro, Paulo 124
Portugal 20–1, 115–16, 121–2, 124
Powell, Colin 67, 69, 187n.57
Power, Samantha 125–6
prestige 2, 10, 39–42, 40*t*, 44, 51, 77, 85
protection of civilians 1–2, 20, 25–6, 88–9, 94*t*, 97, 99–102, 104, 110, 116*t*, 164n.60
public discourse *see* regime change
Putin, Vladimir 122–3

Qatar 70*t*, 72–3, 98–9, 101, 123, 204n.115, 205n.3, 209nn.60,63, 213n.112, 214n.124

Ramcharan, Bertrand 66–7
reference groups *see* peer groups
refugees 17–18, 20, 27, 78–80, 124, 126, 142, 160n.18, 164n.60, 191n.127
regime change 1–4, 6–12, 26, 29–35, 30*f*, 52–3, 55–6, 58, 63–4, 66–8, 67*f*, 72–5, 84, 88–9, 92, 93*f*, 94–5, 102–3, 108–14, 112*f*, 117, 121, 123, 126–30, 135, 137–42, 146–7, 152n.12, 169nn.4, 7, 186n.45, 197n.14, 198n.29, 218n.172
  Chinese sources 29–33
  definition 1–2
  illegitimate 31, 54, 137–8
  precedent 1, 8–10, 33, 138
  public discourse 2–4, 8–9, 34–5, 55–6, 63–4, 66, 88–90, 92, 94–5, 104, 109–14, 121, 138–40
regional organizations 5, 9, 11, 17–19, 43, 50–1, 87–90, 95–101, 104–5, 108–10, 115–18, 127–9, 136, 140–1, 143–4, *see* African Union (AU); Association of Southeast Asian Nations (ASEAN); Global South; Gulf Cooperation Council (GCC); League of Arab States (LAS); Organization of Islamic Cooperation (OIC); peer groups
Republic of Korea (South Korea) 27, 125, 215n.139

reputation 10, 19, 39–41, 40*t*, 45–6, 64, 75–7, 83–4, 87, 104–6, 174n.24
  social reputation 40–1
  definition 40–1
responsibility to protect 1–4, 25–6, 63–4, 88–9, 109, 130, 139–41, 145, 168n.125, 184n.8
  definition 25–6
  prevention 25–6
  reaction measures 25–6
  rebuilding 25–6
  World Summit Outcome Document 25–6
responsible power 24, 48–9
  definition 49
  international obligations 49
  norms 49
Rice, Susan 99–100, 117, 119
rising powers 7–9, 11–12, 39, 44, 48, 116–17, 140, 145–7, *see* China
Romania 71
Russia 10–11, 23*t*, 25–6, 33, 47, 51–3, 55–8, 57*t*, 69–73, 70*t*, 81, 89, 92, 94*t*, 97, 99–101, 108–111, 113–26, 116*t*, 128–9, 137, 140, 145, 155n.48, 168n.125, 181n.133, 195n.166, 205n.9, 210n.71, 212n.97, 218n.172
  axis of convenience 51, 53
  axis of insecurity 51
  axis of necessity 51
  not a peer of China 51–3
Rwanda 19–20, 26, 66–7, 69, 76–7, 86, 125, 130, 189n.82
Rwandan Patriotic Front (RPF) 20

sanctions 1–2, 11, 17, 19, 22, 23*t*, 26–7, 40*t*, 43–4, 50–1, 53–4, 68–71, 70*t*, 74–5, 78, 94–6, 94*t*, 104, 108, 111–12, 115–17, 166n.92, 187n.63, 193n.140
Sarkozy, Nicolas 77–8, 102–3, 113, 196n.191
Saudi Arabia 115, 120, 205n.3, 209n.63, 216n.147
self-image 4–5, 42, 45–6
Serbia 18–19, 23*t*, 29–31
Sierra Leone 26, 166n.97
Sinochem 111
social benefits 40–1, 43–7, 85, 105, 136, 143–4
  definition 45–6
social costs 2, 5, 11, 41, 43, 45–7, 64, 74–7, 79, 84, 86–7, 89–90, 95, 104, 108–9, 115–18, 120, 123, 125, 127, 135–7, 143–4, *see* social punishments
social goods 41, 45–6, 129
social influence 42, 45–6, 56–8, 64, 84–6, 89–90, 104–5, 108–9, 127–9, 135–6, 138–9, 143–5
  definition 45

limitations 129
  mechanism 10, 45–7
social opprobrium *see* social costs
social praise *see* social benefits
social pressure *see* social costs
social punishments *see* social costs
  definition 45–6
social rewards *see* social benefits
Somalia 19–20, 74, 163nn.50, 56
South Africa 15–16, 72, 98–9, 102, 115–17, 116*t*, 121–2, 189n.82, 202n.82
South China Sea 33
South Sudan 24–5
Southern African Development Community (SADC) 26–7, 50–1
Southern Rhodesia 16, *see* Zimbabwe
sovereignty 2, 8–9, 15–16, 18–21, 27–8, 31–5, 39–40, 50, 63, 85–6, 96–7, 105, 115–16, 119, 126–9, 140–2, 146–7, 162n.33, 164n.68, 165n.72, 170n.8
  norms 2, 17, 25–6, 140–1, 220n.31
  protection 21–2, 31, 33–4, 52, 130–1, 172n.35
  threat 2, 17–18, 25–6, 51–2, 72–3
  violation 7, 17–19, 21, 29
sovereignty as responsibility 25–6, *see* responsibility to protect
Spielberg, Steven 65–6, 76–7, 79–80, 83–4, 185n.25, 191nn.124–5
Srebrenica, the Federal Republic of Yugoslavia (FRY) 18, 86, 130, 194n.160, *see* Federal Republic of Yugoslavia (FRY)
Sri Lanka 26–7
stability 1, 8–9, 31–4, 73, 75, 81–2, 90, 104–5, 136, 141, 172n.36, 184n.18
  instability 32, 98
status 4–8, 10–12, 19–21, 39–47, 40*t*, 56–9, 64, 69, 82, 84–7, 89–90, 96, 103–4, 107–9, 111, 118, 120, 127, 129, 135–9, 143–6
  definition 41
  developing state 5, 41, 43
  Global South 6–7, 89–90, 104
  great power 5–7, 25, 41, 43, 48–9, 75, 89–90, 104, 145, *see* peer groups; great powers
status appeals 75, 122–3, 126, 136–7, 143–4
status attribution 6–7, 39, 145–6, 196n.187
status community 4–5, 41, 89, 145–6
status concern 5, 10–11, 15, 27–8, 43–4, 47, 49–51, 85–6, 89–90, 96, 101, 104–6, 108–9, 118, 129–30, 137
status deficits 43–4
status dilemma 7, 11–12, 136, 145
  definition 7
status effects 45, 64, 127, 129–30, 135–6, 143–4, 147

status gains 136
status groups *see* peer groups
status incentives 143–4
status insensitivity 45, 108–9, 137–8
status markers 42, 44–6, 86–7, 145–6
status pressures 41, 74–6, 79, 84, 87, 108–9, 115, 118, 120, 123, 125, 127, 136–7, 144
status recognition 7, 32, 39, 42, 49–50, 77, 85–6, 145–6
status sensitivity 43–5, 64, 89, 108–9, 129–30, 137–8
status signaling 6–7, 87, 175n.34, 222n.51
status trigger 5, 10–11, 43–5, 56–8, 57*t*, 64, 77–8, 84, 89–90, 96, 99–100, 104, 108–9, 127–9, 135–9, 143–4, 176n.47
  definition 43–4
Sudan 1–4, 10, 23*t*, 27, 29, 56, 57*t*, 59, 63–71, 70*t*, 72–86, 88–9, 136, 143–4, 184n.17, 188n.75, 189n.81, 190n.114, 191n.122, 192n.132, 193n.140, 195nn.166–8, 170, 202n.89
  Humanitarian Ceasefire Agreement 72
Switzerland 124, 215n.137, 218n.170
Syria 1, 3–4, 10–11, 29–32, 50–3, 56–9, 57*t*, 98–9, 106–12, 112*f*, 113–30, 116*t*, 136–40, 145–6, 198n.25, 205nn.1, 3, 9, 206n.15, 210n.71, 212n.97, 214n.132, 216nn.147, 153, 218n.170
Syrian Action Group 109, 212n.97
Syrian–Chinese Business Council 111

Taiwan 7–8, 21–2, 33, 39–40, 165nn.78, 81
  diplomatic recognition 7–8, 21–2, 166n.82
Tanzania 15–16, 68
territorial integrity 8–9, 17–19, 34, 52, 97, 105, 115–16, 119, 140–1, 162n.33
Thailand 79–80
Third World 15–16, *see* Global South
Tiananmen Square incident 11, 17–19, 43–4, 86, 97, 176n.47
  Gaddafi's speech 57*t*, 89, 95–7, 103–4, 136, 201n.65
Tibet, China 76, 87, 191n.120, 196n.191
trade 16, 56–8, 64–5, 111, 184n.17, 221n.41, 222n.50
travel ban 23*t*, 26–7, 117, *see* sanctions
Tripoli, Libya 88, 102–3, *see* Libya
Tunisia 88, 98, 197n.10, 204n.124
Turkey 17–18, 117, 124, 213n.112

Uganda 15–16, 98–9, 202n.82
Ukraine 29–31, 33, 51–2, 55–6
United Arab Emirates 98–9, 125, 209n.63

INDEX

United Kingdom 2–3, 5, 31, 49–50, 55–6, 67, 71–2, 77–8, 81, 84, 89–90, 92–4, 96–7, 99, 113–16, 118–19, 121–2, 125–6, 153n.19, 204n.115, *see* great powers; P3 (the United States, United Kingdom, and France); peer groups
United Nations 2030 Agenda for Sustainable Development 142
United Nations Charter 17–21, 47, 101–2, 114–16, 130, 141–2
  Chapter VII 2–4, 10, 15, 19–20, 26–8, 55, 63, 70*t*, 71–2, 115–16, 118–19, 126–7, 136, 163n.50, 182n.145
  Chapter VIII 50–1
United Nations General Assembly 46, 111, 118, 120, 123, 129–30, 137–8, 141–2, 165n.77
United Nations Human Rights Council 114–15, 124, 141–2
  Independent International Commission of Inquiry on the Syrian Arab Republic 124
United States 2–3, 5, 9, 17–20, 24–5, 29–34, 39, 43–4, 46, 48–51, 55, 63–4, 66–9, 70*t*, 71–5, 77–81, 83–4, 89–90, 92–4, 96, 98–100, 102–3, 111–14, 117–19, 121–6, 138–40, 142–3, 160n.18, 182nn.145, 147, 190n.114, 191nn.117, 128, 195n.177, 198nn.29, 31, 204n.115, 219n.17, *see* great powers; P3 (the United States, United Kingdom, and France); peer groups
use of force 1–2, 7, 17–20, 26–9, 43–4, 88–90, 95, 98, 102, 109, 130, 138–9, 170n.8, 210n.71, *see* non-consensual intervention
  against civilians 95, 116*t*

veto 2–3, 16–17, 20, 23*t*, 39–40, 45–6, 52–4, 57*t*, 81–2, 136, 146–7, 205n.1, 218n.170
  on Bangladesh 15–16
  expected 4, 8, 11, 71–3, 81–2, 89, 99–100, 111
  on Guatemala 21
  on Israel 15–16
  on Macedonia 21–2, 156n.60
  moral veto 15–16
  on Myanmar 26–7, 50–2, 137
  on Syria 3–4, 11, 52–3, 56–8, 108–11, 115–30, 116*t*, 136–8, 145–6, 205n.9, 219n.8
  threat 46, 69, 71
  on Zimbabwe 26–7, 50–2
veto cover 25–6, 168n.125
veto option 101
veto player 6
Vietnam 15–16, 164n.68

Wang, Guangya 71–4
Wang, Min 125
war crimes 25–6, 66–7, 81–2, 96, 124–5
Wen, Jiabao 73, 122
Western liberal order 16–17, 51–2, 106–7, 140, 142–3, 146–7
  good governance 16–17
  institution building 16–17
  liberal democracy 16–17, *see* democracy
  open markets 16–17
Western powers 1, 31–2, 34–5, 102, 106–7, 114, *see* great powers

Xi, Jinping 123, 141–2, 214n.120
Xinjiang, China 33

Yang, Jiechi 105, 123
Yemen 117, 139–40, 198n.25
yes vote 16, 23*t*, 45, 53
  on Guatemala 21
  on Haiti 22, 166n.92
  on Libya 11, 57*t*, 88–9, 91–2, 94*t*, 96–9, 101, 104, 136
  on Sudan 10, 57*t*, 70*t*
  on Syria 116*t*, 120, 126–7, 145

Zenawi, Meles 98–9
Zhai, Jun 78, 81–2, 193n.137, 205n.3
Zhang, Yishan 69–71
Zhang, Zhijun 122
Zhou, Wenzhong 63, 192n.129
Zimbabwe 15–16, 26–7, 50–2, 55–6, 98–9